Charles: The Life and World of Charles Acton 1914–1999

For Ninian and Jane

Charles

The Life and World of

CHARLES ACTON

1914–1999

RICHARD PINE

THE LILLIPUT PRESS
DUBLIN

First published 2010 by
THE LILLIPUT PRESS
62–63 Sitric Road, Arbour Hill
Dublin 7, Ireland
www.lilliputpress.ie

ISBN 978 1 84351 165 6

1 3 5 7 9 10 8 6 4 2

A CIP record for this title is available
from The British Library.

Set in 12 pt on 14.5 pt Perpetua by Marsha Swan
Printed and bound in the UK by J.F. Print Ltd, Sparkford, Somerset

Contents

Illustrations

(between pages 204 and 205)

A painting of Kilmacurragh, County Wicklow, after the addition of the wings in 1848.

'Uncle Tom': Thomas Acton (1826–1908) in the grounds of Kilmacurragh.

'Curious Valentine': the travails of landlordism in nineteenth-century Ireland.

Banks Medal of the Royal Horticultural Society awarded to Charles Ball-Acton in 1931.

Colonel Charles Ball-Acton (1830–97), Charles's grandfather.

Isabel Richmond (1876–1970) in 1899, Charles's mother.

Major Reginald Ball-Acton (1877–1916), Charles's father.

Reggie, Isabel and baby Charles, 1914–15.

Notification from Reggie that he had been wounded.

Telegram of condolence from the King (George V) and Queen on the death of Reggie.

Charles with Nurse Hallam, 1915–16.

Charles on the steps of Kilmacurragh.

Charles at home as a young boy.

Charles in studio preparing for school.

Charles (extreme left) during Cambridge Rag Week.

Hugh Digues La Touche (1891–1933), Charles's stepfather.

Charles, Isabel and Hugh.

Reception at Kilmacurragh for Adolf Mahr and crew of the German training-ship *Schleswig-Holstein*, 1937.

Nazi gathering at Kilmacurragh, summer venue for a Hitler Youth camp, before Charles's return in September 1939.

Wedding of Charles and Carol, Monkstown Parish Church, 6 March 1951.

Charles and Polish conductor-composer Andrjez Panufnik at Carrickmines Station, January 1976 (courtesy Camilla Jessel, Panufnik's wife).

Charles and Carol with musician David Carmody, on balcony of the National Concert Hall, Dublin, 1981.

Acknowledgments

Since this book addresses not only the biography of Charles Acton, but also his family background in County Wicklow, I am indebted to many local historians and archivists, and to academics who have contributed significantly to our understanding of Anglo-Irishness and the decline of landed estates in the nineteenth century. Their works are acknowledged in my bibliography, but it is my special pleasure to offer personal thanks to the following.

The co-editor of *Wicklow – History and Society*, Ken Hannigan, and his colleague at the National Archives, Brian Donnelly, were more than helpful, as was John Medlycott, co-editor of the Wicklow volume of the Ordnance Survey letters.

The importance of the Kilmacurragh Arboretum, in the history of the family from 1854, in Charles's memory and in the present day, has been kept alive and actively developed by its present curator, Seamus O'Brien, and also by Myles Reid, whose BSc Hort. thesis, undertaken as part of his work at Kilmacurragh, has been of considerable interest. Dr Charles Nelson, historian of the Botanic Gardens in Dublin was also of assistance.

The staff of the Wicklow County Library were most helpful, and the then County Archivist, Cecile Chemin, was of enormous assistance in establishing the input of William Acton, MP, as a member of the board of guardians of the Rathdrum Union in the late 1830s and 1840s.

Dr W.E. Vaughan (Trinity College, Dublin) and Dr Jacinta Prunty (University College, Dublin) both responded encouragingly to queries about tenants (in the former case) and maps (in the latter), which, like many other enquiries that I directed towards unsuspecting recipients, must have seemed naïve and untutored.

Charles Acton's godson, Barra Boydell and his mother, Mary, enthusiastically enlightened me on several points regarding Charles's relationship with Brian Boydell, at Cambridge, in Yugoslavia, and subsequently in Achill and Dublin. Axel Klein and Gareth Cox also provided insights into this relationship.

ACKNOWLEDGMENTS

On the use of Kilmacurragh by members of the German community both before and during the Second World War, Dr David O'Donoghue and Gerry Mullins, respective authors of works on the subject, and Mrs Jean Medcalf, daughter of Charles Budina, provided invaluable information.

Trevor Lee undertook the copying of rare (sometimes unique) photographic material with professional aplomb.

Conor Brady, who was deputy editor of *The Irish Times* during Charles Acton's last years as the paper's music critic, contributed his personal insight into working conditions at that time.

Michael McGinley, author of a history of the La Touche family, and Michael Digges La Touche, provided information about the background of Charles's stepfather, Hugh Digues La Touche.

Others to whom I am indebted are Katy Astley and Elizabeth Stratton of Clare College, Cambridge; Paul Smith, company archivist at Thomas Cook & Sons; the late Paul Tansey of *The Irish Times*; Anthony Roche (UCD); Catherine Ferris (University of Limerick); Professor L. Perry Curtis Jr.; Professor Roy Foster; Fonsie Mealy; Marie Duff of the Office of Public Works.

Genevieve van Noorden made many valuable suggestions as to the structure and content of the typescript. Neil Holman and Emilie Pine provided essential guidance and assistance in bringing the typescript to fruition.

My greatest practical and personal debt is to my friend Ninian Falkiner who, unhesitatingly, undertook thorough and multiple readings of the book in draft, saving me from some serious errors and helping me to reduce an unwieldy text to the form in which it now appears. His expertise as an historian was only exceeded by his insight, as a former housemaster of a public school, into the mind of an adolescent boy. His interest in, and commitment to, the book was remarkable and the valuable time he devoted to it is deeply appreciated. Needless to say, neither he nor any other person to whom I turned for advice or information is responsible for any remaining errors or infelicities, which are to be laid entirely at my own door. But Ninian's generosity gives me the opportunity to greet him and his wife most affectionately on the page of dedication as two of my oldest and dearest friends, who sheltered me frequently at their home, The Long House, in Connemara, where much of this book was written.

Note on Sources

*W*ith one startling exception, Charles Acton was an inveterate hoarder of family records, a trait inherited from his aunt Irene Ball-Acton. At his death, his widow, Carol, unreservedly placed at my disposal his entire archive, which extended from the earliest extant material relating to his family home, Kilmacurragh, to his bank statements and investment portfolio in the 1990s.

Not only was this material vast in extent, but its evident value as an archive was obvious from the very start. The eventual disposal of the archive rapidly became a source of anxiety, as it was impossible to maintain it in one location, especially as its importance demanded that it should be made available to the public.

With the agreement of Carol Acton and of Peter Acton, the current head of the family, the following arrangements were put in place for the division of the material after it had yielded what was necessary for me to complete this book: all personal family papers, including correspondence and household records, are now known as the 'Acton Family Archive' and remain the property, and in the custody of, the family. Papers and maps relating to the creation and management of the estate at Kilmacurragh and surrounding lands, and to the Acton family's involvement in the local administration of justice, are held at the time of writing by the National Archives in trust for Wicklow County Library (microfilm copies of all estate maps had previously been donated by Charles Acton to the National Library of Ireland). Charles Acton's collection of his own and his wife's music reviews for *The Irish Times*, pasted into guard books, and all his correspondence relating to his work as a music critic, is held by the music section of the National Library of Ireland, to which Charles and his wife had previously donated their collection of concert programmes. Material relating to the military careers of members of the Acton family, including Charles Acton's father (Major Reginald Ball-Acton) and his grandfather (Colonel Charles Ball-Acton) is held by the section of the National Museum of Ireland dedicated to Irishmen at war (Collins Barracks).

One tragedy that occurred when I commenced research was the discovery of a brown paper parcel labelled 'Very fragile – from the basement of Kilmacurragh'. On opening the package, which clearly contained material dating from the eighteenth century, the paper literally crumbled irrecoverably into dust. The loss of this material for future historians is impossible to gauge, but it later became clear that Irene Ball-Acton, realizing the fragile nature of the papers, had had copies made of some of the information, and was assisted in this in 1932 by the Public Record Office.

References will be found in Chapter 2 to 'the Kilmacurragh Book'. This document, which forms part of the Acton Family Archive, is a compilation, begun in the 1880s, by Janet Acton and succeeded by Irene Ball-Acton, consisting of manuscript and typescript notes and (from the later period) photographs and press clippings. As a source of family history, in particular relating to the house and gardens of Kilmacurragh, it is of considerable significance.

The 'startling exception' to which I referred is the fact that, although Charles Acton's mother, Isabel, preserved all her son's letters to her, there is a startling absence of hers to him. In most cases, the content of her letters can be inferred by Charles's replies, but the reason for the non-survival of the originals is unfathomable. Surmise suggests that Charles, who was deeply affected by his mother's death, destroyed them, but Carol Acton had no knowledge of such an act.

Finally, part of the Acton Family Archive consists of the correspondence between Charles Acton's parents, Reggie and Isabel. In reading this I found that, before their wedding, Isabel had written 'fancy any profane eyes reading what was written for you alone'. For his part, Reggie expressed a similar anxiety: 'Some other person might see them & I do not like the idea & possibility of their seeing our sweet intimacy.' The responsibility of a biographer in relation to such 'sweet intimacy' is dangerous ground. I disavow the thought that my reading – and reproducing – parts of these letters could be considered 'profane', and in order to illustrate the unusual nature of their courtship I have considered it appropriate to quote from the letters. In only one instance (see p. 71) have I refrained from doing so: this relates to the letters addressed by Isabel to Reggie in the weeks and months after his death, from which, out of respect for the widow's continuing 'sweet intimacy', I have allowed myself to quote only ten words.

Section of East Wicklow Ordnance Survey Map indicating Principal Townlands within the Acton Estate

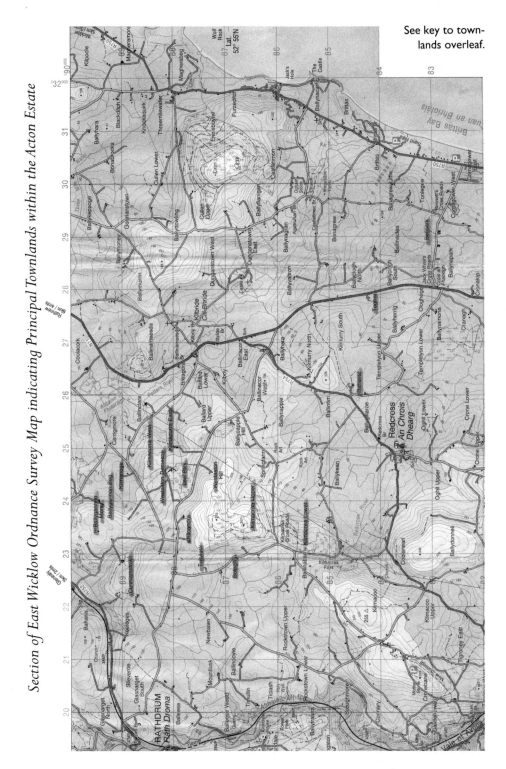

See key to town-lands overleaf.

Acton Estate Townlands, from North to South

Ballygannon More
Ballygannon Beg
Cunniamstown
Kilmacurra West
Westaston Demesne
Kilmacurra East
Deer Park
Kilcandra
Tullylusk
Westaston Hill
Bolagh
Kilmacrea Upper
Kilmacrea Lower
Rahaval
Templeyon Upper
Templelyon Lower
Oghil Lower
Oghil Upper
Bellpark

Charles: The Life and World of Charles Acton 1914–1999

Introduction

*I*n 1990 I recorded three programmes with Charles Acton for broadcast on RTÉ Radio, surveying his life story and, in particular, his career as the long-serving music critic of *The Irish Times*, the function for which he is chiefly remembered today as an opinionated and influential writer. Some months after those broadcasts, Charles wrote to me:

> People, very civilly, go on suggesting that I should write a buke of memoirs or something. Would be delighted to but, in spite of being a writer, I have neither time nor energy. I have often remarked that, although I have met an enormous number of people during my life, in very many different fields, I have always been on the sidelines, and if I were to write a buke I would entitle it 'At a Tangent'.

He went on to ask, at his wife's suggestion, 'if you would care to ghost me'.

His remark about always being on the sidelines was not disingenuous: it takes us immediately to the core of Charles's sense of anxiety about identity, and about his place in the new Irish society which he began to explore in depth when he returned to Ireland as the owner of Kilmacurragh in 1939. His life up to the 1950s may indeed have been 'at a tangent' to social and political realities, but from the moment when he became music critic of *The Irish Times* he was at the centre of opinion and policy-making that he was to enjoy for the next forty years.

Yet this is only part of his *persona* and his place in modern Ireland. *Charles* seeks to account for the way in which his extraordinarily varied life was the fortuitous product of an equally extraordinary family, living in Ireland since

3

the seventeenth century, and playing a major role in local Anglo-Irish politics and society in County Wicklow. This book is therefore much more than the biography of an Anglo-Irish child who happened to become one of the most significant commentators on modern Irish culture. It is also, of necessity, a family history, since it is impossible to appreciate Charles Acton unless one understands the role and status of his ancestors as County Wicklow landowners under the British administration, and the seismic effect on the family of the land legislation, the First World War and the change of government when the Irish Free State came into existence in 1922. Kilmacurragh provided the Actons with the hinterland of hesitant occupancy that, very largely, made Charles who he was.

Charles draws, from his meticulously maintained personal records, a portrait of a singular figure refracted through my friendship with him over a period of almost thirty years, from my first meeting with him and his wife Carol in 1970 until his death in 1999. Charles's increasing lethargy and, basically, his disinclination to 'blather' in any coherent fashion, rapidly ensured that the 'ghost' project never got under way. But when I started to explore his archive, especially his letters to his mother, the richness of the personality I had known so well became even more compelling. In one of those letters (from Cambridge) he had written, in regard to his career choices, 'my soul comes first'. That expression, so vital a part of Charles, leapt off the page for me because much of Charles's life was a quest – which some might call 'spiritual' – for his own meaning, for his 'soul'. Finding his soul, and, to continue the analogy, saving it, was paramount in anything he did, whether it was a pouring out of his musical feelings in a concert review, of his emotional feelings in a letter to his mother, or of his practical frustrations at the realities of everyday life. 'My soul comes first' dominates this study as it dominated Charles himself, regardless of cultural milieu, social position, economic status or professional context. Much of his life was a large question-mark, which may surprise those familiar with the apparent surety of his concert reviews. Yet within every critic is a questioner, constantly revising opinions and revisiting received wisdom, and Charles was no exception, not least because it was the provisional nature of life in all its circumstances which presented itself to him most formidably.

Reading Charles's letters, I came to realize just how exactly the rhythm of his speech was identical with his writing, an idiosyncratic expression of character formed early and carried throughout his dealings with family, colleagues, businessmen and, ultimately, his readers. His personal files reveal the development of a particular sensibility to all the anxieties and apprehensions of his unusual childhood – fatherless, insecure, and suddenly heir to a derelict estate in Ireland.

This has been an 'easy' book to write, in the sense that I was at ease with my subject from the moment when I began to delve into the archive; it has been a 'difficult' book to write, only in the sense that I have obliged myself to rein in my own enthusiasm when it seemed that this might simply appear to be a hagiography of Charles. Presented in all his colours, all his moods, *Charles* could hardly be that. As he himself wrote, 'Fully merited praise is meaningless if there is no liberty to censure also if it seems deserved.' I have followed Charles's view, and have tried to show that, however charming, erudite, committed and persuasive he may have been in print and in human contact, there was also a child within the man, whose anxieties and deep feelings often projected aggressive, petulant and irksome characteristics that did not necessarily endear him to the world at large.

To begin with the earliest extant material from Charles's own life, his schooldays provide us with a glimpse of the man who would develop into one of the central figures in Irish music-making in the second half of the twentieth century. His passions were his curiosity, his insistence on accuracy and truthfulness and his desire to contribute to a developing world. His faults came from those anxieties that I have mentioned: insecurity and a need to find his own identity and sense of purpose, often at the cost of his relations with others. As one commentator, having read this book in draft, said 'this is a psycho-history' – and such it is: of Charles himself, developing from a most unusual context and in a set of quite bizarre circumstances, alien to most of us today, and also a psycho-history of the modern Ireland into which he eventually grew.

When I began to research the Acton family archives, I rapidly realized that the family from which Charles emerged could yield a social history of a cross-section of Irish life through three-and-a-half centuries. While that would have been impossible in the present volume, I hope that the source material listed in the Note on Sources and in the Bibliography could, eventually, help to fill a noticeable *lacuna* in local studies in Wicklow, and especially those of the landed estates, which have been partly addressed at a national level by scholars such as W.E. Vaughan and Terence Dooley.

In many aspects, Charles's life was pre-ordained to be unusual. In social terms, he came from a class and a stratified position that was almost extinct by the time of his birth. His formative years, spent at boarding schools in

the 1920s, coincided with worldwide economic depression and political instability. After concluding that he must part with his ancestral home and estate,
he spent eleven years in the professional wilderness, unable to hold down any
kind of satisfying, remunerative job until, quite suddenly and serendipitously,
he achieved a highly respected and prestigious position at *The Irish Times*. The
stepping-stones from Cambridge to *The Irish Times* were not a natural progression: only after Charles was over forty, and commencing on his principal career
as a music critic, was he able to work, so to speak, in a straight line.

Even then, he was never a member of staff, but belonged to the ranks of
'contributor', paid not a salary but a fee for each piece published. The constant
anxiety not only to prove himself, but also to prove his family, sat on his
shoulder like a dark shadow.

There is much of the Acton family in the Charles of *The Irish Times* columns
– their characteristics were imprinted on him genetically. His mother's constant
presence in his life for nearly sixty years was another dark shadow, inhibiting
him in so many respects, yet that should not be allowed to obscure the fact that
Charles was constitutionally happy even though worried, cheerful even though
anxious, positive even though beset by difficulties.

But it is certain that, whether or not he could ever have followed into
the life at Kilmacurragh, Charles carried throughout his life a deep sense of
loyalty to, and affection for, the context from which his family had emerged.
For some, family background is of little or no consequence in the making of
their character. For others, it is crucial and often decisive. In Charles's case,
it was – given the circumstances of his early upbringing – problematic and
to observe his growth into a sense of Irishness is all the more rewarding. The
ownership of substantial tracts of land brought with it a set of responsibilities
quite apart from the need to derive an income from the estate. These, and
the family interest in arboriculture, made the Actons of Kilmacurragh distinctive players in the life of south-east Wicklow in the eighteenth, nineteenth
and early twentieth centuries. The husbandry of the lands, the maintenance
of a social nexus, the creation of the Kilmacurragh arboretum, were all traits
which, in one fashion or another, found their way into Charles's consciousness.
When, in 1998, I was preparing the 'Notes on Contributors' for the history of
the Royal Irish Academy of Music that we jointly edited,[1] I drafted Charles's
entry, beginning with the conventional 'educated at Rugby and Cambridge…'.
Charles altered the entry to begin 'Of a County Wicklow family…' – his

---

1. R. Pine and C. Acton (eds), *To Talent Alone: the Royal Irish Academy of Music 1848–1998*.

family provenance was evidently more important to him than his academic background. Parnell declared 'I am an Irishman first, but a Wicklow man afterwards.'[2] Charles might easily have reversed the equation.

Charles's overwhelming sense of Irishness was a pervasive influence on anything he undertook. To promote Irish talent, to deflate and combat the inferiority complex that he detected in so much of post-independence Ireland – in short, to make people proud of being Irish – seemed to him the most natural aspect in the world for any Irishman to adopt, however much he may have derided specific examples of bad or inept government, management or decision-making. He was trenchant in his attempt to see Irish people, especially Irish musicians, attain the highest standards. When they did so, he was unhesitating in his praise and in his own attempts to join in that promotion. So much so that when, in 1986, he received a communication from the Bristol Overseas Investors Bond of which the envelope was labelled 'Expatriate', he wrote 'with some distress', 'I am a loyal, domiciled, resident citizen of the Republic of Ireland and not a British or any other expatriate. By implication, to label me on the outside of your envelope is hurtful and potentially damaging.'   When I wrote in *The Irish Times* after his death that 'he could be obstinate to the point of mulishness', I meant that when he was concerned over a particular point he was like a dog with a bone, refusing to let a matter drop until it had been resolved to his satisfaction. One of his preparatory school headmasters recognized the early signs of a character troubled by the circumstances of childhood when he remarked that 'he is childish to the extent that he is easily made angry, peevish and petulant'. The reasons, in Charles's case, were displacement, uncertainty and frustration – affects that would trouble him right up to the time of his marriage to Carol Little in 1951, his appointment to *The Irish Times* in 1955, and even up to the point at which he and Carol found their final home in the converted Carrickmines Station in 1968. This could easily be perceived as peevishness or petulance, and when Charles was angry – for example at someone's inefficiency, stupidity or inaccuracy – he could become very, very angry.

Although he could be said to have blundered his way through his twenties and thirties, as he took up various projects and then abandoned them, most of those projects were occupations to which he was naturally suited both by his curiosity and by his school and university courses. Perhaps only his lack of success as an encyclopaedia salesman could be attributed to his disinterest in

2. R. Foster, *Charles Stewart Parnell* p. 123.

the product, rather than to his avowed 'inability to sell anything', as he once put it. In many ways, Charles's school reports, and the criticism that his own criticism engendered, are complementary: his teachers' complaints about his lack of application mask the extraordinary range of interests, talents and enthusiasms that pour out of his childhood letters to his mother. Similarly, complaints from readers of *The Irish Times*, and from disappointed performers, which judged the judge to have been unfair, hostile or unsympathetic, did not recognize the depth of compassion that often made it agonizing for him to write an unfavourable or dismissive review. Many who received unfavourable judgments of their music-making from Charles will find it hard to believe that he was a generous, deeply caring, encouraging person, but I believe that the evidence of his many kindnesses to emerging artists more than compensates for the image of the grumpy, self-indulgent critic that prevailed, especially in the 1970s.

Charles Acton spent three decades as music critic of *The Irish Times*. I hope to bring to life both the ethos and the extraordinary contribution made by Charles as one of the pillars of its arts coverage and someone whose presence helped to create the vibrancy with which the paper addressed Irish cultural life, and whose value can be measured by the response of his colleagues at the time of his death.

Conscience and belief are the affair of the man with himself, and cannot be taught from without. As the then *Irish Times* columnist Kevin Myers wrote after Charles's death, 'He was confident. He knew his mind, and he spoke it, perhaps more forthrightly than many people found comforting. It would be easy for those who did not understand his manner to think that he was being arrogant. He wasn't. He was being honest. In his world the mind existed that one should speak it. It was that simple.' He was not always as confident as he appeared in later life, and he had to work hard to convince his public that his forthrightness came more from his honesty than from his arrogance. *Charles* attempts a portrait of this man.

The principal personalities in this story are:

Thomas Acton (I), *circa* 1625–1716; his grandson

Thomas Acton (II), 1671–1750, the builder of Kilmacurragh; High Sheriff for County Wicklow 1711 and 1745; his son

William Acton (I), 1711–79; Keeper of the Writs of the Court of Common Pleas; his son

Thomas Acton (III), 1742–1817; High Sheriff for County Wicklow 1781; his son

William Acton (II), 1789–1854; JP, High Sheriff for County Wicklow 1820, MP for Wicklow 1841–48; added the wings to Kilmacurragh 1848; his son

Thomas Acton (IV), 1826–1908, the creator of the Arboretum; JP, High Sheriff for County Wicklow, 1857, Chairman of Rathdrum Poor Law Board of Guardians; his sister

Janet Acton, 1824–1906; family archivist; their younger brother

Charles Ball-Acton (I), 1830–97; Colonel, King's Own Yorkshire Light Infantry; his son

Charles Annesley Ball-Acton (II), 1876–1915; High Sheriff for County Wicklow 1913, killed in action at Loos; his brother

Reginald Ball-Acton, 1877–1916, killed in action at Ypres; his wife

Isabel Ball-Acton, *née* Richmond, 1876–1970; her second husband

Hugh Digues La Touche, 1891–1933; Reginald and Isabel's son:

Charles Ball-Acton (III), later Charles Acton, 1914–99; his wife

Carol Acton, *née* Little, born 1927.

Acton Family Tree

```
THOMAS = Alice Coventry
   |
Edward        Thomas
d. 1656       d. 1716
   |
THOMAS = Elinor Kempston
   |
Thomas Ball = Grace
1671–1750
   |
   +— Jane        William
   |              d. 1794
   |
   +— THOMAS = Elinor Kempston
          |
          +— WILLIAM = Jane            Elinor = Rev. John      Alice = Henry
          |  1711–1779  Parsons                 Blachford              Kempston
          |                                                            her cousin
          |
   Anna Maria = George        Jane = George Meares      THOMAS = Sidney Davis
   b. 1784      Warburton     b. 1787  Drought          d. 1817
          |
   +— Maria    Sidney Caroline   Janet    THOMAS   William = Elizabeth   Charles    WILLIAM = Caroline Walker      Rev. Thomas = Sidney Evans
   |  1819–    1820–    1822–    1824–    1826–    1827–     Robinson     1830–       1789–1854  his cousin          1792–1846
   |  1835     1841     1834     1906     1908     1904                   1897
   |
   Anna Maria = George (Warburton)…
          |
   +— William   Evelyn = Edward   Grace    CHARLES REGINALD = Isabel     Vere    Irene       Thomas Hampden = Lucy      Margaret = Henry  Anna Sophia = George
   |  1871–     1873–    Wynne    1876–    1877–              Richmond    1879–   1883–       1818–            Ussher    1822–      Bayly   d. 1911      Drought
   |  1884      1965              1915     1916                           1900    1966        1843             d. 1899                              her cousin
   |
   Charles = Georgina Annesley        Hampden        Fitzmaurice = Ruby Stevenson      George = Sophia
                                      1870–1888       1873–1920                                 Parnell
          |
   CHARLES = Carol Little
   1914–1999
          |
   Hampden Anthony = Rosemary Charlton
   1913–2000
          |
   Peter = Sarah Bolton
   b. 1952
          |
   +— Gemma        Annabel      Camilla
      b. 1981      b. 1983      b. 1987
```

1. *The Anglo-Irish*

*C*harles Acton's story begins as the story of the Acton family at Kilmacurragh in County Wicklow. It is typical of the lives and fortunes of English settlers in Ireland from the seventeenth century: as landlords, members of parliament, justices of the peace, ministers in the Anglican Church, officers in the British army, riding to hounds, shooting grouse and pheasant over their own lands, and leading the sedentary lives of country gentlemen, they established the quiet and traditional aspects of the so-called 'ascendancy'. But these quiet lives were not easily achieved, and the label of having descended, however remotely, from Cromwell's army of occupation in the 1650s, and one so engraved in the popular memory by virtue of its brutality, was a permanent mark of difference and separation from those among whom these lives were lived.

This Protestant 'nation' took shape in Ireland chiefly on foot of two settlements: one, under James I, from the 1610s onwards, most notably in the 'plantations' of Ulster and Munster; the other, under the Commonwealth in the wake of Cromwell's extensive confiscations of the lands of Catholic gentry, which effectively suppressed large sections of the population in the 1650s. This confiscation or displacement was particularly marked in County Wicklow, where military strategies had included the erasure of many holdings and of their inhabitants. The occupancy of the land by Catholics was reduced from an average of 60 per cent of the land to an average of 20 per cent. Thus there were two 'nations', who had in common the denominator of *land*, which in the popular imagination was the heart's blood of the Gaelic people, and, in that of the settlers, was theirs by right of conquest or appropriation. For two-

and-a-half centuries, the land in fact belonged to neither, but constituted the single most affective entity in their lives; this would become most acute during the period when the 'Land Acts' (1870–1909), which attempted to solve this ineradicable problem, found the Actons, like most landlords, in a form of joint-ownership of the land with their tenantry.[1]

This book is in part the story of a type of people, and of their way of life, which, by Charles's time, had almost completely disappeared from Ireland, due to natural wastage, political change, economic and social circumstances, but most of all, perhaps, to lack of continuing relevance, a loss of *place* in every sense of the word.

Of all the roles of the Anglo-Irish, that of landlord was the most problematic – what it *meant* to Irish people and the Anglo-Irish who owned most of it under English law, land that, within living memory of many at the time of independence, had denied a significant number of its people a basic sustenance during the 'great' Irish Famine of the 1840s, yet continued to exert a visceral call on their imaginations. As Hubert Butler (a friend of Charles and his wife Carol) observed, speaking of 'the disillusionment endured by all Anglo-Irishmen who had given their first love to Ireland', 'sometimes even a few acres of Irish soil can give us an unreasoning obstinacy and the illusion of security… If you are heir to some trees and fields and buildings and a river bank, your love for your country can be more enduring.'[2] And a letter by Charles to his mother, written in 1939, when he was returning to Kilmacurragh to take up his inheritance, expressed similar sentiments: 'in these Wicklow mountains each mountain has its own spirit. The remains of my real history are at Kilmacurra.' Vestiges of *noblesse* would continue to tug at the heartstrings, whatever factors may have led to the creation of Kilmacurragh in the first place.

As W.E. Vaughan has written: 'The landlords in the eighteenth century had been the undisputed economic and legal centres of their localities; in the nineteenth century the state reduced them gradually to being merely rich men who lived in the countryside – their self-evident status by the early twentieth century.'[3] The 'Land Acts', as they came to be collectively called, were a velvet glove which for a time successfully muffled the iron fist of agrarian

---

1. The Land Acts provided for the government to enable tenants to buy their holdings if they so wished, and for the landlord to retain only the land which he himself actively occupied as a farmer.

2. H. Butler, *Escape from the Anthill* p. 96.

3. W.E. Vaughan, *Landlords and Tenants in Ireland* p. 12.

agitation that had been known as the 'land wars'. The violence – principally the destruction of great and middle-sized houses – would erupt again during the war of independence and the civil war, although Kilmacurragh would escape destruction in 1921–23, as it had in the Rebellion of 1798.

By the early twentieth century, land had ceased to be of any great significance as far as the former landowners were concerned. Yet the Actons at Kilmacurragh had been a remarkable succession of thoughtful and productive landlords of a middle-sized estate, noted for the unusual extent of their tenanted farms. This continued through six generations, up to the point where Charles's uncle Charlie (Charles Annesley Ball-Acton, 1876–1915) inherited Kilmacurragh. Although Kilmacurragh was a considerable distance from the 'great houses' of Wicklow – the Wingfields at Powerscourt, the Tottenhams at Woodstock, the Tighes at Rossanagh – they held the places in Wicklow society traditionally assigned by history to the landlord class.

In the preface to his edition of *Burke's Landed Gentry of Ireland* (1958) my father, the genealogist L.G. Pine, referred to the 'natural disappearance of old landed families from the Irish scene'. This was amplified in an essay in that volume, which he commissioned on 'The Changing Picture of the Irish Landed Gentry' from Mark Bence-Jones.[4] One might even perceive it as 'the changing *landscape* of the gentry', or even *mindscape*, since in both senses of the word – literal landholding and metaphorical ways of looking at the land – the outlook for the gentry was concerned with their future place in society, in physical and metaphysical terms: did they 'belong'? Had they ever 'belonged'? Did they any longer have viable estates or farms? Did they have a role in modern Irish (as distinct from 'Anglo-Irish') society? The 'nation within a nation' is today virtually extinct, and those of its members who started a new life in the new state have, like Charles himself, come to terms with the Irish Free State, which evolved, under Éamon de Valera, into the Republic of Ireland and is now largely integrated into the European Union, a process with which, as we shall see, Charles was entirely in accord.

The irony, and perhaps the tragedy, of the 'land question' in Ireland was that the *deus loci* – the adhesion to the *idea* of what the land meant to them – affected equally the tenantry and the landlords. Until the period of political agitation (both national and local) from 1879 onwards, there had been little

---

4. Later the author of *Twilight of the Ascendancy* and himself the descendant of an Irish landlord, William Bence-Jones of Lisselane, Clonakilty, County Cork, who published (1880) *The Life's Work in Ireland of a Landlord Who Tried to Do his Duty*.

articulation at a national level of this spirit on the part of the tenants and the land-less – no peasant voice to express feelings about the land.

Charles was acutely aware that it was his own class that featured in the history books of those days, rather than that of his ancestors' tenants. In his own reflections on the Acton estate and of the Wicklow landscape generally, he showed clearly that there was an unspoken, and probably unspeakable, history of those who had had no voice.

> If I gradually amassed details about life in our own neighbourhood, an inter-esting book might come out of it. The actual details about how people lived. What people ate, and how much, and how done, and what in winter? What they wore, what their houses, what they grew and how much of it they got per acre, and how they got it. Their implements. Their customs and prac-tices, prices of everything. How they travelled to what. Where the roads went to. What their domestic animals, breeds, sizes, yields. What birds beasts and insects and weeds and flowers they noticed or were bothered by. Not so much the gentry, about whom one knows something, as the ordinary people, artisans, and labourers and farmers.

These unwritten people were those whose descendants would continue to call the young landowner 'Master Charlie' long after he and his family had left the estate. Charles – maybe from a residual sense of guilt – wanted to know about the landless, who were unknown to history *because* they were landless. This, perhaps, was what he meant when he referred to 'the remains of my real history'.

Charles's letter betrays a degree of insecurity about his status on the land that was certainly characteristic, by the early twentieth century, of the Anglo-Irish as a whole. He joked that an Anglo-Irishman was never so much at home as on the mailboat between Dublin and Holyhead, but that in itself is a jocular way of echoing Arland Ussher's statement that 'an Irish Protestant never quite knows to what country he belongs'.[5] As Declan Kiberd has observed, 'The Anglo-Irish were *similar* to both the Irish and the English, but never felt *iden-tical* with either.'[6] When Charles came to live at Kilmacurragh, he was faced with the challenge of living in it as a real rather than an imagined place.

The fulcrum upon which the identity of the settler-family balances at a time of political change such as that of Irish independence is the question of

---

5. A. Ussher, *The Face and Mind of Ireland* p. 75.

6. In a programme note for a revival of Lennox Robinson's *The Big House*, Abbey Theatre, Dublin, 2008.

hyphenation: the issue is whether one continues to regard oneself as 'Anglo' or decides to become 'Irish': to move, irrevocably and without equivocation, from one side of the hyphen to the other.

Charles was 'a Wicklow man' or, as Charles said himself, 'of a Wicklow family' – the county projected its own character onto the individual. This character contributed to many factors about the Acton family: residency on their estate rather than absenteeism; conservatism in politics but compassion towards the tenantry; a much lower rate of tenant evictions than in other parts of the country; and an almost passionate concern for the landscape, especially where forestry was concerned.

Charles's eventual disposal of Kilmacurragh in 1944, and his search for gainful and meaningful employment in Ireland is in fact typical and characteristic of those Anglo-Irish who decided that there was a viable future for them within the new political entity and its changing society, however suspicious they may have been of the new politicians and however critical of the operations of the fledgling state. Charles found his place in modern Irish society, even though it was far removed from the spheres of landowning or the adherence to Church and Army, which had been the remit of most of his ancestors, because he had decided, without hesitation, to move across the Anglo-Irish hyphen.

One of the most striking facts about the Actons is that, unlike some others of the Anglo-Irish, they were resident, rather than absentee, landlords, and were closely associated with their tenants – mainly, one suspects, because a high percentage (80–85 per cent) of those tenants were Protestants (see Appendix). Moreover, during the period for which most of the Acton estate accounts survive – from the late eighteenth century to 1917 – only two or three tenant evictions appear to have taken place, for persistent non-payment of rents, while in several instances rents were deferred (an 'abatement'). This was against the background of judicial downward adjustments of existing rents as enabled by the Land Acts.

After 1854, when Thomas Acton IV inherited the estate, the family story diversified: integrated participation in 'ascendancy' affairs, and close-knit relations with neighbours (into whose families many of the Actons married) continued to be the superficial norm, yet – if a pun may be permitted – the seeds of a new direction in the life of the family were sown with Thomas's and his sister Janet's creation of the arboretum at Kilmacurragh (one of the most important in Europe, which continues to occupy a space of international significance)[7] and, two generations later, with Charles's decision to divest

---

7. Significant exceptions being the nearby Mount Usher at Ashford; Fota House in

himself of the burden of the estate and his finding a new life in the world and the politics of music. To confine oneself to reviews of classical music-making within a distinct cultural milieu would have been a convenient way of living in Anglo-Irishness. To move the argument into modern *Irish* society by discussing the politics of music-making was another aspect of Charles's *transitus*.

The changes were in many ways significant as far as the role of a former land-owner was concerned: generations of Actons held the office of High Sheriff of the county, right down to Charlie Acton in 1913. They had been justices of the peace, members of the Poor Law administration, and, in the 1840s, a member of parliament (Colonel William Acton). During the nineteenth century, exten-sive legislative reform reflected the growing power of the Catholic nation: preceding the Land Acts came the inexorable march of cognate legislation, beginning with Catholic Emancipation in 1829, the continued extension of the franchise to Catholics in the period 1865–84, and the abolition of tithes with the disestablishment of the Church of Ireland in 1869. The Local Govern-ment Act of 1898 established elected local authorities to replace a hierarchical system, maintained almost entirely by the landowning classes up to that point. If there was an 'Anglo-Irish nation', it ceased to exist when its members no longer had positions of authority in the structures of local government and the administration of justice, and when the land they owned passed, by means of the enabling legislation, into the ownership of their tenants – a transition that was to permeate the lives and fortunes of the Actons at Kilmacurragh up to the time of its sale by Charles in 1944. With the new State in 1922, very few landed families had any further association with local administration – the Actons' neighbour at Glendalough, Robert Barton, a signatory of the Anglo-Irish Treaty, being one of them.[8]

Perhaps only in the arts has the presence of the Anglo-Irish hand and voice been maintained, and here Charles and his close friend Brian Boydell provide outstanding examples. They occupied a new form of centrality to Irish society through their seminal contributions to Irish culture and cultural politics. In this

---

Cork; the Actons' distant relations, the Annesleys, at Castlewellan in County Down; and another distantly related family, the Parsons (Earls of Rosse) at Birr.

8. Robert Childers Barton (1881–1975), a cousin of Erskine Childers, was Minister for Agriculture and then for Economic Affairs in the first (pre-independence) Dáil, in the period leading up to the Treaty negotiations; he signed the Treaty but subsequently repudiated it, leaving politics for a legal career. He was chairman of the Agricultural Credit Corporation 1935–54.

they were typical of the 'new Ireland', but atypical of their class and education; it is therefore difficult to say whether they were, as Roy Foster says of Parnell, 'the logical outcome' of their context or a temperamental reaction to it.

Much of the foregoing is a commonplace in the Irish history books, but a letter from Charles to his mother, written in March 1940, expresses essentially the same notion of an Anglo-Irishman finding his way into a feeling of Irishness and of purposefully being Irish:

> I don't think I am likely to get narrower and narrower by living in this parish. From that point of view my class and generation are lucky. For we are to some extent stateless. A few of the Anglo-Irish continue to live like such of their parents as are left. There are a few of the modern generation who refuse to face reality, and dream that they count for something in this new Ireland. But of course we count for nothing in it. We are regarded tolerantly as foreigners, pityingly described as West Britons, and it is made plain that comments on the country are NOT wanted. An Anglo-Irish is regarded as purely Anglo, unless, like Yeats, Parnell, Pearse, Gregory they have done something which the Irish feel is an asset: then they call them Irish, and forget the Anglo. We are by circumstances made to feel stateless. Occasionally in the evenings earlier on, I listened to the conversations [at Kilmacurragh Park Hotel, as it became] and occasionally suggested small points or larger points where the country might in some way be improved, or mentioned that the present national education, or the graft and corruption, or the censorship, or the tariff on gramophone records, and so forth, were bad. The answer has always been, 'If you can speak like that *you're no Irishman*: anyway you're English' [*my italics*]. I pointed out that feeling myself somewhat Irish I found these things regrettable. But no, they are still in the stage that because it is theirs, Irish not English, therefore it must be perfect. Therefore anybody with any intelligence, any foreign experience, and a Protestant (or enlightened Catholic as opposed to Irish Catholic) upbringing, if he has any intelligence must feel himself slightly alien.
>
> You see, the older generation of Anglo-Irish grew up in the country when to be the Gentry meant that you were the dominant force in the land, that you were in the middle of what was going on ... Now all that has gone.
>
> In the fullness of time... the wheel may turn. Then our generation could be intensely useful, since by having been made to be international and detached, we can criticize constructively. Some day the country may listen: now if one of us were to write to say such constructive criticism, we should be banned and stoned out of the country.

There could be few more explicit acknowledgments by a member of the former landlord class of both the closure of the age in which they had enjoyed privilege and the need to seek a new life in what was without doubt a troubled and vulnerable environment. 'You're no Irishman' rang in his ears and in his conscience for many years, because it was untrue and yet unanswerable; such was the rhetoric of nationalism.

For the senior member of the family (usually the eldest son), the house and lands were often the only world he knew. For the younger sons, it became a distant home for most of their lives: Charles's grandfather, Charles Ball-Acton and his brother William made their homes in England once their careers as army officers had ended. An occupation in the clergy, the army, or in colonial service was the option for all except those few whose families were so wealthy that they could afford to live as country gentlemen. As Hubert Butler put it, 'they were stupid and defenceless simply because since the Union they had exported all their brightest and their bravest to England. They had generalled her armies, governed her provinces, dominated her newspapers and her theatres, written her plays. Many of those who remained behind had been educated in England and knew nothing of Ireland's problems.'[9]

Charles was an only child – and, at the age of two, fatherless. His grandfather commented on the fact that the four surviving children of William Acton II experienced an isolated childhood, to which the character of the house seems to have contributed. For the house itself Charles had little affection. But for the concept he had a passionate attachment. The idea of exploring one's relation to history was one that fascinated and compelled him.

From Charles's schooldays he exhibited many of the characteristics that made him into the concerned citizen who saw himself in a particular role in Irish society. Like Hubert Butler, who might be regarded as a keeper of the Protestant conscience of Ireland, he made it clear what he thought, even when that was painful to both himself and those to whom he spoke. In the Actons, and in Charles in particular, the love of country, at first local and later of much wider significance, becomes manifest and open to exploration and debate on many levels.

---

9. H. Butler, *Escape from the Anthill* p. 87.

2. The Actons of Kilmacurragh, 1697–1915

i: 1697–1854

Origins

*W*ho were they? And where did they come from? All settlers display anxiety about origins: in relation to both the point of departure and the time of arrival; in particular, an anxiety about responsibility. It is therefore important for them not only to establish a stable regime of their own and, if possible, to reach some accommodation with the society into which they have arrived, but also to maintain knowledge of where they have come from, which will always have an ambiguous meaning as 'the home place'. 'Home' is two places: where you are now, and where you originated, where you have put down roots and the roots from which you came. Both can pull in different directions, and for Charles this was no less significant than for other members of his family and his class. The account in this chapter of the Acton family over the course of more than two centuries occupied Charles himself, a man of ancestral images and memories, whose studio at Carrickmines was lined with the very images of those ancestors, and whose bookshelves were laden with their library.

It was conventional to believe that the first Thomas Acton, who established the family in Ireland, had been given lands in Wicklow as a reward for serving in Cromwell's army of conquest (1649–50), and this was the starting point for the family's genealogy (of which the principal authors were Charles and his aunt Irene, in the 1958 edition of *Burke's Landed Gentry of Ireland*).Yet a parallel and alternative version always existed, which absolved Thomas Acton I from political land-grabbing and situated him in the Kilmacurragh area in the decade *before* the Cromwellian occupation. As Charles observed, Irene 'is determined that we are Cromwellian; I suppose if we are we are, but one doesn't like the idea much!' He himself, on at least two occasions, asserted that the family's arrival in Ireland was pre-Cromwellian. [1]

The Actons of the late nineteenth and early twentieth centuries showed considerable interest in their 'home place' – the point from which their current life was derived. Three possible English counties – Cheshire, Shropshire and Worcestershire – had been home to branches of the family. Charles believed that they emanated from the Shropshire village of Acton Burnell, where the family has been traced to the twelfth century. [2]

In the Shropshire branch the forenames of William and Thomas are evident

---

1. In a letter to *The Irish Times* in 1984, in which he stated that the Actons had been in County Wicklow in 1640, and in his obituary in *The Irish Times* that, unbeknownst to the newspaper, had been written by Charles himself and successfully filed to await his death.

2. The Shropshire family gave rise to a baronetage, established in 1644; members of this branch later lived in France and became Catholics. One of them, Sir John Acton (1736–1811), became prime minister of Naples under Ferdinand IV, married his own niece, and became the father of a cardinal, Charles Januarius Acton and the grandfather of the first Baron Acton of Aldenham, John Emerich Edward Dalberg Acton (1834–1902). Lord Acton, while still a commoner (he was ennobled in 1869), was liberal MP for Carlow (in Ireland) 1859–65, and for Bridgnorth (near Aldenham) 1865–66; he was appointed Regius Professor of Modern History at Cambridge in 1895, and, in connection with the doctrine of papal infallibility (which he unsuccessfully opposed in 1870) was the author of the aphorism 'Power tends to corrupt, and absolute power corrupts absolutely'. Charles was mistaken in believing that 'being a highly scientific, teutonically scientific historian he wrote "tends to" in each half of his remark'. The Italian connection was always a matter of fascination for Charles, especially as, very distantly, he was related by this connection to his long-term friend, Goffredo di Biondi Morra, Prince of San Martino and Duke of Belforte, who served as Italian ambassador to Ireland for many years, and who frequently came to Charles and Carol's home to pore over the family tree, which they spread out across the drawing-room floor. The Italian branch of the family included Sir John Acton's great-great-grandson, the notable aesthete Sir Harold Acton (1904–94), but his parentage has recently been disputed. A minor Neapolitan composer, Carlo Acton (1829–1909) was also a member of the family.

in every generation, where they occur from the fifteenth century onwards. The fact that, among the elder sons, between the 1660s and the 1870s, four generations of the Irish Actons were named Thomas, and three William (and many more among the cadet branches), suggests that these were traditional forenames carried over by the first Actons from their place of origin.

Thomas I and his wife, Alice Coventry, had two sons, Edward and Thomas. Edward predeceased his parents, and his mother probated his will (dated 1654) in 1656;[3] he bequeathed £10 to his brother Thomas; his horse and, most significantly, his arrears of pay, to his father; he was described in the probate as 'Edward Acton of Loughill, County Longford'. The significance of Edward's leaving his arrears of pay to his father lies in the fact that the Cromwellian solution to rewarding the army was by means of land which had been seized from the native Irish, a policy that was continued after the restoration of the monarchy in 1660. Many who were dispossessed of their land by the 'adventurers' (as the incoming forces were conventionally as well as legally termed),[4] were given compensatory land west of the Shannon, but in Wicklow some, such as members of the Byrne, or O'Byrne, family who had held Kilmacurragh, took to the stony and less fertile uplands. The Byrne family would continue to be associated with the area, eventually settling in Cronybyrne. The two families in fact lived in a form of symbiotic captivity, the possessor and the dispossessed moving over the same landscape but with different mindscapes.

The basic dichotomy between the position of the landlords and the tenants consisted in the fact that those Irish who had been displaced in the seventeenth century (such as the Byrnes) believed that they had a moral and inalienable right to the land they had occupied up to that point, whereas the settlers/landlords who held their land under what was effectively English law regarded themselves as entitled to continue to occupy those same lands as of legal and proprietorial right. The dispute was between two completely different mindsets. The collision between them not only suggested independence for Ireland from 'the traditional enemy' but also meant the extinction of a people who in

---

3. It was witnessed by Edmund Walsh of Clonmannon, age twenty-two, and William Byrne, age nineteen.

4. The 'Adventurers Act' of 1642 (i.e. legislation enacted during the reign of Charles I) was a measure to raise funds for the suppression of the Irish uprising of 1641, by means of which an investment of £200 would be repaid by 1000 acres of Irish land. 35,000 Cromwellian soldiers were to receive land in lieu of arrears of pay; many of these sold their interest to the officer class, and approximately 7500 eventually settled.

most cases had by now only tenuous connections with the country that had originally sent them to Ireland as 'adventurers'. Both parties had suffered from the deep psychic structures that bind *land* to *memory* in the folk mind.[5] The displacement of the native Irish in the 1650s would be undone 250 years later by their reinstatement, as the descendants of the 'adventurers' were themselves displaced.

The founding of the Kilmacurragh estate, 1690s

Thomas Acton I had a house at Bog Hall, near 'Deputy's Pass', in the townland of Ballygannonbeg. He subsequently had a house at nearby Kilcandra, which had all but disappeared by 1883. Like most of his descendants, he had a house in Dublin (his was in Peter Street) where the winters were commonly spent. The Ballygannon and Kilcandra lands remained a central part of the Acton estate up to the time of its dispersal. These lands were the context and the hinterland of Charles's love of Wicklow in general, and the Kilmacurragh demesne in particular, and of his interest in the local history and pre-history of the area.

The lands acquired by the Actons were imbued with ancient local history. Kilcandra and its neighbouring land at Kilmacurragh, in the parish of Dunganstown, was an historic site that still shows evidence of neolithic activity. By 1839, when Eugene Curry's work for the Ordnance Survey had brought him as far as the parish of Dunganstown, he reported that 'there is an ancient rath on the townland of Cuniamstown and two others very near it on the townland of Kilcandra'.[6] (Cunniamstown, lying south-west of Ballygannon-beg and -more, became another significant part of the Acton estate in the eighteenth century.)

An early eighteenth-century map of the area clearly shows a church of St Mochura, two fish ponds and an orchard, which were part of the original monastery on the site.[7] Maps would become an important part of the estate records; at one point, a textbook (which may have belonged to William I) was employed at Kilmacurragh to instruct in the exact measurement by trigonometry of the acres, rods, poles and perches of the lands let to the Actons' tenants

---

5. This is discussed in T. Dooley, *The Big Houses and Landed Estates of Ireland*, pp. 1 off. and in his 'Landlords and the Land Question' in Carla King (ed.) *Famine, Land and Culture* p. 126; *cf.* also Philip Bull, *Land Politics and Nationalism* (pp. 67, 93, 95).

6. *The Ordnance Survey Letters — Wicklow*, p. 115.

7. In 1275 Kilmacurragh was known as 'Kilmechur'; in 1531 as 'Kilmethur'.

— a bivalent symbol, making tangible the evidence of the occupier's holding and the fields of the dispossessed.[8]

The building of Kilmacurragh began less than forty years after the restoration of the monarchy and only seven years after the decisive battle of the Boyne; the Actons had been in possession of land in the area for less than thirty of those years, yet not only was a deer park decided upon, suggesting a high degree of permanent residency, but Kilmacurragh was one of the first houses to be built without fortifications.[9]

Thomas II, who started the building of Kilmacurragh in 1697, was born in 1671. He was, in effect, the founding father of Kilmacurragh.[10] The earliest extant documentation in the Acton family papers relating to the years immediately before the building of Kilmacurragh is a notebook by Thomas II, in which he recorded his buying and selling of sheep and cattle in the years 1694–7. It also included the fact that he grew flax, which permitted a considerable quantity of linen to be made at home – in the late nineteenth century, part of the immediate Kilmacurragh demesne was denoted as 'the Bleach Field', indicating the area where the bleaching of the linen took place. The notebook also proves that his father (also Thomas) was still alive at this date, suggesting that there was no straightforward succession to the land by Thomas II, but that he was in fact starting out on his own at Kilmacurragh, while his father continued in residence at Kilcandra. The memoranda pre-date the building of Kilmacurragh, indicating that Thomas II had a residence of some kind on the site before the new house was begun. Thomas's account book is punctuated with the record that 'My father dyed at Kilcandra on Saturday ye 10th day of Novemr 1716 & was buried in Rathdrum Church on Tuesday ye 13 of Novr 1716.'

The family interest in trees is in early evidence in a single entry by Thomas senior, reminding his son to prepare for grafting walnut and chestnut, oak and ash, and also 'to get w[hite] oates ych [which] can [be] threshed & made money of'. The coincidence of commercial potential and aesthetic appreciation is evident

---

8. Microfilm copies of the Acton family maps were deposited by Charles in NLI in the 1980s; the originals are now in the Wicklow County Archive.

9. Although the 'Kilmacurragh Book' records that 'as was usual in houses in Ireland at that time, a small loophole was made in the hall door for the purpose if necessary of firing from'. Another entry in the same book states that the hole was cut into the door at the time of the 1798 Rebellion.

10. He is also credited with having at least contributed significantly to the building of Wicklow workhouse in 1715.

in the cherishing of trees such as the alders in the Deer Park, which Frederick Moore (Director of the Botanic Gardens in Dublin 1879–1922) considered to be the remnants of a primeval forest. In time, Clara would provide a commercial interest in timber that continued up to the 1930s.[11]

Thomas II, who was only twenty-six years old when he started building Kilmacurragh, was very much 'on the way up'. He was not yet a 'landed gentleman' since his personal involvement in buying and selling sheep, cattle and horses at the local fairs indicates that he was still a 'hands-on' farmer, but within thirty years the family had moved from being minor landholders to the threshold of the 'gentry' class. Thomas II already had approximately a dozen tenants of his own in the late 1690s, whose surnames include some that would continue to figure in the estate records right up to 1916/17: Byrne, Bradshaw, Taylor and Farrell in particular,[12] while William Hudson, a member of a family closely associated with the Actons for two centuries, was working at Kilmacurragh from as early as 1714. Many smallholders also sold produce to Thomas II, or were employed by him in labouring work.

The cost of building the original house at Kilmacurragh was £1500— a remarkably small outlay even for a moderately small house. The wood carving on the staircase was undertaken, probably by an Italian woodcarver then working in Dublin, at a cost of £6. It is unclear how Thomas, with or without his father's contribution, commanded sufficient capital to invest in the building of Kilmacurragh. From 1707 to 1709, and again in 1720, a total of £3000 was spent on improvements to both the land and the house; work on the land included levelling the ground, building garden walls, and making a courtyard. £142 was spent on building the wall around the Deer Park, which extended to over forty acres. Later, in 1730, two masons were employed to build another seven-feet-high wall around the deer park. According to the 'Kilmacurragh

---

11. Clara had been owned by Thomas I since at least 1758, when he advertised its timber for sale in *Saunder's Newsletter*.

12. Thomas I's accounts record 'William Farrell, Loghlin Farrell, Hugh Standun and Widdow Pluck' as tenants at Cunniamstown in 1705. Patrick Byrne had grazing land with a house and garden at Ballygannonbeg in 1705. Other names which occur as renting land in the first decade of the eighteenth century include George Tomlinson (land at Ballygannonbeg and Kilmanoge), William Manley (Kilcandra, 1704), Patrick Doyle (Kilmanoge, 1707), Jacob Williams (Bolagh and Tullylusk, 1704), Richard McDaniels (Cunniamstown, 1707). One of the first instances of a lease being mentioned is in connection with William Ashenhurst in 1747 for land at Kilmanoge. For continuation of many of these tenancies, see Appendix.

Book', in a time of famine in the area, in 1822, local people were given employment in digging a ditch to further prevent escape by the stock.

> 1822. Famine in west of Ireland, thousands died of starvation & famine fever. The jails were full as the starving people broke windows & all sorts of things to get into prison for the food. Absentee landlords made it worse spending their money in London instead of Ireland. The famine was caused by excessive rain… During the fearful famine, all the potatoes died in the ground & the corn sprouted in the ear. Every house had a little scoop, to scoop out the eye of the potatoe [sic], reserving the greater part of the potatoe for the table. About 100 people came for work here, work which was never refused by Colonel Acton. The poor were employed making the large sunk fence round the deer park… The work took a year to do.[13]

Another version of this story, also within the family, relates that the digging took place during the 'Great Famine' of 1845, and that the employment was given to men who came from the west of Ireland: 'the starving people came in multitudes to the eastern counties for help. Our dear father [i.e. William II] gave them the work of digging the fence.' The 'Kilmacurragh Book' also refers to relief work during the Great Famine for local people who 'were reduced to the brink of famine & most abject want'.

If the term 'big house' is the common term for a landlord's residence, then it requires qualification, since Kilmacurragh was, until at least 1848, when its two wings were added, decidedly *not* a 'big house'. But, as Terence Dooley observes in his account of the decline of such houses, 'the *raison d'être* behind the building of these houses [was] to announce the economic and social strength of their owners in their localities and as a class as a whole…'[14] The physical size of Kilmacurragh was not as significant as the fact that it had been placed, as a symbol, at the centre of Thomas Acton's rapidly growing estate.[15]

---

13. One supposes that deer had in fact jumped the wall, as, after the ditch-digging, the park was re-stocked with deer from the Evans family at Portrane, which itself had originally been supplied by Kilmacurragh. In 1900 there were still a hundred head of deer, but after the First World War the wall was not maintained, and they again escaped. Today, the deer park is part of Coillte's Tree Improvement Research Station (as is the walled garden nearer the house).

14. T. Dooley, *op. cit.*, p. 9.

15. There has been considerable confusion about the name of the Kilmacurragh estate due to the change of name by Thomas III to 'Westaston', which has often been assumed to be an incorrect spelling of 'West Acton'. The family explanation, supported by local historian Stanley Lane-Poole, is that Thomas Acton II had a close friend named Aston,

It is also noteworthy that Thomas II began the planting of trees that would become so characteristic of the demesne. In his important 1933 lecture to the Royal Irish Academy on 'Tree Planting in Ireland during Four Centuries' A.C. Forbes asked, 'When did settlement and the relative permanency of land occupation advance sufficiently far for planting to be regarded as a reasonable undertaking?' Settlers might easily assume that the political situation would remain unstable, and that they might be as promptly displaced as they themselves had taken, or been granted, the land on which they built.

So far as the actual tree-planting is concerned, Thomas II distinguished himself as a planter, adding to the 300–400 yew trees, which Myles Reid believes to have been part of the original monastery gardens. Much later, in 1780, Thomas Acton III planted an avenue of silver firs towards the lower gate lodge, which earned a £10 prize from the Dublin Society.

The Actons as local officials

With Thomas II we see, in 1711, the appointment of the head of the family to the position of High Sheriff, a post to which he was re-appointed in 1745, and in which he was followed by his future male heirs.

One of the first appointments of an Acton in the local government system was on foot of membership of the Grand Jury. This body, consisting of approximately twenty of the county's largest landowners, assembled twice yearly at the summons of the High Sheriff, with a semi-judicial function at the assizes, and with a growing responsibility for infrastructural works such as the repair of roads and bridges, the building of courthouses and gaols, sewerage and destroying vermin, and tax-raising to pay for such works.

In many cases, members of the gentry undertook improvements as part of their contribution to the community, although it is unclear whether they were always reimbursed for their outlay. On at least one occasion in the Acton family history, a road was built for amatory reasons, as George Drought found

---

who built his own house near Jack White's Cross, approximately three miles south-east of Kilmacurragh and a mile east of Redcross. By mutual consent, the geographical locations of these houses and the respective names of their owners were commemorated by Mr Aston calling his house 'East Acton' to complement 'West Aston'. Since the Actons later came into possession of a house at Bell Park, only a short distance from Jack White's Cross, supposition that this was in fact the previous 'East Acton' is not unjustified.

the road from Glencarrig to Kilmacurragh through the Deputy's Pass so bad that (as Charles recounted the story) he persuaded the Grand Jury to rebuild it in order to facilitate his wooing of Jane Acton. Whether he recouped the cost is not known.

The 1798 Rebellion

County Wicklow was less affected by the 1798 Rebellion than many other parts of Ireland. However, Janet Acton noted in the 'Kilmacurragh Book' that her grandfather, Thomas III, sent his wife and children for safety to his Dublin house in Peter Street. She recorded the family memory that 'on their way to Dublin the children, looking out of the windows of the carriage, were horrified to see the dead bodies of the rebels, but the sight was so frequent that at last it ceased to attract their notice'. Thomas had called for soldiers from Dublin to protect Kilmacurragh against insurgents, and he also enlisted the help of the family's music teacher, William Manley.[16] Thomas gathered the families of his Protestant tenants into the stableyard '& two fat oxen were killed for them to eat'.

Janet Acton's memoir continued: 'In defending the house against the possible arrival of the rebels the window frames were taken out & filled with sods, a square hole was cut in the middle of the door, in order to shoot the rebels from it.' Kilmacurragh was not in fact attacked, which Janet attributed to the rebels having been defeated locally at the battle of Arklow on 9 June. Only one estate worker, John Bolton of Clara, the Actons' woodranger (an early term for 'gamekeeper'), was killed by the rebels.[17]

Although there were few serious incidents in the immediate vicinity, Janet recorded that 'the heads of three men who had aided the rebels... dipped in

---

16. The surname Manley or Manly would appear fifty years later among the tenants on the estate, holding land at Kilcandra and Cunniamstown.

17. According to family legend, passed on by Charles to Fr. James Murphy, parish priest of Barndarrig 1985–96 and local historian, the forename was James, but the facts as stated by Ruán O'Donnell (*The Rebellion in Wicklow 1798*) seem to be more accurate. The latter mentions that in some records Bolton was listed as a weaver working in Clara and Rathdrum: there is no reason why he should not have been engaged in the weaving trade in addition to his work for Thomas Acton, especially as, at a later date, one of his descendants operated the forge at Kilcandra as well as being an Acton tenant.

tar, were put on pikes in front of Flannel Hall Rathdrum'.[18] Another rebel was hung between two ash trees beside the Dark Lane at Kilmacurragh and his ghost is said locally to continue to haunt the place: 'the natives still shout & whistle when passing the quarry after dark'. 'After the rebellion was all over … the rebels brought their pikes to T. Acton who was a magistrate; the sweep in front of the house was covered with pikes.' A family legend (recounted to Charles by his cousin Muriel Walker of Tykillen) has it that 'the butler was told to hide securely the family jewels but that before he had had time to tell his master after hiding them he died or was killed and the secret died with him'. A further tradition held that there was 'a cache of treasure under the thorn tree in the Oak Row' – which Charles himself disbelieved. Yet in the 1950s, Charles and his wife Carol would extensively survey the grounds with an early form of metal detector, without result.

A Wicklow Estate

East Wicklow was regarded as a 'conservative', rather than a 'radical', county, due to the high proportion of Protestants in the population. Ken Hannigan notes that, whereas a 25–50 per cent occupancy might be the norm in other parts of the county, some of the townlands on the Kilmacurragh estate in the 1830s were entirely occupied by Protestants, a situation that continued up to the 1901 census, in which it was a cause of comment.[19] This may account for the less than usual demand on the Kilmacurragh estate for 'tenant right' ownership that would develop into the 'land war'.

Of the more than 150 specific tenancies that I have been able to trace in the surviving Acton estate records (some of them leases, others year-to-year agreements), sixty-six date from before the Famine (some as early as the 1690s). Forty-two were started in 1848–49 and forty-eight in subsequent years (up to 1916, in fact). This suggests that there may have been a recognition on the part

---

18. The Hall had been built in 1792, principally by Lord Fitzwilliam, at a cost of £3500 in order to stimulate trade in the area. The Chevalier de Latocnaye (*Promenade d'un Français dans l'Irlande* 1798) believed that £4000-worth of flannel would be sold at the monthly fair.

19. 'Wicklow before and after the Famine', in Hannigan and Nolan, *Wicklow – History and Society*, and in 'The Barndarrig Band: life and death in an East Wicklow village of the 1890s' in the *Journal of the Wicklow Historical Society* 1995.

of William Acton II, his agents and perhaps Thomas, his heir apparent, of the need to put their tenants' occupancy onto a more secure footing. Since only ten tenancies were negotiated in the years 1845–48, it may, however, simply indicate that it was only after the Famine had subsided that tenants felt sufficiently recovered and secure to enter into new agreements with their landlords.

The Actons appear to have been exceptional in the number of leases that they granted. In Ireland as a whole, approximately 25 per cent of tenants were leaseholders (135,000 out of 540,000). The vast majority had yearly tenancies, or tenancies for a term of years or for the lives of named persons. Barbara Solow points out that 'although the yearly tenancy sounds precarious, such tenancies in fact existed for generations and were regarded by tenants as a perpetual interest'.[20]

William Acton II (1789–1854):

HIS FAMILY

Considering the duration of William's ownership of Kilmacurragh (almost forty years) and his political career, it is surprising that we know comparatively little about him. The crucial factor in his life seems to have been his marriage to his first cousin, Caroline Walker, which took place in 1818, a year after he inherited the estate. Caroline, who was to survive him by twenty-five years (he died in 1854, she in 1879), seems to have been the focus of attention and affection for her surviving four children. Two elements permeated the marriage: firstly, the fact that Caroline brought considerable funds to Kilmacurragh, and secondly the evidence in the family lore that this was a love-match with deep devotion between husband and wife.

William and Caroline had four daughters, three of whom died prematurely (Maria, 1819–35; Sidney, 1820–41; and Caroline, 1822–34). These three deaths within a space of seven years may have contributed both to the intensifying of the Actons' religious feelings and to the reticence of which their youngest child, Charles, would write in 1860. The fourth daughter, Janet, born in 1824, died unmarried in 1906. She recorded in the 'Kilmacurragh Book' that 'our dear father made the fine garden for us, saying as a child he never got fruit enough & that if ever he had children he would insure their having an abundance of it'.

---

20. B. Solow, *The Land Question and the Irish Economy* pp. 7–10.

The births of the girls were followed by the eldest boy, Thomas IV (born 1826), who would become 'Uncle Tom' to the family and would inherit the Kilmacurragh estate, outliving his younger brothers and dying unmarried in 1908. The second eldest, William (born 1827), appears to have been reclusive and unsocial, although he did serve in the Crimean war, fighting at Sebastopol and Inkerman. [21] Although William married, he, like his elder brother, would die (in 1904) without issue. The youngest child of the marriage, Charles, who seems to have been his parents' favourite, would become grandfather of our chief subject, and would inherit considerable wealth on condition that he

---

21. The second son of William and Caroline, also William, no doubt realizing, as did so many younger sons, that his future lay not with the family estate but farther afield, opted for a military career, as would his younger brother, Charles. In the same week as his father's death, William was aboard ship in the Black Sea with the 77th (East Middlesex) Regiment, describing their passage through the Bosphorus and arrival at Scutari. On 14 May 1854, the army proceeded to garrison Varna. He commented on a fire in the stores at Varna 'It was the vile Greeks did it. They did not all escape. An English sailor passing with a hatchet chopped one scoundrel's head in two, a Zuane bayoneted another, two more were thrown into their own fire, and two others hanged, all these fates were not bad enough for them, the whole race are villains.' In September he had been under heavy fire from the Russians at the battle of Alma, and had injured his knee, but he was nevertheless able to continue in this engagement and, six weeks later, at Inkerman. Between the two battles, at almost the exact date that Florence Nightingale was *en route* to Scutari, William was able to observe the hospital conditions there: 'our sick and wounded are dying at the rate of 25 a day – I believe in a great measure from want of care & medical attendance. The French really take care of their sick & wounded – it is a disgrace to England the neglect of our wounded. Many men told me no doctor saw them or dressed their wounds for 5 days after the battle. The French carried nearly all our sick to the beach at Alma. I was carried by them – we had no means of carriage almost.' As a lieutenant in the 77th regiment, during the battle of Inkerman on 5 November 1854, he was ordered to advance on a Russian battery with the remaining fifty or sixty men of his detachment; as related by Alexander Kinglake in his *Battle of Inkerman* (1875), when the soldiers indicated that they were too few in numbers to carry out the task, William declared 'I'll go by myself', and proceeded to march off some thirty or forty yards towards the Russians before his men decided to follow his example. Having got under the range of enemy fire, they succeeded in putting the Russians to flight, thus earning him the knickname 'the hero of Inkerman', and promotion to the rank of captain. He required convalescence for his injured knee at Scutari before being sent back to England in 1855. The injury was a permanent disability, and as late as 1894 Janet noted that 'he is so feeble he had to [sit] in a wheelchair'.

adopt the additional surname of Ball. It was due to Thomas IV having survived both his younger brothers that, on his death, the estate passed to Charles Ball-Acton's elder surviving son, also Charles.

On the home front, William and Caroline seem to have encountered severe problems in attracting – and, more significantly, keeping – domestic staff. This was no doubt partly due to the isolation of the house, deep in the Wicklow countryside, and partly to the sombre atmosphere that pervaded the family.[22]

HIS SOCIAL AND POLITICAL POSITION AS LANDLORD AND MP

The most frustrating fact about William's career is that the estate records are silent for most of his tenure. This is disappointing for the reason that his later years spanned the Great Famine of 1845–48. There are almost no surviving records or diaries from Kilmacurragh for the Famine years,[23] although there are extant records for the Poor Law union at Rathdrum, of which William was the inaugural chairman in 1839.[24]

---

22. Cooks and maidservants came and went with considerable frequency; 'staid 6 days' is a not uncommon record of a new servant's arrival and departure. In 1832 a cook was hired at the standard rate of £10 per annum and was discharged eight months later, 'not sober and most abusive'. Another was 'a bad cook & very ill-tempered'. Also in 1832 Mary Dalton, housemaid, was discharged for being 'a most dangerous and deceitful person'. In 1834 Mary Baker was let go, 'having assaulted with a hatchet & otherwise conducted herself in a most outrageous manner'. Of the outdoors staff, a groom was discharged after less than two weeks: 'threw himself off mare, said horse reared & fell on him, a lie as Bowes saw it – let the mare run away – a cowardly liar'. Another stable-boy, Patrick Thwaites, was discharged in 1847 for 'absenting himself at night & sleeping in the stables after drinking'. On the other hand, some staff were treasured for their long association with the family: Catherine Redmond, for example, came in 1790, married Christian Bolton in 1798 and remained in service until 1821. Later, Thomas IV would advertise for staff in specific terms: 'Wanted, able-bodied country girl, Protestant, not out before preferred, £12 a year, if able to dairy £15'. Wages in 1783 were £4 per year for a house servant, £5 for a labourer. In 1839–40 the following annual wages were paid: kitchen maid, £4; cook, £14; housemaid, £6; laundress, £4; lady's companion, £12.12.0; coachman, £12–14; woodranger, £10; gardener, £10.

23. A similar gap occurs in the estate records for the Parnells at Avondale.

24. Cf. Terence Dooley, The Big Houses and Landed Estates (p. 28), who comments on the lack of literature on the topic: 'given the centrality of the landed estates to Irish rural society and economy, it seems remarkable that in this outpouring of works [on

William's election to parliament was by no means a foregone conclusion: he was unsuccessful in his attempts at the 1832 and 1837 general elections, but was elected in 1841 and re-elected in 1847. His six years as an MP were not notable – he spoke only three times, and never on matters directly pertaining to the Famine.[25]

William's attendance at Westminster was seasonal, and suggests that local business may have been more important to him than merely supporting the government in parliamentary divisions. His maiden speech was a most unfortunate affair, since he had inadvertently entered the wrong lobby on a division on the government grant to St Patrick's College, Maynooth. This had led him to support the government, whereas his intention had been to oppose it.[26]

An indication of William's involvement in local administration in the county in general and in Rathdrum in particular, was his third speech in the Commons, on 5 May 1843, in support of the Poor Law relief system.

> Colonel Acton said he had for many years been anxious to rescue the unfortunate and destitute hundreds and thousands of his fellow-countrymen from their long dependence on the casual charity of their fellow-countrymen ... He had gladly hailed the enactment of a legislative remedy for Irish distress ... He had been at great pains to ascertain the working of the measure ... and from the result he was enabled to congratulate the country on the amount of good that had been achieved.[27]

---

the Famine] there remained a dearth of focus on the effects of the Famine on individual Irish estates, big houses or landed families'.

25. William had stood in the 1832 general election, when he polled 661 votes as against the elected MPs, his distant cousin, James Grattan (717), and Ralph Howard (710) – a member of the family at Shelton Abbey (Earls of Wicklow). He did not stand in 1835, but in 1837 he received 623 votes, again being beaten by Grattan and Howard (the latter was related to the Parnells). In 1841, he topped the poll with 663 votes, Howard (who had succeeded to the family baronetcy) receiving 603, and Grattan being defeated with 563. He held the seat unopposed (along with Viscount Milton, son of the Earl of Fitzwilliam) in 1847, but resigned the following year when, in the consequent by-election, Howard won back his seat in company of C.S. Monck. The diaries of James Grattan (NLI) would repay study as to the cut-and-thrust of party politics in County Wicklow at this time, not least the exploitation of landlords' power over their tenants' voting patterns and the pragmatism with which candidates such as Grattan changed their policies from one election to the next.

26. His speech of explanation and self-exoneration is at *Hansard* vol. 54, col. 692.

27. *Ibid.*, vol. 68, cols. 1346–7 on the Poor Relief (Ireland) Bill.

However, even though he appears to have been present, William did not speak during the week-long 1846 Famine debate on 'Famine and Disease in Ireland', when Sir Robert Peel avowed that the victims of the Famine were predominantly dependent on 'the spontaneous charity of the landed proprietors' on whom there was 'an undoubted claim' and who, Peel was sure, 'will not fail to come forward at this period of great general distress'.[28] It is important to note that other Irish MPs were in fact absent: when it was complained that William Smith O'Brien was not present to pursue his arguments about Famine relief, John O'Connell pointed out that 'it was more important for him to be in his constituency', and it may well be, especially during the worst years of the Famine, that William had the same priorities. He was absent in April 1847 when the House debated the 'Landed Property (Ireland) Bill' to tax property so as to fund Famine relief, and was back at Westminster at the end of that year, to vote against the establishment of a committee of inquiry into the 1800 dissolution of the Irish Parliament and the effects of 'continuing the legislative union between both countries'.[29]

William's elevated positions not only as MP but also as vice-lieutenant of the county, and as a justice of the peace, as well as holding a colonelship in the Wicklow Militia, would have exposed him both to the major famine of the 1840s and to that of 1822. Although there is nothing to prove it, the building in 1848 of the two wings of Kilmacurragh, considerably enlarging what had previously been a relatively small house, may also have been partly motivated by compassion for out-of-work labourers. It was certainly not undertaken in order to enhance his status, since 1848 was the year in which he resigned his membership of parliament (probably on grounds of ill health), nor was it done to provide space for his family, since by that time only his son Thomas and daughter Janet remained at home.[30]

---

28. *Ibid.*, vol. 84, col. 782. In fact, approximately 25 per cent of landlords were bankrupted by their attempts to succour their tenants during the Famine. Peel was no doubt completely correct when he said that 'without their aid, without the local efforts of those who are acquainted with the particular circumstances of the district, the intervention of the Government would be useless.'

29. In December 1847 he spoke on the Crime and Outrage (Ireland) Bill regarding the intimidation of jurors.

30. Charles (letter to Roger Hill, 5 February 1976) stated that 'the moral and economic principles of the day were that relief must not be given, but must be provided in return for work; and that the work should have no economic significance, so that both the economy as such and those in employment should not be harmed by relief work.'

Local government and the Poor Law

A highly practical and extensive involvement in community affairs was the operation from 1839 of the Poor Law relief, including the workhouses, under the authority of Poor Law 'guardians'. As Eva Ó Cathaoir tells us, 'This was the case in County Wicklow, where the officers of the first Rathdrum board were landlords: Acton of Kilmacurragh, Parnell of Avondale and Synge of Glanmore.'[31] William's chairmanship in the inaugural year of the Rathdrum Poor Law Union in 1839 is indicative of the Acton family's status within the Protestant community and, indeed, of the wider county establishment at that stage. The 'Union' was a euphemism for *workhouse*, and in two respects it was a radical reform, in that it created a new tier of local administration, and brought into existence a phenomenon that had a profound effect on the minds of those most likely to find themselves as its clients.[32] County Wicklow was divided into three unions: Baltinglass to the west, Rathdrum in the centre and east, and Shillelagh to the south. Rathdrum seems to have had the most extensive remit, and as it was so close to the estates of the Parnells, Actons, Synges and Dicks, their *ex-officio* membership of the Rathdrum board was inevitable.

The Irish Poor Relief Act of 1838 was designed to achieve a balance between those members of the community who, by reason of major land-holding, were appointed *ex officio* members of the boards of guardians (as they were called) and those elected. The Act gave the vote for the first time to many small land-holders and businessmen, although the franchise was restricted and based on the value of property held.[33] This was the first opportunity for non-landlords to become involved in a very locally based form of government, which would continue until the system was subsumed by the Local Government Act of 1898, which created the county councils and, thereby, also ended the Grand Jury system which was another fiefdom of the landed classes. In the sixty years of their existence, the boards of guardians became increasingly dominated by

---

31. 'The Poor Law in County Wicklow' in Hannigan and Nolan, *Wicklow – History and Society*.

32. *Cf.* J.M. Synge, 'In Wicklow, as in the rest of Ireland, the union, though it is a home of refuge for the tramps and tinkers, is looked on with supreme horror by the peasants. The madhouse, which they know better, is less dreaded': *Collected Works*, vol. II, p. 30.

33. In Rathdrum, there were 10 *ex-officio* members and 24 elected; of the latter, two described themselves as merchants, two as millers, one was a schoolmaster and five were tenants.

elected representatives in areas experiencing more severe poverty, but this was not the case in counties with a conservative tradition. [34]

One perspective from which to view this incipient democracy is to say that in Wicklow the beneficent nature of landlords earned the respect and support of the tenantry. Another is to acknowledge that where, as in the case of the Acton estates, there was a strong Protestant element in the farming community, the landlord class was almost certain to be re-elected. Deference to the gentry was endemic: the 'Kilmacurragh Book' contains an example of William Acton and his brother-in-law George Drought acting to control a potentially dangerous situation that seems to have occurred in 1840:

> In Rathdrum there were two breweries. One of these was turned into a factory for making starch out of bad potatoes. The poor people fearing that their chief article of food was to be used for manufacturing purposes, began to raise a riot. Colonel Acton & George Drought & some other gentlemen rode into Rathdrum to try & pacify the people. George Drought began to speak to them, but the people with one voice cried, 'We will not hear you. Colonel Acton the friend of the poor is the only one we will listen to.' He reassured them & promised them that as a magistrate he & George Drought would not allow the manufacturing to continue. The people trusted the word of the 'Friend of the Poor' and quietly dispersed.

William was initially appointed chairman of the Union on the proposal of John Synge, with John Parnell as vice-chairman, keeping that position for most of his life. Parnell[35] and Edward Bayly served as vice-chair and, while he was able, William attended approximately half of the weekly meetings.

Most of the farms on the Acton lands averaged 100 acres, and this may have been a major contributing factor to the relatively harmless effects of the Famine on their lands. Unfortunately, due to the almost complete *lacuna* in the estate records for the 1840s, we know nothing of the rate of emigration from any of the Acton lands, although the county as a whole witnessed substantial emigration both before and after the Famine; before it, the Fitzwilliam estate had assisted emigration to clear uneconomic holdings; after it, Elizabeth Smith records that local men and boys were 'pouring out in shoals'. [36]

---

34. Cf. W. Feingold, *The Revolt of the Tenantry: the transformation of local government in Ireland 1872–1886*, *passim*.

35. John Henry Parnell chaired the Rathdrum Union from 1852 until his death in 1859.

36. In the records under Thomas Acton IV's ownership, there is mention of only three individuals leaving the lands – two to America and one to Australia. William

It is inconceivable that William Acton was not deeply affected by famine conditions. Many of his contemporaries and neighbours in the county must have experienced conflicting emotions when faced with the emancipation of the Catholic population, the need to derive an income from their estates, and the responsibility to provide relief for the starving population. As Protestants they believed in the need to maintain both the primacy of the Church of Ireland and the union with Britain.[37]

William's health seems to have declined rapidly in 1848, possibly as a result of a stroke, but he lived another six years. From 1851 he was unable to conduct his own affairs, which were taken over by the twenty-five-year-old Thomas IV. William's youngest son, Charles, wrote at one point to say how glad he was to hear that his father had been able to be taken out of the house in a wheelchair, knowing how much he enjoyed the outdoors. For his part, three months before he died, William wrote to Charles signalling the incipient arboretum: 'we have lately heard of wonderful trees in California some of them over 120 feet high 22 feet in girth'; these were almost certainly the *sequoia* that were in fact planted at Kilmacurragh around this time, and with this letter he enclosed a copy of Thomas Moore's poem 'Fairest put on a while':

> Fairest put on a while
> The pinions of light I bring thee
> And o'er thy evergreen isle
> In fancy let me bring thee.[38]

He told Charles that the poem was 'the best description I ever met of the beauties of Ireland in a few lines'. Apart from his religious devotions, it is the only personal expression that has come down to us to show that William had feelings for poetry or the landscape.

Brennan worked in the stables 1852–54, before going to Australia: 'honest sober quiet & careful of horses & cleaned them well'. A stable-boy who left in 1847 to go to America received a loan of £12.

37. One member of the family, Jane (d. 1794), youngest daughter of William I and Jane Parsons, was shunned by her relatives because in 1787 she befriended John Wesley and became a Methodist.

38. The poem was included in Moore's *Irish Melodies* vol. 9 (1824); it is based on an eighteenth-century air on the theme of nature and Ireland's natural beauties, and contains references to the Skelligs and Glengariff: I am obliged to Moore's biographer, Dr Ronan Kelly, for this information.

ii: 1854–1915

Succession of Thomas IV and the growth of the estate

Kilmacurragh in the mid-nineteenth century has been described as: 'a good example of Wicklow's middle gentry families: resident, involved in local administration and military establishment, energetic promoters of silviculture and high farming'.[39]

By 1840, the Acton estate, with almost 5500 acres, was the seventeenth largest in the county, comparable to the lands of the Synges, Kemmises, Tighes, Whaleys, Hoeys and Byrnes, the latter four being the Actons' immediate neighbours. It was very small, however, when compared to the Meath (23,000 acres), Downshire (15,000), Powerscourt (21,000), Hugo (20,000), Beresford (23,000) or Carysfort (16,000) estates, or that of the Earl of Wicklow (21,000).[40]

It is easy to accept William Nolan's observation that 'landlords strode imperiously across early nineteenth-century Wicklow'. Given the principal interest of the man who became known within the family as 'Uncle Tom' – the acquisition and breeding of rare plants and trees – it is difficult to see Thomas Acton IV 'striding imperiously' around the county. Yet, despite the family perception of him as a shy, retiring bachelor, there is also a local folk memory of him as a stern Justice of the Peace, and although the estate records show him to have been a friendly landlord, he was clearly resourceful and reasonably successful in maintaining his property. It is significant, however, that Charles recalled the family image of Thomas as 'perfectly beastly to his tenants', despite 'his habit of distributing everything left over from dinner to his employees to take home with them'.

Thomas's was a much more complex character than might at first be supposed, and both his home environment and the accelerating decline of the landlord class are contributing factors in his apparent ambivalence towards the land and its occupants. Even Thomas's idiosyncratic choice of burial place

---

39. William Nolan, 'Land and Landscape' in Hannigan and Nolan, *op. cit.*, p. 661.

40. However, the size of an estate did not necessarily indicate its value, since, for example, the Hugo estate was largely mountainous and of poor quality, despite ranking seventh largest in the county, after the enormous holdings of Fitzwilliam (79,000), which dwarfed even those of Beresford, Wingfield or the Earl of Wicklow.

(beneath his favourite tree, a *Pinus ponderosa*, at the entrance to the deer park) was due partly to his devotion to his trees and partly to the fact that in 1900 he had had an acrimonious dispute with the select vestry at Dunganstown, where he was parish treasurer and nominator to the rectorship, which seems to have decided him not to be buried with his ancestors in the family vault there. Janet had already been buried in the same spot, and Sir Frederick Moore told Charles forty years later that 'Your Uncle Tom made me promise to see that he & Miss Acton were buried in the deer park, & himself marked out the spot when Miss Acton died [in 1906]. I was with him and when he died I was present at his funeral.'[41]

Around the world in fifteen months, 1859–61

Between December 1859 and March 1861, Janet and Thomas, aged thirty-fve and thirty-three respectively, undertook a journey that, by the standards and conditions of the time, was truly remarkable. They sailed from Cork on 18 December 1859 and landed at Halifax, Nova Scotia, on new year's eve. They moved on to Toronto and Niagara and by 3 February they were in New York, at the Fifth Avenue Hotel which Janet thought 'magnificent & good, vertical railway to convey guests up & down stairs'.[42] Yet Janet was none too impressed with the dirtiness of the city and commented on the number of fatalities due to the many wooden buildings taking fire. Philadelphia, which they reached on 27 February 1860, was, by contrast, 'a very beautiful & large city really superior to N York'. Here they met Thomas Keegan, who had worked at Kilmacurragh

---

41. When Kilmacurragh was leased to Charles Budina in 1932, the piece of ground surrounding Tom Acton's and Janet's grave was specifically excluded from the lease; when, in the 1940s, the question arose of a possible sale of the house and gardens, Charles was anxious to ensure that the site should be protected from 'inquisitive and inconsiderate sightseers': 'My own feeling was that the place where Uncle Tom rests is a private matter … and that this privacy should not be invaded by the curious multitude … Uncle Tom's own desire was that he should rest in and be part of his Deer Park and place without mark or indication save for his tree.' Charles had the railings removed, and a 'tree protector' placed around the pine tree. His aunt Irene, however, objected strenuously to the removal of the railings, a scathing attack on Charles himself.

42. The safety elevator was built by Elisha Otis in 1853, and his first elevator in New York was installed in 1857.

in 1848 as a footman before emigrating. Janet got the impression from him that it was 'very difficult for servants to live with Americans [as] they are so overbearing & treat them as slaves!! T.K. has lived with his master 8 years, gets 12 dollars a month.' Memphis was 'a horrid town' and she recorded 'in the first hotels in the country [I] am disgusted by people at every side at breakfast & dinner spitting on the floor filthy beasts'.

They were in San Francisco for several weeks, using it as their base for extensive excursions. It had 'beautiful shops & goods, somewhat like Paris' but Janet again noted that wooden houses frequently burned down. The highlight of the American part of their holiday was a horseback excursion to the Yosemite area. This horseback holiday took the Actons through snow-filled valleys, and demonstrates remarkable courage and a sense of adventure on the part of both brother and sister.

Most of June 1860 was spent in San Francisco, until on the 28th they embarked for Hawaii. During this visit they demonstrated the Acton family's penchant for volcanoes. The Kalauea volcano, today part of the Hawaii Volcanoes National Park, is considered to be the earth's most active volcano. 'Started from rest house for descent into crater sides of which are said to be 900 ft in height & 3 miles across … wonderful lake of fire in which is the movable island of rock. The boiling up of the liquid fire … surges … many feet of a fine red, like blood.'

The Actons continued west on a voyage of almost a month into the tropics, including a visit to Fiji. On 15 October Janet recorded 'half way round the world today!!!' The rest of their holiday was comparatively uneventful. On 3 November they sighted the coast of Australia, landing at Melbourne on the twentieth. In mid-December they took boat for Ceylon, proceeding *via* Aden and the Gulf of Suez to Cairo, where they climbed to the top of the Great Pyramid. They took ship for Malta and Gibraltar, reached Southampton on 24 February, and London the next day, meeting their brothers Charlie and Willie, the latter of whom had been managing the estate in their absence. On 5 March they were on the *S.S. Leinster* to Dublin. The total cost of their round-the-world trip was £1400, of which, as Thomas recorded in his account book, each paid half. It is notable that not once in her travel diary does Janet mention her brother by name. In her domestic diaries she refers to him by the sign '=', and very occasionally by the letter 'T'.

Life at Kilmacurragh: Janet Acton's diaries

Life at Kilmacurragh was lived at a slow and regular pace (Janet's domestic diaries survive only for the periods 1861–68 and 1886–99). Apart from a regular annual visit of six-eight weeks to England to visit her brother Charlie after his marriage in 1869, Janet's life was, one might say, 'humdrum at Rathdrum'. There is no mention of any agricultural aggression, indeed very little indication of Janet's awareness of the world beyond the demesne; her diaries are a domestic chronicle of visits, the weather, meticulous household accounts,[43] the attendance every Sunday morning at Dunganstown church and at Kilcandra hall each Sunday evening (in the latter case, after its establishment in 1863),[44] inspections of the school at Kilcandra, and the absences of '=' on his duties as Poor Law guardian, justice of the peace and treasurer of Dunganstown parish.

Janet was a conventionally devout Anglican, and her understanding of God entered into many of her notes. Some of her remarks strike a modern mind as bordering on the ghoulish, but are revealing of mid-Victorian piety. Thus on 3 August 1891 a neighbour, John Neale, had 'a wonderful death bed, he was so happy not a word of sorrow or regret, only happy to go to his Saviour, a beautiful life & a beautiful deathbed'.[45]

---

43. Janet's accounts show that household expenses in 1855 were £231.5.1¼d, and that through the 1850s they averaged £250; this was approximately matched by income from sale of butter and eggs. Wages for dairymaids were £18 p.a.; for kitchen maids £12; for housemaids £24; and £30 for the cook. Typical prices for bought-in poultry were: a duck, 9d., a chicken 5d., a goose 1s6d.-2s., a turkey 2s6d.-3s. A pound of tea cost 3s8d., of coffee 7s., and ten gallons of ale – sufficient for the servants for one month – cost £1, with a dozen bottles of porter 2s3d. Mutton sufficient for three months cost £2.17.11¼d. Approximately seven pounds of coffee were consumed each month. Corduroy was supplied for the clothing of the farm labourers costing £9.18.6d for 222 yards, while 100 yards of calico for house blinds and quilts cost £1.5.0.

44. Charles wrote (letter to Ken Hannigan, 18 August 1995) that 'the building at Kilcandra was a schoolhouse, built by Uncle Tom. The rector of Dunganstown always took an afternoon service there on Sundays.' The schoolhouse was built by Thomas Acton at a cost of £500. Ken Hannigan ('The Barndarrig Band') notes that neither Kilcandra school nor that at Dunganstown was part of the National School system, but were privately funded (in the case of Kilcandra, by the Actons).

45. Her concern for the dying moments of the tenants seems to have been inherited by her niece, Grace Ball-Acton, who, in 1914, gave a pamphlet, 'The Traveller's Guide to Heaven', to 'old Bolton'.

Visits were paid to the Ball cousins at Sea Park, the Drought cousins at Glencarrig, the La Touches at Bellevue, the Revells at Ballymoney, the Gun Cunninghames at Mount Kennedy, the Bartons at Glendalough, Julius and Maria Casement at Cronroe, and visits were received from a Mr Drew of the botanical gardens at Kew in London, the Earl and Countess of Wicklow, the Byrnes of Cronybyrne, and solicitor Alfred MacDermott, who came frequently, sometimes bringing his children (who were half-Parnell and thus remotely related to the Actons).[46]

Shooting was naturally a major part of the social year, and Janet regularly noted the size of each bag; for example on 12 August 1890 eighteen brace of grouse and woodcock were shot, and the following day twenty-two brace of grouse. On the next day 'Mr Wynne staid to shoot a stag. The others to the mountains – brought back 9 brace grouse'. 'Mr Wynne' was a regular visitor, Edward Nixon Wynne, of Wentworth House, a JP and secretary of the Wicklow Grand Jury, who in 1892 was engaged, and in 1898 married, to Evelyn Acton, Janet's niece and the elder daughter of Charles. Another frequent visitor for the shooting (in addition to his horticultural interests) was Frederick Moore, who was often accompanied by one of the family solicitors, Edward White.

As might be expected, an occasion as significant, for a loyalist family, as Queen Victoria's golden jubilee in 1887 did not go uncelebrated by the Actons. Janet's evident enthusiasm sits to an objective eye in contrast with her naïveté in her relations with the people of the locality:

> 21 June 1887. Jubilee Day. To Kilcandra with cake & lemonade – we arrived at 3 with medals & flags. About 70 children walked in procession to school-house, where the C[atholic] children stood outside. Mr Harrison had a nice service & an excellent sermon & 1^d for the children to whom he asked questions. G Watts & T Winder answering very clearly. Marched back to J Bolton's where all had lemonade & cakes. Every one said they enjoyed the day. I distributed 38 copies of the Life of the Queen. I planted a tree, yew, to commemorate the day. The poor people were all very very happy & said they enjoyed themselves so much. The people staid till one a.m.!!! At night the hills were lighted up & many of them took fire & burned for many hours – 50 acres of mountain at Macreddin were burned, from top of hill 42 fires were seen.[47]

---

46. MacDermott had secretly married Charles Stewart Parnell's sister, Sophia, in 1862. He was solicitor to both the Parnell and Acton families and had been agent at Kilmacurragh as early as 1863.

47. See Appendix for details of the Bolton and Winder families.

Thomas Acton IV's management of the estate 1851–1908

William Acton's health had declined rapidly; in the same year that he added the wings to Kilmacurragh (1848) he resigned his seat in Parliament. By 1851, Thomas was running the estate. Following the establishment of the Irish Republican Brotherhood (IRB) in 1858, and its support organization, the Fenians, in 1859, agitation for land reform gained momentum, culminating in the abortive 'Fenian Uprising' of 1867. The 1860s saw a growing rift between landlords and tenants, as the issues of land and nationality, an 'ideology' to which Terence Dooley refers, gained considerable political and social currency.[48] The place of the Anglo-Irish in that nation was by no means assured, nor was their exclusion a definite outcome. In 1865, Thomas received the following letter:

> The Head Centre
> Dublin
> 27.11.1865
>
> Acton
> We are creditably informed that you are going to join the crowbar brigade well, we give you <u>timely notice</u> that we will have the same mercy on you as <u>you</u> will have on your tenantry mind tho in Dublin we know, we know your <u>self</u> and <u>place</u> very <u>well</u>. Of this take particular notice.
> Yours,
> O'Mahony.

The 'Head Centre' was the term used by the IRB to denote its governing body, and the 'crowbar brigade' was its term for landlords who evicted tenants. What relation the signatory may or may not have been to the O'Mahony of Grangecon cannot be established; the Grangecon family was embedded in the county establishment, so it is unlikely, but not impossible, that the writer was Peirce O'Mahony.[49]

---

48. As Terence Dooley puts it, 'the nineteenth century witnessed the consolidation of the ideology that promoted land as the basis of the nation': *op. cit.* p. 10. Ken Hannigan ('A Miscellany of Murder', *Journal of the Wicklow Historical Society* 1/7) points out that agrarian violence was far less prevalent in Wicklow than elsewhere in Ireland, although in the earlier nineteenth century 'Ribbonism' – violence perpetrated by secret societies – was a feature of rural life.

49. Why the letter should have been signed is unexplained. A similar instance is the fact that Hampden Evans, father of the girl who married Rev. Thomas Acton, was a

Of a more serious nature was a letter with Wicklow, Ashford and Rathdrum postmarks dated 17 April 1867 (that is, just five weeks after the attempted Fenian risings, some of which had taken place in Wicklow). Written on the reverse of a cartoon cut from a magazine was the following:[50]

> crooked decrepit buck tooth Acton I send you your Image you flaming old scoundrel you infernall drunkard you damnable rogue you bloody Kip keeper you humpy back bastard you imp of the devil blazes to your soul if I can leave my hands on you I will tear you in quarters the time is drawing near when all your iron bolts and bars wont keep me out and I will paste the walls of your kip with your infernal blood you lowsy whelp you tyrannizing hell hound you curse of god blasted cur I will make you know what a gentle man is what you are not hells fire everlasting to your dam rogish soul prepare your coffin.

On the envelope of which Thomas wrote 'Curious Valentine'. One 'curious' feature of the letter is that the writer refers to 'the walls of your kip' – that is, a brothel.

Tenant strength and landlord decline

It was during Thomas's fifty-four year ownership of the estate that the decline of the family's fortunes inevitably took place. After 1881, with the passing of the Land Law (Ireland) Act, one can detect, in the somewhat terse accents of his correspondence with his tenants, the frustration and recognition that the family's 200–year tenure of this significant tract of land had lost its certainty. From this point onwards, because Thomas had the compensation of his and Janet's rapidly developing arboretum, we cannot call him a 'broken' man, but he was probably disillusioned.[51] Charles wrote that

---

prominent member of the United Irishmen in 1804, despite his family being equally elevated socially.

50. Although the cartoon superficially suggests the type of simian features employed by British journals such as *Punch* and *The Illustrated London News* to depict Fenians and other Irish peasants, it in fact bears no detailed resemblance to such caricatures, which can be studied in L. Perry Curtis Jr's study *Apes and Angels: the Irishman in Victorian Caricature*.

51. But *cf.* W. Vaughan, *Landlords and Tenants* p. 39: 'The decline of the gentry was not an inevitable result of the destruction of landlordism, for it was envisaged that they would survive the sale of their tenanted land.'

His entirely Irish passion for land was so affronted by what he conceived to be the misguided efforts of his neighbour Parnell to strip him of his lands that, in his old age, he probably became a bad landlord. However, such was his devotion to trees and to the importance of forestry that he would reduce a tenant's rent for planting hedgerows or shelter-belt timber or for planting unusual species.[52]

With legislation increasingly taking over traditional landlord-tenant relations, the scene was being set for a drastic reconfiguration of Irish society. The 1881 Act represented a revolution in relations between landlord and tenant, effectively putting them on a parallel footing. The achievement of 'fair rent' effectively meant a rent reduction, averaging 20 per cent across the country. It was one of the 'three Fs': fair rent, fixity of tenure, and freedom to sell; but the concept of 'dual ownership' – a shared responsibility for the land between landlord and tenant in a social rather than a strictly legal sense – meant that (as Philip Bull notes) the Act 'set down the terms for a new phase of conflict between landlord and tenant'.[53] In a sense, the Acton estate was typical of those areas where landlord and tenant shared the same religion and a similar political outlook.

Nevertheless, as Barbara Solow observes, the Land Act of 1881 and the Land Law (Ireland) Act of 1887 'gave the tenants so much that the question arose whether the advantages of land ownership amounted to anything at all'.[54] It was on this realization that Thomas made his remark to his gardener: 'When I am gone this place won't be worth a penny to anyone.' It was partly an admission that he was running the farm at a loss in order to give local employment, and partly a realistic view of the elimination of the landlord from the land. In the 1930s Charles would record that a neighbour, Dick Jones, had told him that on Thomas's death the land itself was in 'a ruinous state', but that his uncle, Charlie, after inheriting the estate, would have turned around the fortunes of Kilmacurragh if he had lived another five years.

The gradual erosion of rental income due to the operation of the Land Acts affected the Acton estate very seriously, and if there had not been substantial funds from other sources in the family it would probably have been necessary for much more land to be sold. By 1876, the size of the estate had reduced to 4845 acres, with a valuation of £2730 and was now the thirteenth largest estate

52. Letter to Eric Joyce, custodian of Kilmacurragh, 28 August 1980.

53. P. Bull, *op. cit.*, p. 92.

54. B. Solow, *The Land Question and the Irish Economy, 1870–1903*, p. 184.

in the county. The rental income on all the lands in 1893 was £1625, dropping to £1582 and £1564 in the next two years, when it seems to have stabilized until 1899, when it dropped further to £1486. By the year of Thomas's death in 1908, the estate was bringing in only £1234, and in the year that Charlie became High Sheriff (1913), this had dropped to £887. These, however, were the *gross* figures, and much less was available after the estate costs, including agents' fees, were deducted.

Despite his convinced unionism and his strictness on payment of rents, there is no reason to think that Thomas was not a compassionate landlord. The estate records for the 1880s show that he frequently granted abatements, and one might deduce that his understanding of a tenant's inability to pay was due to humanitarian principles. But this understanding was a shrewd one, and Terence Dooley explains how, in the years of the 'land wars', abatements were often granted by landlords 'as a pre-emptive strike against the withholding of all rents',[55] until at least the passing of the Arrears Act of 1882.

Much of the drop in income was attributable to the 'judicial rents' fixed by the Land Commission Courts and 'judicial' decisions were partnered by 'judicious' arrangements on the part of landlords such as Thomas Acton in granting abatements to tenants in arrears. From 1889 onwards, there is an increasing incidence of notes on the estate accounts: 'rent fixed by sub-commission. Notice of appeal served'. But while it may have been a matter of course for such appeals to be made, they were seldom successful. Landlords had to acknowledge that in order to remain 'rich men who lived in the countryside' (as W.E. Vaughan describes them) they could not rely on rents to sustain their way of life.[56] The operation of the Land Acts 1870–96 resulted in 74,000 holdings, amounting to 2.5 million acres (10 per cent of Ireland's total acreage), being purchased by tenants, at a cost of £24.78m.

After the passage of the 1881 Act, Thomas's correspondence with his tenants becomes increasingly terse. He insisted on strict observance of this unwelcome legislation, since, as a counter-balance to the tenant's right to a reduced rent, it gave the landlord the right to receive that rent on the due date, a point on which he was aggressively adamant. To Thomas Richardson, of Ballykerrig, Redcross, he wrote 'The first clause of the Land Act 1881 by which you deprived me of part of my property says reduced rent must be paid the day

---

55. T. Dooley, *The Big Houses and Landed Estates*, p. 44.

56. Cf. T. Dooley, 'Landlords and the Landlord Question' p. 116: 'in just over half a century landlordism as a way of life had disappeared in Ireland'.

it is due.' Thomas frequently stated, or implied, that the tenant, by exercising his rights under statute, was 'depriving' him of his property. To members of the Hudson family Thomas threatened 'if you have not sent [the rent] an early call will be made on you. Receipt in one hand, writ in the other'. To several others he stated, 'I believe you are better off in your line of life than I am.' It is an indication of Thomas's mixed feelings on the subject of his lands and his tenants that these seemingly bad-tempered missives were addressed to tenants with whose families the Actons had successful and long-standing relations.

Whatever the rights and wrongs of a situation that had been allowed to develop over the past two centuries, one can understand the bitterness with which landowners such as Thomas Acton regarded their displacement in Irish (or at least Anglo-Irish) society, and saw unionism as not only their natural political orientation but also as a possible strategy to avoid Home Rule. From 1879 onwards a sequence of landlord associations sought to defend land-lords' interests. There is some evidence that on one occasion Thomas Acton attended a meeting of the Irish Landowners' Convention (founded 1888), and he certainly attended (in the company of Lords Wicklow, Carysfort and Powerscourt and members of the Tottenham, La Touche and Casement fami-lies) the inaugural meeting of the 'East Wicklow Loyalists' Union'.[57] But it appears from his diaries that it was an isolated occasion. Thomas's relations with his tenants may have been litigious at times, but he seems to have kept his affairs within the estate rather than associating openly with others of his class on such matters.

While Roy Foster tells us that Parnell's own political strategies had caused an 'unbridgeable…rift' between him and his neighbours,[58] Thomas Acton's diaries (which are in any case extremely terse) simply recorded on 6 October 1891 'Parnell died'. 'Home Rule' to Thomas definitely meant 'Rome Rule': in 1885 he wrote to one supporter of Home Rule that is 'means the exter-mination of all creeds except Roman Catholics', while he addressed H.C.E. Childers with the accusation: 'If you are as I suppose a member of the Church of England, if you vote for handing over the government of Ireland to the majority who are mostly unable to read or write as they are entirely under the direction of the priests of the Romish clergy, you assent to drive out of the country all outside the Pale of the Romish church.'[59]

---

57. Cf. R. Foster, *Parnell: the man and his family* p. 208.

58. *Ibid.*

59. *Ibid.*

Creation of the arboretum

Although planting of trees and rhododendrons had begun at Kilmacurragh as early as the 1820s, the creation of the arboretum as it exists today was the achievement of Thomas and Janet Acton, he for the trees, especially the conifers, and she for the rhododendrons. The 1850s onwards was an era when new species were being introduced to the British Isles from all over the world – especially from South America, Australia and the Far East. The conduit for much of this traffic was the 'Royal Exotic Nursery' owned by the Veitch family in London, with which Thomas would have considerable dealings in the coming decades.[60] With Thomas's and Janet's emergence as the gardeners of Kilmacurragh, we can see a quantum leap in both the extent and the depth of interest in arboriculture and horticulture.

In 1893 a frequent visitor – 'to see the wonders of this place' as Janet Acton recorded – F.W. Burbidge (curator of the Trinity College botanic gardens, author of a work on narcissi and a plant-hunter for Veitch in south-east Asia), noted that 'they include one of the most complete series of the Sikkim and Bhotan [sic] and Nepalese species that is known.' He listed 'the rich blood-crimson bells of Royle's Rhododendron [Rh. roylei] as they hang in great clusters among its leathery leaves… the bouquet-like masses of R. falconeri… the moonlight effect of R. triflorum… the splendour of R. kewense x thomsoni'.

When the Danish writer Signe Toksvig visited Kilmacurragh thirty-five years later, in the spring of 1928, she wrote in her diary:

> Saw the rhododendrons in full magnificence. O words! How describe the white ones? A living wall of dusters of creamy white, each cluster made of great bells, doubly spotted inside. Four pearls in each bell, black in some, crystal in others. Backs of leaves rich bronze. The pink ones with bluish green glassy calyxes. The avenue of scarlet ones. Like another sphere where flowers were kings. Majestic flowers. If music came out of them you wouldn't be surprised.[61]

---

60. One of the associates of the Veitches was the collector William Lobb, who supplied a *Podocarpus nubigena* (from Chile) to Kilmacurragh as early as 1846, a *Saxegothaea conspicua* ('Prince Albert's Yew') in 1847 and a *Fitzroya patagonica* (Patagonian cypress) and *Libocedrus tetragona* in 1849.

61. S. Toksvik, *Signe Toksvik's Irish Diaries 1926–1937* p. 108. The white flowers described by Toksvig are the *Falconeri* and those in the avenue (i.e. the Broad Walk) are the *arboreum* which Janet had planted in the 1860s, alternating rhododendrons with yews.

The close association of the Actons with David Moore and his son Frederick from the Botanical Gardens in Dublin may have started with a professional interest on the part of David in the work of Thomas at Kilmacurragh, but it clearly ripened into a friendship: during the shooting seasons, Janet Acton recorded the frequent visits of the Moores, father and son, to shoot. Frederick Moore, who was a fine shot, once woke in Kilmacurragh to find outside his bedroom door, in addition to the usual jug of hot water, a bottle of champagne with a note from Thomas asking him to drink the wine and then shoot a deer in the park so that they could enjoy venison the following week.[62]

David Moore (1808–79) and his son Frederick (1857–1949) were central not only to the development of the botanic gardens at Glasnevin, of which they were successive curators/directors (1838–79 and 1879–1922 respectively) but also to the growth of the Kilmacurragh arboretum and gardens. Frederick's succession to the post coincided with the takeover by the State of the gardens in 1922, which had previously been administered by the Royal Dublin Society. Grace Ball-Acton recorded that he visited Kilmacurragh in 1913 with Lord Headfort, who was personally interested in the cultivation of conifers. Charles recorded his childhood and adolescent memories of Frederick Moore: 'Sir Frederick was one of the family household gods when I was growing up … My memory of [him] is of infinite kindness and patience.' Moore continued as a private consultant and in fact nearly brokered a deal for the new government to purchase Kilmacurragh. Charles recorded that 'as long as he was alive, Sir Frederick worked behind all sorts of scenes to have Kilmacurragh become the calcifuge branch of Glasnevin – after all, it has been that in effect for three quarters of a century at no cost to the State'.

One of the attractions for the Moores in visiting Kilmacurragh was the Actons' success with rhododendrons, since at Glasnevin, with its heavy alkaline boulder-clay soil with a pH level of 7.9, these could only be planted in specially prepared peat beds, whereas at Kilmacurragh the pH level of 5.7 is well below that at which rhododendrons find it hard to thrive. Moreover, they require a moist climate, and Kilmacurragh has 44 inches of rainfall per year, whereas Glasnevin enjoys only 28. For example, Kew had held specimens of *Rhododendron delavayi* since 1889, but they had not flowered until transplanted to Kilmacurragh, where they flowered in 1904. Furthermore, Thomas had planted a massive laurel hedge to the east side of the east-sloping grounds to

---

62. It was said in the family that Frederick Moore proposed to his wife, Phylis, in the gardens at Kilmacurragh.

give extra protection. When Frederick Moore remonstrated with Thomas that the latter had diminished the value of the rest of his land in order to enrich the garden soil by taking all the available manure, Thomas responded 'I hate commercial, Freddie, don't talk to me about it. I hate commercial.'[63]

The family was, understandably, particularly proud of the hybrid *Rh. actonensis*, although some uncertainty attaches to it. Variously referred to as '*Rh. actonensis*' and '*Rh. actonii*', it has in fact never been officially registered as a variety, and therefore technically its existence cannot be referred to other than parenthetically. An article in *Irish Gardening* of 1914 recorded that it was 'a hybrid from *R. arboreum* crossed with *R. campanulatum* which flowers in early April', with the white flowers spotted with crimson, and named it simply as '*arboreum x campanulatum* "Thomas Acton"'. Charles, on the other hand, said that it flowered in May, and believed that one of its 'parents' was *Rh. loderi*. Moore himself wrote to Irene Ball-Acton (12 April 1916), 'it was raised by my father, named by me, a cross between R. campanulatum and white arboreum. It gets the nice close heads from arboreum, and the spotting and the colour on the under sides of the leaves from campanulatum.'

Kilmacurragh conifers were awarded the Banks silver medal (first prize) of the Royal Horticultural Society in 1891 for the most outstanding collection of conifers in private ownership; again, in 1931, Charles (as the then owner) was awarded bronze – the silver having gone to the Marquess of Headfort – out of a worldwide entry of 600 specimens. 'My mother and I', Charles recalled, 'tried hard to get the RHS to put Sir Frederick's name on it, as he deserved, but he had more influence with the RHS and got my wholly undeserving name on the medal.'[64]

---

63. In 1913, specimens of *Tricuspidaria lanceolata* [today, *Crinodendron hookerianum*] and *Libocedrus tetragonal* [today, *Pilgerodendron uviferum*], from Chile, were considered the finest in the British Isles. In fact *Libocedrus tetragona* was thought in 1904 to be the only specimen in Europe. Among the conifers, three species of Tasmanian *Athrotaxis* and the Mexican *Cupressus lusitanica*, 'one of the rarest of silver firs', were admired and the Australian evergreen beeches *Fagus cunninghami* (at 40 feet) and *Nothofagus moorei* ('a very rare species' at 25 feet) were 'probably the finest trees of their kind in the British Isles'. The *Nothofagus moorei* was named after David Moore's brother, Charles, who is credited with its discovery.

64. The saga, beginning in the 1920s, of whether or not the gardens would be taken into state ownership, continued into the 1930s and thereafter. In 1937 Éamon de Valera, as Taoiseach, determined that the interest of the then lessee, Charles Budina, should be bought out, and the property vested in the Minister for Lands, but the

Charles Ball-Acton (1830–97): Charles's grandfather

Charles's grandfather, also Charles, the youngest of his generation, was born at Kilmacurragh on 17 December 1830. Like his own son and grandson, he was called 'Charlie' within the family, and was known as such to his wife. Although a younger son, he achieved significance not only as a brave soldier but also as a shrewd commentator on the Afghan campaign, a complex and all-important element of world affairs, and at that time a vital key to the fate of British India. As the father of two men who would take their places as Kilmacurragh landlords, his personality, characterized by profound reticence and self-doubt, has a significance for his family out of all proportion to what might have been expected from someone born into his position.

A significant *lacuna* in the children's lives at Kilmacurragh, according to Charles's widow, Georgina, was the company of other young people: they were 'almost entirely cut off from companionship with children of their own age'. This would perhaps account for William's unsocial nature, and Thomas's reserve may also have stemmed from this childhood inhibition. It is clear from the account of the day-to-day happenings at Kilmacurragh, derived from Janet Acton's diaries, that there was no lack of social contact in later years (by which time of course young William and Charles had already departed to pursue their military careers), but the suggestion is that in William and Caroline's time their surviving children saw little of their contemporaries. It may be that the deaths of the three older girls caused a withdrawal on Caroline's part, and the five years of William's illness may also have deterred visitors.

In 1842, at the age of twelve, Charles followed his two brothers to Rugby, but in 1844 the three Acton boys left Rugby for Cheltenham College, which had only been founded three years previously, perhaps because of the emphasis placed at the latter on Christianity and public service. The Actons at Cheltenham introduced the game of rugby from their previous *alma mater*, where it originated in 1823. (While the two younger boys went on to military college, Thomas went to Emmanuel College, Cambridge.)

---

economic austerity of the time prevented this. Eventually, the Land Commission purchased the property from Dermot O'Connor in 1974 (he having owned it for thirty years), and the Forestry and Wildlife Service (later Coillte) partially restored the arboretum. In 1992 the property was again privatized, being bought by Bill Dolan, who in turn sold it to the Department of Arts, Heritage, Gaeltacht and the Islands in 1996 for £250,000, with the proviso that the house be retained as a ruin.

Georgina's account is certain: her husband's inhibited childhood made him extremely shy. Charles was a serious, introspective person, with the same deep religious sense as his sister. It is significant that in her editing of her husband's diaries, Georgina retained and published the revealing fact that, at the age of thirty, Charles reflected that at home, discussions of faith 'have always been avoided, and I cannot think by accident, for if such were the case they would come out sometimes. We have always been a very reserved family amongst ourselves, and not intimate in our exchange of thought and feelings.' Whether this reserve was, ironically, due to his parents' deep religious faith we cannot tell. But the silence ensuing after the deaths of his three older sisters, accompanied by Caroline's banishing all music from the house, suggests an inward-looking view of the world which, in the case of the soldiers in the family, worldwide travel did nothing to dispel. His grandson may well have inherited some of this gloom, exacerbated by living at close quarters with his widowed mother. Nevertheless the older Charles's reservations about discussing religion at home did not deter him from playing a significant role in his army appointments, which included much pioneering work in the fields of religion and teetotalism, and his own diaries record many instances when he exhorted brother officers to have the scriptures in their minds when behaving as soldiers.

Charles was gazetted as a lieutenant to the 51st King's Own Yorkshire Light Infantry (in which his third son, Reginald, would serve) just five days before his twenty-first birthday in 1851. 1855 saw him at Malta, from where he obtained leave for a tour of Italy, visiting Naples, Paestum, and Rome. He recorded his journey to Rome in a crowded carriage with three Italians: 'I begin to dislike the whole race. Seldom made a more tiresome journey.' He was 'not much struck' by the Coliseum, and the catacombs elicited 'the usual amount of groping in the dark, damp and old bones'; even the Sistine Chapel was 'so dark that I could see nothing'. He carried away with him a 'Roman fever' that laid him low in Malta on his return, so critically that he was sent back to Portsmouth and thence to Kilmacurragh, with serious fears for his life. By 1858 he had been promoted to Captain, but he was very despondent and lacking in self-confidence, despite gaining entry to the Staff College at Sandhurst, where he spent the years 1861–62, resulting in his promotion to Major.

At the end of 1864 the regiment sailed for Bombay, when Charles's real career as a British officer came into focus, and the shape of his life became more determined. In order to see active service, a knowledge of Hindustani was required, and Charles successfully set about learning it. It was during these years that his strong religious belief deepened considerably, and he began to reflect on the significance of holy communion: he wrote 'There is to my idea a tangibility about it, and without form of some kind one's religion is very likely to become very visionary and speculative'. And we encounter, in his self-examination, an expression of faith which is also an expression of anxiety, which we will meet in the principles on which his grandson would base his work as a music critic:

> Two strong and active causes are with me (and I fancy with many) preventing the discussion of such subjects; one, the fear of being supposed to set one's self up as better than one's neighbour, and the other, the most proper and natural, though I suppose, exaggerated, dread of cant.

In June 1869 Charles met Georgina Annesley, became almost immediately engaged, and married in London on 31 July at Christ Church, Lancaster Gate. Georgina's family was distantly related to that of Lord Annesley at Castlewellan, County Down, but she herself was of the English branch of the family which held the manor of Clifford, near Stratford-on-Avon.

The six-week honeymoon was spent in Germany and Switzerland, followed by a further three months in various English resorts, before Charles rejoined his regiment, which then transferred to Ireland, stationed variously at Clonmel, the Curragh, Athlone, Castlebar and Fermoy. The Actons' first child, William, was born on 21 March 1871. The first daughter, Evelyn, was born on 29 January 1873, while her father was *en route* to Fyzabad. A year later, in 1874, a second daughter, Grace, was born at Dalhousie (she died unmarried in 1923).[65] The second son, Charles Annesley, was born at Peshawar, in February 1876, and the third, Reginald (Charles's father), unlike most of his siblings, at 'home' at Kilmacurragh in 1877. Vere was born in 1879 and Irene, the 'baby' of the family, in 1886.[66]

---

65. Grace died suddenly from a gastric ulcer and a blood clot in the heart.

66. Although the youngest of the four Ball-Acton brothers who survived childhood, Vere was the first to die in combat. He had won a cadetship to Sandhurst in 1898, and was posted as second lieutenant in the Oxfordshire Light Infantry the following year. Like his older brother Reggie, he wrote short stories, but he was the first of the three surviving brothers to die on active service. At the beginning of the Boer War, he was sent out to South Africa, and wrote home, 'I hope you will try & not be anxious about me.' Just three weeks before his death he told his sister Grace 'I have come to the conclusion that campaigning is not much fun as it appears at present we

Despite the inhibitions of their father's childhood at Kilmacurragh, and the fact that, for most of them, he was a remote and unfamiliar figure, the boys in the family seem to have enjoyed a 'normal' childhood. When he lived at Kilmacurragh himself, Charles learned from his aunt Evelyn that 'although Reggie and Charlie liked tennis, it was impossible to get them willingly to take part in Rugger or Cricket, while they were boys, and that they loathed compulsory games. Reggie's room was always an awful mess, and no one could make him keep his clothes tidy, although Vere and Charlie were very tidy. Reggie as a boy was nearly always late for everything and then he had usually left something behind.' Evelyn remembered them 'toughing' on the lawn: 'Reggie was nearly always underneath because Charlie was older and therefore larger, and Vere was always thick and heavy.' Charles commented, 'I was wonderfully glad and interested to hear Evelyn reminiscing like this since I have never been able to know what they were like as boys, and had always had an idea that putting together their dislike of school, the santimonious books their parents lavished on them and their sisters the result was a bit sanctimonious until they got out into the world. Irene shewed me her photographs of their youth, and I was so interested. Whereas Irene always looked heavy and sulky, and Gracie daft, Charlie looks shy but otherwise splendid, and Reggie always delightful.' In a sense, this conversation with his aunts was for Charles an essential homecoming to Kilmacurragh.

At the end of 1873, Georgina had travelled out to India to rejoin her husband. Shortly afterwards, Charles inherited property ('ancient meadow or pasture lands') at Syddan, near Slane in County Meath, worth £500 *per annum*,[67] from his distant relation Elizabeth Ball, whose surname he was required to prefix to his own by deed-poll,[68] a procedure that his second son (Charles)

---

shall not see a Boer for some time yet.' He was killed on the first day of the battle of Paardeberg (18–27 February 1900), shot through the head and dying instantly, while leading his men on an assault that brought them within fifty yards of the Boer lines. He was buried where he fell. His commanding officer told Georgina that 'on three separate occasions he assisted wounded men when under heavy fire and his coolness and courage were beyond praise' – action that would be characteristic of his brothers at the time of their own deaths.

67. This land was sold in 1912 following the death of Georgina Ball-Acton, who had inherited it from her husband.

68. 'I, Charles Acton, Major and Brevet Lieutenant-Colonel in Her Majesty's 51st Regiment of Light Infantry, now stationed at Dalhousie, in India, hereby give Notice, that I have taken as a Prefix to my Surname the name of BALL, and shall henceforth call myself and be known as CHARLES BALL-ACTON' – *Times*, 2 June 1875.

and his grandson would reverse in due course. Elizabeth was a wealthy woman, the only child of James Ball and his wife Elizabeth of 28 Clare Street, Dublin, whom Janet had visited with some regularity since at least 1863. Whether this family was related to the Acton's Ball cousins is uncertain but seems probable. On her father's death in 1851 Elizabeth inherited two houses in Clare Street and two more in the adjacent Clare Lane, and another in Charlotte [today, Camden] Street, which she left to friends.[69] Even though he continued as an eminent army officer, Charles's financial security was assured by this inheritance.

Colonel Ball-Acton was soon posted to Afghanistan, where he mistakenly expected a short campaign – it was to be the most significant period of his military career. The Afghan empire had long been a pawn in the balance of power between Britain and Russia, and British troops had previously occupied the Afghan capital, Kabul. The emir at that time, Shir Ali, was bargaining with the Russians and refusing to negotiate with the British, occasioning the order to move the army towards the border. Thus, for the first time, Charles Ball-Acton was in battle, as the regiment proceeded up the Khyber Pass, connecting Kabul with Peshawar, one the most strategic straits in the north-west of Asia, giving, as it does, restricted access between Afghanistan and what is today Pakistan. From 1839 onwards, it had been the focus of British manoeuvre and intelligence-gathering, as the protection of the Indian sub-continent became increasingly vital to British interests.

Military intelligence and strategy were not distinguished, however. Charles's record of the engagement at almost the highest point in the pass, against the fort on the hill of Ali Musjid, shows his distrust of the orders that he received; of one order, he wrote, 'I did not like it at all, as I thought it quite a mistake and throwing away life for nothing.' In January 1879, after two months dug in at Ali Musjid, he wrote home: 'I do not think it an unjust war, but I think our Government for the past twenty years has made an awful hash of it.' Georgina recorded in her memoir that he 'was noticed by those who saw him in action for his admirable coolness under fire'. She included in her memoir the evidence of a fellow officer who observed Charles being advised to take shelter when under heavy fire: pointing to heaven, he replied, 'No, my man,

---

69. In addition to the property left to Charles, she bequeathed £300 each to Caroline Acton and Janet Acton, who also became her residual legatees; other moneys were bequeathed to friends and servants. Not only did Charles benefit to the extent of £500 per year, but his mother and sister, as residual legatees, received slightly less than £2000 after all other bequests had been fulfilled.

thank you – there is One up there who is taking care of me.' That capacity for coolness was evident also in the circumstances in which the three surviving sons met their deaths in the Boer and First World Wars; the 'throwing away life for nothing' would be a feature of the appalling conditions during which two of them, Charles and Reginald, would meet their deaths in Flanders.

Charles's experience of the Afghan campaign was punctuated by the death of his mother, on 11 April 1879 (he received the news on 13 May), and the birth of his fourth son, Vere, on 22 April. On his periods of leave from India, Georgina noted in her own diaries that Charles was almost a stranger to his children, and the distance – both physical and emotional – between them may not only have stemmed from the familial inhibitions but also have been passed on to the next generation.

After the massacre of the British mission at Kabul in September 1879, the regiment was ordered to advance once more up the Khyber, where it was expected that they would winter again. 'No one in the least knows what we are to do. Everyone in India thinks we should hold this country.' A premonition of developments in the twentieth century came in January 1880:

> I expect we shall be out of this country by May, as England won't stand our keeping it, which I say we ought to do. A great number of the inhabitants would, I believe, like us to stay. The Hindus, of course, would. The Hazaras living about Ghazni we believe would, also the Kazil-bashes who are, I think, Shiah Mussulmans, and therefore hated and oppressed by the Sunni Mussulmans, which the Afghans are.

On the day of his promotion to Lieutenant-Colonel, one of his messengers died under enemy fire, and Charles's disillusion was such that he wrote, 'this is one of the saddest days of my life'.

In 1878, Charles had noted in his diary: 'Are my sins little? Sloth, self-indulgence, envy, anger, inattention, wandering thoughts and sleepy when in Church. I seem to get a glimpse of what a delightful state it would be to live altogether for Christ – to be perfect.' Now, in 1881, the year in which he was decorated as Companion of the Order of the Bath (the third most ancient British order of chivalry), his work saw him conducting Bible-readings and temperance meetings. Leaving aside the question of religious belief, there is, in his self-examination, more than a hint of self-doubt and hesitancy.

A shadow was cast over Charles's retirement by the death of the first-born child, William. 'Willie' had been at Monkton Combe school near Bath, and seems to have been a bright child. On 29 March 1883, just after his twelfth birthday, he reported in a letter to his mother that 'my neuralgia [is] a little worse', and 'tell Papa I have finished the first book of Euclid'. Less than three weeks later, having been sent home from school with meningitis, he was dead. In failing health, Charles himself died from pneumonia on 3 February 1897, aged sixty-six. He did not live to have to cope with the death of his youngest son, Vere, during the Boer war three years later, at the age of twenty.

Charles Annesley Ball-Acton (1876–1915)

Vere's eldest surving brother, Charlie, also held a cadetship at Sandhurst (in 1895); he was gazetted second lieutenant in the Royal Welch Fusiliers at the age of twenty in 1896. The following year he was serving in Malta at the time of his father's death, moving on as part of the international force of occupation in Crete (shortly after the attempted revolt against Ottoman rule). In 1900 he was in Hong Kong and mainland China towards the end of the Boxer Rebellion, before the regiment was posted to Agra in India. From Agra he pointed out that with pay of £13 per month, a mess bill of £10 and the cost of servants at £5, officers subsidized the army, quite apart from having to bear the cost of their own uniforms: 'never recommend any one to go into the army', he wrote home.

By 1904, Charlie, as heir presumptive, was visiting Kilmacurragh, aiding Uncle Tom in the administration of the estate. Charlie was in Burma when Tom died in 1908. Having inherited Kilmacurragh, he resigned his commission and moved, with his mother and sister Irene, into occupation of the house and demesne. Henceforth, until he rejoined the army in 1914, he was to all intents and purposes principally a farmer and secondly a landlord; the Kilmacurragh demesne was 'very nice but too much for an amateur' Charlie wrote to the estate agent, Louis (or Lewis) Kemmis.[70]

The home farm, or 'demesne', amounted at that time to slightly more than 1000 statute acres, of which the Hill (behind the house) of 150 acres was practically useless except for grazing. Ballygannon accounted for over 300 of the total acreage, and Bellpark another 110, which explains why Charlie was so reluctant to see them disposed of. His attempts to retain as much as possible of the remaining

---

70. Louis Kemmis, of the Wicklow family of Ballinacor (one of the seven estates in the county sized between 5000 and 10,000 acres), had succeeded Alfred MacDermott as Thomas IV's agent in 1895; the Actons and Kemmises had been on visiting terms since at least 1866. He continued as agent until after Reggie's death in 1916.

tenanted lands, and to return the home farm to profitability, would probably not have succeeded, even if he had not died in 1915. The last parts of the old estate (with the exception of Ballygannon) were acquired by the Land Commission under the compulsory purchase powers of the Irish Land Act of 1909, despite Charlie's last-ditch (and somewhat risible) tactics of 'evasion', as his agent, Louis Kemmis, put it. (He tried to pass off his mother as the *bona fide* tenant of Bell-park, even though she was quite clearly *not* farming the land herself.)

When, in 1910, he was asked formally by the Land Commission whether he had any untenanted land which he was prepared to sell, he replied that he was 'occupying [all the land] on my own account' – a blatant untruth. In that year he asked Kemmis to calculate the value of the total estate at the rates provided for in the 1909 Act, which appear to have amounted to £36,000 gross or £24,000 net. But if sold without compulsory purchase, the £24,000 would yield less than £500 per year from stocks, or £700 if sold for cash. It is impossible to be more accurate, as there were four different ways of calculating the proceeds, depending on the method of transition, resulting in four different possible outcomes, all of which were unclear to landlords and their agents, and which continued to puzzle his nephew Charles and Charles's mother Isabel in later decades, when a substantial part of Isabel's income was derived from Land Stock. It is quite understandable that landlords should resent a situation in which they not only did not know which estates the Land Commission intended to redistribute, but also could not accurately compute their future financial position.

The annual running costs of the staff in the house and on the home farm (including the schoolmistress at Kilcandra) amounted to £800 per year,[71] which was equivalent to the annual rental from the vestigial estate. Moreover, he found himself, like Uncle Tom before him, obliged to honour a will which (in this case) forced him to mortgage land on an estate already in deficit.[72] In addition, death duties amounted to £1560, payable in eight instalments of £195, so that, by the time they were discharged, two more sets of duties had been levied following the deaths of Charlie himself (1915) and Reggie (1916).

71. Farm steward, £50; farm labourers, £520; two men in the stable yard, £48; the woodranger, £30; schoolmistress, £30; butler, £24; three maids, £66; pensions, £45.

72. Thomas IV left his sister-in-law Georgina, his nephew Reggie and his niece Irene £500 each, £300 to Frederick Moore, £500 and a gun to his solicitor, Edward White, £500 to his agent, Lewis Kemmis, and £100 and his clothes to his steward, Robert Taylor. Other bequests included £3 per year to each of his gardeners. Georgina and Irene agreed to forego their legacies, although Reggie accepted his; Frederick Moore wanted to forego his, but Charlie was insistent that he should accept it.

By 1913 – the year in which he became the last Acton to hold the position of High Sheriff – Charlie noted in his account book that 'for me to live or exist must try and live on £30 per month'. It was all that was left to him after the house expenses had been paid out of the net rent receipts. In 1913 Reggie wrote, for his brother, a piece of doggerel that sums up the land situation: 'My oatless husk of Tullylusk/Barren rocky acres/Very nearly breaks me/But Bellpark's hay & Ballinaskea/Pay the rent that makes me.'

Charlie had applied to the Land Commission for a loan to make repairs to Kilmacurragh's drainage and roof, and 'to make the servants' wing habitable', for which he received £230; in this he was fortunate, as the loans were intended for repairs to farm buildings. Charlie's excuse, that 'I admit the dwelling house is in the nature of a mansion, but I wd also point out that I am a farmer & consider a farmer's house is still a farmhouse', strikes one as peculiarly weak. A further application, for funds to improve and extend Kilmacurragh (inscribed by Charlie 'a man's reach should exceed his grasp or what's a heaven for?') was rejected out of hand. Nevertheless, family traditions were upheld: on 29 December 1912, twelve Protestant tenants, including the Taylors, Keegans and Farrars, were entertained to Christmas dinner (turkey, roast beef, pudding and mince pies) while on 1 January thirty 'RC labourers and wives' came to a tea of cold salt beef.

With Charlie's ownership (followed immediately by Reggie's short-lived tenure) we see the opening of the penultimate chapter of the Actons' history as landowners – the last phase being Charles's own attempts to 'make a go' of the home farm in the early 1940s. As Charlie's agent pointed out regarding the Land Commissioners, 'altho' we may withstand for some time their effort to take [the lands], in the end they will get them.' Even so, there was a grey area, not least because the funds available to the Commission were limited, and there had yet to be a test case under the new law relating to compulsory purchase: 'then one will know exactly how far it can be evaded', as Kemmis put it. 'It is all more or less a lottery', added his lawyer, Edward White.

Since Thomas had allowed the land to deteriorate, Ballinaskea was of use only for recreational shooting and Charlie was advised to wait for compulsory purchase, which had the advantage of providing cash rather than Land Stock – cash which could then be invested in restoring the remaining lands at Bellpark and Ballygannon. But it seemed to White that 'some Nationalists' wanted the good land at Bellpark, which suggests that, within the deliberations of the Land Commissioners at that time, political influence and social deference were each playing their part in this final act of land redistribution. Charlie did, in fact, save Bellpark temporarily, making it inevitable that Ballinaskea would be appropriated: 'You can I think put out of your mind the possibility of obtaining any sympathy on our position, as having taken the cream (Bellpark) from them, and left them the skim milk, they can't be expected to be anxious to go out of their way in our favour', White told him. Charlie said that he would sell Bellpark at 10 per cent discount on its market value if he could find a Protestant purchaser.

A few days after the outbreak of war in August 1914, Kemmis still found it necessary to explain to Charlie that 'questions of "fair" rent in Ireland are not decided from a "fair" point of view & landlords have to do the best they can for themselves'. Charlie seems to have inherited his uncle's jaundiced view of tenants – perhaps imbibed during his apprenticeship in Thomas's last years: 'One has to look on these men as trained to get the last 2/6d out of a cow if it takes a whole morning to do it.'

But tenants also had their deep-seated anxieties: in 1914, Thomas Hudson, one of the Actons' longest-standing tenants, wrote from Kilnamanagh, 'I am most anxious to know if you would be inclined to sell your property to the tenants. The time has now come when people must decide whether they will stop in Ireland or not. Unless I can buy at a reasonable price so that I shall have a perament [sic] interest in the place I shall clear out of the country altogether.'

Perhaps one of the most telling ironies of the dual lives of the Actons as the Land Acts took their toll is that, in the same period when Charlie Acton was trying, by every conceivable strategy, to prevent the compulsory purchase of Ballygannon, Bellpark and Ballinaskea, he would become the last Acton to occupy the position of High Sheriff for County Wicklow. It seems from the views of Charles, as expressed in the 1940s, that – at least in moral terms – he would have been entirely in sympathy with the concept of 'fair rent', meaning, of course, reduced rent, even though this, along with tenant purchase, meant the gradual extinction of his family's role as landlords.

After six years of painstaking dedication to the family lands, Charlie must have been torn in different directions at the outbreak of war by two competing factors. On one hand, his desperate need to 'make a go' of Kilmacurragh put family matters above conscience, but, as a soldier and (presumably) as a unionist, he must have seen war as a *force majeure* which he could not shirk. Charlie not only re-enlisted, but pressed to be sent to the war front. From the trenches he continued to write home about estate matters, noting the details of the harvest and movements of sheep, while giving descriptions of life in the trenches themselves and in the periods when on a break behind the lines. One notes, as with his brother Reggie's similar epistles, the light-heartedness with which the grim realities of trench warfare, especially the juxtaposition to the enemy lines, were cloaked.

In October 1914, writing from Salisbury, he said, 'My dear sisters, don't dread the worst until the worst occurs which it never may.' When Charlie died in action, two months after promotion from Captain to Major, a common remark in the many letters of condolence received by the family was his gallantry. It was clearly the family characteristic that came to the fore with his uncle William at Inkerman, his father in the Khyber Pass and his youngest brother at Paaderberg. He was, in fact, killed while trying to save another soldier; although he did not die instantly – death came after two hours, during which he struggled to write a farewell note to his sisters – he said he was in no pain, and, it was reported, he had a smile on his face.

Frederick Moore, who had continued to take an active and helpful interest in Kilmacurragh, wrote that he was 'gentle, kindly, generous, always with a good word for people, and devoid of any malice or littleness'. Writing from Anna Liffey House, Lucan, Rebecca Shackleton said, 'he was just the type of man this country can least afford to lose'. The Sharpe family, of Ballinaskea, asked for Charlie's photograph: 'we adored him as a landlord, and had every right to do so'.

Reginald Ball-Acton: Charles's father

Reginald Thomas Annesley Ball-Acton was born on 2 October 1877. He followed family tradition by attending School House at Rugby and then the Royal Military College at Sandhurst, and was gazetted to the 1st battalion of the King's Own Yorkshire Light Infantry in 1897. His former commanding officer, Colonel Johnson, later wrote that 'Captain Ball-Acton served under my command in the 1st Batt. Yorkshire Light Infantry, from January, 1898, to November, 1899, and during that time he was attentive to his duties, and I had no fault to find with his performance of them; careful in his habits, and a strict teetotaller. He was fond of out-door sports, and a good rider.'

Reggie then served as a Lieutenant with the 2nd battalion in the South African (Boer) War from April, 1900, to October 1901, and in the 3rd battalion from then until the end of the campaign in June 1902, and received the Queen's Medal with three Clasps and the King's Medal with two. In 1900, with his first experience of battle, he wrote home that 'I *think* I did all right but was very afraid of making a mistake & the shells frightened me dreadfully.' He would have had in mind his younger brother's recent death in the same war, but this is the only evidence surviving of Reggie being afraid: his letters from the Ypres trenches fifteen years later convey no such fear.

Reggie was promoted Captain in 1901, and was partly responsible for the search for 'a man called Botha' as his diary records, this being Christopher Botha, brother of the politician Louis (future President of South Africa). Eventually, he tracked down Botha in order to deliver a communique from Lord Kitchener. 'A Visit to the Boer Lines', his account of the meeting, was published in the regimental *The Bugle*.

Retiring at the end of the war, he spent two years farming in South Africa, in the Barberton district of the Transvaal. 'From the time you took up land there in 1902 to January, 1904 the assiduous manner in which you applied yourself to the cultivation of your land was, besides being particularly noticeable by me, a matter of general comment to the inhabitants of the district, to whom it gave a splendid example of what could be done by keen application', wrote his former superintendent, Captain R.H. Vyvyan. Reggie had some ambitions as a journalist, and several of his articles from South Africa were published – in the *English Illustrated Magazine* and the *Morning Post*, possibly as an antidote to the arduous business of farming, which was most unattractive: 'I am working at present like a common labourer.'

When he did leave South Africa, he had no job and no prospects. Somehow, while Reggie was, in his own words, 'slacking it' for three years at Kilmacurragh (from 1904), there was sufficient income to support him there. But he felt the possibility that Kilmacurragh might offer him a future: in 1910 he told his mother, 'It seems that the Liberals will get in. Then the Budget & Home Rule & Charlie sitting in Dublin a member for Wicklow with me writing his more excellent speeches.' The idea of the Acton brothers having a role in an independent or semi-autonomous Ireland was both harking back to their grandfather (as an MP) and looking forward to the new political reality as it seemed before the First World War and the war of independence.

Despite their unionism, Charlie and Reggie would have acknowledged Home Rule if not accepting it, much more so than their uncle: and in the person of the youngest Charles, the Acton family came to accept and embrace the concept of Irish independence in a new political and social climate.

3. *Reginald and Isabel 1908–1916*

Isabel

*I*t was a protracted and hesitant courtship: an almost unemployable Reginald pursued a reluctant and uncertain Isabel. Despite the intensity of his wooing, there were moments over the five years of their courtship when it seemed that his siege would be unsuccessful: they would not marry, Charles would not be born, the Acton line would die out with Reggie's death in 1916, and this book would not be written.

Reginald and Isabel's family backgrounds were neither complementary nor necessarily conducive to a happy and prosperous partnership. He is a soldier, the younger son of a younger son, biding his time in idle pursuits and unsuitable employments, until soldiers should be called upon again. Yet as a junior member of a cadet branch, Reggie's status as a member of the Acton family had nevertheless made him familiar with the land and its social environment.

She is a spinster with several possible suitors,[1] whose parents' marriage was a warning against the commitment required of man and wife. Isabel Richmond's family came from a different part of Ireland both physically and intellectually, and from a completely different social and cultural *milieu*, even though she enjoyed a greater financial independence than her suitor. As it was, Reggie's was a death foretold, and, despite her second marriage, Isabel's life was largely a long widowhood complicated by her relationship to her only

---

1. One of whom, Ponsonby Sullivan, continued to press on her his own attentions right up to Isabel's engagement to Reggie in 1912.

child. Although Reggie's place in this story is brief and poignant, Isabel's is central because of that long-lasting and problematic relationship.

By a strange coincidence, the Richmond family came from the parish of Acton, near Poyntzpass in County Armagh in the north of Ireland, which was named after Iron Acton, near Bristol, from which the Poyntz family had originated,[2] and where Isabel would be living at the turn of the century in her grandmother's house, 'Holm Ray', to which she became deeply attached.

Isabel's father, William, born in 1827, was educated at Trinity College, Dublin, was ordained, and held a curacy at Leeds before becoming rector of Philipstown, County Louth, after which he moved to Lewcombe in Dorset and Rockhampton in Gloucestershire. His first wife, Isabel Perchon, who died early and childless,[3] was an heiress who left her husband an annual income of £2000 – a very considerable sum in those days. William's youngest daughter, Dora, later recalled that her father decided to forego the luxuries that such an income might provide,[4] and to invest half the proceeds – thus providing generously for the future welfare of his three daughters by his second marriage, in 1872, to Harriet Marshall. Dora also recalled that the childhood and home life of the three Richmond daughters (Eva, born 1874; Isabel, born 1876;[5] and Dora, born 1877) had been a happy one: 'he was a lovely Papa to have, & devoted to us all'.

Revd William Richmond died shortly before Isabel's marriage, while Harriet herself lived on to become a surrogate mother to baby Charles. Isabel herself never liked Rockhampton – 'this loathed place', she later called it, and she spent much of her time living with her grandmother, Mrs Marshall, at Iron Acton. Some of the spirit of 'the manse' may well have entered her young mind due to other causes, not least the strictness with which Protestantism, with a northern Ireland bias, was conducted, and this in turn is suggested by her descriptions of a rectory childhood in her unpublished novel 'Rent Cordage'.

---

2. The Poyntz family had come to the north of Ireland as part of the 'plantation of Ulster' referred to in Chapter 1, and is reputed to have brought families from Iron Acton to settle in the new parish.

3. Her dates of birth, marriage and death are unknown.

4. Dora discovered only later that her father had been able to afford an orchid house and a yacht.

5. Isabel was born at Baronstown, Dundalk, County Louth, on 8 July 1876; Baronstown was the home of her mother's Marshall cousins, where Isabel frequently visited before her marriage.

There is no doubt, however, that, in her own words, as she wrote to Reggie, Isabel was a 'frightened and bewildered child', and this gave her the determination in later life to serve the needs of others who were also frightened and bewildered. Charles would exhibit the same sense of bewilderment and a passion for discovery in his absorption with physical phenomena and in his pursuit of the essence of music. It was all to do with finding a 'place', a 'home' where one could be safe and at peace. In Isabel's case, as a child of the manse, with her familiarity with the basic texts of Christianity, she was also engaged on a spiritual quest. Many of her letters were concerned with her striving towards a *credo* – perhaps because her family background had allowed her to take conventional Christianity for granted and now, in conjunction with her letters to and from Reggie, she was questioning the meaning of life.

Courtship

On the envelope of Reggie's earliest extant letter, dated 9 August 1908, Isabel wrote 'The beginning', but it is clear from the letter itself that they had already known each other for some time. They had attended a dance that week, and Reggie had proposed to Isabel, clearly without success. In addition to his own personal circumstances in the marketplace for gainful employment, Reggie was inhibited by the family 'reserve', tentative yet longing. Despite the necessary reserve in the etiquette of the time, Reggie's letters are clearly passionate, placing Isabel on a pedestal and casting himself as her faithful knight. Isabel, for her part, was by turns teasing, timid and self-deprecatory. Yet until they entered into their engagement in 1912, nothing was written to suggest or imply or betray the fact that love was ever considered. By Christmas 1908 the pedestal had become a throne, and Reggie referred to Isabel as 'Your Majesty', while she sometimes signed herself 'Isabel Regina'. His tone is characteristic of the playful yet bashful aspect of their courtship.

The dissimilarity in their backgrounds may well have accounted for the hit-and-miss aspect of their correspondence. Reggie seems to have been less able to express his thoughts and feelings, while Isabel's letters often gushed with emotion. Reggie was hesitant not only because his financial circumstances made it difficult to envisage marriage, but also because the inhibitions in his family background caused him to question whether he was able to make an emotional commitment.

Isabel's hesitancy and lack of self-confidence and Reggie's persistence became increasingly obvious: 'I do want friendship', Isabel told him, 'and I should be very glad indeed if you would give me yours, as I gather from what you said that you don't want anything more – and that it does not hurt you to go on knowing me. Will you let us be friends, real friends, always?'

In March 1909 Isabel was nursing a young cousin, Bobbie,[6] 'who is suffering from nervous depression, a very bad case, and who has come here on purpose to get all the magnetism, or whatever it is, possible, out of me. I've got that, you know, a valuable gift, & he is already better – but it's hard work and uses up all my available energy.' (Bobbie would appear again in the story nearly thirty years later, when Isabel was trying to join Charles in Palestine.) She saw her friendship as 'a job': 'I am so dreadfully faithful and am capable of an absolutely unswerving devotion to my job – once I undertake it.' Whether that devotion was to her friend or to her cousin, the intensity of her application was astonishing, and it was one of the qualities that would be inherited by Charles, along with Reggie's diffidence.

Isabel was clear on the relationship she imagined between husband and wife:

> Want me always, & so help me God, I will never fail you. And oh, my heart is hungry for you – lonely, dissatisfied, everything is dull and empty wanting your arms round me – for lack of you. Don't you realize that a woman is born to give – herself, her strength, her life – to the One Man? That *that* is what she is homeless for want of, till she meets him? And in return I claim as my right the First Place – I must be your first thought, wish, consideration – anyone & everyone must go to the wall for me.

Isabel was laying down ground-rules which, in the first place, positioned her as a giver, but at the same time also claimed that in that role she would be ruthless in its performance.

Reggie's employment at this time, in Argentina, seems to have been similar to that which he had in South Africa, of a form of estate management, though farming in South Africa after his war service there, had effectively closed off any interest Reggie might have had in pursuing it as an avenue for investment. Working for Menzies Neild and Co., a firm of merchants with extensive estates run by two long-established British expatriates, he found Montevideo 'rather frighten[ing], the men looked like unshaven monkeys & the women

---

6. What the exact blood relationship was between Isabel and her 'cousin' is difficult to determine: there was no 'Robert' or 'Bobbie' among her first cousins or their children.

worse. Here [Buenos Aires] they are better, more mixed with English. I have met some rich Argentines & they are very friendly, but rather humbugging in their flattery. The country is full of death & blood but this means it is also full of life'.

By October, Reggie had written to both his mother and Isabel, surveying his options. 'I am bored to death with doing nothing. So I want to clear out. Where to?' One possibility was to herd cattle from Argentina to Chile or Bolivia; another, to take a job in the nitrate mines in Chile. Like his son forty years later, he seems to have lacked any self-confidence in his ability to secure 'a decent job' but 'I *will* not spend all my days in this country'. In reply, Isabel told him 'You *ought* to write. I've always said so. Here you go hunting for employment, when all the time your talent lies buried at your very feet.'

Just before he returned to Europe, from late May to early July 1911, Reggie took a river journey to Asunción in Paraguay, and wrote one of the more heartfelt and positive accounts in all his letters from South America. 'I feel in a happy glow from the music & the singing of the native passengers & the joyous dancing. It is a wonderful river about a mile broad & bright & shining with thick wooded banks & disappears here & there to the horizon.'[7]

A home for Isabel?

When Isabel's grandmother, Mrs Marshall, died she left Holm Ray itself to Isabel, but her remaining estate was divided between Isabel, her two sisters Eva and Dora, her mother and a maternal uncle, making it likely that Isabel would have to let Holm Ray and move about, staying with friends and relatives. 'I have always had a home – I dread having none – I am a very homesick person.' The loss of Holm Ray would be a marker of the loss and displacement that Isabel would feel for the rest of her life.

Immediately Reggie heard this news, he invited her to stay at Kilmacurragh with his mother. 'There wd. be nothing to do but look at flowers, crocuses then, probably, & few people.' By July 1910 Isabel was staying with cousins at the fishing village of West Lulworth in Dorset, which would be a feature of her and Charles's summer holidays – 'a dear little place where one can be as happy as the day is long'. She also often visited her parents at Rockhampton

---

7. The would-be journalist succeeded in having his account of this river journey published in the South American supplement of *The Times* after his return to Europe.

Rectory. 'Wander, wander. I feel as if I could never settle down to live in one place again.' In January 1911, having apparently found a tenant for Holm Ray on a twenty-one year lease, Isabel was nursing her sister Dora through appendicitis and peritonitis, and bringing her to recuperate at Weston-super-Mare ('not a place I'm fond of'), a seaside resort near Bristol where Charles would attend his first school. In the meantime the death of Isabel's father offered the prospect of Isabel and Reggie being able to live reasonably comfortably once his estate was settled in about a year's time, on an income which was in the region of £600 per year.

> I'd rather live in a cottage with you than in a palace without you. Let's live in a cottage & you can write. And we will rejoice when you get anything published & love each other & damn the editors when they send things back. Couldn't you be happy with your wife in a little wee house, my dear? Even if it meant you couldn't afford to hunt & we had to count the pennies rather carefully?

Isabel demonstrated an ambivalence about Ireland that was partly touristic and partly a revisiting of her family roots. She was puzzled by Irish domestic customs, charmed by their picturesque (even though sometimes uncouth) manifestations: visiting Marshall cousins in 1906 she said 'I am going to find this a strange quaint land', and called Castle Ring, near Dundalk,[8] home of her Bolton cousins, 'dark & dirty, the oddest mixture of grandeur & shabbyness, the food execrable'. She was travelling, as it were, in an unknown and unknowable land to which she nevertheless felt some atavistic ties. Despite his English schooling, such ambivalence was not evident in her son's behaviour in relation to Kilmacurragh, suggesting that, although it was his mother who was responsible for that schooling, he was much more responsive to ancestral echoes on his father's side of the family. After his mother's death (in 1971) Charles would recall that 'she ended her days as fervently British, standing up every time she heard God Save the Queen on the wireless' but 'she was proud to have an Irish passport and taught me as a child to be a republican (lower case).'

Engagement and marriage

Isabel and Reggie were able to renew their physical acquaintance after his two years' absence when he returned to Kilmacurragh *via* London at the end of July 1911. She wrote after their first reunion 'I never knew you before and I

8. Cf. Bence-Jones, *A Guide to Irish Country Houses*, p. 75.

was rather afraid of your coming back, lest you shouldn't be like the writer of the letters of my imagining, but you are, every bit & more so'. Reggie, for his part, thought that Isabel had changed 'from a wonder-round-eyed girl to an imperious eyed woman which is equally attractive & much finer'.

Within three weeks of Reggie's return, the writing between the lines of their correspondence had become explicit, and by the end of August each was close to making a declaration of love, yet Isabel continued to press the claims of friendship over those of love, and Reggie, while protesting his passion for her, was still painfully conscious of his inability to support a wife financially.

Less than a week after she had seen Reggie, Isabel asked him 'Wouldn't it be best for you in the long run, to forget about me? If you didn't see or think of me anymore, you might find the one really right girl. I *think* you only want me, really, to idealise, to weave your poetic fancies round – and to set on a pedestal & decorate with attributes I don't really possess. I'm so afraid of your getting hurt over it.' Reggie, who was at Kilmacurragh enjoying grouse shooting, picnics, the Dublin Horse Show and messing about with motorbikes, immediately reassured her that he had no interest in any other woman, and asked her to engage a room for him at Lulworth so that they could be together for the last week in September. But his own doubts about marriage were not merely financial: 'I do not feel that I could keep a woman happy & my fear of watching your regard change to scorn or contempt is extreme.'

At Lulworth, it appears that Reggie made a major effort to persuade Isabel that their relationship was more than friendship, but it seems that Isabel refused to discuss the idea of love or marriage. Isabel admitted that she had invited Reggie to Lulworth to put him to the test of seeing her at close quarters: 'If it wasn't going to prove firm and solid I'd rather know it at once.' But while Reggie had pursued the topics of love and marriage, she had retreated to her pedestal, keeping her 'faithful knight' at bay. It is easy with hindsight to recognize the *pathos* in Reggie's reply: 'Your reassurance that my life has a value is most comforting. I know I am going to live long by heredity & a strong & cunning instinct of self-preservation.'

When Reggie's mother intended to invite Isabel to stay at Kilmacurragh during the summer of 1912, Isabel's nerves exerted themselves: 'Does your mother *really* want to ask me? ... I am so horribly shy that I am *quite* miserable if I think I'm where I'm not wanted.' It was at this point that Reggie seems to have made his last, and successful, attempt to propose to Isabel, who was terrified that his family would assume that the visit was more than one of friendship. 'Will they think our sort of friendship queer? And can I be natural if they do!'

On her way to Kilmacurragh that summer, Isabel stayed with cousins at Woodsgift, County Kilkenny.

> This is a Paradise of a place. I now long to be a millionairess & own an Irish estate. I think one would need tons of money – I've been in England too long to bear to have it so untidy. But this place is not untidy *for Ireland*! And it's heavenly – the most gorgeous trees. The beauty of it all just breaks my heart. I'm told Wicklow is the 'garden of Ireland' – so I am expecting your place to be even more lovely than this, *if possible.*[9]

Shortly after this first, intimidating, visit to Kilmacurragh, all became clear, and the vocabulary of the letters became more intimate and open: on 1 August Isabel wrote simply: 'My very dearest, I love you better than all the world and I am glad I am engaged to you and I do not want to break it off & I knew it the minute your dear face came in this afternoon. Yours Isabel.' Nevertheless, throughout September and October both of them vacillated on the subject of the engagement, Isabel being the more outspoken in her view that Reggie would be happier if he 'regained his freedom'.

Isabel was excited about the prospect of accompanying Reggie back to South America, where he had been offered another job, but he was also chasing a job with the *Daily Standard* in London and a Resident Magistracy in Wicklow, which he thought would, for both of them, be preferable to Buenos Aires. The prospect of a job in Argentina faded, too. Reggie eventually determined that his salary would be insufficient – 'the cost of living is very high & I am afraid it would mean your going without a great deal that you ought to have'. When he had some success with newspaper articles – for example, a piece on emigration in the *Standard* in September 1912 – it began to seem as if a career as a writer, or at least a journalist, might be opening.

Almost immediately after her return to Iron Acton from Kilmacurragh, Isabel wrote again with the financial solution to their problem, which involved her now widowed mother: 'My Best Beloved, Mother says I am to suggest that you marry me & come and live here [Holm Ray] in my own little house. Mother will build on a couple of rooms to be her own – she will live with us and of course be together for meals and all that, but she says she knows you'll

---

9. Woodsgift was destroyed by fire very shortly after her visit: Mark Bence-Jones states (*A Guide to Irish Country Houses* p. 286) that the fire occurred prior to 1914 and that the house was subsequently demolished.

want your house & your wife to yourself so she would have her own part of the house to herself.' An awkward reminder of this situation would arise when Charles married Carol, and Isabel, perhaps unconsciously reviving this idea of a *ménage à trois*, hoped that they could all make their home together.

It is painful as well as ironic to read today what Reggie and Isabel had expressed in their letters just before their wedding. He wrote to her: 'Dear love, that we may spend many many years together, & that they may get better & better if it is possible. Mine have been increasingly splendid since I knew you.' She replied: 'I feel that it will take years to say all we're wanting to say to each other. So lovely to think of *all* our years with each other & always more & more to delight in.' Months before they were married, but while the prospect of war was increasing, she had written 'I am so glad I didn't know & love you before the S. African war. I always wondered how the women whose men were out there lived through. Too awful to endure, I thought.'

They were married at Iron Acton on 17 April 1913, by Isabel's brother-in-law, Rev. Frank Leigh; 270 villagers were entertained to tea afterwards. The six-week honeymoon was spent mainly in Italy. The day after the wedding, they travelled to Paris *via* a rough crossing Newhaven-Dieppe. Then they moved on to Dijon, Montreux, through the Simplon, to Stresa. In Milan, their next stop, 'The Queen feels rotten' – a frequent complaint of the honeymoon. 'Walking is harrowing because Reggie will stroll in front of the rapid electric trams – and I do not wish to be buried in the cemetery of Milano, or return to England a widow.' Arriving at Venice,

> I was very ill & worn out but the first view of the lagoons of Venice, and crossing the railway bridge built on 222 arches was so interesting & exciting I forgot it for a while & arriving at the station and being packed into a gondola kept up the excitement. We arrived at the hotel after a most romantic row through canals at night, the high mysterious houses, the picturesque bridges & the light on the water were enthralling. Arrived here, I attempted dinner, but feeling faint & sick, went to bed. Poor Reggie!

They returned home *via* Milan, where Reggie took over the diary, mainly, it seems, because Isabel was suffering from cystitis. This contributed to their early return, under doctor's instructions, and they arrived back in Iron Acton on 3 June. (Isabel was frequently unwell following her marriage and especially after the birth of Charles.)

Almost ten more months would pass before Charles would be born, and a little more than a year before the great powers would engage in the mass slaughter that would rob Kilmacurragh of Charlie, and rob Isabel and Charles of husband and father. Once they returned from honeymoon Reggie and Isabel would, in fact, have that one year together; thereafter, their physical together-ness would amount to little more than six months.

Charles's birth and Reggie's death

Charles Acton was born at Iron Acton on 25 April 1914. His father reported to Irene and Grace that the baby 'weighed 9½lbs. Hair very fair & curls. He dribbles & is sick occasionally & snorts his milk in his nose & Isabel says he is the dead spit of brother Charles – also of me.'

This episode of the Acton chronicle is perhaps the most poignant, because it sets against Reggie's short and tragic war the home environment enjoyed by his infant son during his first two years of life, sometimes with Isabel (when Reggie was not at the war front) and sometimes in the care of his grandmother and a hired nurse. Reggie's accounts of trench warfare sit in awkward but telling counterpoint with the idyllic village life of Iron Acton; between them is Isabel's commuting from son to husband, both in her physical relocations when Reggie is in England, and in her correspondence in which she speaks to Reggie of both Charles's daily progress and her care and anxiety for Reggie's safekeeping.

Before their marriage, Isabel and Reggie had discussed whether or not it was prudent to start a family, when war, and the consequences of war, loomed so strongly over Europe. But, as she wrote to Reggie on the day she received notifi-cation of his death, they *had* decided 'to give the gift of life to our little son'[10] – a son who had only just celebrated his second birthday when his father was killed – and, on reflection, Isabel knew that they had made the right decision.

Isabel had no fear of death itself, regarding it as the prelude to another phase of life. But with the likelihood of war, and the concomitant probability that Reggie would be killed, she clung to the hope that they might die together. For example, before their marriage, she had written that, had they been together on the *Titanic*, she would have wanted to die with him. 'I'd much rather go with you into the next life than go on with an earth life alone.' After his death it was only her sense of responsibility to Charles that maintained her resolve to stay alive. In very old age, she would tell Charles, and his distant cousin the

---

10. As indicated in my Note on Sources, these are the only words I have quoted from the most intimate part of Isabel's correspondence with Reggie – after his death.

Rev. Billy Wynne, that she was not afraid because death would, at last, reunite her with Reggie who had gone before, fifty-five years previously. But at that time, the hope that life with Reggie and baby Charles would continue after the war was at the forefront of Isabel's pious thoughts. 'I would like to send your brother Charlie a line. I will hold the hands of the little heir together so that he may pray God to take care of his uncle & keep him here to do his work in Ireland many many years.' When Reggie went to the front, she reported that 'Whatever the news or the weather, there is one face in the house that is always cheerful, one bright smile always ready, & that is little son's.'

On 1 August 1914 Reggie wrote, 'War still seems imposs. with all Western Europe hating it', while Isabel wrote that the officer in charge of the local militia thought the war would last 'about 3 weeks – pray God he may be right, but I fear not'. Reggie was mobilized, and his regiment was stationed in Yorkshire, where the men were digging trenches to defend the river Humber. This may have seemed unnecessary work, but in December 1914 German warships would bombard towns on the English east coast, killing and wounding several hundred.

Isabel hoped that Reggie's poor eyesight would prevent him being sent to the front, but his company was sent to the Ypres battlefield immediately after the first offensive in October-November. The idea that the war would be short and sharp was already becoming an empty notion, as the first Ypres offensive led to a standoff which would see fighting over the 'salient', as it was called, continue right through the war.[11]

From Iron Acton, Isabel would ruefully comment on the lack of volunteers for 'Kitchener's Army' – the makeshift assembly of largely untrained recruits, most of whom would simply become cannon-fodder for the German machine-guns. 'My beloved village is not showing up well as regards volunteering – the farmers' sons seem to be a disgrace to the country – a set of cowards – if they knew how scornfully the village talks about them they'd be surprised.'

Reggie was introduced to the trenches at the beginning of December 1914. 'We are some 3 miles from trenches, which I hear are quite quiet now. I & my warriors go in tonight for 24 hrs & then we go to the rear for a rest for

---

11. There were three 'battles' of Ypres: 'Ypres 1' occupied late October and early November 1914; 'Ypres 2' took place in April 1915, and 'Ypres 3', otherwise known commonly as the battle of Passchendaele, resulting in an allied victory, in October-November 1917. In the interim periods, both sides were literally entrenched, each striving to resist the yard-by-yard attempts of the other to gain a precious piece of ground. This stalemate was, however, the continuity which made the Ypres offensive such a protracted battle.

a matter of [a] week. They are 130 yds from Germans. Charcoal stove fried bacon, toast, big dugouts. Quiet Germans. Every luxury... So strange this war is... Pheasant and pate de foie gras when we got here. I enclose a will witnessed by my subalterns.' He also reported that his regiment had performed well at the first Ypres battle: 'Several generals have said the YLI is the best regt. out here.' The trenches in fact became the defining characteristic of the war, and the figure of speech 'over the top' was the signature of hundreds of thousands of deaths. As Patrick MacGill wrote, 'the scaling ladders were placed against the parapet, ready steps to death'.[12]

'I do not understand war,' Reggie wrote. 'Across Belgium by 50 steps is so very slow & costly.' As Charles would tell his mother many years later, '[his aunt] Evelyn told me in 1938 that my Father left the army after the South African war, partly because he strongly disapproved of the discipline imposed in the army and the way the privates were treated, and partly because he could not reconcile his religion with fighting.' This was echoed after Reggie's death, when one of his soldiers wrote to Isabel: 'It seems hard to reconcile to one's idea of God & religion ... that such a fine, gallant Christian gentleman should meet his end in a way so unmistakeably brutal.'

'It will be delicious to be together again in peace. Perhaps the war will end from everybody's disgust with it', Reggie wrote on 11 January 1915. Less than two weeks later, he was wounded at Lindenhoek and invalided back to England. On 24 January he sent the regulation communication card to tell Isabel that he had been wounded in the right arm, the bullet passing through 'leaving big holes in his arm & all his sleeves & covering his clothes with gore' as Isabel told her sister-in-law Gracie. 'It is really a clean sort of wound & nearly all trench wounds are in the head.' His brother Charlie hoped that 'it may just put him out of the firing line. It may save his life.' Where Reggie's eyesight had not proved a deterrent to his being sent to the front, Isabel now hoped, unsuccessfully, like Charlie, that the wound would enable him to remain in England for the duration of the war. After his death, at least one letter of condolence would bewail the fact that wounded men were being returned to the front to fight again.

The correspondence between Reggie and Isabel resumed when he went to Ireland in October 1915 to put Charlie's affairs in order. He discovered that where the combined death and estate duties on his uncle's death seven years previously (on a valuation of £40,000) had amounted to £4800, the

---

12. P. MacGill, *The Great Push* p. 33.

corresponding duties now, on an estate valued at £30,000, would be £3600. Irene would look after the estate for the foreseeable future.

Reggie's return from Ireland meant that, again, letters ceased until a startling letter from Isabel on 4 March 1916 (by which time Reggie had rejoined his regiment at Ypres) indicates that there had been some disagreement between them: 'Certainly by all means let us live apart in future – you in the horrible Ireland, I in my little home here.' All that can be inferred is that Reggie foresaw himself bound to live at, and try to manage, Kilmacurragh for at least part of each year, once the war had ended. Reggie's replies indicate that he expected to be told of another pregnancy but Isabel miscarried in early 1916. If the pregnancy had taken its course, the child would have been born in August 1916, just two months after its father's death.

While Isabel was with Reggie in Hull (from March 1915 until he returned to the front, with the one short break when he went to Kilmacurragh), Mrs Richmond and Nurse Hallam cared for Charles either at Rockhampton or at Iron Acton, and the almost daily reports of his welfare abound with descriptions of his moods and his growth. Just before Charles's first birthday his nurse, Miss Hallam, reported,

> what meals Charlie demands. At 7a.m. I give him a bottle, milk & albulactin,[13] & a sponge cake. About 10 a.m. or 10.15 he says he is ready for his breakfast – he sucks his thumb & smiles! He then has egg or bread & milk or (when I get it) groats or oatmeal with heaps of milk. After that he sleeps most of the morning & is quite happy till about 2 o'clock & then he sucks his thumb again. He has his pudding & occasionally meat juice & water to drink. He eats it quite slowly & enjoys it thoroughly. [Waking about 7pm] he then has his savoury.

Mrs Richmond would comment on 'the merry bright face, & crowing laughter, & the hearty appreciation of his breakfast', and his evident enjoyment of days spent in the garden in his pram or playpen. But it also appears that Charles suffered from bad dreams, which it was thought he might have inherited from his mother, although generally the reports remark on his consistently enjoying a good night's sleep. Miss Hallam also thought that his 'nervousness' was associated in some way with Isabel's tendency to worry.

---

13. Albulactin contained pure milk albumin, which replicated human, rather than cow's, milk. How Miss Hallam obtained it in 1915 is unclear: it was said to be unavailable in Britain until late 1916, since it was produced by the German-owned Sanatogen company until it was bought by a British consortium.

Charles's development, including the increases in his shoe sizes, were all faithfully relayed to Hull. Perhaps the most frustrating for his absent parents were the reports of his walking abilities and his general transition from a baby into a child: 'Miss Hallam tells Charlie he must walk before he wears his pretty new coat, in which he will certainly look a little *boy* – he has made a step or two inside his pen, holding only one hand of Miss Hallam's.' Walking was soon mastered, but Charles was lazy and needed encouragement. His appetite developed also, Miss Hallam writing that 'Charlie had his first taste of poultry yesterday. He had minced chicken for dinner & when he realised that it really was something he might swallow he thoroughly enjoyed it.' A few weeks later 'he had a little fish for the first time & he thoroughly enjoyed it.' As his grand-mother noted, 'there is a good deal of perseverance in the little scamp.' Her comment on his perseverance was apt, and many would say that later photo-graphs bore out her view of a 'scamp' with his 'roguish expression'.

It appears that, apart from missing Charles and wanting to be with him, Reggie and Isabel felt that Charles was developing too strong a love for Miss Hallam, and she for him, and that they themselves might lose that love. But Miss Hallam reassured them: '*Of course* Charlie will know you. He always does. As for not loving his mummie, it is utterly impossible. I would never never steal a child's love, but endeavour to pass on to him a little motherly love in the absence of his mother, which he returns *to his mother* – that is an *inborn* quality in a child.' The choice Isabel had had to make – whether to be at home with her son, or at Hull with her husband – must have been painful and the pain and anxiety must have been continuous. Charles never mentioned his early child-hood (although the surviving photographs suggest a strong sense of happiness in his surroundings and companions) but it can be reasonably surmised that he may have been confused emotionally by the loving care bestowed on him by his grandmother, by his nurse, and by his mother – the latter, of course, coming much more strongly into focus after Reggie's death.

After a visit from his parents in the first week of 1916 (the last time Charles would see his father) Isabel seems to have written to Miss Hallam that Charles had been 'disagreeable', but in reply the nurse said 'he is neither whiny nor disagreeable. I'm sorry he disappointed you' – but she defended her own training of Charles and pointedly said that things might have been different: 'I've had to do what I believed to be best, since you were not here.'

Meanwhile Reggie continued, right up to the day of his death, to describe life in the trenches. 'A beautiful fine morning. One of our aeroplanes up 1st thing pursued in the blue sky by some 200 little white puffs. They all look from our point of view absolutely hopeless misses. But it is very fascinating & pretty against the blue sky.' He also sent his son a short letter for his second birthday, 'although it's a long time before you will be able to read it'. He mentions 'the apparent waste of good lives in this horrible war' and hopes that Charles will grow up 'as near as possible to the ideal of a Christian gentleman. May you be as good as your Mother & remember that we love you.'

Reggie was killed on the night of 22 May 1916. He had insisted on accompanying a patrol into no-man's-land and was looking for two wounded soldiers when he was shot through the head, dying instantaneously. One of his fellow officers attested to his courage, remarking that he was 'a thorough gentleman, chivalrous, keen and brave, of more than ordinary force of character', while another said 'I don't think I ever met a man in the army who was so truly a soldier and a gentleman, and with it all there was a true humility'.

The harsh reality of Reggie's death meant that Isabel's letters to him dated 20th May (enclosing a photograph of Charles), and 22nd and 23rd May were returned to her with 'Killed in Action' written on the envelope in red ink. That of 20th May ended 'The red May trees are just coming into flower here & the fields getting golden with buttercups. All is lovely, if only my dear were with me. My dear own man, when shall I see you again[?]' On the twenty-third (Reggie had died the previous night) she wrote that, despite her inherent dislike of the place, she was 'full of eagerness to garden at Kilmacurragh & breed ponies & farm & even take an interest in your horrible cows & bulls! Why can't it all be nice & peaceful & let us all be happy & me with my dear husband, without whom it seems not worth while to be doing things. My own dear man, God keep you and bring you safely home.'

On 26 May Isabel received 'the telegram' – the official notification from the War Office that Reggie had been killed, another signature of war brought home to the parents and widows of so many men: 'Deeply regret to inform you that Major RTA Ball-Acton was killed in action 22 May Lord Kitchener expresses his sympathy'. Four days later: 'The King and Queen deeply regret the loss you and the Army have sustained by the death of your husband in the Service of his Country. Their Majesties truly sympathise with you in your sorrow'. On the day of the War Office telegram, Isabel commenced a series of letters. For a week, she wrote each day, sealing the letters in individual, dated envelopes. For the following four months, up until Reggie's birthday on 2 October, she continued to write similar letters in a notebook.

The posthumous correspondence is an extraordinarily moving dialogue between Isabel and her dead husband, the main thrust of which is that she knows he is near her, and is able to read what she has written. She declares her absolute desperation at this new separation, and her frustration that she cannot die and join Reggie. Her determination to stay alive is due entirely to her sense of responsibility towards Charles, and she tells Reggie that she would be happy to die when her son reaches the age of twenty-five. She is extremely anxious about the best way to bring him up, how to be at once firm and gentle. At first, she expects that, as the mother of the heir to Kilmacurragh, she would be doing so in Ireland (but that was not how matters evolved). As a whole, these letters constitute the testimony of a woman torn between inconsolable grief at her loss, and her equally insuperable sense of duty to the infant child who now represents her love for her husband: Charles now belonged to her, and became a real subject to give meaning to her life.

Many recognized that Charles would provide Isabel with a focus for her future: 'I feel so thankful', wrote another cousin, 'to think you have his dear little son to think of & to console you.' A close friend underlined the deep relationship which was to develop between mother and son: 'He will be a comfort indeed to you, the greatest you can have, & will indeed be something for you to really live for & for your life's work.'

As far as the family and the 'grand inheritance' was concerned, Irene (with whom both Isabel and Charles would later encounter difficulties over the fate of Kilmacurragh) was exceedingly concerned for Isabel and to give a good account of her stewardship. Gracie comforted her by writing 'my one comfort is that I know you made him very very happy, & love lasts for ever'.

What did Reggies's death mean to the Acton family, and to Charles in particular? In Palestine in 1937 Charles would tell his mother 'I am very flattered to think that you find a resemblance between my photo and my Father. The next thing is to try and live up to it! which has always seemed to me quite impossible. I have no illusion about my own character, and I have occasionally thought that I must be rather a disappointment, since I fall so far short of him, though I have that curious mixture of faith and scepticism, belief in essential goodness and cynicism, that you both have, though in me I tend more to the rational end of it. The thing I lack is courage, which is a pity: it is the one thing that worries me about my pacifism, since the essential thing for pacifism is supreme courage, the ability to face the worst without fear.'

Like many a tiny child deprived of his father, Charles's circumstances now saw him becoming the exclusive focus of his mother's emotions, which would have deep consequences in his school years and in his later development, up to and after her death at the age of ninety-six in 1971. But conversely it also deprived him of the father with whom most boys experience a growing relationship of trust, respect and affection. In Reggie's case, even though it had been a very brief tenure, this younger son of a younger son had, fortuitously, become the master of Kilmacurragh. It had been bequeathed to Isabel in Reggie's will, and in time it would become Charles's inheritance by deed of gift from his mother. But the continuity of family feeling, lore and attachment was broken. Although Aunt Irene would do everything to ensure that Kilmacurragh was handed over to the heir in as healthy a state as possible, the political and economic realities dictated otherwise, and Irene's own prejudices, and her apparent dislike, or disapproval, of Isabel, were factors in pushing Charles away from an intimate appreciation of Kilmacurragh, however much he may have resisted Irene's influence. Until he came to Kilmacurragh as its owner in 1939, it was an 'other' place for a young man who in fact had no 'place' of his own, but who carried a great deal of emotional and intellectual baggage.

Isabel attempted to replicate, or provide an alternative for, the father-figure in Charles's life by her marriage in 1920 to Hugh Digues La Touche, but, despite the passionate outbursts in their correspondence, it was more a marriage of convenience than any other kind of union, and its effectiveness in providing Charles with this father-figure was dramatically reduced by Hugh's sudden departure from the marriage for a period of five years between 1921 and 1926, a crucial time in Charles's formative years, when he was aged between seven and twelve.

As far as Charles as the heir to Kilmacurragh was concerned, the almost complete hiatus between his father's death in 1916 and his arrival as heir in 1939 meant that, instead of growing up in County Wicklow under his father's tutelage during the historic phase of Ireland's move towards self-determination, he in fact developed slowly and uncertainly with the over-compensatory affection and concern of his mother, his stepfather's unorthodox character and beliefs, and his own exposure to the English public school and university system, with an idea of 'Ireland' somewhere at the back of his thoughts.

4. *Childhood and Early Schooldays*
1916–1928

Childhood

Charles said very little in later life about his childhood. Luckily, his voluminous letters to his mother were preserved, so that we do have snapshot images of his life at preparatory schools, at Rugby and Cambridge, which reveal a great deal of his own perception of himself and the world into which he was growing. But later in life, he wrote that 'whatever does make an adult, we all of us feel that our childhood, as we recollect it, played a great part in that process'.[1] The words 'as we recollect it' are crucial, because, whatever suppressed emotions and experiences may also be at work, it is only those elements in childhood which we choose to recall that we consciously allow to shape our adult lives.

It may seem unfair if not unkind to send an eight-year-old boy to boarding school, yet in Charles's view (expressed in the 1940s), 'boarding schools are better than day schools, since there is more time and more scope for voluntary community occupations – in which the methods and results of cooperation are more apparent than in ordinary urban life where the community is so much larger'. Charles's letters, whether they concern group astronomical observations or a frog-breeding club, indicate that he was not the solitary type

---

1. He was writing in 1980 to Gertrude Tree, the sister of composer A.J. Potter, with whom there was some dispute concerning factors in Potter's own childhood (Potter had recently died).

one might expect to develop from his earliest circumstances. But also, as a class-conscious youngster strongly influenced by his communist stepfather, he could add 'Just as I fully appreciate the benefits I have received from a very good public school, I am also aware that from the point of view of the whole community they are to a large extent "socially undesirable". Public school education does at present tend to produce almost another nation.' Charles, as an Anglo-Irishman, was already conscious of belonging to 'another nation'; to have followed his grandfather and father to Rugby was not so much a matter of becoming a part of an England which (at the time when he was within its educational system) was in severe social and economic crisis, as of discovering what his difference meant to him within his family context.

Charles's school reports suggest that his difficulties in accommodating himself to the system were not simply those of an only, fatherless, child, in reaction to an unfamiliar, and potentially hostile, environment. Charles, from a very early age, became a skillful observer, alert to dangers and possibilities, ready to close the door firmly on the one and to open it eagerly to the other. Insecurity in Charles's case stemmed from loneliness and a sense of loss, the first of which set him on a quest for connection, love and acceptance, the second of which obliged him to seek compensations beyond those normally sought and obtained by boys of his age. The need to belong fought against a fiercely independent spirit who felt an equal need to control his environment and to live successfully within it. Most of Charles's life, up to the time of his marriage and his joining The Irish Times four years later, would see him commuting between the need to belong and the equally compelling need to be oneself.

The future of Kilmacurragh

With Reggie's death, Isabel, as Reggie's widow and young Charles's mother, moved centrestage as far as the Kilmacurragh estate was concerned. By the cruel accidents of war, the younger son of a younger son had inherited, and within a year lost, the family estate which now passed to his widow who would eventually gift it to Charles, the last in the senior male line of the descendants of Thomas Acton who had founded the dynasty in the 1640s.

Isabel's ignorance of management skills or of how to find them in others hampered any chance the estate might have had of finding its financial feet. The rental income at that stage was slightly over £700. Charles would later refer to 'the mess you [his mother] came into', which was attributed partly to Louis Kemmis's mismanagement of affairs but more to Uncle Tom's long-term neglect of the land in favour of the arboretum. By 1930, as the Irish Free State's policy of land redistribution came into effect, ownership of almost all the remaining estate of 3600 acres had been transferred and the Actons were left with what Charles later called 'a rather poor farm'.

Irene (who had been caretaking Kilmacurragh) appears anxious in her letters not to seem to be pestering Isabel, but at the same time equally anxious to gain her approval for what had been done since Charlie's death. The tone of her letters perhaps explains why, in later years, she would exhibit marked disapproval of Isabel's custodianship of the Acton family home, and outright hostility to the presence on the estate of Hugh Digues La Touche.

In 1917, the year following Reggie's death, Isabel went to live at Kilmac-urragh. She lived there until at least 1920, when she remarried, and references by Charles in later life suggest that she may have retreated there again for a further two years after her five-year separation from Hugh began in 1921. Clearly her time there was miserable. Her previous encounters with Irish country houses had not endeared her to a life in which she felt uncomfortable in every sense. Discomfort and local conditions would have prejudiced Isabel and suggested to her that selling Kilmacurragh was the most sensible option. Her acquired Englishness would have outweighed any residual affection that she may have entertained for an Irish country estate on behalf of her infant son – Charles was only three years old when she went to live at Kilmacur-ragh, and eight at the most when she gave up the attempt and moved back to England to supervise his schooling. The fact that the existing legislation, and the political climate of the period 1917–22, was anathema to any land-owner would have also contributed to her reservations about the future of the property.[2]

When she was told later by Hugh that she was highly thought of in the locality, Isabel, in a startling admission, betrayed the same lack of self-confi-dence that she had expressed in her letters to Reggie: 'One reason I hated living

2. During the period covered by this chapter Isabel composed words for the national anthem of the Free State, which she dedicated to W.T. Cosgrave and the late Kevin O'Higgins (in fact it is probable that the verses were written immediately in the wake of O'Higgins's assassination in 1927): 'Raise our Irish flag on high/Wave it on the breeze/North and South and East and West/Till it reach the seas. // Let no party discord tear/Let no malice stain/Ireland's flag float free and fair/Ireland one again.'

there was that I thought all the people disliked me ... They think one must be rich to own such a place ... I'm sure it's psychological – the old bullying from the Irish servants when I was a cowed child & so frightened & afraid. It's their animosity that has made me dread living at Kilmacurragh.'

Isabel had been left with debts at Kilmacurragh and on Reggie's death received an *ex gratia* payment of £300 and a war widow's pension of £140 per annum, with a 'compassionate allowance' of £24 in respect of her child – the pension to cease in the event of re-marriage. But this had little to do with the domestic situation at Kilmacurragh where, as Isabel wryly said to her young son, 'all a grateful government did after two officers laid down their lives for it was to charge their heirs death duties'.

The principal fact hanging over the family was the financial consequences of the deaths of Uncle Tom, Charlie and Reggie, since on Reggie's death a further tranche of death and estate duties had to be paid, in addition to the two previous exactions of £4800 and £3600. Thus in a space of less than a decade Kilmacurragh was impoverished to the extent of £12,000, which could only be raised by selling much of the remaining estate, by mortgaging against future rents, or disposing of capital on which Irene and Grace, and to a lesser extent their married sister Evelyn, depended for income. Isabel herself was not affected financially by the levy of death duties, since she had her own income from Richmond family trusts and the rent of Holm Ray, but the future welfare of Charles had been irreparably jeopardized by history.

Later, when the sale of the house and the remaining lands was definitely being discussed, Irene would urge that it should somehow be kept in the family, perhaps – on a temporary basis – being rented by herself and Evelyn. 'Even if Charlie does not care enough about it now [c. 1928] to keep it ... he would at any rate be more likely to have a chance of having it in later years than if it passes into other hands.' Irene's sense of family tradition weighed heavily, but in the meantime, making a success of Kilmacurragh in financial terms was an obstacle with which she was unable to assist.

Isabel's main motive in marrying Hugh (on 28 August 1920) was to provide Charles with a father-figure, a development in which she seems to have partially succeeded. We know nothing of how they met. Hugh (born in 1891 to a family with origins in County Wicklow) was the son of a geologist, James Norman La Touche (1857–1939) who, like several others of his family, had worked in the service of the Indian railways. James's father and grandfather had been rectors of Stokesay, in Shropshire, where his grandfather, Thomas, had emigrated from Dublin, and, effectively, from the main La Touche family, in the early nineteenth century.[3]

After his retirement, Charles fondly recalled Hugh as 'my best friend' but acknowledged that he was 'a super-magpie collector of useless but enjoyable facts, a shell-shocked victim of the First World War's trenches; a reformed alcoholic who knew what it was to survive in London by remaking and selling cigarette butts picked up in Hyde Park; and a card-carrying member of the Communist Party of Great Britain.' He also noted that 'in sheer exasperation my mother once remarked that Hugh was the definition of the difference between intellect and intelligence'. One is inclined to wonder what Isabel saw in Hugh that fitted him either to be her husband or to be the step-father of Charles.[4] As Isabel's later correspondence indicates, she was only too well aware of Hugh's character: 'you, I know, won't work unless your alternative is starvation.'

From the surviving evidence, we know that Hugh was educated at Cambridge, and that he, too, worked briefly for the Indian Railways.[5] A single reference to Hugh as 'Captain La Touche' suggests that he had been commissioned during the war, from which, on his own as well as Charles's evidence, he had suffered greatly. It seems that Hugh was an inveterate outpourer of his political and social emotions – his surviving pages, besides the various chapters of his novel 'The Travail of Man', consist of essays on the themes 'Why I am a Socialist', 'Why I am a Communist', world disarmament, 'Organization of the World Commonwealth', the abolition of national frontiers and of organized

---

3. Hugh was the seventh generation in direct descent from David La Touche (1671–1745) who, like Isabel's own ancestor, had come to Ireland as a refugee from the oppression of the Huguenots in his native France and, as a very young man, had fought in the army of William of Orange at the Battle of the Boyne (1690). Hugh's branch was the junior, descended from David's younger son James, while the senior branch, which by the mid-eighteenth century was well established in landholding and banking in Dublin, listed six members of the Irish Parliament before its dissolution in 1800. The junior branch had held two large houses in south Dublin: Belfield (now part of University College Dublin) and Sans Souci in Booterstown, which had been acquired by Hugh's great-great-grandfather William (1747–1803). Other cousins had settled at Bellevue, in Delgany, and at Luggala, both in County Wicklow.

4. Hugh's down-and-out experiences would find their way into 'Rent Cordage', the unpublished novel by Isabel which, it appears, he co-authored.

5. As part of an inspection team in the provinces of Kathiawar, Junagadh and other parts of Rajputana.

religion; Charles would, at least temporarily, adopt some of Hugh's views, and absorb some of them deeply into his political thinking.

Quite apart from the separation almost immediately after their marriage, Isabel and Hugh spent very little time together in the remaining seven years of their marriage. Just before his sudden death in 1933, Hugh wrote to Isabel from a London address 'Very many thanks for putting me up. I had a most enjoyable time at Grata Quies [Isabel's house near Bournemouth]',[6] which is hardly the expression one would expect from husband to wife.

In fact the exchanges between Isabel and Hugh, when they were not indulging in recriminations (from her) and defensive replies (from him), were love-letters without love. One of the considerable puzzles over Isabel's own character is the fact that the inconsolable widow, whose every emotion was strained towards the memory of her husband and the raising of her orphaned son, should, within four years, have married someone whom she knew at the time to be completely unlike Reggie in character and temperament and unsuited to the harsh conditions in which their lives were to be lived.

There is only patchy evidence of the cause of the separation of Hugh and Isabel shortly after their marriage. It was apparently engineered by Hugh's sister Marjory, who had set out to break up the marriage by persuading Isabel that Hugh was a wastrel and philanderer; Isabel herself would come to regard Hugh as a wastrel, after their reconciliation. 'When you were down & out, in rags almost, & half starved, when I took you back – well, the condition you were in didn't look as if Marjory & her husband had done much for you when you needed help. Did she even give you a home when she had got you away from mine – no, she left you in a miserable boarding house. There is no place for her in the lives she did her best to ruin.'

Once Isabel and Hugh were reconciled, she found that she was linked to a man with boundless ideas and mental energy which might possibly rescue the fortunes of her son's ancestral home. Even though he was prevented, by his managerial ineptitude and early death, from making a success of Kilmacurragh, he did secure, firstly, a reliable tenant in Lucy Phillimore, followed by a long-term lessee in Charles Budina, who would, at least temporarily, turn around the fortunes of the house.

---

6. The letter was written on 3 August 1933; Hugh died in Dublin two weeks later.

Charles and his early schools

Nothing is known of Charles's life between the ages of two and eight, other than the photographs which show his growth from a baby into a child. Since Holm Ray was sold in 1918, we assume that Charles accompanied his mother to Kilmacurragh from age three to six. But in 1922, two years after his mother's remarriage, he was sent to the first of a succession of preparatory boarding schools, a junior establishment at Petergate, Weston-super-Mare, on England's western seaboard, from where the headmaster wrote on 23 February 1922:

> His behaviour has been excellent &, *though he seems to regard life as somewhat strange* [my italics], he is most evidently very happy & greatly interested. He has been thoroughly obedient even to the extent of keeping silence after the light has been put out in the dormitory, & has shewn not the slightest sign of rebellion unmanageableness of any kind; in fact his manners have been quite charming. I think the boy has a great deal in him & I am quite sure that the discipline & routine here combined with the training that contact with other little boys must give him, will do wonders for him.

When Charles was one month short of his eighth birthday, he wrote one of his earliest recorded letters to his mother (14 March 1922) in a babyish way, on lined paper with little punctuation:[7] 'My dear Mother, Now I can write I am writing you a letter. I am getting on finely at school We played football on the sands one morning, and I kicked a goal I had tea with Grannie on Sun day On Princess Mary's Wedding-day we went on the Pier and saw the life boat, which was being painted. Lots of love from Charlie.' Most of his letters began 'My dear Mummie' and were signed 'Love from Charlie', until a point, during his years at Rugby, when he began occasionally to sign 'Charles' rather than 'Charlie', signalling his eventual decision to delete the 'Ball' of 'Ball-Acton' and to insist that he be called 'Charles' by all. His mother, on the other hand, continued, in her few extant letters, to call him 'My own dear little son' right up to, and after, his marriage in 1951.

Charles was achieving average marks at Petergate, being placed sixth out of a class of twelve: 'he is backward but shows great aptitude to learn'. By the time he left Petergate, his end-of-year report recorded that 'His writing &

---

7. Peter Acton informs me that, when opening the letter-box from Kilmacurragh (which he inherited on Charles's death), he found inside it a stamped letter which read: 'Dear Mummy, Just to tell you Mummy dear that your Charlie is a very good boy with love Charlie'.

spelling are very backward but he shows considerable aptitude'; he had difficulty with arithmetic, showed interest in Latin, and 'shows little natural aptitude for games & almost total inability to run or jump'. 'We have found him straight and plucky but quarrelsome among other boys. He certainly tries to improve.' However, at his next two schools, and at Rugby, he would demonstrate a keen interest in games, but his academic record would continue to prove problematic until he entered Rugby at fourteen.

It was intended from the outset that Charles would be sent to Rugby School at the standard age of 13–14 years, on the basis of a War Exhibition, 'awarded to the sons of Old Rugbeians or others who were killed or incapacitated... in the War'.[8] The regulations further stipulated that 'no son of an Old Rugbeian who fell in the War shall be debarred by lack of means from being educated at his father's School.' Parents or guardians were required to indicate 'what proportion of the total expenses [£240 p.a.] would need to be met' from the War Memorial Fund, 'and also what assistance, if any, would be required towards educational expenses at a Preparatory School.'[9] In May 1922 Isabel was informed that Charles had been awarded £10 per term (£30 per year) by the Rugby fund, towards the costs of preparatory education: 'I hope that this will help you through the difficult time,' wrote W. W. Vaughan, the headmaster of Rugby. Her personal finances were always precarious during these years, contributing to Charles's own sense of anxiety for his mother's well-being, besides a general awareness of the impecunious nature of family life. He was destined for School House, which had been attended by his father and uncle. He was actually 14½ when he entered Rugby in September 1928.

The intervening years (1922–1927), which almost exactly coincided with his mother's separation from Hugh, would see Charles moving first to Boxgrove and then Great Ballard schools. Rugby itself had to be consulted, as the school would not accept a boy unless it approved of the preparatory school which he had attended. There is no indication of whether Rugby regarded Petergate as unsuitable, but Isabel had contacted Boxgrove School, near Guildford in Surrey, as an alternative, at a cost of 150 guineas per year. The headmaster at Petergate, Arthur P. O'Connor, and his wife Mary, remonstrated that Charles should remain at their school:

> You are overlooking the great cardinal point in the child's development namely his extreme backwardness – backwardness not only in his lessons,

8. Rugby School prospectus, March 1922.

9. 'Rugby School, War Benefactions' January 1922.

but in his general ability to consort with, & hold his own among other boys. Charlie is not a normal ordinary boy yet, & this fact must be reckoned with.

Nevertheless, it is clear that Isabel's decisions about Charles's schooling were closely connected with her own domicile, since she was anxious to be as close to his school as possible – even, when he went to Cambridge, contemplating a move to a house nearby.

Isabel persisted, and Charles entered Boxgrove in September 1922, even though his new headmaster had also advised that Charles should not enter the school until mid-1923. It is clear that she was concerned not merely about his academic progress but about his health, since the headmaster of Boxgrove was at pains to put her mind at rest about the sanitary conditions of the school: 'we have had no illness here of any importance since the flu epidemic of 1918!'

Charles's first letter from Boxgrove informed his mother that 'I am very well, and not at all homesick. Please Mummy may I have some stamps for extra letters. With love from Charlie.' It seems that, despite the O'Connors' fears and warnings, Boxgrove suited him, since, after only ten days in the school, the matron told Isabel 'he is settling down splendidly and is so happy & loves everything. He is just full of joy. I do hope he will grow out of all his little ailments.'

Charles's first foray into music criticism came on 19 November 1922: 'Last night the Masters gave a concert which I liked very much.' Three weeks later he told his mother 'we had a Gramophone Concert. It was the *Pirates of Penzance*. The song I liked best was the Major-General, which was very funny. I will bring home my music so that I can play it to you.' Charles reported to his mother that he enjoyed football, dancing and boxing lessons, as well as instruction in music (piano) and drawing, at which he became proficient very early and pursued for much of his life. 'I have got on nicely with my Dancing so if I go to any parties it is nice to be able to dance.' At his next prep school, Great Ballard, he would play hockey and fly a kite (which, along with the headmaster's passion for music, was a major school pastime), and it was noted that 'he is very plucky in the water and shows no fear at all', while at Rugby he would take up ice skating and fencing, as well as the mandatory sports of football and Rugby which, of course, had its origins at the school.

Very soon he was achieving better reports than previously: at mid-term (November 1922) his reading and spelling were 'decidedly good for his age', although writing presented problems; he showed 'a quick brain' at maths, but progress in music was slow, 'chiefly because he does not practice steadily'. By the end of summer term 1924 Charles was top of his class overall, and top also in each subject except classics (second) and maths (fifth). At the beginning of the new school year his English teacher was reporting that 'he has a complete grip of his own language' – a factor in his journalism which would become evident to his readers as they accustomed themselves to the idiosyncrasies of his style. This is demonstrated by one of three short essays, which are the only extant examples of Charles's work as a schoolboy:

> Short account of Queen Elizabeth after 1588
> Queen Elizabeth was getting old & practically all her friends had died.
>
> In 1598 there was a rebellion headed by O'Neill, Earl of Tyrone which he was successful in and in '99 an army of 7,000 men was sent over from Spain – and at the same time Earl of Essex had come over with an army of 20,000 men. Essex was a very bad general & O'Neil killed everyone practically in the army. Then in 1601 things were better for the English who made Ulster a horrible smelly dessert then they put in some Scotch and English soldiers which made it a much better place.
>
> In 1600 the East India Co. was founded which lasted up to 1858. Then Elizabeth died & that is the end.

This essay was marked: 'This is very bad work: 5'. At the end of the Summer term Charles had dropped back to eighth place out of eleven.

Charles seems to have been anxious for his mother to visit him at school ('You needn't come and see me if it is aguad [*sic*] for you'), and an even greater anxiety regarding where the school holidays were to be spent: 'I think we had better go to that place in Devon if it is a cold spring like last year. I do remember how cold it was last year. I hope we shall have good weather.' He hoped very much that his mother would attend the school concert, but was disappointed, as he was again in July when she failed to visit him on her birthday. But he was proud to tell her that he had come 'third in geography, top in history and English grammer [*sic*] and third in French.' This was a continuing problem for him, since he seemed to receive a series of disappointments as far as visits from his mother were concerned. (In March 1929 we will find him writing from Rugby in obvious disappointment: 'Of course I don't mind you not turning up at the [school] play if it is your health!') Isabel's health remained delicate, with arthritis and a series of injuries incapacitating her for considerable periods and provoking extremely solicitous letters from her son. He was constantly wishing his mother's health to improve. She had an unspecified operation in January 1924, and his anxieties over her health continued to feature in his letters: 'I am so glad that you are lighter but I hope the life you are leading is not too strenuous and that you will not have a breakdown'. The phrase suggests that her illnesses were not entirely physical – something we might attribute to her financial worries and the responsibility of a single parent bringing up a highly strung young boy.

As young as nine years old, Charles was aware of the family's precarious financial position which made the upkeep of Kilmacurragh almost impossible: 'I think we had better sell Kilmacurragh because we don't want to lose it without the money, as you say'. The youthful sense of purpose is followed immediately by that of the child: 'I do not want to let it go with my toys that I want such as:– the rocking-horse and the musical-box etc and some books, you had better look after your things and a bit of mine.'

Towards the end of the summer term of 1924, the headmaster was writing to Isabel (in the letter from which I quoted in the Introduction), clearly in response to her enquiries as to Charles's development: 'he is, as you know, rather highly strung, and of course I cannot bring myself to whip him, and, indeed, I do not think he requires it, because he knows how to behave himself perfectly'. Isabel was clearly outraged at the idea that Charles might be whipped, and the headmaster responded to her letter 'I am sure you are right that Charlie is a boy who ought not to be whipped.' The headmaster maintained that 'he would enjoy life so much better if he wd. conform & play the game as practically all the others do'. To think that Charles might 'conform' may have been a reasonable expectation in respect of most pupils, but in Charles's case it was quite unrealistic: it was only as his teachers became aware of his interests and his disinterests, that they gradually became able to advise him and his mother as to his future prospects.

The reports of prospective pupils were sent to Rugby for inspection, and Charles's report and his headmaster's letter were regarded as satisfactory; A.E. Donkin wrote from Rugby 'I attach no importance to the word "babyish"; after all he is only 9½. The letter is a kind and sensible one. Charlie must be a very interesting little lad.'

Perhaps his abiding curiosity for, and interest in, the natural world was part-and-parcel of his worry about where holidays were to be spent, quite apart from the financial considerations which often saw mother and son spending his school holidays either in her current lodgings or, very occasionally, at Kilmacurragh. In June 1924, anticipating his summer holidays, he asked his mother: 'I have being [sic] thinking about things for Woolacombe [a town in Devonshire] next hols … A Sunday preferable. Do not come on purpose.' The following month he wrote again on the subject, spilling out his earliest ambitions: 'As you are very much better I hope to go for some walks. I do not mean "umpteen" miles but strolls for some time taking our tea out or whatever meals we are missing & do some wandering all over the place avoiding as much as possible roads of any sort because I have decided to be a naturalist when I grow up & I like watching various interesting things.'

There is more than a two-year gap in Charles's letters to his mother, from summer 1925 to late 1927. In September 1925 Charles had been transferred from Boxgrove to Great Ballard, another preparatory school near New Milton in Hampshire, which had been founded the previous year by its inaugural head-master, Ivor Poole, who assured Isabel that his clientele 'are without excep-tion boys of the right type. We have no Jews or foreigners among them.'[10] This transfer was possibly due to a change in Isabel's address, from one near Boxgrove at Guildford to 'Grata Quies', a large house which had formerly been a hospital, at Branksome, near Bournemouth in Dorset (which was appreciably nearer to New Milton). Isabel appears to have rented it, later purchasing the house and letting it out, with variable success, as flats. On one occasion Isabel stated that Grata Quies was bought with capital of £3000 which she inherited on the death of Elizabeth Acton (the widow of Charles's great-uncle William) who had died in 1928. In 1931 she told Hugh that a story was going the rounds in Bournemouth that it had been bought 'with money paid to her husband by the Russian government for doing propaganda work in England.' (Hugh was a vigorous apologist for the soviet system.)

Gramophone recitals were quite regular, and towards the end of 1925 the nine-year-old Charles was reporting that he had heard Tchaikovsky's '1812 Overture' 'and a bit of Gossec's gavotte which Kreisler plays'. And stamp collecting was clearly becoming a passion, with particular interest for the overprinted British stamps in use in the earliest days of the Irish Free State, an iconic introduction to the political changes taking place between his two coun-tries. The largely solitary pursuits point to a continuation of Charles's unease with company, and his sense of the need for privacy, but in early 1926 his head-master noted that in Charles's 'demeanour and relations with other boys [there had been] a very marked change for the better. I am very pleased with the way he has tackled the difficulties that beset him'.

Isabel had gone into the confectionery business in a modest way in order to eke out her income (which she also did by winning frequently at bridge

---

10. The school moved from New Milton in 1940, first to Iwerne Minster in Dorset and since 1961 has been located at Eartham, near Chichester in West Sussex.

tournaments), and Charles was clearly concerned about her. At the time when she and Hugh were reconciled he wrote: 'If you are very pressed for help it is quite likely that Mr Poole might let me come home early now that my exam is over. Can't you rope Hugh in some time when you are doing sweets and ask him to help you then because he can't very well refuse to can he?' His mother sent rejects from her sweetmaking, but Charles pointedly asked for cake in preference, although he appreciated the sweets as well: 'I would like to be supplied with the not-elegant-enough-for-sale sweets but do not make them so on purpose will you.'

At this stage he also had the first inkling of changing his surname, since on occasion he signed as 'CA' rather than 'CB-A' as previously, and was filling in forms as 'Charles Acton', although at Rugby, as his father's son, he would have to revert to his full surname. When in 1929 (as a fifteen-year-old) he had a letter published in *The Listener*, he had a reply from the BBC: 'Unfortunately they write to me as Bale-Acton, How much simpler it will be when I am Acton without the "Ball".'

Apart from schoolwork, Charles had a typical young man's interest in popular sensational literature. Hugh had sent him *The Final Count*, featuring the hero Bulldog Drummond.[11] In the same year he was pursuing his interest in Bulldog Drummond with *The Female of the Species*, followed by John Buchan's *The Runagates Club* (1928) and, by the time he reached Rugby, the adventures of another popular sleuth, Sexton Blake.

A major development – more for its financial than its academic consequences – came in June 1928, in his final term at Great Ballard, when he wrote home excitedly: 'My dear Mummie, I do not know if you have heard the joyful news. I have won my scholarship [to Rugby]. It is the forty pound Ralph Evers scholarship.[12] Do you think you could send me 2lbs of plain biscuits – try "Petit Beurre" because I want some for bathing.' On foot of this news, his headmaster wrote to Isabel

it is not a very valuable scholarship but I think that it is as much as he could expect to get, taking into consideration all the circumstances. Charlie is able

---

11. The author 'Sapper' (Herman Cyril McNeile, 1888–1937) created his fictional hero in *Bulldog Drummond* (1920); this was followed by *The Black Gang* (1922), *The Third Round* (1924) and *The Final Count* (1926). *The Female of the Species* (1928) was first read by Charles when it appeared in serial form.

12. One of the scholarships provided by the Rugby War Memorial Fund. Ralph Evers was an Old Rugbeian who had been killed during the First World War.

and intelligent but he is a poor candidate from a scholarship point of view. Although he has improved his handwriting it is still unusually bad and the papers which he did in the examination were messy and untidy. Moreover I have not cared to work him too hard for the simple reason that I could not accept the responsibility for pressing a boy who came to us in such a highly nervous condition. Until quite recently Charlie has not been a great worker, nor did he come here particularly well-prepared. He stood no chance at all of winning an open scholarship at Rugby, where the standard is very high, and I really think that he is rather lucky to get anything at all there.

Obviously aware of Isabel's circumstances (he had already reduced Charles's school fees from the regular figure of thirty guineas per term), Poole suggested that, if the £40 scholarship was insufficient, she should approach Rugby for extra assistance, adding 'It might be a good idea for Charlie to do a little work during the holidays but I should not insist upon his doing very much; his first term at Rugby is likely to be somewhat trying and I think it is important that he should arrive as fit and fresh as you can possibly make him'.

Hugh at Kilmacurragh

In 1926, when Isabel and Hugh were reconciled, Hugh was working at Barker's, a London department store. Later, he would acknowledge 'I am exceedingly fortunate really – for I don't know what I should have done without you. You took me back, looked after me and gave me a job when the world looked pretty bleak.' His communism (or at least socialism) is always at the fore: in May 1926, in the middle of Britain's short-lived General Strike, he writes 'What do you think of the great struggle against tyranny? The government's latest dope is telling the workers that they will look after them – just as they did in 1914, and with about as much intention of carrying it out. The sleeping giant is at last shaking himself.'

The reconciliation took place early in 1926; in the middle of February Charles wrote 'I am so glad you & Hugh are friends again. I have quite forgotten what Hugh looks like' – hardly surprising, since Charles had been only six or seven when the separation took place. The relationship between husband and wife was passionate as far as literary expression was concerned, but distant in terms of physical contact. 'I am missing you dreadfully', Hugh writes. 'Sometimes I lie awake at night, I am so lonely. O darling, I do long so for you – but I advise you to stay where you are. You are better off there

[Isabel was staying at Milford, in Hampshire] than you are here in London.'
In September 1926, when Isabel and Charles were holidaying at St Columb
Minor in Cornwall, she wrote: 'There is a piano!! Charlie's performances on
it with several notes missing & two or three sticking, are enough to excruciate
the most hardened.' She and Charles wished that Hugh could be with them,
but his absence suggests that there was, in fact, little domestic liaison between
them, with the exception of the winter of 1926–27. Nevertheless, a fond
relationship still succeeded in establishing itself between Charles and Hugh,
partly by way of correspondence and partly during their brief reunions, when
they would play flute and piano duets together. Hugh may have been an eccentric, and a useless one at that, but Charles's acceptance of him, as his mother's
companion and as his own stepfather, whether or not a figure of authority,
speaks much to us about his later tolerance of some types and his intolerance
of others.

By the spring of 1928, Hugh was at Kilmacurragh, where Isabel and Charles
visited at Easter. His role seems to have been exploratory at first:

> In the autumn, if the house is not let or sold, I should be quite capable of
> taking on the agency – the letting of the lands, and everything else, and
> would save expense and not run you into any. I understand and can deal with
> the people – and you yourself say that I have grown up! I am a good bit less
> nervy and stronger in body and mind than I was a year or two ago – thanks
> entirely to you – and I intend to use my powers to the utmost. I intend to
> make money for both of us, God willing.

In Ireland, he believed, 'It isn't the republicans who are putting obstacles in
the way of progress – far from it. The real obstacle is the imperialist tory
English government (who are taking the money for "annuities" you ought to
be getting from the Land Purchase) and bleeding Ireland – and their organ the
Irish Times.'

By the middle of 1928 Hugh was deeply involved with development plans
for the Kilmacurragh estate, which included discussions with Charles Budina,
the German businessman who would become the lessee of Kilmacurragh
in 1932, the possible sale of part of the house's library, and letting fishing
rights on the Ennerilly river to a Major Bayly.[13] In the middle of 1929 he met,
among others, Sir John Keane, a director of the Bank of Ireland, whom he
intended as a director of Irish Resources Ltd, Hugh's anticipated engine for

---

13. He managed the ancient post-hotel at nearby Woodenbridge; in the 1940s
Charles formed the view that Bayly (a very distant cousin) was an idiot.

the revival of Kilmacurragh.[14] Another member of the proposed syndicate was Batt O'Connor, a Cumann na nGaedheal TD, author of a memoir on his close friend Michael Collins.[15]

Hugh described Budina as 'a chap of about five foot ten, fair, broad open face, full of ambition and undaunted by anything. Has been in business all his life, and has been in Ireland a long time. Fancy his father brought him here as a boy. He has heaps of brains and also sturdy physique and courage. Just the combination required, specially in conjunction with me.' When Budina complained that, as a foreigner, he was subject to more intense questioning on business matters, Hugh pointed out 'that his very nationality is an asset in this country, as the people of Ireland have an almost superstitious reverence for the business acumen of Germans.' Budina had in fact been raised in County Dublin; his uncle had a tobacconist's in Blackrock and he himself was a hairdresser by trade, working at Prost's in St Stephen's Green, Dublin. Charles thought 'he had a most fertile imagination and vision for the future of Ireland, which he might have started to realise if it had not been for the [second world] war'.[16]

'There is iron on Bolagh as well as Ballard', Hugh wrote, 'and there is the Macreddin stone – and there is money available for these activities and I am going to try my utmost to get Kilmacurragh industrialized. Factory chimneys and mines are what we want to see!' Another meeting was with Gordon Campbell of the Department of Industry, which seemed to promise government support for some of Hugh's schemes. 'Budina and I intend to try and make it the "Garden of the Western World".' An annual rent of £180 would represent a yield of 4½ per cent on a valuation of £4000. Hugh reported 'He comes from a family of working farmers, and wants to bring over his brother and sister from Germany'. Budina did in fact operate the Kilmacurragh hotel in association with his brother Kurt up to 1939, carrying out his original intention of farming pigs and cows to produce delicatessen goods 'for the German, Jewish and foreign population of Dublin'.

---

14. Sir John Keane, 5th baronet, 1873–1956; barrister, member of Seanad Éireann 1922–34 and 1938–44, where he opposed the censorship of publications.

15. *With Michael Collins in the Fight for Irish Independence* (1930/2004).

16. Budina had returned to Germany in order to fight in the First World War and had been interned after being captured by the Irish Guards, returning to Ireland after his release. It appears that he had a daughter by a first marriage, and that he had married her governess in the late 1920s. Nothing is known of his first wife.

A notable feature of Hugh's work as Isabel's agent was his assiduous application to the parallel questions of forestry and mining. He was quite sure that the granite quarry at Macreddin could be made profitable, and it was in fact a central factor in his concept of 'Irish Resources'. Macreddin had long been considered a possible source of income, and even as late as 1944 Charles, with his interest in mineralogy, was receiving professional reports of the potential for mining in the Wicklow area. But however significant the potential for industrial development in Wicklow, into which Hugh and his associates might gain an entry, there was neither the capital resource nor government will to enable it to be realized at that time.[17]

With increasing investment by both government and private enterprise in Irish industrial enterprises, some of Kilmacurragh's natural resources, especially a granite quarry and the potential to mine for manganese (an essential ingredient in steel production) appeared very profitable. But in April 1930, the entire set of schemes was in jeopardy as Ireland faced into a general election. As Hugh observed, 'I have to wait until I know whether President Cosgrave will return;[18] as otherwise I don't know who I am dealing with.' Two years later he was correct in his prediction that Fianna Fáil would win the next election.[19]

Isabel was, even if wryly, supportive of Hugh's general attitude, and respected his political views. She commented 'By the time you've worked up the Industrial Development of Ireland schemes & got things going, you may be a very prominent man.' Life alone at Kilmacurragh intensified Hugh's longing for Isabel. 'Without your letters I should be like a man on a desert island. Sunday here is a complete *dies non* – even the excitement of the post is missing. I used to like Sunday in London – a change to see the shops closed – but now one might be on Pitcairn Island!' But we also find him writing 'I love Kilmacurragh, my work and the country; if you could only see me there, and the changes! There is life and work in the place now – it no longer looks derelict.'

17. Roy Foster tell us (*op. cit.*, pp. 155–65) that quarrying had, by the mid-1880s, captured the imagination of C.S. Parnell, who had granite on his land at Ballinaclash (much of which went to build O'Connell Bridge in Dublin) and who was intensely interested in industrial development in his native county.

18. Cosgrave had led the government of the Irish Free State since its inception in 1922.

19. On the other hand, Edith Somerville, who was endeavouring to make her home farm viable, wrote in 1932, 'This last disastrous year of Mr de Valera's government has brought to me, as to very many others, what is very little short of ruin... My present difficulties are wholly attributable to the state of my [nb] country': G. Lewis, *op. cit.* p. 377.

He was deeply conscious that he owed his existence to Isabel. 'I know and have always said I owe everything to you and am trying my best to justify your love. I know from bitter experience the difficulty of getting jobs.'

Apart from the brief reunions, Hugh and Isabel were indeed fated to live separately, she caring for Charles and he caring for Kilmacurragh. But perhaps the separation served to deepen their undeniable affection for each other. Hugh wrote: 'I miss you so much that I feel utterly lost without you. It is awfully hard to be apart like this … But I am sure you couldn't live in Ireland. It's altogether too damp for your health and too provincial for your mentality.' After a visit by Hugh to Bournemouth in February 1930, Isabel wrote: 'My poor little husband, it's very sad to think of you so lonely without your big fat warm cushiony wife.' She had always been conscious of her weight, and now her husband advised 'Please eat properly, even if you have to go out to lunch to save cooking. To try and get yourself thin by starving is awfully bad for you. Better be plump and strong than thin and weak.'

Hugh also relished the English papers which Isabel sent him: 'One gets so fed up with the local papers – the *Irish Times* is deadly dull and there is too much illiteracy and religion in the *Independent*!' He was clearly conscious, as an Irishman, that the Free State could be managed much more efficiently. 'Ireland is still in the pioneer stage. As yet it needs lots of licking into shape, and the local "gentry" are a singularly dud crowd. No doubt their ideas and orientations have been totally upset; they still long for the "ascendancy" and are out of touch with modern times.' And he shared Isabel's revulsion at hunting: 'I don't mind fishing or shooting for the pot, or for the markets. But to look upon hunting a poor offensive little creature to death with overwhelming odds as the highest delight of life; it makes you sick.' And he contrasted the landowners with the tenants: 'Look at men like Kerr and Bradshaw and Nolan and Farrar, illiterate plain farmers, never fail in an obligation; ask permission even if it is only to put a hayrake in a shed, and give help whenever needed ungrudgingly.' Isabel agreed:

> Irish provincialism is extraordinary. I was simply bored stiff with the few people I knew socially at Kilmacurragh – it isn't that I ever have any profound or intellectual conversation here – no such treat comes my way – but it's an attitude of mind – all their mind cased up in a little compartment & so absolutely contented to be inside its enclosing walls they don't even want to think there's anything outside them. It makes my mental clostrophobia [*sic*] rampant!

One of Hugh's first actions on moving to Kilmacurragh and inspecting the accounts was to try to eliminate, or at least reduce, the tax liabilities. In April 1929 he wrote:

> Charlie is too young yet to make up his mind; the property will increase in value. With capital to run it, it would be worth £2000 a year; the sheepmen's rents alone are over £300 a year; they make 3 times as much themselves. A man with capital could stock with sheep and make £800 or £900 a year out of that alone. Beet is the most paying crop in Ireland – apart from sugar, the leaves are cut and fed to cattle. With capital for seeds, tillage, and labour, a profit of £10 an acre is made out of this. Kilmacurragh is ideal for beet.

Although he would not sell Kilmacurragh until 1944, Charles was constantly alert to the disadvantage of owning a house which he could not afford. In 1929 the weight of Kilmacurragh was already on his fifteen-years-old shoulders: 'How about advertising in an American paper so that if some Irish-American millionaire wanted to buy an estate in Ireland he would see the advertisement and write?'

A tenant at Kilmacurragh

The idea of letting Kilmacurragh to a suitable tenant had been discussed extensively among the family. In 1925, Irene and Evelyn agreed in principle to rent the property at £100 per year, but this had fallen through, mainly because Hugh rejected it as unacceptable. For sentimental reasons, Isabel and Hugh agreed to offer Irene the purchase of the hall at Kilcandra and a cottage there for £100, which had been part of the original Acton estate, in order to maintain it as a place of worship for the few remaining Protestants.

But by September 1927, Lucy Phillimore, a novelist and friend of Lady Gregory, was renting Kilmacurragh on a seasonal basis; W.B. Yeats stayed there with her in convalescence the following year and W.T. Cosgrave often visited, amond many others including the former Governor-General James MacNeill, the publisher Jonathan Cape and G.K. Chesterton.[20] Hugh had written to Isabel: 'The best we can do with Kilmacurragh I think now is to let it to Mrs Phillimore

20. Lucy Phillimore was the anonymous author of the novels *By an Unknown Disciple* (1918), *Paul: the Jew* (1927) and *Paul: the Christian* (1930), and *In the Carpathians* (1912). Born Lucy Fitzpatrick, she married (in 1895) Robert Phillimore, son of the first Baron Phillimore, who died in 1919.

– if she could be induced to take it on a five year lease it would be good.' When the house was let to Mrs Phillimore, who moved in with six maids and a chauffeur, Hugh moved into summer quarters at Dunganstown Castle. 'One solitary woman! She excuses this on the plea of humanity to the lower orders.'[21]

But the idea of selling the entire estate remained foremost in Isabel's mind, and she even contemplated buying another, more easily maintainable, property in Ireland in which she and Hugh could take up more profitable farming. As with Charles's own attitude to Kilmacurragh during the years he lived there, there is an ambivalence due in part to the determination to wrest a profit from the land that was left after tenant purchase, in part to a loyalty to the ancestral acres, and in part to the latent acknowledgement that the age of the great landed estates had, literally, died with the Land Acts and the First World War. Hugh's views seem to have swung between the profit motive and the need to realize a shrinking asset which was fast becoming a liability.

Although she definitely ruled out living at Kilmacurragh, Isabel did occasionally feel a sentimental attachment to her son's property:

> Oddly enough your description of the view from Cunniamstown Plantation – 'desolate to a degree' gave me a sudden feeling that I would be quite happy with you over there – trudging round the place, and coming in to the log fires. Now that you are doing it all & seeing to things, so that I would not be crushed by the burden. But I really couldn't live in the house unless I could either have a full staff of servants with a competent cook-housekeeper or have it quite to myself.

Nevertheless, Isabel constantly vacillated on the question of whether or not she wanted to end her physical separation from Hugh by moving to Kilmacurragh. 'I am not at all satisfied to live apart like this. Then I think of the dark house, the damp, the dirt & discomfort of it – the big cold kitchen – & I feel sure that I would get so depressed you'd wish I'd never come. And then, there isn't a good doctor anywhere near, is there?' Almost in the same breath, she validated the separation: 'You being there makes all the difference to me – I never worry about Kilmacurragh at all now – it isn't the great black menace

---

21. The Danish writer Signe Toksvig, who lived nearby, visited frequently and recorded in her diary: 'big old 18th century house, dismally gloomy, all furniture as if bought at third-rate auctions… But a garden like romance itself… judicious neglect… Curious shabby dark dingy dignity… but superb prideful views… Sculptured black yews, all gigantic. Vegetation is noble. It owns the place.' *Signe Toksvig's Irish Diaries 1926–1937* pp. 103, 108, 116. The interior of Kilmacurragh features in her novel *Eve's Doctor* (1937).

standing always at my elbow which it was before you took it in hand. That is a tremendous relief to me.' In reply, Hugh told her 'I don't think you could ever stand the life here, no matter how we did the place up ... And the mental atmosphere here is a rotten and decaying one. Provincialism and narrowmindedness to the nth degree. One's brains seem to shrink in it.'

'Don't think I am a quitter,' Hugh explained to Isabel,

> but the fairest thing for you and Charlie is to give up this place. Here is a place where neither you nor Charlie are ever likely to live. It is too encumbered, and is a millstone round your necks. Apart from actual practical considerations, by the time that Charlie's grown up there is likely to be a great change in general world conditions, and it is very improbable that there will be any more private ownership of large landed estates.

The costs of running the house were: wages of £500, rates £30, tax £50, repairs £25, ancillary costs £60 – a total of £665, against which there could only be set the rent from Mrs Phillimore of £80 and sale of garden produce £70, leaving an annual deficit of £515, not allowing for travel expenses, or loss of Mrs Phillimore's rent; whereas the lands themselves showed a net profit of £600, after tax and collection costs had been deducted. To the deficit of £515 Isabel would have to add the costs of servants and gardeners, adding another £400 to the overall annual loss.

Hugh proposed to sell the house and grounds, and for Isabel and Charles to enjoy the income of £619 payable by the Land Commission, giving each of the four workmen on the grounds, including Robert Taylor, a pension of ten shillings per week, leaving an income of £500, plus a capital sum of whatever could be got for the house. 'You two people are the greatest things in this world to me, and my whole being is entirely engaged in doing my best for you. I look to Charlie to carry on the torch of light in succession to my somewhat murky beams; and you are all in all to me.'

Isabel took this advice immediately, and practically assumed that the house had been disposed of already. 'I feel lighter & brighter altogether now that it is decided to sell Kilmacurragh (unless Charlie objects).' She was certain that Charles would agree to the proposal. But she hoped that Hugh would continue with Irish Resources. Hugh responded that 'I mean to get into the great world, and so I am sure does Charlie. He couldn't bury himself alive. You have the most wonderful talent of homemaking.'[22]

---

22. There was a further possibility during this period that the house might be rented, firstly, by a Robert Kennedy, who apparently knew it well, and secondly by a member

Kilmacurragh had been previously advertised for sale in *Country Life* and attracted no interest. Now, the obvious principal candidate for a purchaser was Mrs Phillimore, but Isabel thought it might be better to give Irene first option to purchase. This she did, but Irene realized that, despite her best intentions and affections, the responsibility as well as the financial burden would be greater than she and her sister could bear. Isabel tartly commented,

> If they [the Acton family] subscribed, say four or five hundred a year, they'd have a say in the matter – but no, they want to scrawl about 'our family estates' at my expense … The Actons are sentimental but not practically helpful about 'the family estates'. She wouldn't care if Charlie was crushed flat by it – his whole career sacrificed to its voracious acres. I want Charlie to rise by his own endeavours, to be worth something through his own merit & ability – not a nonentity dependent for his "honourable position" on the reflected glory of his estates.

At approximately the same time, Isabel exhibited another mood swing in respect of what she saw as Hugh's dilatoriness, but the violent manner in which she discussed it is remarkable:

> I'm afraid, if I sell Kilmacurragh, & you come here, you'll just idle. Or what will you do? You never stuck to anything or really tried to work till you went there. What will you do – and what will you live on? Not on me, I won't have you. I won't have you go back to being the useless creature you were and whom I had to get rid of by going off & leaving you … It sounds harsh, but I learnt through bitter experience & I don't want to return to having to despise you when I've just been able to change my opinion of you.

In about 1932 (the dating of the letter is Charles's own) he wrote: 'I think it would be better to sell Kilmacurragh. Even if I do retire into it what on earth would there be to do[?]. It is not as if we were a large family is it?' But Isabel performed yet another a *volte face* and began to talk constructively of living at Kilmacurragh. 'If instead of selling it we lived at Kilmacurragh, which gives you interest & occupation & an outdoor life, which would be a beautiful home for Charlie to come back to & ask friends to, it wouldn't be a question of making it pay, but of running it within our means & having a nice home & a beautiful garden – which, after all, is Charlie's inheritance & if you & I lived there & kept it going, he might some day value it very much and retire to it after his life work was done, & watch his sons go out to do their work in the world.'

---

of the Mansergh family (both in 1928, when Mrs Phillimore was wavering about whether or not to renew her lease) but neither proposition materialized.

As an ironic preview of the ultimate fate of Kilmacurragh, in 1931 Hugh suggested that the State might buy the house and arboretum: 'it would become a sort of country Glasnevin. The authorities of Glasnevin certainly would like to acquire it' and indeed Hugh received a letter from Sir Frederick Moore indicating that he hoped the estate would not be sold, but turned to further horticultural use; officials from the Department of Agriculture were investigating the lands in January 1932. It appears that Mrs Phillimore based her firm offer, to purchase the house for £4000, on the condition that the Government would maintain the grounds as an adjunct to the Botanical Gardens ('she and Sir Frederick are negotiating with Mr Hogan, Minister for Agriculture, about this', Hugh told Isabel) – but the change in government in February-March 1932, marking the accession to power of Fianna Fáil, caused Mrs Phillimore to abruptly withdraw her offer. Hugh told Isabel: 'The new Government here has a hell of a hard job in front of it. There is one difference already, a mental one, and that is the lifting of that awful feeling of coercion and repression of thought and opinion.' But the new circumstances did nothing to solve the problem of Kilmacurragh. There is nothing in either Isabel's, or later in Charles's, letters to suggest a sense of closure or even an ending; and the estate continued to occupy a major role in Charles's – and his family's – thinking and activities for some time to come.

5. Rugby, Cambridge, Germany
and Palestine

Rugby

Rugby, like many of the major English public schools, had emerged from
the doldrums of the early nineteenth century, but at the opening of the
twentieth century it remained in need of modernization, which was introduced under the headmastership of Albert David (1910–21) and William
Vaughan (1921–31). They were followed by P.H.B. Lyon (1931–48). One of
Rugby's historians, J.B. Hope Simpson, considered that with Lyon's appointment 'the School entered a period of less authoritarian and, some would say,
more humane direction'.[1]

Charles later said that he 'hated' his first term at Rugby (in 1928) – 'I was
a nasty little boy.' But he acclimatized very rapidly. Although he was conscious
of the public school system creating 'a second nation' as he called it, he nevertheless recognized the value of thought that was instilled in its subjects, even
though he may have resisted its politics. He later wrote 'I am glad to consider
myself as part of that minority that has been brought up to *think* and who
therefore have from a sociological point of view profited from what can be and
sometimes is the finest education that there is'. In this development of an independent mind, and in his crucial contact with Marcus Beresford, his mentor at

1. Lyon (1893–1948) was, among other accomplishments, a poet (he had won the
Newdigate Prize at Oxford) whose 'Wild Geese' Brian Boydell would set while at the
school, as his earliest extant work (1935).

Rugby, we can discern the beginnings of the critical faculty that would distinguish Charles as a music critic in later years.

It is noticeable that, from the age of fifteen onwards, Charles easily developed the ability to express himself in terms of music criticism. One of his first experiences of a professional symphony concert came shortly after his start at Rugby, when, he told his mother (October 1928), he heard the City of Birmingham Symphony Orchestra playing Weber's overture 'Oberon', the first movement of Beethoven's third piano concerto, Mozart's g-minor symphony and the last two movements of Beethoven's fifth – 'a wonderful work'.[2]

> By special permission I and several others were allowed to sit behind the orchestra ... However by a stupid oversight I sat behind the trombones, trumpets, cornets, horns instead of behind the less pretentious flutes & clarinets. Thus it did once or twice happen that a trombone would suddenly put in an unexpected note which would temporarily drown the flutes & violins. But I thoroughly enjoyed the concert and am very glad that I did sit in the 'orchestra stalls' ... The overture to Oberon is [a] lovely thing and they played it very well indeed. Next came the [Beethoven concerto]. This is a nasty one for the pianist as he has to sit through over a hundred bars without playing a note. When once he does begin and did begin he played it wonderfully, it being [a] remarkably difficult thing to play. Fury did it wonderfully.[3] The first movement [of the Mozart symphony] I do not myself very much care for as it is neither one thing nor the other it just IS. The tunes I like very much but there are many things I like better ... The last movement is also very good. Then after two gavottes by Bach which were very very nice and lively and so unlike Bach, and a Scherzo by Mendelssohn we came to the 'piece of resistance [the last two movements of Beethoven's 5th symphony].

Unfortunately, Charles did not record his feelings about the Beethoven. He was sufficiently interested in music, a great deal of which he heard on the radio, to write to the BBC, asking for the texts of Sir Walford Davies's talks on 'Music and the Ordinary Listener', a subject on which he himself would excel when he came to give lectures to local gramophone societies throughout Ireland. Concerts at Rugby were a frequent feature of the evenings: in May 1931 he heard the 'Wireless Singers' (forerunners of today's BBC Singers),

2. On a later visit, Adrian Boult and the CBSO ended a concert at Rugby with the Brahms Academic Festival Overture, 'and got the 600 of us to sing the Gaudeamus at the end.'

3. R.B. Fury, at Rugby at the time. He later (1931) played the César Franck Symphonic Variations with the CBSO at Rugby.

conducted by Stanford Robinson, and in the same term the legendary Irishman Harry Plunket Greene:[4] 'He had one defect it seemed to me in that when he sang he sang very very soft, too much so in fact'. When he heard him again at Cambridge a few years later, Charles thought that 'he owed his reputation to his musicianship and interpretation, since apparently the old dear never really had a voice, and yet he was so wonderful'.

Science

In his second term at Rugby, in 1929, Charles reported his excitement at seeing the airship 'R 101'.[5] This was one of the first manifestations of Charles's interest in the natural sciences, which would develop considerably at Rugby and constitute his courses at Cambridge. His early declaration, *I like watching various interesting things*, may have been naïf, but it sums up his comprehensive fascination with the world which he had found 'strange to him'. In 1929 he wrote from Rugby, 'I think that after all biology, whether plants or insects is the best line to take up. For Kilmacurragh [it] would be very useful. When I get into the lower Fifth I should go on to the science side and specialize in Biology. I read in the paper that biologists of this type are greatly needed and that the demand greatly exceeds the supply.'

By 1930, astronomy, in which Rugby was very advanced, was taking up a great deal of his attention: 'Today', he wrote to Hugh, 'there was a meeting of the Astronomical Section [a school society]. We have decided to write to Greenwich and ask if there is any particular star or stars they want observing (Double-stars, I mean). Last term we observed β Cygni about 20 times and have results which agree fairly well. We thought therefore that instead of confining our activities to β Cygni & Andromedae we might do some useful work.' At the same period he was also wondering about the usefulness of shorthand, tuition in which would cost an extra £1 per term, which would

4. Harry Plunket Greene (1865–1936), bass-baritone, became a favourite interepreter of Schumann and Brahms in England from the 1890s onwards. He sang in the premiere performance of Elgar's *Dream of Gerontius* (1900). He recorded four 78rpm discs in 1934 and wrote *The Interpretation of Song*.

5. The R 101 airship, the largest flying craft ever built (surpassing the *Graf Zeppelin*) was built in 1929; it almost crashed at the Hendon airshow in 1930, and did crash on 5 October 1930 at Beauvais in France in the course of its flight to Karachi, with almost total loss of life, including that of Lord Thomson, Secretary of State for Air.

necessitate sacrificing boxing lessons. German was another subject adopted at school: later, Charles was certain that German would be essential if he were to pursue a career in natural science, and this in turn would determine his decision to study in Germany after Cambridge. In all this, we can detect the vagueness of a child who is aware of his passion for the natural world but also undecided as to which branch of science to enter, as one enthusiasm gives way to another. During Charles's years at Rugby, in particular, his ideas crystallized towards an academic career at Cambridge, followed by entry into the professional world of industrial chemistry. A neat combination of his dual interests in music and the natural sciences is the fact that in 1932 he was awarded the senior prize in astronomy at Rugby, receiving the three volumes of miniature scores of Beethoven's symphonies.

Many letters describe Charles's experiments in the physics and chemistry laboratories; one of them seems to have been so tedious that he wrote:

I had thoughts of the assembly at the [last] judgement:

The Lord: Where is Charles Ball-Acton.

St Peter: I haven't seen him come up & we have taken everybody up here, on earth, on the sea, in Hell...

Recording Angel: Oh, it's alright, he is still adding Ammonium Carbonate to 50% Acetic Acid in Rugby School chemistry lab.

The Lord: Oh, leave him at it: I am sure he would like to see the action go to completion.

On one occasion he made silver acetylide by passing acetylene through an ammonial solution of silver nitrate. 'The latter we all knew to be an extremely dangerous explosive substance, but we made it because we knew that the master, who had not seen that the book said so, would not on any account allow us to make it if he had known.'

Generally Charles's letters to his mother began with an expression of regret for their lateness and ended with an apology for their brevity. Occasionally his letters expressed frustration or annoyance in very outspoken terms, suggesting a recurrence of his petulance (typical of Charles in later life when exasperated by stupidity or a failure to follow his instructions) and Isabel obviously thought so, since quite often a contrite Charles was at pains to exonerate himself and eat humble pie when his mother complained about the tone of the letters.

School activities

A feature of life at Rugby was that the boys were often shown films of first-world-war topics, such as re-enactments of battles like Verdun, which those of them, including Charles, who had lost fathers in such encounters, must have viewed with distinctly mixed feelings.

Charles was – compulsorily – a member of the Officers' Training Corps (OTC) common to all English public schools, and told his mother 'I wore uniform for the first time. It is very comfortable indeed – in fact much more so than the clothes I have on now!!' Although he had mixed feelings about warfare, he appears to have taken part in OTC manoeuvres quite willingly, however much he may have found them pointless or too time-consuming. When the corps was subject to General's Inspection (a thorough survey by a British army general of the corps' appearance and abilities) Charles reported that the general in question

> displayed great sense by saying that he did not care two hoots for our turn out & not much for our drill, though both were good … It takes about 2 hours to fug [Rugby slang for 'prepare'] one's uniform & equipment & boots etc. This time is 'spare time'. A great many people take it out of prep & quite a number make up for it by cheating in form. There are 440 people in the corps: that is 880 hours wasted.'

Those who encountered Charles in his later life would find it difficult to believe in his interest in sports or other outdoor activities including skating on a frozen canal near Rugby.

> Most of the week I have merely slid: but this morning we were allowed to skate and I borrowed some boots and skates and tried to skate … I could not go backwards and when I began to move I fell very hard onto my behind and simply could not get up for minutes. Still after that I managed to get along very slowly and next time I hope to do considerably better.

So too, unless they knew of his interest in fine art and his own proficiency as an artist, they would not be immediately aware of his skill at carpentry, which he took up enthusiastically, making small standard lamps in the school workshop for various family members. He also made a mahogany case for his two clarinets which had been a gift from his stepfather, with whom he played duets. Later, he undertook a lot of carpentry, including picture frames which became a useful skill in connection with another of his passions, photography. In summer 1929 he was busy photographing his house rugby and hockey teams, making the frames himself.

Another interest which one would not automatically associate with the later Charles was electricity. In July 1932 he was stage electrician for a performance of *Hamlet*: 'we were using 7,600 watts i.e. 7½ kilowatts; sufficient to run a moderate sized broadcasting station or three Bournemouth stations! I did enjoy pushing up & down the resistances, dimming on and off the lights.' In March 1933, near the end of his time at Rugby, he was in charge of lights for the house play with a boy named Michael Weizmann, who was to become a friend and to open his eyes to the Palestinian situation.

Hugh

Hugh Digues La Touche was an extraordinary figure. He continued living at Kilmacurragh, trying to run his own company, Irish Resources Ltd., had written several stories and a novel, and was a prolific writer on social and economic affairs. At the end of 1929 he visited Isabel for Christmas, and typed the first version of her novel: 'It *is* very good, and it gives a real impression of atmosphere & reality.' But Isabel was still working on it two years later, when she told Hugh 'I am writing in quite a lot extra & altering it. If by any chance this book is a success & if I can go on & write another, I must arrange my life differently – regarding my writing as real work & devoting proper uninterrupted time to it. I do envy men, I think they are *so* lucky – a man wants to do something – say write a book – and he settles down to it in peace – his wife runs his home, sees to his meals, sees he isn't disturbed at his work – in fact makes everything so easy for him. He's only got to get a wife & there he is. But a woman, poor soul – has to do everything – think of a hundred things at once – snatch time to write.' In April 1932 she was still working on the book, and accepting suggestions from Hugh as to new episodes; of the three extant typescript copies, one states that the novel is by 'Isabel Digues La Touche and Hugh Digues La Touche'.

During 1931 Charles had been offering support and advice to his mother regarding the possible publication of her novel, *Rent Cordage*. Charles had to ask: 'I am afraid that rent cordage is too deep for me – what *does* it refer to?' When Isabel explained that the phrase came from *Hymns Ancient and Modern*,[6]

---

6. 'Safe home, safe home in port!/ Rent cordage, shattered deck,/ Torn sails, provisions short/ And only not a wreck:/ But oh! The joy upon the shore/ To know our voyage perils o'er'. Cordage refers to the ropes used in a ship's rigging.

he retorted 'I must say that if I came upon a real rent cordage it would strike me as the names of some American films do, little connection with the story but I feel enlightened now.' He was also enlightened about one episode in the novel depicting police escorts for workers brought in by landlords to work the farms of evicted tenants: 'Now in history we are doing all about the Irish troubles and the Irish nationalists in Parliament during Gladstone's second ministry. In your novel I never could understand why the new tenants had to be escorted to and from the church by the policemen. Now I fully see it.' He was also getting to know about Ireland in other ways: in class he was studying – and loving – Yeats's poem 'The Song of Wandering Aengus'. Yeats would become a lifelong passion (Charles often recited Yeats's poems with deep emotion). He believed 'Of course someone will publish your book. If as we have often said the stuff that one reads does get published, yours jolly well ought to. Even if the English publishers did not your name would be enough to publish it in Dublin, irrespective of the great intrinsic merits of the book, wouldn't it?' When it seemed that Isabel was having some difficulty in finding a publisher, Charles suggested 'Failing H[odder] & S[toughton], which of course I hope you won't, I should try Victor Gollancz: I am told that he is the most go-ahead & considerate publisher of the lot.' As a romantic fiction, 'Rent Cordage', with its background in Isabel's own experience of life in a vicarage, reads today as a period-piece, set against the political situation, especially the land wars, in late nineteenth-century Ireland.[7]

In November 1930 Hugh travelled to the Soviet Union, visiting Moscow and Leningrad. His open espousal of communism obviously ran him into trouble with the authorities of the fledgling Irish Free State and on 30 November 1931 Charles wrote: 'Dear Hugh, I was surprised to read of your letter's seizure by the Irish Government. Can't you talk to Mr Blythe[8] about it & ask him to get you off these unpleasantnesses. I don't think they need take all this bother over you for really, in spite of your wild Communism, I am afraid I cannot imagine you really having a revolution – leading the mob up O'Connell Street – or anything like that.'

Under Hugh's guidance, Charles became fascinated with communism and contemporary events in the still-young Soviet Union. It left him with a lifelong

---

7. Hugh's experiences as a down-and-out in London also feature in the revised edition of the novel.

8. Ernest Blythe had become Minister for Posts and Telegraphs in 1927 in addition to his portfolio as Minister for Finance.

concern for world affairs and the concept of open and equal government. At the same period, Hugh was writing to encourage Charles to consider 'Science in Socialist Reconstruction'. 'I am convinced that this is going to be the field of work in the future, and in every country in the world.' The whole capitalist world was experiencing the crisis of the 'Great Depression' in these years, and the correspondence between Hugh and Charles suggests a trusting and affectionate relationship.

When *The Soviets in World Affairs* appeared in early 1930, Charles asked Hugh for a loan.

> I have read so far this term Stepniak's *Underground Russia*⁹ which I found a very good book indeed, but I am sure you have already read such a classic as Stepniak. Next I have read 'Life under the Soviets' by Alexander Wickstead. It is a very good book published in 1928 about his life in the Union from 1923–1927. All the time he noted a definite improvement going on thro' everything and as that was before the 5–Year Plan started things in Russia ought to be getting quite luxurious! If you have not read it, you ought to. Next I read a book, lent to me, called 'Certain People of Importance' [1926] by A.G. Gardiner, a Liberal, a contributor to the Daily News. He is very good on Lords Beaverbrook & Rothermere, Jix¹⁰ and Winston Churchill. Amongst other things he calls Churchill 'a genius without judgment'. Lastly I have read Bertrand Russell's *Theory and Practice of Bolshevism* [sic].¹¹ With every respect to the eminent scientist, it seems to me that his arguments were not very strong. In fact even I seemed to be able to pick holes in them. Furthermore it was written in the lean years of 1920–1.

In 1931 he asked for a loan of another title, which might also find its way into the hands of some of his fellow readers: 'Those who might see the book would be those who know my sentiments already. There are three or four boys in the house (at the most six out of eighty-six) who are interested in politics if you know what I mean to the extent that I am. I often argue and discuss with them such things. But I don't try to disseminate Communist literature nor any other! Nor do I stand on a soap box in the quad & harangue the House or anything like that! Of course I get a certain amount of chaff, but then it is all in fun and I enjoy it. There is no objectionable or disagreeable stuff in it. Of

---

9. 'Stepniak' [Sergei Kravchinski], *Underground Russia: revolutionary profiles and sketches from life* (1883).

10. Nickname of William Joynson-Hicks (1865–1932), Home Secretary 1924–29.

11. Bertrand Russell's influential book was actually *The Practice and Theory of Bolshevism*.

course I dare say if I tried to force things down people's throats I would obviously get [it] in the neck and elsewhere. But I don't.'

After Hugh's return from Russia (in November 1930), he wrote (at Isabel's prompting) a lengthy letter to Charles that is worth quoting extensively, since – as an eye-witness account from an Irishman – it has in common with many other visitors to Russia at that time a fascination with the apparent productivity of the Soviet system. Hugh wrote:

> My impression of Russia is of intense activity. The streets were swarming with people, of every conceivable nationality. The population of Moscow has almost doubled in the last few years. There is no unemployment, but a labour shortage. But the streets are always full, at all hours of the day and night. These are the people off duty. They have a five day week – four working days of eight hours, and then a day off. But nothing ever stops. There are three shifts of everything, and even three performances of everything. Operas, cinemas, theatres, etc., and these performances each last about six hours! There are no days of the week, only dates. One gets caught up in a ceaseless flow of energy, for the climate is most bracing, and Russians appear quite tireless. Women are on exactly the same footing as men in USSR, and seem if anything the top dogs! I saw factories, schools, new flats, whole new blocks of workers' buildings, and went to the slummiest quarters of Moscow. We were shown everything, nothing was hidden. The Russians said 'you mustn't mind the outward shabbiness; we have gone through hell – from the outside world – and when we have proper housing for the people we shall have time for paint and powder'. You can see that they are a people engaged in a gigantic task of construction, full of determination. Whilst at work, strict discipline. When off duty, perfect social equality. There is no starvation; if there is a shortage, it is never allowed to affect the children.

As Hugh was so much respected and befriended by Charles, it is easy to understand how his enthusiasm for the Soviet system projected itself onto Charles's own political views, especially when supplemented by one of his teachers, who reported on his own visit: 'He said that the 5 Year plan is the plan of youth. He does think that the Bolshevik experiment is a great thing and a success & it might well be applied here without the Communist things. He thinks besides that all this scope given to youth has a fine reaction on the arts. The modern Russian music seems to him far more tuneful than ours.'

Charles wrote regularly to Hugh on Soviet affairs and assiduously kept cuttings from *The Observer* and the *Daily Herald* on subjects such as food shortages, labour conditions, and the collective farm system in Russia. Asking Hugh whether he could receive radio output from Moscow, he commented, with obvious reserve about such affairs: 'Probably you have been too busy listen[ing] to the new Jerusalem in Russia's white & chilly land to listen to the talk [on the BBC] by Maurice Dodds on "Looking at Russia"', and asking Hugh fairly searching questions, for a sixteen-year-old, about the show trials, the number of political prisoners, and alleged 'slavery in [the] Russian timber trade.'[12] His reading included D.S. Mirsky's biography of Lenin and Stephen Graham's study of Stalin (both 1931). On a lighter note, he was also reading Maurice Walsh's *The Small Dark Man,* Shaw's *Back to Methuselah* and, as an 'antidote', Axel Munthe's *The Story of San Michele.* His very wide reading continued from that time right up to his final illness, and late in life he recalled that at Rugby, at Hugh's suggestion, he had read Shaw's *The Intelligent Woman's Guide to Socialism* because of its appeal to the idealism of young people.

> I think that that book had a far greater influence on what has now become ordinary thinking than is realised. The strength of Shaw's idealism resonated with the idealism of my own youth to produce a lifelong optimism. And I do not believe that anyone can be a competent critic who does not believe that, somehow, we all want things to be better for our neighbours as for ourselves and can help, in however small a way, to make them.

While he came to reject 'the sheer intolerance' of communism, Charles's view of Hugh as a close adult friend, rather than a father-figure, marks Hugh's own idealism as a factor within his personal growth. There was a tragic, but perhaps characteristic, end to the marriage of Isabel and Hugh: at the beginning of 1933 when Budina started to operate it as an hotel, Hugh left Kilmacurragh and appears to have started work in London as a translator, remaining there until the end of July, when he visited Isabel at Bournemouth. Then he returned to Kilmacurragh. He died suddenly in August 1933, having experienced some form of seizure, and was taken to a nursing home in Dublin, where it proved impossible to save his life.[13] It appears that such a seizure might have occurred at any time, although Isabel had been unaware of it. Charles (in what appears to be his only surviving mention of the subject) wrote to her 'My poor poor Mum what an awful shock it must have been.' Isabel had now lost two

---

12. Hugh had told Charles that in India, out of a population of 330 million, there were 45,000 political prisoners, while Charles had heard that in Russia there were 660,000 political prisoners out of a population of 168 million.

13. A death notice appeared in *The Irish Times* of 19 and 26 August 1933, with no details of place or time of funeral or burial.

husbands, and Charles both a father and a mentor. At this stage, with Kilmacurragh operating as an hotel under Charles Budina, and Charles trying to decide on his future career, mother and son were largely without guidance; but in Charles's case both Marcus Beresford and the headmaster, Hugh Lyon, were available for advice and support.

Beliefs

Charles reported regularly to his mother on the house debating society, taking a keen interest in the contemporary politics reflected in its proceedings. In February 1929 he told her: 'The motion was that "Empire Free Trade is contrary to the best interests of the Empire": so that those who voted *for* the motion voted *against* Empire Crusade & Lord Beaverbrook. I voted *for* the motion – against our Daily Express.' He seems to have spoken only once, on the motion 'That the breaking of records in speed and distance with risk of danger to life should be declared illegal'; the motion was lost 16–12.

And towards the end of 1929: 'Last night we had a debate on "Short of a change in human nature war is inevitable". It was a very popular motion, for there were more than a hundred people present. It was one of the very few occasions on which a motion has been won. It was won by a hundred and something votes to fifty-seven. I was one of the fifty-seven.' Another occasion when he found himself in the minority was that 'the possession of India is more trouble than it is worth' which was lost 19–17: 'it seemed to me that the motion was deserving of my support'.

One debate, that 'It is better to be a discontented philosopher than a contented pig' was lost 36–8. Charles considered that this proved the saying 'The school does not think because the school is conservative in politics'. He was delighted to be called 'a discontented philosopher' by one of his fellows. But on the matter of thought, he must have been dismayed when the outgoing headmaster, W.W. Vaughan, spoke after chapel 'on the subject of thought and thoughtlessness "Ireland became troublesome when it began to think: India in these the last 10 or 20 years has become troublesome because it has begun to think: & Russia is the most troublesome country in Europe because it thinks".'

As he came towards the end of his time at Rugby, Charles's philosophical leanings became clearer.

Man seems doomed to exist in a long useless fight against cold like a species of animal fleeing from the hunters guns into the backwards recesses of the mountains, all the time doomed to final extinction. Then to think of the isolated settlements in the Himalayas, never having seen other men, living their own happy lives fighting with nature probably just as truly happy as European man with his culture, his arts without which now he could scarcely live. And would they not be just as truly happy asleep[?] NOT that I would be as happy asleep as doing something. And yet with all the purposeless unwise God must have a purpose for it so we come back that where knowledge ends faith begins and we must carry on believing in God's ultimate purpose & strive all out for him. This all sounds very morbid but it does not worry me.

Over fifteen years later, in 1950, Charles put these beliefs and convictions in a letter to Carol, just six months before they were married, and during a long separation when he was mostly in Dublin and she in the family home in Clabby, County Fermanagh:

God as such has seemed unreal since I was about 10 or so – for most of the usual reasons: the creation of evil, the contradictions, the unnecessity of any creation & so forth. A stream of ideas that has since about 15 so strongly appealed to me includes: the unity of all forms of energy; the unity of all forms of matter; the unity & interconvertibility of matter & energy; the unity & indivisibility of all living things: there is no dividing line between or means of determining what is life & what not life – in other words all things of which we have cognisance are one, are built of the same primeval stuff. And now we ourselves have found our own oneness. I have always thought of this unification from a purely materialistic point of view. Though as a child I often tried to make myself believe I believed, or that I was having religious experience, I never did. In music & other arts and in beauty I have had many experiences of the spirit, but never felt any of that religious, nor felt the need of anything religious; and I have had no reason to regard such manifestations as not a part of all material unity. The beauty of the English liturgy, of an English cathedral, evensong at King's, the first chapter of John, & so forth I was overwhelmed by; and I could feel mystery & wonder; but never anything specifically religious, anything that could convince my emotions let alone my mind & that there was God or any God.

Music

Marcus Beresford was a young music teacher at Rugby (barely five years older than Charles himself) and a distant member of the family of the Marquess of Waterford. He became one of Charles's closest friends in these years, and someone on whom Charles looked with the deepest respect; Carol would later say that one could not emphasize too strongly Beresford's influence on Charles, and Charles himself attributed to Beresford the fact that he became a music critic.[14]

Perhaps Beresford's influence was most important because Charles's academic progress was not encouraging, and music became a valuable discipline, even though Isabel would not necessarily agree. Charles's report at the end of the summer term of 1929 shows that he was regarded as slipping from previous standards. His form master wrote that 'He does not admit that he has been trying to live on his reputation, but I fancy he has been taking things a little too much for granted.' In music, he was judged 'A hard worker. When practising he must think more of his hands & less of the music he is playing. His difficulty is an inability to relax the right muscles for a sufficiently long period.' Music was to be the most important outlet for his energies apart from his academic studies. He had taken piano lessons from an early age, and by April 1930 he had decided to take up the clarinet. 'Today [18 May 1930] I had my first clarinet lesson. I got on very well. I shall never I imagine be able to be a "famous" clarinettist since Mr Pierce said I have too short an upper lip.' A month later he was being threatened with having to play the slow movement of the 'Mozart 10th clarinet sonata' for the House Music Competition; this was an obvious joke on Charles's part, since Mozart wrote no such work, but in June he was definitely learning the sonata for flute and piano by Purcell (presumably in a transcription for clarinet), and was making efforts at composition: 'I tried to compose an accompaniment for "Let Erin Remember" and "The Minstrel Boy". I did it almost entirely in common chords. I disregarded the rule in 4 part harmony that one may not use consecutive octaves since it seems not to apply to piano accompaniments. They sound all right and Hugh will be able to sight read them.' On a visit to Oxford he met Balfour Gardiner, 'the composer of largoes and also one or two comic operettas' – who had transcribed many of Delius' manuscripts. 'An awfully nice man, elderly & plump but very cheerful.'[15]

---

14. Marcus Beresford taught at Rugby 1931–1969.

15. Henry Balfour Gardiner (1877–1950) had studied at Frankfurt where he was influenced by the musical styles of Wagner and Tchaikovsky. His career as a concert

After some success with the clarinet, he moved on to the bassoon, despite his mother's reservations. He persisted, and soon found himself in the school orchestra, playing in works such as the Brahms Requiem or Bach's St Matthew Passion. In one concert they played gypsy songs by Brahms, the Children's Overture by Roger Quilter, and a polonaise by Sergei Liapounov[16] – 'this is a very fine piece to hear but fiendishly difficult to play. However it is loud and an "all-in" piece – i.e. the second bassoon is not of great importance so that when I get tied up I can sit & *look* as if I am blowing & noone will be any the wiser! A comforting thought.' At the annual CBSO concert for the school in November 1931 'I had a long talk with the 1st bassoonist. He is a very nice man. He showed me several tweak fingerings.' Charles's last appearance as a performer at Rugby was at the Speech Day concert in his final term in 1933, when he played in the virtuoso Poulenc trio for oboe, bassoon and piano.

By the end of 1932, when his mother was worrying lest his interest in music was interfering with his preparations for the university exams, he wrote passionately and indignantly: 'I have NOT let music at all outcrowd my work, I am sure. What I gave up for music was everything else save work. I have given up nearly all interest in politics here, I gave up astronomy, I gave up all light recreation such as reading books & so forth to work & music & only do music when I have done my work. You wanted me to learn singing, but I would not because I have not time.'

A career

While Hugh had been alive, working on the establishment of Irish Resources, Isabel had told him that Charles was 'deeply interested' in the work at Kilma-curragh, and asked him 'What prospect do you see of Charlie going on with it – I mean, in another few years will there be room in your schemes for Charlie, can he come on in your footsteps as a man's son often does?' Hugh replied that

---

pianist was cut short by muscular paralysis and he devoted himself to composition and to championing the work of English composers such as Bax, Holst and Vaughan Williams. He gave financial support to Holst and particularly Delius. By 1925 he had ceased composing and in 1927 had moved to Dorset. Contrary to what Charles had been told, Gardiner wrote no comic operettas and most of his music has been lost.

16. Sergei Liapounov (1859–1924) had attended the last class of Tchaikovsky at the Moscow Conservatoire as well as classes with Taneyev. He was one of the circle of Balakirev and Liadov, and emigrated to Paris in 1923.

'His scientific mind ought to fit in well in any business where figures come in. If he wants to make money, he had far better, on leaving Rugby, get apprenticed to some big business ... I quite agree that sending him to Oxford or Cambridge would be a loss of money and time, unless he wants an academic career.'

By the summer holidays of 1930, Isabel could tell Hugh 'Charlie thinks he had better just go into business, try to get into some good firm where he can learn office routine & work up & become au fait with business methods, & in time learn company law & so forth. I think it sounds a good idea – he does not seem at all to regret giving up science, it is quite probable that was only youthful interest & while it will always remain an interest & resource to him he seems to think he would like to take up a commercial career & is getting on quite well with his German.'

At last Charles's mind was concentrated, for over two years, on the subject of his career after school – on the practicalities of university courses and where they might subsequently lead him. On 9 March 1931 he wrote to his mother: 'I have been thinking furiously and it seems to me that what with the Irish Resources Ltd and all and the fact that if I go definitely for science it would be best for me to go straight into some business. Perhaps Hugh might know or see some good place in Ireland as isn't England rather crowded with young men looking for jobs[?]' At which point, Isabel asked Hugh point blank 'is Irish Resources a fait accompli or is it just a beautiful dream & nothing to build upon? He [Charles] has a pathetic faith in you.' Perhaps it was as well that Hugh's death closed that particular avenue of possibility.

In early December 1931 (eighteen months before he actually left Rugby), Charles was in Cambridge for the entrance exams to Trinity College and met his putative tutor, Mr Dykes, a lecturer in engineering. His headmaster, however, told Isabel that in his opinion Charles 'does not seem to me at all the type of boy to go into business, especially as he has such intellectual interests.' During 1931 and 1932 there was considerable confusion as to whether Charles would be able to enter Trinity College Cambridge, due not least to the financial consequences. In September 1931 he told his mother: 'It looks certainly as if I won't go to Cambridge. It is really true that no matter how hard I try & work, I could not get a scholarship there.'

A year's further preparation seemed to be necessary. Much of this year's delay seems to have been encouraged by Marcus Beresford, who had stayed for two weeks at Kilmacurragh during the summer holidays in 1931 and had taken Charles to the Three Choirs Festival at Worcester that year, when he heard the Bach B minor Mass, Elgar's 'Dream of Gerontius', Mendelssohn's 'Elijah' and Holst's 'Hymn of Jesus', with artists including Keith Faulkner, Harold Williams, Isobel Baillie and Astra Desmond.[17]

Charles's determination to accept Marcus Beresford's invitation to the Three Choirs Festival, and to take up driving lessons under Beresford's tuition, as well as his unilateral decision about postponing his entry to Cambridge, may all be attributed in some part to Beresford's friendly influence. Heretofore, Charles had referred everything to his mother (or, where appropriate, to Hugh) for approval: now he was set on making his own decisions and finding his own way. Perhaps recognizing this, Isabel wrote to Hugh 'Rugby has done a tremendous lot for my nervy boy – made him quite different. To be at a first class public school gives a sensitive boy a feeling of selfconfidence & assurance which is very valuable to him.'

Shortly before he left Rugby for Cambridge, he wrote his second extended consideration of a music recital, when he heard violinist Isolde Menges play, among other works, a Bach unaccompanied chaconne:[18]

> It struck me that it must say a tremendous lot for composer & performer – both, that the school audience sat absolutely motionless, tense, completely absorbed, so that you could have literally perhaps heard a pin drop; sitting on Speech Room chairs listening to this which was entirely without accompaniment and lasts for more than ¼ hour! It is, I am told, about the most difficult violin work written. Yet she put it across marvellously, making it a work of tremendous splendour & not a bit of tricksy fireworks. At least so it all seemed to me – in fact her whole recital filled me with a sort of ecstasy!

---

17. 'It does seem unnatural now to call Marcus Mr Beresford, though fortunately he dislikes anybody calling him Sir!' Charles hero-worshipped Beresford ('I bathed in the light of Marcus'), and later recorded that the holiday at Kilmacurragh was 'the happiest I have ever known'. Keith Faulkner was later the British Council representative in Rome and Director of the Royal College of Music; Harold Williams (1893–1976) was an Australian baritone specializing in performances of *Elijah*, *The Dream of Gerontius* and Elgar's *The Kingdom*; Isobel Baillie (1895–1983) was a Scottish soprano, with a reputation for the interpretation of *Elijah*; Astra Desmond (1893–1973), contralto, was closely associated with Elgar and the Three Choirs Festival, particularly in *The Dream of Gerontius*.

18. Isolde Marie Menges (1893–1976), English violinist, studied with Auer, made her London concerto début in 1913; played under Mengelberg and Landon Ronald (with whom she made the first complete recording of the Beethoven concerto in 1922). Founded the Menges Quartet in 1931 and taught at the Royal College of Music.

Sitting on hard chairs, making honest judgments that would entertain and enlighten his readers, and expressing his deep-seated and deeply held convictions – these would be the experiences and responsibilities which Charles would bring to his later work at *The Irish Times*. His last report from Rugby recorded the fact that he was 'honest and amicable' – perhaps that best sums up his character and points him towards the next phase of his unorthodox career.

Cambridge (i) 1933-35

Charles 'went up' to Trinity College, Cambridge, in the first week of October 1933, to read Chemistry, Physics and Mineralogy. For his first two years, the college provided rooms at 26 Sydney Street, and he lived in college for his third year. As soon as he arrived, he immersed himself in the cultural and social life of the university, joining the Amateur Dramatic Club (ADC), which was to be his principal focus for the next three years, and both playing in and attending concerts. Cambridge was the occasion for his first foray as a music critic, the forum for the development of the political ideas he had already formed at Rugby, and the opportunity for the development of his friendship with Brian Boydell, the Irish composer and teacher whose relationship with Charles was one of the determining factors in his formative years.

Charles's immediate adhesion to, and immersion in, the world of amateur drama was no accident. Theatre offered Charles the possibility of finding himself by creating an 'other' self; it was a world of enchantment, and Charles entered it in a philosophical and intellectual spirit. It was the foil to his scientific explorations, allowing him to keep the practical and the imaginative moods in one framework.

The tentative, schoolboyish contact with stage management in which Charles engaged at Rugby now became a major passion. There is no evidence that he was ever seriously interested in being an actor, but his work at the ADC as a facilitator found him at a meeting-point between the amateur and professional worlds of drama, where, as with future generations, careers were launched and connections made with the international acting community. In the musical dimension, he did continue to play at an amateur level, as he would on his return to Dublin in the 1940s, and this activity also gave him an insight into the theory and practice of music-making and music management.

The deep affection which Charles exhibited for, and to, Isabel (whom he more than once described as a 'contemporary') thrived on physical distance.

He was, as always, deeply conscious of Isabel's good nature and the stresses that that induced in her: 'It seems to me that your life apart from being worried by disasters and worries unavoidable by you, has been made up of helping other people, putting your strength, in all senses, into actions of love, and getting not only nothing out of it at all, but losing all along.' Her widowhood, her love for her child, her care for her family, her financial anxieties, her up-and-down marriage to Hugh, and the constant question-marks over Kilmacurragh, were all factors in Charles's understanding of his mother's character and condition, yet 'I know that you will live to an enormous age'.

While Charles's letters are replete with details of his social life, he also continued to provide didactic proof of his studies, limited though they were by his other passions. Whether or not he intended to persuade his mother that a leisurely and social life was the norm, he did inform her shortly after settling in at Sydney Street that 'anyone can do as much work or as little as he likes: those who come here to do sport entirely, or propose to be good at it, are the people who do no work, as a whole ... No-one makes you work, except in the subjects where it is essential, such as science and some languages and maths.'

While on a visit to Oxford he met Joseph Cooper, a friend of Marcus Beresford, who at that time was organ scholar of Keble College and president of the university's music club. This 'very brilliant pianist' as Charles described him was also a composer of jazz songs which he published under the pseudonym of Joseph Elliot.[19] Typical of Charles's diffident attitude to his exams, the trip to Oxford immediately preceded his end-of-year exams; returning to Cambridge he spent the night before 'in last minute revision of essential formulae.'

Charles's inquiring mind led him into the world of the visual arts, which he had not previously appreciated, being more interested in design than in representation. His lack of visual art appreciation evaporated as he came into contact with practising artists such as Anthony Reford (who would make an impact on his life in Dublin during the war years). He read R.H. Wilenski's *The Meaning of Modern Sculpture* which had appeared the previous year (1932) and found that 'the more I see of this modern furniture & decoration the more *I love it*'. He found 'a tremendous peaceful beauty' in Jacob Epstein's work, and thought that modern architecture 'is far the most awe-fully beautiful since the Gothic & especially the Norman'. He thought the college chapel 'like the

---

19. Joseph Cooper 1913–2001, had been a pupil of Egon Petri. He became a household name in Britain due to his appearance as the host of a BBC quiz show *Face the Music* 1966–84.

attempt of man to put ornamental beauty on to forms that otherwise would have little. The result makes me think of the craftsman rather than the work. It seems the difference between the ornamental tone of an operatic soprano & the pure unadorned gorgeous beauty of a boy's voice.'

The local cinema introduced him to a wide selection of continental films, including *A Nous la Liberté*, *Morgenrot*, *Mädchen in Uniform*, *Le quatorze juillet*, *Der Traumende Mund*, and Eisenstein's *Thunder over Mexico*. Later, in 1936, he would see Liam O'Flaherty's *The Informer*: 'it does not introduce [Irish] Nationalism as a propaganda, fortunately, but the atmosphere & the types of the leaders are so good. It ought to be a good film to take Irene to if one were feeling mischievous.' He would no doubt recall this jibe when, living in London in 1936, he invited Irene to see Eliot's *Murder in the Cathedral*: 'I thought it ought to suit her, being religious.'

But it would be in Munich that Charles's eyes would really be opened to the meanings of modern art. There he would see originals of Cézanne, Gauguin and van Gogh (the 'Sunflowers', the 'View of Arles' and a self-portrait) – 'brilliant things that just take one's breath away' – which excited him in contrast to the German art of the nineteenth and twentieth centuries which he thought 'heavy, dull, uninspired and uninspiring, and in fact bad'. When he visited the International Exhibition in London in 1936 there was again an air of excitement in the presence of modern art: 'It was the first time I had ever seen any of the originals of modern art, having only seen photographic reproductions.' He was particularly impressed by the work of Paul Nash, whose pictures he would continue to mention in his letters in later years.[20] He realized that at that time his contemporaries were remaking the aesthetic world in music, drama and in the visual arts: 'It is unfortunately as yet a thing of the intelligentsia, but in music there is this enormous creative outburst, a freshness of outlook and advance and sufficient appreciation to make it go. In theatre there is now a lot of movement to produce a living drama, and here there is a great deal of appreciation from the people.'

At Cambridge, Anthony Reford and Charles had known Nigel Heseltine,[21]

---

20. Paul Nash (1889–1946) was a contemporary of Ben Nicolson, Stanley Spencer, Mark Gertler and Dora Carrington at the Slade School; he became a war artist in 1917 and subsequently became an influential pioneer of modernism; he was a co-founder, with Herbert Read, of the Unit One design studio.

21. Nigel Heseltine (1916–1995) was the son of Philip Heseltine/Peter Warlock, composer of 'The Curlew', a setting of W.B. Yeats which had had such an effect

although it seems that Charles had disliked him. Reford intuited that Heseltine shared Charles's impulsion to '(1) desire for complete independence, (2) to do something that will be for the good of some part of humanity, (3) to achieve some small measure of fame, the desire for self-respect, (4) to go places & see things'. In Charles's case, these, Reford believed, amounted to

> the fundamental desire to attain unity & the peace which comes of unity. The ordinary fellow attains a certain unity & calm through marriage, a recognised place in society, etc. But the person with more spiritual & emotional awareness, although by virtue of it enjoying potentiality for greater peace, stands more chance of getting bloody muddled up with his values. The desire for complete independence & to go places & see things is the desire to complete oneself; to experience all the things worth experiencing to the full capacity of one's senses.

Perhaps no other single statement better sums up two aspects of Charles's character: his natural curiosity, which made him such a passionate traveller; and the indecision which held him back from the potential turning-points in his life.

Given that Cambridge, earlier in the 1930s, had been a recruiting ground for disaffected young Englishmen with a social conscience and an inclination towards communism, it can be legitimately questioned whether there was any likelihood that Charles, had he been approached, might have become a candidate spy for the Soviets. The lasting influence of his stepfather, combined with the empty childhood that was such a factor in the lives of characters such as Guy Burgess and Donald Maclean, might have inclined Charles towards the view that world-government by a post-imperial Russia could provide the end to such conflicts as had wiped out his father's generation and a solution to the international economic chaos.

A further question was whether Charles's almost complete exclusion from the society of woman contemporaries might have persuaded him that homosexuality was preferable to the problem of finding 'the right girl' for the heir to Kilmacurragh. Certainly, his close friendship at Cambridge with Brian Boydell, who at that stage was displaying bisexual characteristics,[22] and Charles's own

---

on Charles and Brian Boydell. Nigel Heseltine also spent some of the war years in Dublin, where, as 'Michael Walsh', he worked with actor-director Shelah Richards and contributed at least four articles to *The Bell*; there is no evidence that Charles renewed his acquaintance with Heseltine during that time. In 1948 he married Jean Stoney, previously the wife of Louis le Brocquy.

22. Information from Carol Acton.

disdain for anything but serious talk with women, suggest that, intellectually, sexually and socially, he might have turned away from the privilege of his ancestral acres and his scientific enthusiasms and towards the dissemination of information in the cause of world peace. Nervous and vulnerable all his life, Charles was susceptible to a 'cause' that could offer him a place to put his trust.

Yet in his failure to obtain a degree or any other professional qualification, Charles would in fact have been less than useful to the spymasters who recruited in Cambridge. He could not have occupied any position of either influence or insight which could have made him a convincing informational conduit. In a sense, his enthusiasms, which largely defeated his professional prospects up to 1955, also declared him a non-joiner of anything more dramatic than the ADC.

Within a month of arriving at the ADC, Charles was 'doing the lighting' for Beverley Nichols's *Avalanche* which was being staged by a visiting professional company, and preparing for the ADC's own production of *Treasure Island* for which he was not only building the sets but acting as prompter – 'it was offered to Bolton & me, we tossed, I lost, I am prompter'. He was very conscious of the different styles between Oxford's dramatic society (OUDS) – 'the long haired arty aesthetic type' – and Cambridge's ADC which 'is just full of people who are marvellous fun and like the rest of the University delightfully childish'. Other productions on which he worked included *Anthony and Cleopatra* and *Androcles and the Lion* – 'all kinds of most extraordinary props' – in which Charles 'was a female Christian, as a super'.

It was a major disappointment that he narrowly missed Terence Gray's work at the Cambridge Festival Theatre, and knew it only by reputation.[23] In 1934 Gray's successor, Gordon MacLeod, presented Shaw's *Arms and the Man*, *Othello*, Edgar Wallace's *Frightened Lady*, *Uncle Vanya*, Ben Jonson's *Silent Woman*, Farquhar's *Beaux' Stratagem*, Strindberg's *The Father* and *John Gabriel Borkman*, Eugene O'Neill's *Anna Christie*, Webster's *The Duchess of Malfi* and a Russian play, *Cyril Comes Over*. *Othello* 'was rottenly done', but Coward's *Hay Fever* 'was an absolute scream'. *Anna Christie* was 'very sad and tragic although it does have a more or less happy ending, like most Eugene O'Neill it is very sordid, but I

---

23. Terence Gray (1895–1986) was an Irishman and a cousin of Edris Stannus [Ninette de Valois] who worked with him at the Festival Theatre in Cambridge, encouraging his understanding of ballet, on which he wrote a book that accompanied Charles on his trip to Germany. He renovated the Cambridge theatre, which he named 'Festival' and opened it in 1926, but his participation ended in 1932, after which it ran for two more seasons under his influence, and was then taken over by a commercial management and closed in 1939.

found it in spite of its first appearance of sheer sordidness, a very good play.'

Probably the most significant drama that Charles experienced at Cambridge was Denis Johnston's *The Moon in theYellow River*,[24] which he saw at the Festival Theatre in 1934 and again in 1935 – 'very odd play; very funny play; but also is a serious play'. Charles's interest in Irish drama would have received a fillip from the fact that the play had the setting of the Ardnacrusha hydroelectric scheme on the Shannon. And late in 1935 Charles would actually be stage manager for Johnston's next play, *Storm Song*. *Yahoo*, Lord Longford's complicated portrayal of Swift,[25] came on in mid-1935. 'It might have been an extremely good play, but somehow all the time except the very end it just failed to grip one. Pity. Still very interesting, since it did teach me something of Swift's life, of which I knew nothing and had a little bearing on Irish history.' In this way, Charles became familiar with both the experimental drama being staged in Dublin and the current state of new Irish writing.

Charles also joined the university music society (CUMS), from which he borrowed a bassoon which gave him a lot of fingering problems ('AWFUL but I hope to persevere') and played in the college orchestra as well as the CUMS orchestra who, with the choral society (which he also joined), were to perform Handel's *Jeptha* and Bach's B-minor Mass. The conductor, Cyril Rootham, 'digs up for the judgement of the modern world some such oratorio each year that had been forgotten'.[26] Steuart Wilson (whom Charles would meet personally two years later) sang the title role,[27] with two additional professional solo-ists, Margaret Field-Hyde and Irene Flanders.[28] Charles did not appreciate the work: 'the various arts used do not combine'. The chorus members 'are not

---

24. First produced at the Abbey Theatre, Dublin, in 1931.

25. First produced at the Gate Theatre, Dublin, in 1933.

26. Cyril Rootham (1875–1938) had been a student of Stanford at the RCM; he was organist of St John's College, Cambridge 1901–38, and conductor of the CUMS. Among his students were Sir Arthur Bliss and C.A. Gibbs. His 'Septet' was performed in 1930.

27. Sir Steuart Wilson (1889–1966) had been a student of Rootham and later of Jean de Reszke; the dedicatee of Vaughan Williams's *Four Hymns*, he became one of Brit-ain's leading tenors, after retirement teaching at the Curtis Institute (Philadelphia) and becoming music director of the BBC Overseas Service 1942–45 and of the Arts Council 1945–48. Director of Music at the BBC 1948 and deputy administrator of the Royal Opera House, Covent Garden, 1949–55.

28. Margaret Field-Hyde (1905–1995) created the part of Angelica in Vaughan Williams's *The Poisoned Kiss* (which Charles reviewed at Cambridge); Irene Flanders also sang in another Handel revival, the oratorio 'The Choice of Hercules'.

people who are interested in theatres or stageing or acting.' He thought that musically Oxford would have made a better job of *Jeptha* – 'Oxford is more artistic than Cambridge. Cambridge is on the whole more practical or material. On the whole Cambridge does more work than Oxford.' But whatever his personal feelings, Charles was conscious that it would have been inappropriate for a professional reviewer to criticize an experiment (at that time, only Handel's *Samson* had been given such a treatment). 'The critic knows that it is not good to criticize in an experiment of this sort, things which are due to the ignorance of amateurs' – it was one of the rules of his own professional conduct as a critic, embodied in his lecture 'A Critic's Creed'.

He would remain grateful that he had been introduced to the bassoon at Rugby, and in his college orchestra there was another Rugbeian bassoonist, R.B. Fury. 'Now it is that I realize more the benefit of a rare instrument. There is a surfeit of clarinets & flutes.' With the choral society he was practising Bax's 'This Worlde's Joie' – '15th century words set modernly'. In his second term he played in Vaughan Williams's 'Sea Symphony'. He felt that the bassoon was an important progression from the clarinet and told his mother 'it is merely a question of plenty and plenty of practice'.

Among the concerts he heard was a CUMS event with Prince Chavchavadze[29] playing Beethoven's fourth piano concerto. Due to a lecture commitment, he had to miss Rafael Kubelik's concert, the second time this misfortune occurred, as Kubelik had also visited Rugby when Charles had been in the sanatorium. A visit by members of the legendary Dolmetsch family was disappointing: 'the whole four of them turned up and played all manner of instruments, but I was so surprised how badly: it was extremely interesting hearing these kinds of music on their different instruments, but it would have given much more musical and emotional pleasure if they had played more accurately and more in tune. This surprised me very greatly, since I had known of them as so great and famous.' Charles, as stage-manager for the concert, also found them difficult to deal with. 'They told me they wanted to tune up on stage for four minutes or so before the curtain went up, so they came on stage at the time the curtain should have gone up, then spent 12½ minutes tuning.' It would be many years before he would experience the thrill of early music at the first Dublin concert by Musica Reservata, conducted by John Beckett, and which was followed by the creation in Dublin of the Consort of St Sepulchre,

29. George Chavchavadze (1905–1962), born in St. Petersburg to the Troubetzkoy family, made his London début in 1927.

a leading light of which was his godson, Barra Boydell. On a visit to London he heard Delius' 'Mass of Life' conducted at Queen's Hall by Sir Thomas Beecham. 'He does the whole thing from memory, with no conductor's desk in front of him. My impressions and feelings are beyond words.'

The attention to gramophone records was an extremely important part of his musical education at this time, with an introduction to a work that would become very significant to him and Brian Boydell: Peter Warlock's 'The Curlew', a setting of four of Yeats's poems. He was told by someone who brought it to his attention that Warlock 'committed suicide [in 1930] because he thought he had outwritten himself, and was a failure and musically unwanted'. And he also heard that it had been difficult for Warlock to persuade Yeats to allow him to set the poem, because Yeats 'had heard 10,000 boy scouts singing 'The Lake Isle of Inisfree' – one can well sympathise with Y.'

At Cambridge he met his cousin Tony Acton and began entertaining, and being entertained, on a regular basis ('I have met all Rugby!'). Isabel's cakes were a useful ingredient in his tea parties, and a decision had to be made about alcohol. He called the practice of offering expensive sherry 'the drink bribe', and decided 'in order not to have to give everyone 6/6d sherry I keep two bottles, one of 4/6d for acquaintances & one of 6/6d (Harveys) for my friends. The former is quite good enough for the former – it is very nearly the same, save that it stings one's throat a little.'

Charles was acutely conscious that his family's traditional schooling had equipped him better than most: 'the outstanding merits of Rugby appear almost describable when one looks at all the Etonians & other unpleasant people'.

Apart from the lectures relevant to his curriculum, Charles heard many others that he considered relevant to his personal development. One was by Sir Frederick Gowland Hopkins, 'the discoverer of what he firmly called "vitamins", [which he pronounced veit-a-mins] who said "I invented the word, I know how to pronounce it"[30] – a point which Charles, with his insistence on accuracy, would frequently repeat.

Another notable lecturer was Alfred Adler: 'he said that people use "inferiority complex" to depict the sense of inferiority, whereas "I invented the expression and I know what it means".'[31] This made a considerable impact on

---

30. 1861–1947, Professor of Biochemistry at Cambridge from 1914, having published papers on the existence of vitamins since 1912. Joint winner of the Nobel Prize, 1929.

31. 1870–1937, an associate of Freud, published his controversial study of organ inferiority and its psychical compensation in 1907.

Charles, who was frequently able to identify those affected by the condition.

On the scientific front, he also heard Alfred (Lord) Rutherford on 'Heavy Hydrogen and its Effects on Transmutation of Elements'. In 1936 he heard Sir William Bragg speak on the amenability of viruses to X-ray crystallography, which led him to speculate on the 'indeterminate boundary between living and non-living' and, even further, on Marx's 'Dialectical Materialism'. However far Charles's mind and imagination may have strayed from the confines of his academic curriculum, he was never in doubt as to the possible convergence of science and the arts, or of science and philosophy, and told his mother that Bragg's lecture partly coincided with his own fumblings towards the concept of the electron microscope.

In addition to scientific topics, Charles also heard a lecture by sculptor Henry Moore, and one on the Soviet cinema:

> it seemed to me that they go a little *too* far in the materialistic conception of history, in saying that *all* art is a manifestation of the economic conditions of contemporary life, and that such a thing as absolute, abstract art, "Art for Art's Sake" has never and does not exist'. And T.R. Henn 'from Sligo' lectured on 'Yeats and the National Revolution': 'a most vividly informed man who knew Carson & Countess Markiewicz & Lady Gregory and was all through the troubles.[32]

Germany, 1935

In the summer of 1934 Charles had contemplated a holiday in Austria. He was very conscious of the contemporary political situation: 'of course we would be the souls of discretion in the matter of politics, not allowing them to stray onto our tongues. I gather that if you do not allow yourself to mention politics on any account, and never *never* mention Dollfuss's name, then all is all right.'[33]

Charles was 'unclassed' in his 1935 end-of-year exams at Cambridge, meaning that although he had not exactly failed the year, he had merely been treading water. At this level of engagement, Charles would be heading for a 'pass' rather than an honours degree. His chief stumbling block was poor memory for accu-

---

32. T.R. Henn (1901–74) was President of his *alma mater*, St Catherine's College, Cambridge, 1951–61. Directed the Yeats International Summer School at Sligo 1959–69.

33. Engelbert Dollfuss (1892–1934), Chancellor of Austria 1932, was assassinated during an attempted Nazi putsch in Vienna.

mulated facts in general, and mineralogy in particular. His tutor, Kitson Clark, told him that 'with determination the entire position will be recovered'.[34]

Realizing that a career in science required a working knowledge of German (which he regarded as 'the language of science'), Charles had already decided to spend the summer vacation of 1935 in Munich. After his time there, he reported to his aunt Eva that 'though to say I spoke German like a native or anything like that would be a gross exaggeration ... There are too many words in the language that mean too many things all at one and the same time.' And fifty years later, in a Radio Éireann interview with myself he put it more bluntly: 'I didn't learn very much German, but I had a whale of a time. Met too many Anglophones. Spent too much time playing pontoon in English instead of learning German.' The dialects were another major problem: 'instead of speaking correct German, the south German aristocracy speak dialect, and are gloriously careless of grammar. In the shops they either speak Bayerisch [Bavarian] which is fairly unintelligible or else English which I don't want.'

Having spent a week with his mother at Grata Quies, and seen the Vic-Wells ballet in Vaughan Williams' *Job* ('it was one of the most wonderful things I had ever seen'), he travelled via London, where he saw the *Ballets russes de Monte Carlo* at Covent Garden in *Les Sylphides*, *La Boutique fantasque*, and *Les Présages* (Massine's 1933 ballet with music from Tchaikovsky's fifth symphony, which Charles described as depicting 'man's struggle with his destiny').

He arrived in Munich at the end of June, and stayed in a boarding house in Arcisstrasse run by a woman he later described as 'a formidable Bavarian' who 'ought to be Irish', named Bertha von Gietl – her uncle had designed the recently-built Deutsches Museum in the city. The intention was to learn both scientific German, by reading learned journals, and conversational German from his companions in the boarding house, including Fraülein von Gietl herself, who had little English.

He found Munich a charming venue, 'the entertainment town of Germany'. He admired the spacious layout of the city 'with an enormous number of public buildings, palaces, gardens, fountains and trees in a vast royal manner. It is a wonderfully pleasant town ... Altogether this is a wonderful country, the people, the climate, the public services & everything. So much better than England in so many ways.'

But it was a country climbing back to self-respect and economic viability after the humiliation of defeat in the First World War. Writing from Palestine in

---

34. The historian G.S.R. Kitson Clark (1900–75) had become college tutor in 1933.

1937, Charles gave his own honest opinion of the economic versus the political situation, as he had seen it two years previously:

> There was not much interest taken in the condition of Germany before Hitler: unemployment figures, even when the number of unemployed workers without their families are 7 million out of 63 million, or one ninth of the whole population, are not exciting reading. But Nurnberg speeches and atrocities are good reading. I do not like Hitler's ideas, but even on the evidence of anti-Nazis it looks to me as if Germany is materially no worse off than before him. Now, though I may be mistaken, I see in Hitler a sincere man, with fairly practical, or anyway reasonable, from his point of view, ideas who puts them straightforwardly and I cannot see how Hitler could want war if he could give the people enough food, shelter and self-respect without it.

This was a widely held misjudgment; domestic and international policies seemed at variance; from May to September of 1935 what has been called 'the new wave of anti-Jewish violence' was evident in Germany,[35] culminating in the Nuremberg laws in the latter month.[36]

Shortly after his arrival, Charles was at a 'midsummer day, neo-pagan display. Der Führer was there himself', with approximately 100,000 onlookers. It was not Charles's only view of Hitler; in fact, he saw him on a regular basis. At the time, he told his mother that 'opposite this house Hitler has pulled down a large private house, and is building, for the last year & a half, new Nazi administrative buildings. He is in München [Munich] practically every weekend. It seems as if he is here too often for people to take much notice ... Last weekend I saw all three [Hitler, Goebbels and Goering] here.' It was this 'glory' of poverty that made Adolf Hitler so significant, as Fraülein von Gietl made clear, in Charles's recollection of their conversations:[37]

> CA: One thing was very odd about it, I was living with a remarkable old battleaxe called Fraülein von Gietl,[38] immediately opposite where the Nazi

---

35. Ian Kershaw, *Hitler 1889–1936: Hubris* p. 559; I am indebted to Ninian Falkiner for drawing this to my attention.

36. The 'Nuremberg Laws' of 1935 promulgated racial discrimination against Jewish people under a genetic classification.

37. The following quotations are from my radio interviews with Charles broadcast by Radio Éireann in 1990.

38. Charles was allowing his hyperbole to mislead his memory – Fraülein von Gietl was 44–years-old at the time, but he described her in his letters as looking only 35.

headquarters, the Braunhaus,[39] was being built, and it fascinated me that every Saturday afternoon the top bottlewashers came down to see how the thing was going, Hitler and Goering and Hesse and Goebbels, and if I had had a reasonable gun, and been a reasonable sort of a shot, I could have picked them off with the utmost ease, and escaped at the back into the basilica, and everything would have been alright.

RP: Is that the only reason you didn't kill Hitler?

CA: Well I hadn't a gun and I was a no good shot, but I also put this to Fraülein von Gietl – why does nobody do it? – and she, who was viciously anti-Nazi, and a real Bavarian, said to me 'Well, look, this is 1935 – since 1918 we have had five revolutions, an inflation and a deflation, at the moment we've got a certain amount of stability, Hitler and all his works are terrible, but let's just wait for another four or five years, come back in 1940 and shoot him then.'

This assessment of Hitler's importance to Germany between the wars was by no means unique to Fraülein von Gietl: at Kilmacurragh, Charles Budina's wife would tell Charles that she was hoping for a partial German victory.

The major experience of his two months in Munich was his exposure to music-making at the highest level. Each Saturday a 'Serenade' was given in the courtyard of one of the palaces, and Charles heard the Norwegian soprano Eidé Norena, at that time a resident star at the New York Metropolitan:[40] 'a soprano with a loud-soft voice. She sang Handel, Mozart and Schubert brilliantly, though she unfortunately finished with a little coloratura that was quite out of place.' He also heard Julius Patzak singing Mozart songs 'that sounded like something from another world'. But it was the opera festival that gave him the greatest rewards, that he would recall in detail and with enormous affection fifty years later. For part of this experience, he was joined by Brian Boydell, whom he had visited in Heidelberg on his way through to Munich.[41] Despite being on a tight budget, Charles was able to attend almost everything

---

39. The Braunhaus would be the venue for the meeting between Hitler, Chamberlain and Mussolini in 1938.

40. Eidé Norena (1884–1968) sang at Covent Garden from 1924, at the Paris Opéra 1925–37 and at the Met 1933–38.

41. Before going up to Cambridge, Boydell stayed in Heidelberg for six months, according to Axel Klein: 'though his stay was primarily motivated by a wish to broaden his general education, learn the language and to hear as much first-class music as possible, in retrospect the violence experienced after, for instance, coming across a burned-out Jewish village, was extremely disturbing' – *The Life and Music of Brian Boydell* p. 2.

he wanted to hear, since the cheapest tickets could be got for the equivalent of eight shillings. He later told his aunt Eva that 'I had never seen any opera before I went to München and was absolutely overwhelmed by the Wagner'.

The Wagner Festival took place in a theatre modelled on Wagner's own at Bayreuth. 'It is the most sensible theatre anyone ever planned & like all really good inventions so simple. Everyone can see & hear everything perfectly. The orchestra is well buried & hidden so that one is not glared by their lights.'

The title role in *Lohengrin* was sung by Julius Patzak;[42] 'the whole is supremely dramatic; the music of course, needless to say, was wonderful. It is to me now incredible that Wagner was ever considered not to have written music.' The following evening Mozart's *Die Zauberflöte* was given at the Residenztheater and was 'complete anticlimax – very light, fluffy, pantomimy, in which plot mattered nothing ... I found myself emotionally incapable of appreciating both Mozart and Wagner on alternate days, and as the Wagner was making the larger emotional impression I dropped the Mozart.' But he was 'VERY disappointed' by *Die Meistersinger*: 'As I saw it in the first act Wagner had written a comedy, in the strict technical sense, and the music being Wagner was far too noble, far too dramatic; more fitting a serious drama, or a tragedy – that the plot was an anticlimax from the music.' Equally, he did not enjoy *Tannhäuser*, which he considered 'the complement of *Meistersinger*'. The title role of *Parsifal* was sung by Julius Pölzer, who had a distinguished career at the Vienna Staatsoper before leaving the opera house for dentistry. 'This man, besides having a wonderful tenor voice, just as good as Melchior or better ... he is also a very good actor, and gives the appearance of being a born dancer.' The religious intensity of the opera seems to have restored Charles's faith in Wagner. The production of *Tristan und Isolde* he thought could have been presented just as well in a concert performance. 'There is even less action than in some of Bernard Shaw's plays, but the most exquisite music is absolutely ravishing: sheer unalloyed beauty.'

But he was preparing himself for the marathon of the *Ring* cycle – *Das Rheingold*, *Die Walküre*, *Siegfried*, and *Götterdämmerung*, conducted by Hans Knappertsbusch. 'I am determined to take many handkerchiefs to the Ring.' 'I had thought that an opera taking 5 hours must be interminably dull and longwinded, but when it came to the point, I was just as it were knocked over.'

Charles said little about the first three parts of the *Ring*, but the climax, *Götterdämmerung*, was 'superlative. Handkerchief well needed.' *Siegfried* was

---

42. Julius Patzak (1898–1974) sang at the Munich Staatsoper 1928–45.

Julius Pölzer and Brünnhilde was sung by Frida Leider (1888–1975), who performed the role at Covent Garden every year from 1924 to 1938, and during the same period was a star at the Berlin Staatsoper. 'It is no use my trying to give any impression of what I felt about it, save that it was the greatest piece of dramatic art or music that I had hitherto experienced.' The 'message' of the *Ring* had struck home to Charles in a spiritual sense where conventional religious practices never would.

> It was Wagner's chief philosophy that the world is to be redeemed. It keeps on coming in to all his operas. The Flying Dutchman is redeemed by the love unto death of the lady concerned – I forget her name – Tannhäuser is redeemed by Elizabeth's love. In Lohengrin the Duke of Brabant is redeemed by Elsa's love for Lohengrin. In the Ring the whole world – that includes the Gods – is to be redeemed by the man who has no fear. But the world is not redeemed, so everything, gods, mortals, giants, Nibelungs, Valhalla, crashes to destruction & flames save the Rhinemaidens who regain their gold, and the Rhine. But all through, a redemption motive. Had Wagner lived longer than Parsifal he would have written a cycle on Christ, the Redeemer of the World, and though it certainly would not have been the Jesus, meek & gentle, it almost certainly would have been bad. Wagner's ideal was the Redemption of the German people through culture: that not until they took in & appreciated the high forms of art would they be saved from dullness.

If immersion in Wagner were not enough, a further bonus to Charles's education and enjoyment of the season was a week in which the 80–year-old Richard Strauss conducted many of his major works. 'Remarkable thing – he having a week of this otherwise only Wagner & Mozart festival to himself. When one considers it, he is, with Ravel in a slightly smaller way, the only world-heard & world-appreciated composer of the present day.' Charles did not enjoy *Elektra* – 'disappointing. Not dramatic really – too many women, and one screeched – the first screech I have yet heard. But music *magnificent*. An *enormous* orchestra of which Strauss makes full use. Very good conductor, does practically nothing & gets the results.' *Salome* came next. 'Very very good. Text Oscar Wilde & therefore wonderful. Makes magnificent drama. Music very good … Rantzack takes the part extremely well.'[43] *Die Frau ohne Schatten* 'is very rarely done, probably because it requires terrific staging. Very good fairy plot, which Strauss & the author Hofmannsthal work out extremely well. Wonderful music, with just the right number & degree of cheapish obvious

---

43. I have been unable to identify the singer Rantzack.

fairytale thrills, all carried out so remarkably well.' Of the Strauss works that week, this was the only one not conducted by the composer.[44] A double-bill with an early opera, *Feursnot*, and the dramatic ballet *Josephslegende* came next. Charles thought *Feursnot* 'a short rather pointless fairy story with light inconsequential music', but greatly admired the portrayal of Joseph resisting the guiles of Potiphar's wife. He 'could not face *Rosenkavalier*' on the grounds that it was an early work, 'rather Johann Strauss'.

Despite the intensity of the two-week festival, and his exposure to Wagner and Strauss, Charles would regard his expertise as an opera critic to be his weak point at the time when he joined *The Irish Times*, but he would always look back on this time in Munich as a very special part of his musical life.

There were also opportunities to drive out into the surrounding lake district and see the mountains and the popular bathing resort of Tutzing. One five-day trip, after he had met a Cambridge friend, Jon Wainwright, took Charles and some friends to Garmisch, Mittenwald and Oberammergau. Another day trip took them across the border into Austria and to Innsbruck. 'The Germans have discovered that if you build a perfectly straight road, it gets so boring that one goes to sleep; so they put slight artificial bends in it every three kilometres: very good idea, but somehow dreadfully typical.' It was a phenomenon with military overtones which he would encounter three years later on a trans-European drive with Brian Boydell.

And although he does not seem to have enjoyed much German food (and certainly hardly ever mentioned it) he was introduced to the traditional dip of *Liptauer* cheese from the Liptau region of Slovakia, which was also popular in southern Germany and Austria:

> stiff orange-coloured cream cheese, which is given on a plate with red peppers, olives, anchovy, caper, chopped onion & lemon, & the inevitable caraway seeds & butter. One mixes all this together with a little *bier* and eats it as cheese; it is magnificent & very thirsty & makes *bier* taste better than before, very sustaining, very good & very profitable for *mein host*, even though itself only costs 40 pfennigs [4d.].

Charles's renewed interest in mineralogy received a boost when he met a German chemist who had discovered in Lower Bavaria a unique specimen of a mineral which had previously been known for its bleaching powers, but which, it was thought, could be used (through the process of 'adsorption') as a

---

44. Axel Klein (*op. cit.*) seems to be mistaken in stating that Brian Boydell attended this opera.

medicine to cure acidity and rheumatism. Charles's interest was not, however, philanthropic, but of practical advantage in that the discovery might be used in his final exams, and also as a possible source of profit.

Cambridge (ii) 1935–36

Returned from Germany, Charles had to go to Kilmacurragh on business and then resumed his studies at Cambridge. It was important for Charles, as the eventual heir, to keep an eye on what his (or strictly speaking his mother's) lessee was doing at Kilmacurragh, even if his own future might lie in a career in Britain. At this point all the land except for the home farm had been acquired by the Land Commission, which held the residual £16,000 of purchase money in land bonds, which were a continuing source of bewilderment to Isabel, Charles and their solicitor. For his part, Budina, whose lease had commenced in August 1932, and who had immediately opened the house and grounds as 'Kilmacurragh Park Hotel', had made major developments, installing a golf course in the deer park and a swimming pool which involved digging out the original monks' pond in front of the house,[45] and building a large 'pavilion' or dance-hall on the side of the house which could accommodate up to 400 visitors who would arrive in buses on 'works outings'. Charles was forced to 'acknowledge a virtual fait accompli'. He would later also acknowledge that Budina had a flair for attracting such clientele, while expressing reservations about his *métier* as a true hotelier. According to Budina's advertisements, Kilmacurragh was 'the most beautifully situated hotel in the Garden of Ireland', containing 'the rarest collections of conifers and rhododendrons in Western Europe, visited by eminent botanists from far and near for scientific purposes'. The hotel was suitable for families with children and for invalids: 'doctors recommend a week-end or a few weeks' stay. Prominent men in the Dublin medical world are frequent visitors.' Bed and breakfast was 6s.6d., full board was three guineas per week. Tea was two shillings, with 'Meat Delicacies for the first time introduced from the continent, all foodstuffs grown and manufactured on the Estate'. The hotel succeeded in attracting passing trade, especially lunches and teas at weekends, until in war-time the petrol shortages severely limited this clientele.

---

45. His sister-in-law would later drown herself in the pool.

Irene, somewhat predictably, objected, complaining to Charles that the Britska had been placed on the gravel sweep as an attraction.[46] 'What desecration, but no worse of course than the fate of the old house, to be the abode of not only a German, but a barber, and to be "licensed" for the sale of drinks. It is indeed a tragedy, or is he an Italian!' It may have been a tragedy in the eyes of the new keeper of the family dignity, but to Charles it was a godsend. Against his better judgment and his mother's advice, he wrote to Irene 'what came into my head – a fairly snorty one'. Exchanges would continue to exasperate both aunt and nephew, especially when Irene attempted to have Budina's liquor licence revoked.

At the beginning of 1936, as his finals loomed, Charles visited the Cambridge Appointments Board, an early version of today's career guidance office. He was advised that pure chemistry was 'not a very promising job' and was only suited to brilliant students. An opportunity seemed to arise with the linen business of William Ewart in Belfast at a starting salary of £200–250, but Charles could not decide whether his eventual goal of a job in southern Ireland would be prejudiced if he had previously worked in the Six Counties. 'Ireland we keep on hearing is a new country. It is perhaps untrue to say it is in a mess. Muddle, though perhaps a trifle strong, seems almost to describe it. Where there is development and some muddle, would there not be opportunity with work & some ideas & some luck to carve out some of it to oneself?' When he was offered a job with a soap manufacturer, Charles had puzzled over the social implications. 'Thirty years ago, one could not do much beyond distilling, without losing caste, ten years ago one could brew, and by now so many people of the right kind are earning money in the most varied of ways that one can do a great deal more.' He would rapidly learn that life did not consist of merely mixing – and working – with 'people of the right kind'.

An occupation of some sort was, of course, essential, even though Charles did prove, during his years at Kilmacurragh, that he was able to live within the very modest income from his family trust funds. 'The problem of what I want to do with life' was more important than the mere earning of money, although 'from a practical point of view one has to secure a reasonable income in a reasonably short time, anyway by the time the right girl comes along,

---

46. A Britska [diminutive of *bryka* – a goods vehicle] was originally a Polish/Russian four-wheeled vehicle with a long wicker-work body and a hooded top; it was introduced to Britain from Austria in the nineteenth century; the Kilmacurragh model had been acquired as early as 1863.

and without keeping her waiting too long'. He hoped for an intellectual life, stimulated by change: 'when people stop changing their mental attitudes they stop thinking.' If he were to be employed by Guinness (a possibility through the Boydell family's business connections), he would nevertheless look out for any opportunity that would allow him to 'do as much living as possible' while also being able to support a wife and family:

> when I reach retirement, to be able to do so with a not uninteresting life behind me with enjoyable, worth-while memories, and with sufficient mind left still to be able to think and capable of meditating on the problems of those days, and to appreciate the culture and thoughts of people of those days. This is not the road to knighthood, nor do I think it is the Road to the Nirvana, but it may be one of the roads to heaven. *My soul comes first.*

That expression is less of a statement than a *cri de coeur*, a calling out for under-standing and appreciation, for a space within which to make himself.

And at precisely this point, Brian Boydell did make an intervention in Charles's life which would eventually allow him to discover his *forte*: concert reviews. As Charles later recalled it 'A slightly scurrilous weekly *Varsity Weekly* gave what all critics value – free tickets – though you had to work for it.' One of his first assignments was a musical comedy performed by the Cambridge Amateur Operatic Society: it taxed his tactfulness, since he had straight away encountered the critic's dilemma of how to bring professional standards to amateur performances. 'Being used to ADC shows, where there would be considerable indignation if a show were reviewed on any but a professional standard, until I gathered that I was expected to judge the show as "courageous amateurs" and that they expected it. I found it difficult to combine flattery with some regard for the truth.'

Charles found in the role of critic the position of authority which allowed him to answer and fulfil that *cri de coeur*. In commenting on the performance of another, Charles was judging it but also to a certain extent identifying with the performer's own need to find him- or herself. This is the inevitable burden of the critic, who is required to be the arbiter of taste: to reach sound judgments but at the same time to relish the infinite possibilities available in performance.

Charles and Brian jointly reviewed, among other events, the first perfor-mance of Vaughan Williams's opera *The Poisoned Kiss*. He wrote to his mother that the opera itself 'was very good. Not a good libretto but wonderful music, although slightly marred by Rootham's conducting which was appalling.' Other assignments were recitals by pianists Artur Rubinstein (they commented on his 'unpleasant metallic tone', Alfred Cortot (they complained that the promoters had scheduled insufficient Chopin) and Walter Gieseking, the latter playing Debussy 'as nobody has played Debussy before or since'. In Charles's recollection 'we chatted about it and I did most of the writing, but since I became music critic of *The Irish Times* Brian's never approved of music critics, and I rather doubt if he remembers that he was one himself once!'

In February 1936, Boydell gave 'the first and probably last public performance' of his opus 4, 'Cathleen the daughter of Houlihan', with Yeats's words, and dedicated to Charles. 'Although it went well, it is not a song for performance. It is written in no established key and completely free rhythm. Feel certain that Yeats should only be set without any ordinary rhythm, letting his own rhythm control it entirely. Am therefore exceedingly glad that Brian has done this without any rhythm intrinsic to the music.' Charles was at this time reading Yeats's 'Red Hanrahan' – 'it is some of the most wonderful English I have ever met. It has the simplicity & beauty of the Bible & all the time full of Irishness.'[47]

Charles's final exams were not a cause of celebration, and he seems to have regarded them as he had those of previous years, taking music as an escape valve to ease the tension of an ordeal which he found constitutionally irksome. His last paper, on 9 July, lasted seven hours 'in a badly ventilated lab with everyone including myself disgorging unpleasant gases into the room', after which he still had enough energy to type a five-page letter to his mother. He had written an essay on 'Chemistry and Civilization': 'I thought it would be rather a good idea to discuss the idea that the greatest chemist and the man who will do the most to benefit civilization is the man who is not merely a machine for investigation, but who is something of a philosopher.' He had incorporated Flecker's quotation 'A fool believeth nothing till the proof; the wise man believeth everything till the disproof', and later reflected 'so no wonder I failed my degree'. He thought he had done neither well nor badly in most of the papers, but his mind went blank in the mineralogy paper. 'It was odd; although I was going to bed early, and eating properly and not working between the theoretical exams, I came out of each weary and shivering with coldness.' In fact he had used the time between the papers to attend the Vic-Wells ballet – Walton's *Façade*, with *Carnival* and *Rendezvous*, and *Swan Lake* and

---

47. Charles also considered that Boydell's 'Hearing of Harvests', op. 13, written in 1940, to text by W.H. Auden, and dedicated to Charles, had been completed at his behest.

The Rake's Progress choreographed by Ninette de Valois (he probably did not know at that time that she was in fact born Edris Stannus and a near neighbour from Baltiboys in their native Wicklow).[48]

At the end of his time in Cambridge, Charles heard the St Matthew Passion, with Reginald Jacques conducting the LPO and the Bach Choir, once again encountering Steuart Wilson:[49] 'No tragedy I have seen in a theatre or opera house moves me so deeply or seems such great theatre as this oratorio.' An Irish singer, who never gained the international renown she deserved was Renee Flynn, whom Charles heard also at this time in the premiere of Vaughan Williams's forewarning of war, 'Dona Nobis Pacem', which he described to Flynn over thirty years later as 'one of the most moving memories of my life'.

London and Palestine

Charles had two weeks to wait for his results, during which he was told of a job as a travelling salesman with a soap and candle manufacturer in Newcastle-upon-Tyne, and, to add to his 'irons in the fire', an opening with the international travel agency, Thomas Cook & Son. Without a degree, Charles needed a job which did not require university qualifications. 'I knew somebody who was a director of Thomas Cook and Son: "If you'd like a job as a booking clerk I could get it for you", so, as any job was better than no job, I was for a year in the High Holborn office, and then they suddenly sent me to Palestine, as assistant manager in the Haifa office. That was one of the most fascinating periods of my life.'[50] What his mother thought of her son, the heir to an Irish estate, working as a clerk in a London office, is not recorded. Nevertheless, it was indeed a 'most fascinating period' in Charles's life, not only for his immersion in the international *débâcle* of the Middle East, but also for his travels in Yugoslavia and Jordan, before returning to Ireland at the beginning of the war.

By July 1936 he was working at Cook's office in High Holborn, and staying in Roland Gardens in South Kensington, a considerable distance from his place

---

48. Edris Stannus (1898–2001) changed her name officially in 1921 to Ninette de Valois; worked with the *Ballets russes* and the Abbey Theatre Dublin before establishing the Sadler's Wells (today the Royal) Ballet 1931.

49. One of the other soloists was Joan Cross, at that time principal soprano at Sadler's Wells.

50. My interview with Charles, Radio Éireann 1990.

of work. It was dreary work as a desk clerk, except that – he later believed – it equipped him for dealing with 'difficult' people and, moreover, it brought him into contact with the exotic.

> I in trepidation am asked by the customers most esoteric things like 'which is the best way from Jerusalem to Baghdad?' or 'I want to book tickets to go from Cheb, via Vanigrovska to Algiers'. Though I am making several mistakes at first, I think I shall pick it up. I would much rather have my time full to bursting than have a slack time, since in the latter case there is nothing whatever to do, and even if one fills it up by reading timetables it is impossible to acquire any appreciable amount of useful information.

Introduction to the work included lectures, one of which concerned the company's business in Egypt:

> apparently Upper Egypt depends almost entirely for its trade on tourists brought by us. Recently the King of Egypt went to the Upper Egypt, which was most unusual, and the first visit thereto of the head of the Egyptian State for as long as anyone could remember. Being rather pleased with himself, he asked a small boy among the crowd who was the greatest in the land. Small boy replied 'Allah'. This did not please the King much, though he had to admit the truth of the statement. 'Well, who is the next greatest in the land?' Small boy: 'Mr Cook'.

He expected to be transferred during the winter to head office in Berkeley Street, but that would deprive him of the contact with customers, and he hoped to be stationed in one of the company's in-hotel offices,

> where they might have some use for social qualifications, since I gather that these are good jobs since the customers are far more friendly and courteous.[51] I am glad to say that I have mixed well. There may be a little friction at some time with the chief clerk who is a doddering old fool. I unfortunately committed the tactical mistake of correcting him … when he was landing a customer rather up a tree, and it was in the interests of the customer and our relations with him, that I should point the matter out.

Charles always had an eye for the odd or the bizarre, and Cook's provided him with plenty of examples of this, such as an information leaflet which instructed that when shipping items, cats and dogs should be counted as three packages, horses as six, cremated remains as ten and corpses as twenty.

---

51. Cook's had offices in such hotels as the Cumberland, Dorchester, Grosvenor (at Victoria Station), Langham, Savoy, Regent Palace and Strand Palace.

This humdrum and uncertain existence contrasted sharply with Charles's solitary evenings when he debated with himself (and, in writing, with his mother) his beliefs. At school he had been a great admirer of Sir James Jeans, author of the best-selling *The Mysterious Universe*, but he was sceptical of the fact that 'Jeans sat down in 1920 and "proved" on the laws of probability that there was a Creator-God. If there is a God, he must contain all the attributes he is able to create in others.'

From the window of his lodgings across the rooftops of Knightsbridge, Charles saw a similar city to that evoked by Eliot in the lines on 'Unreal City' in the first section of *The Waste Land*, and sent his mother his poem portraying the 'undead' of London life: the wind 'calls to the dead to awaken / And live their joyous years/ But these dead are not in the graveyards / But the grave of their own fears./ They sit by the fire doing crosswords / These grey respectable clerks...' This life of respectable clerking was not for Charles, and, after a year in the London office, he must have leapt at the offer of transfer to Cook's in Haifa.

Charles travelled out to Palestine in October 1937, *via* Paris, Venice, Brindisi and Alexandria. The boat from Brindisi brought him down the west coast of Greece, towards the Peloponnese:

> the shape of the mountains rising up like kings on their thrones – they are not the soft little mountains of Wicklow, nor the perpendicular mountains of the Alps ... They do not lie like the Irish mountains peopled with Sidhe ... nor are they as the Salisbury plain downs waiting in divine silence till man shall turn again and worship the sun and themselves ... but they are the immortals who do not need recognition.

In Alexandria he had his first encounter with African Asia, and the Levantine *mélange* of cultures which he would meet head-on in Palestine. 'The quay looked like a collection of noisily badly organized ants about to build a bad ants nest ... Alex is NOT Egypt. It might be described as Cité moderne, cosmopolite, européen rôti sauce Egyptienne'. Arriving in Palestine, Charles saw Jaffa and Tel Aviv – 'they merge into one another like Bournemouth & Poole without any obvious division, they are the fiercest of economic & political rivals. Jaffa the home of Arab Nationalism, Tel Aviv the mushroom Jewish port built to be the chief port of Palestine.'

The situation in Palestine was very delicate, the subject of a series of strategic political manoeuvres as the legacy of the First World War and in the context of the slowly evolving social, economic and cultural situation which led to what remains, to this day, 'the middle east crisis'. In the case of

Palestine, two instruments of international diplomacy had created an impossible situation: in 1916 Britain and France, represented respectively by Mark Sykes and François Georges-Picot, made a secret understanding (the 'Sykes-Picot Agreement') which would define their territorial interests at the end of the current war, on the assumption that the Ottoman empire would have been dismantled at that stage – it 'provided for Britain and France to divide up the Arabic-speaking Middle East'.[52] Under this agreement, Jordan, Iraq and the area around the strategically important port of Haifa were mandated to Britain. Palestine itself was to be administered by an international consortium of the powers, but this was made impossible by the Russian revolution the following year. The Sykes-Picot Agreement effectively denied the 'promised land' for Arabs. Meanwhile, in 1917 another secret agreement was made between the British Foreign Secretary, Arthur Balfour, and Walter, second Baron Rothschild, a leader of the British Jewish community, allocating Palestine as the Jewish 'national home' following the partitioning of the former Ottoman empire (the 'Balfour Declaration'). This had been effected by the intervention of Chaim Weizmann (of which Charles had particular knowledge from Weizmann's son Michael), and was the basis of the mandate for the League of Nations – a position which Britain would find it impossible to maintain. As Charles wrote later to his mother, 'Even if the Mandate were indisputably legal that would have little bearing on the actual state of the million and a half people in Palestine, and it is after all they who finally should count. Just as the legal form of the Act of Union did not make the Irish any more British, or the legal form of the Home Rule Act make Carson and the Oranges particularly satisfied.'

In the words of the influential Maude Royden, whose *The Problem of Palestine* appeared in 1939, 'we all believe that Palestine is the Holy Land, yet between us we have made it most unholy... Palestine is one of the most unhappy countries in the world. It is torn with hatred, its roads and even its cities are unsafe'.[53] Charles possessed a copy of this book, with which he entirely concurred; and from practical experience when he drove around the countryside, he was acutely aware of the dangers from the operations of four sets of vested interests – the British, mandated to administer the territory, chiefly through the Palestine police force; the growing populations of the Jews; the Moslem Arabs; and the Christian Arabs, to all of whom the land was 'holy' and 'promised'.

---

52. David Fromkin, *A Peace to End all Peace* p. 257.

53. M. Royden, *The Problem of Palestine* p. 125.

Royden attributed the Balfour Declaration of 1917 to three factors, one of which was the fact that 'Dr Weizmann, who is not only the President of the Zionist Association but a very distinguished chemist, made a discovery of importance to modern chemical warfare, put it at the service of the British Government, and thus earned the gratitude of all patriotic British people.'[54] Whether or not Royden knew the exact details of the 'discovery of importance', Charles thought that he *did*.

> I was a close friend of Chaim Weizmann's son Michael, who unfortunately was killed in the war, and a very nice guy he was, and he told me for what it was worth, that Chaim Weizmann, who was a chemist, had perfected a system of getting explosives out of the residue of malting barley for beer, and at that time, in 1916/17, the British were in a terrible state, for lack of high explosives, so Weizmann, having evolved this, went to Lloyd George and said "Here you are, you can have it in return for the Jewish homeland in Palestine", and Lloyd George wouldn't play, so Weizmann said 'Right, if you don't want it, I'll sell it to Berlin'. That clinched the thing, therefore the British government agreed, and made the Balfour Declaration which with the Sykes-Picot Agreement of 1916, put the whole cat among all the pigeons. Today the residue goes to make marmite, so Michael told me.[55,56]

By the time Charles arrived in Haifa in October 1937, the rejection by the Arabs of the British attempt to facilitate Jewish settlement had led to guerrilla warfare throughout the country. As he and his mother would become very much aware, 'Arab and Jew remain facing each other. Terrorism continues. British troops still try to preserve "law and order". Terrorism is met by terrorism. Movement about the country becomes more and more restricted, curfews more and more common.'[57] By the time he left, in 1939, the 'Arab revolt' had ended, and Palestine was relatively peaceful, although Arab and Jewish leaders still refused to talk directly to one another.

Arriving into Haifa, Charles found Mount Carmel 'where Elijah did his stuff most uninspiring. I had hoped for a mountain, not merely the Harbour Heights Hotel'. Here he was met by the Cook's representative,

> an Arab, very cordial & charming, who with that magic that one associates with Cook got me through the passport people first and took me on shore,

---

54. *Ibid.*, p. 94.

55. See the note at the end of this chapter.

56. My interviews with Charles, Radio Éireann, 1990.

57. Royden, *op. cit.*, p. 106.

[then] I met the manager, a little Welshman, Jeffries, with a face rather like an Irish-American policeman ... His slight over-efficiency of manner was explained when I went to his home for a drink & saw that his bookshelf contained apart from novels only 'Personal Magnetism', 'Business Efficiency', 'A Practical Manual of Psychology' & 'Pelmanism'.

Charles lodged initially in the brand-new Grand Hotel Nassar, leased from Cook's general manager for Palestine, who owned the site. To his surprise, an authentic Irish stew turned up on the menu, and later on a dish of beans, carrots, peas and cucumber with rice:

> it was called Legumes à l'Anglaise. Strange the things that one country attributes to another. The waiters are, of course, Arabs, very dark dressed in tarbushes, white linen night gowns with a red or green sash around their chests. There is a German chamber maid with whom I have made friends. She borrowed my Van Gogh illustrations, & now she has on its return been lent Feuchtwanger's *Erfolg*, a very heavy German novel which should keep her happy for a long time.[58] There is also an Arab chamber maid whose English does not go much further than Good Morning, and a page boy who sits at the bottom of the lift (automatic) has a smile three times the size of his face & answers any enquiries I address to him, with 'speak little engleesh'.

Charles was also encountering Arab music, and his attempts to understand it were the prelude to his discussions of it with Seán Ó Riada. 'Entirely melodic, strongly resembles plainsong, but has a lot of ornamentation in the form of trills & appoggiaturas, & makes a great point of returning to the dominant or tonic with great emphasis.'

The staff of Cook's consisted of Jeffries, the manager, 'a chap of 20 called Lewis who is learning to be a booking clerk ... an Arab cashier – too much pre-pituitary gland – a Jewish typist girl, a Jewish messenger boy, an Arab of about 25 who is filing clerk & maid-of-all-work.' His working environment was a ready introduction to the mixture of cultures, languages and nationalities which made the Levant such a fascinating and dangerous place. Charles immediately asked for a week's sightseeing holiday – it was refused. Jeffries 'gave me a house-master lecture against Wein und Weib. I gather that predecessor was over-given to both. When I told him that you were coming out too, after saying a lot about what a good idea it was, he said "I shall be very glad too, since your mother will have the responsibility & not me".' Charles had to admit that 'I know the

---

58. *Erfolg* [Success], published in 1930, was critical of Nazism and led to persecution of Lion Feuchtwanger, a German Jew (1884–1958).

difference between mild flirtation & lerve, and between lerve & love. I have already indulged in a certain amount of mild flirtation, found myself at one stage getting somewhat sentimental, recognized the unpleasant symptoms of lerve.' Flirtation, it appears, was in contrast with 'vamping', in which

> I can give as good as I get, and am at present in that very youthful stage of regarding it all in terms of psychology, biology & the unpleasant light of reason. I am told that even expert vamps are disconcerted by deflation of sentimentality. I have in this respect another advantage – namely laziness. Although I have left behind three girls [in Cambridge] where there were omens of quite promising romances, or anyway suitable fields for experiment in sociability, I find it takes so much time & energy to make light conversation about nothing & to behave as the perfect little gentleman that I have not been bothered – although I *had* intended this winter to pursue the matter, I find heavy conversation comes to me so much easier than light, and in girls of my age brains seem usually a substitute for S.A. [sex appeal].

His social life consisted of meeting police officers of various ranks, including the district commissioner, the bank manager and his wife ('very nice "not quite" people'), a woman who organized amateur theatricals – 'I hope to get in on that' – and a judge. Social appearances were very mixed. Although Charles was concerned about dress codes (when to wear black tie, and when to wear white) and the etiquette regarding leaving visiting cards, he reported to Isabel that

> the few people there are who have money, such as the heads of the IPC[59] and so forth, are nearly all I gather gentlemen by birth, so that even though they are earning several thousands a year, they have no reason to display it. There are also various strata of people, who in England would not mix, but who here are all the same, roughly speaking, that any formality beyond the minimum would sort them out into classes according to incomes.

Charles was invited to meet Colonel Frederick Kisch,[60] who was honorary treasurer of the Palestine Orchestra, and – more importantly – head of the Jewish Agency in Palestine. He had in fact been at school with Kisch's nephew, and was to find that between Rugby and Cambridge a large number of those he met shared the same background. Charles mentioned the disagreements among Jews themselves about where the Jewish state should actually be. Many,

---

59. IPC: a British-controlled international consortium for oil exploration from Iraq; chief partners BP, Shell and Gulbenkian.

60. Later killed in action in north Africa.

including Theodor Herzl, the father of modern Zionism, would have settled for land in Brazil or Uganda (the latter having been offered by Britain in 1903), but hard-line Zionists had insisted on the biblical interpretation of the homeland: Palestine. Charles agreed that if there were fifteen million Jews in the world, even to settle half of them in Palestine would be impossible, and that in order to create a modern state, the Jews would have to engage in manufacture and exportation, which would be physically difficult even if there were sufficient capital investment. Anticipating his 'short story' or reflective memoir 'New Wine', he suggested that 'unless they are going to live as a simple rural community, without modern civilization, which seems unthinkable, when one sees how much of modern civilization is mixed up with the Jews – to such an extent that Hitler bans modern architecture and art and music because the leaders in Germany were Jews – they will only be able to live on what they can get from Jewry outside Palestine. It is absurd anyway to try and settle in a country like Palestine which is always between rival powers. In the old days it was between Assyria and Egypt: now it is still an important trade route. For England it is a very important link in the Empire. For Italy it would be a great asset in controlling the Mediterranean. It will always therefore be a potential battleground, and if ever independent will only be so on sufferance.' As a Belfast Catholic, working in the harbour docks in Haifa, said to Charles, 'they bloody well serve each other right'.

Musical fare was much less in both quality and quantity than in Cambridge and London, but interesting nonetheless. In October 1937 Charles heard the one-year-old Palestine Symphony Orchestra (later the Israel Philharmonic), founded in order to give a musical home to Jewish musicians who were being increasingly persecuted in Europe. It had given its first concert, under Arturo Toscanini, the previous December. Its founder, violinist Bronislaw Huberman, had had an accident and was unable to conduct as planned, and the concert, consisting of Beethoven's pastoral symphony, the triple concerto and the eighth symphony, was conducted by principal conductor William Steinberg. It is a measure of musical awareness at that time that Charles had not previously known of the triple concerto (for piano, violin and cello). He didn't like it: 'one of the few works of his which is conventionally in his manner, and even the fact that he has a lovely tune in the slow movement does not make it worth while.' He liked the strings, but thought that the woodwind was the worst section. 'Their tone is rough and somewhat harsh. But I dare say this is due to their German upbringing – in spite of the exquisite woodwind passages written by their great German composers, the Germans tend to regard a woodwind instrument as one for filling out orchestral tone, or for adding volume, and do not cultivate that excellence of tone that is such a joy in England. Oh to be in England now that Goossens there.'[61] He thought Steinberg 'is a competent man, rather in Godfrey manner,[62] and has not at all a clear beat. There was not nearly enough contrast between loud and soft. It takes a first class conductor to make a full orchestra play *piano* and a Toscanini to make it play *pianissimo*.'[63]

> In the eighth symphony Steinberg did put it across. This symphony is one of the most playful and lovely things written. Very delicate, not that rough boisterous heavy humour one expects of the man, but a joyful, almost Disney dancing. I sound awfully critical of this concert – I know that I ought to be jolly thankful that it exists at all, and indeed I am, but I was worked up with an excess of local patriotism to believe that it was as good as the great orchestras of the world. Had I been told that it was as good as the Bournemouth, or even the LSO, I would have been most agreeably surprised, whereas I went expecting the BBC or the Berlin orchestra.

It appears that Isabel's cousin Bobbie, whom she had previously nursed out of a nervous breakdown, had suffered a relapse into alcoholism: Isabel was proposing to bring him out to Palestine as a kind of rest cure, under the pretext that he was her secretary/chauffeur. Charles told Bobbie's fiancée, Dorothy, that if Bobbie remained in England the responsibility for his welfare would be hers, and that Isabel would be freed from the burden she had carried during 1937 – it is clear that he hoped that Isabel would travel alone to Palestine, leaving Bobbie in the care of Dorothy. If Bobbie had in fact travelled out with Isabel, Charles recommended that he himself should offer to abstain from both alcohol and tobacco so as to give Bobbie the moral support he would need. He felt that it was much easier to abstain from drink in Palestine, whereas

---

61. Leon Goossens, 1897–1988, leading British oboist, member of an extensive musical family.

62. Sir Daniel Godfrey (1868–1939) founded the Bournemouth Municipal Orchestra in 1893 and conducted it until 1934.

63. Charles had heard Toscanini conducting the BbC Symphony Orchestra in London the previous summer. 'Toscanini will not have in his performances anything that is not absolutely perfect. Every man under him follows his beat exactly, and he gives them the clearest indication, then one realizes what this inappreciable difference does. Then there is an inspiration in the performance, the fortissimos astound one and the pianissimos amaze and thrill one.'

in England drunkenness was regarded 'with as much loathing as prostitutes, thieves, murderers and other criminals, unless they can carry it off brilliantly like Birkenhead'.[64]

Charles and his mother moved into a house with a garden on the slopes of Mount Carmel. He told her in prospect that 'in a month's time it would be the nicest house in Haifa – the home you make always is'. Isabel's arrival in Haifa had two effects: it meant the cessation of Charles's letters home, and it brought mother and son together, with the effect of increasing the tensions between them. Even though Charles had assured his mother 'we are going to have a grand time together', it seems that it was not the best of years for either of them. He had been very lonely in Haifa but although he regarded his mother as his 'best friend', their proximity was craved on both sides yet it made them both uncomfortable when it was achieved.

Two journeys

In 1938, Charles made two quite different journeys from his base at Haifa. The first, in July-August, was to Yugoslavia with his Cambridge friend Brian Boydell, which he recorded in a 120–page typescript letter to his mother; the second, in November, was to the ancient site of Petra in what was then Transjordan, in which he was accompanied part of the way by Isabel.

He left Haifa by an Ala Littoria seaplane, having asked that the plane would fly over the town so that his mother could signal to him by flashlight. In Athens, he and his travelling companions stayed overnight at the King George hotel. 'Athens is a somewhat squalid place for a capital city, and a good deal of it smells "Palestine" ... I think that the people who talk so disparagingly of modern Greece only do so because they start with the extremely exaggerated idea of "The Glory that was Greece".' The flight next morning passed over mainland Greece towards Brindisi, where they re-embarked into a 'landplane' which took them on to Rome, and where Charles strolled around in his *kuffia*, the traditional Arab overgarment. 'Rome is not a great city – in general it seems to

---

64. F.E. Smith, 1st Earl of Birkenhead (1872–1930), Lord Chancellor, Secretary of State for India, one of the British negotiators of the Anglo-Irish Treaty, and notorious drunkard. He remarked to Michael Collins at the signing of the treaty that he, Birkenhead, was 'signing his political death warrant', to which Collins retorted that *he* was signing his 'actual death warrant': Tim Pat Coogan, *Michael Collins* p. 276.

be a heavy eighteenth-century city in retirement, though the hand of Il Duce [Benito Mussolini] is often visible. There are some lovely fountains, but it does not seem to be as living as Dublin.' His view of the city as a whole was not unlike that of Colonel Acton in 1855: 'The trouble with the Colosseum and the Forum is that they are not complete enough to have beauty and as spectacles – well, one has seen Baalbek.' St Peter's basilica was 'absolutely dead'.

The next day the journey was resumed and, after refuelling at Marseilles, passed over Arles, Nîmes and Avignon, to Paris, 'a long sprawl dominated by a toy Eiffel Tower and the twin spires of whatever church it is', to land at Le Bourget, transferring to an Air France plane which brought him to Croydon.

Charles and Brian Boydell made contact at London's Dorchester Hotel; they had kept up their correspondence in the meantime, with Brian sending regular letters 'about the biochemical aspect of life, pacifism, music and general gossip'. They set out for Dover in 'Medusa', Brian's soft-top Ford V8 two-seater, accompanied by Alan Leeke, a Church of England priest and chaplain at Clare College Cambridge, in his Alvis. The ferry brought them to Ostend, whence they drove to Liège *via* Ghent and Leuven, and then on to the German border, where they alarmed the customs officials – Charles in his *kuffia* and Brian in 'an immensely tall Mexican cowboy hat' which his mother had given him. Their route took them to Aachen, Cologne, Koblenz, and Bonn. 'The Rhine itself was disappointing. The river is very fast and broad and carrying all manner of traffic, but the scenery is of the same type as that of the Wye valley but not so good.' Mainz came next, followed by Ludwigshaven and Darmstadt, where they joined an *autobahn*. After visiting some friends of Brian at Heidelberg, they moved on to Stuttgart, and Augsburg, which made Charles feel 'once more at home, with the nice Bavarian houses, painted outside, and the nice Bavarians in their nice Bavarian clothes, and a marked decrease in Hitler flags.' This was the exact time of the Austrian 'Anschluss' (unification with Germany), when the crisis over the annexation of the Czech Sudetenland was taking shape.

Munich was bypassed in favour of a detour to Oberammergau, and Charles reminded his mother of his letters describing the lake of Walchen See: 'it started raining which enhances the beauty of this lake since under cloudy skies it is pure emerald, but under sun it is a postcard peacock blue.' On to Garmisch, where 'the whole town was full of Hitler Jugend from Thuringia', and *via* the Fernpass into Austria and Innsbruck. On the road to Kitsbuhel they stopped at a village where Charles bought a pair of *lederhosen* for seventeen shillings 'which sounds a lot for a pair of shorts, but they are tremendously useful and will last not only one lifetime, but several.' Next day they crossed into Italy at San Candido. 'The frontier was very simple. We simply had to fill up the money forms and show how much tobacco we had, which was not much since our tin of 50 Players was almost exhausted and we had only a few German penny cigars left. It was a pity we had not got more as Italian tobacco is worse than brown paper as we soon discovered.' Here

> Brian did not do so well because the menu was Clear Soup with Spaghetti, Ravioli au gratin, Steak (he did eat this, but it was rather tough and there were no potatoes only butter beans which he does not like) cheese. Brian was rather miserable, since there is very little that he likes. We used to say that he likes nothing but joint and two veg. and tea. This is an overstatement but he is like Marcus with cheese, won't eat anything of the spaghetti type because he does not like the feel of it in his mouth, and will only eat clear soup if it has no bits in it, etc. etc. He is NOT the person to take on a Voyage Gastronomique and will never try anything new to eat because he thinks he won't like it.

They then moved on over the Dolomites.

> The mountains are simply grand and very thrilling. The trouble here is that the Italians behave like the Welsh who always seem to put the most hideous villages into the most lovely country. All this would not matter but for the smell. One's idea of what a fish shop in the Suk [*souk*: Arab market] in summer should smell like, is absolutely nothing. The general impression is rather like this: one is motoring along the road in this perfect mountain countryside and then without seeing anything one is suddenly aware of the smell and one says 'We are coming to a village' and sure enough round a corner within the next kilometre one comes to the village through which one hurries.

From Trieste they drove on down the coast and, on 14 July, five days after leaving London, they crossed into Yugoslavia, with 'a sentry in a very chocolate soldier uniform' and soon others 'also in various Ruritanian uniforms'. They discovered that local cigarettes were cheap and good quality – 'this seemed to be a grand start to the country'. Yugoslavia at that time was a fragile democratic monarchy, which had been created as a nation-state in the aftermath of the Balkan wars of 1912–13 and the routing of the Ottoman empire. As Charles would discover, this state was an uneasy *mésalliance* of Serbia and Montenegro, Slovenia, Croatia, and Bosnia-Herzegovina, in which the Croat people in particular suffered from maladministration.

The first stop for Charles, Brian and Alan was Ljubljana, capital of Slovenia, where 'we had a first class meal in the German manner with the Jugoslavian vin ordinaire, pleasant with a curious sharpness in it, with a pleasant string band all for 5/-, 1/8d each.'

> Ljubljana has a nice large treed square in which people walk about and what very much impressed me was the clean simplicity of the whole town ... The women were excellently dressed but nothing garish or loud ... In fact this was a lasting impression of the rest of the country through which we passed, that it is a country of very high, polite, quiet civilization and at the same time of a great freedom. There is a very lovely atmosphere about it.

They moved on to Bled which, Charles noted, has a lake the size of Glendalough, in which, with some difficulty, he washed his *kuffia*. Charles found that in this idyllic setting he had become oblivious to the day and the date – 'I found it grand not to have the slightest idea of times or dates after Cook's, where they had been so all important.' They proceeded in the direction of Zagreb, the Croatian capital. 'The further on the road we went the more Russian the villages looked, and often the impression was definitely Chekhov, as the Macadam road would end at the village and give place to enormously broad streets of solid uneventful but not unpleasant houses with a cobbled pavement and a mud street. Zagreb itself is quite a pleasant city, I suppose the same size as Stuttgart or Birmingham. Large block buildings in various types [of] baroque, and all clean and orderly.' From Zagreb they went on to see the lakes and waterfalls of Plitvice, which they had been told were 'second only to Niagara'. Charles remarked on how the landscape became very like that of Palestine, infertile and barren, while the people were 'very reminiscent of Palestinian Arabs. The people were much darker. Many of the women looked very Araby. From looking at them I would say that the type of civilization was very similar to that of the fellahin.'

Arriving at Split, Charles wrote 'The SEA! Thalassa, Thalassa'. The town, he thought, was 'a dullish town with a very Brightonish sea front. The general impression was of a second rate Italian seaside town.' Moving on, they found the 'real' Dalmatian coast: 'a Riviera village, all done with a broad promenade, overhung with vines, and with spacious houses and people bathing.' Taking an inland road which wound up and up, they came to a mountain top from which they could see the sea. 'A gorgeously dark blue. There was a kind of impossibility about that view, it was too big and too beautiful to be true.'

Dubrovnik (where the ex-King Edward VIII arrived in his yacht at the same time) was, in Charles's opinion, 'an improvement on Venice, though without the canals'. 'Everything is more restrained and dignified, and there is none of the past glory stuff from which Venice suffers. The buildings, the city and the people alike have this quality of aristocracy. Dubrovnik must be revisited without doubt.' The slight acquaintance that the travellers had had with Hitler's Germany was renewed at Dubrovnik when they met a Czech family from the Sudetenland, where Hitler was fomenting trouble which would, two months later, lead to annexation. 'They thought that it was mostly bluff on Hitler's part. They do not think that in spite of all he said Hitler would eventually do anything about it, but that if he did they were very confident, because the whole country was united.'

Charles attended an Orthodox service, and 'though I did not understand a word I felt to be a real part of the congregation, and that the congregation was individually and collectively making a very real worship to God. It was the most impressive and sincere and soul-inspiring service I have ever been to, and the only one where I really felt that I and everyone else was making a piece of real worship, praise and prayer.' And a foretaste of later times after the death of Marshal Tito was provided by a Croat who told the three trtavellers that the Serbs were suppressing the Croats, whom they outnumbered 7:6. 'All the central government is done by the Serbs, and there is not a single Croat minister in the cabinet. It seemed a very great pity that in this lovely land, among these lovely people, there should be dissensions and bitterness.'

They left Dubrovnik on 'an evening with such a light on these lovely islands and mountains as absolutely to fit in with the Slav singing we had heard. It was a beauty that made one weep, quite apart from our sadness at leaving this so beautiful place. Ever since getting onto the boat, I have been homesick for the country. I long to drive you up and down it.'

The return journey had all the air of an anticlimax. From Bari, Charles again found himself in his grandfather's steps at Paestum, followed by Salerno, Amalfi, Pompeii, and an ascent of Vesuvius as his grandfather had done before him. In Pompeii, Charles told his mother,

> It must have been an extraordinary civilization ... The amount of sheer obscenity and pornography is staggering. And it is not as though they kept the pornography to the brothels, or the bridal rooms, or anything like that. That would be natural, and pictures of the classical mythical romances in the public rooms of the houses would also be natural and right, but the exposure in the courts and passages and living rooms of the most crude and exagger-ated pornography and obscenity seems so odd and unnatural.

From Naples they returned to Rome and on to Pisa and Genoa, and over the Alps to drive through France *via* Nice, Lyons, Orleans, Chartres, Rouen and

Dieppe. Charles witnessed a Mass at Chartres, which 'was somehow very like the last act of *Parzifal* – I felt myself to be watching a wonderful mistery [*sic*] which was very beautiful, though without quite identifying myself with it.'

One memorable meal in a French village celebrated their return to the 'voyage gastronomique':

> it started with an excellent hors d'oeuvre of raw smoked ham very well cured, with liver sausage, followed by melon glacé, followed by good potage, followed by trout fried in butter served with the butter round the fish still frying the fish, then cold chicken, then a sweet had we wanted it, then excellent cheese and excellent fruit. The whole meal costing twenty francs or 2/4d including service. There is no doubt about it, that the French do know how to cook better than anyone else, and how to serve it.

On 8 August the party reached Newhaven, and, en route for London, stopped at a roadhouse at East Grinstead where reality reintroduced itself as they lunched on thick oxtail soup, lamb chop ('quite good') with boiled potato and cabbage, rice pudding and prunes, costing 2/– without either alcohol or service charge.

'It was as you can gather an absolutely wonderful month, and some time we must go there together', he told Isabel. For Brian Boydell, however, the trip had not been so 'wonderful', and it signalled a cooling off – on his side at least – of the deep friendship with Charles. He later recorded that he had not seen Charles since the time they had spent together in Munich, and

> I was longing to see him again, for we always managed to find enough to say to each other to talk the sun round. It turned out that I was greatly disappointed in both Charles and Alan, whom I thought would be admirable companions on a trip. Charles had been changed by Palestine. He was arrogant, and sure of his wisdom to the extent of angry contradiction. He made me feel the ignorant youngster of the party, by combining with Alan against most of my decisions. It was a great disappointment to find Charles so changed. A devil had entered a soul which had been so charming.[65]

Between his Yugoslav and Jordanian journeys, events brought Charles briefly back to Kilmacurragh.

> I travelled to Ireland on the evening of Hitler's speech at Nurnberg, and before I left London it seemed generally agreed that there might be war

---

65. I am indebted to Dr Barra Boydell for making available this portion of his father's diary.

before the night was out.[66] It does seem that a war is possible before the month is out, though probably not afterwards. If such an event were to take place, I should most certainly endeavour to go to Palestine to you. My actual plans in such event are so much confused in my mind that I do not feel I could sort them out without you, and I should wish to be out of England at the time, since in England the only two moral alternatives are the front or the concentration camp. Budina, although he has told me that he was not naturalized, does not seem at all worried by the idea as far as Kilmacurragh is concerned, because he says that nothing in the world would make him fight, and that he will carry quite all right the Kilmacurra Park Hotel on.

(Events would soon prove otherwise.) At Kilmacurragh Charles heard 'the wireless bulletins from England, Germany, France & Prague [in the last week of September], and although they seemed black enough there was a general optimism about the final outcome until the news of the Czechoslovak mobilization came through.'[67] Charles was anxious to secure his mother's return to Ireland, amid a certain sense of helplessness as the news seemed to change day-by-day. 'All my various thoughts and worries of this last fortnight have been most instructive. The world has been on the edge of war to settle a problem that has been left till too late. Apparently we may hope and trust that war has narrowly been averted but the danger of war has by no means been lessened.'[68]

During three weeks in England, he compiled his 120-page travelogue for his mother, and went to Worcester once more for the Three Choirs Festival. He was sorry that this meant having to miss the drama festival at the Abbey Theatre (which has since become renowned for, among other elements, Yeats's discussion of eugenics in connection with his play *Purgatory*). The Three Choirs Festival involved a music camp for fourteen people which Charles ran with Marcus Beresford and expected to continue successfully in future years, deriving great satisfaction from the fact that he had been one of its instigators, with one of his closest friends. 'So much of the beauty of the camp is Marcus' personality.'

66. Hitler's speech on 6 September 1938 was mainly concerned with cultural nationalism and the renaissance in German art having rejected the Jewish contribution to art, but it precipitated the 'Munich crisis' which was the catalyst for the war.

67. On 23 September the Czech government ordered troop mobilization, but Czechoslovakia capitulated on 30 September (the day Charles's letter was written), to Germany's demand for the ceding of the Sudetenland.

68. It was averted for the immediate future by the Munich Agreement of 29 September between Germany, Italy, France and Britain, permitting Germany's ultimatum to the Czech government regarding the Sudetenland.

He then spent a fortnight at Kilmacurragh, where, in order not to shock either the Taylors or his aunts, he shaved off a beard that he had recently grown, but retained the moustache. Farming had been disastrous: the deer park had been partly ploughed to plant vegetables, which had been eaten by rabbits, and the farm had made a loss of £500. Mrs Taylor regarded Budina's loss on the farm as a kindness, since it gave employment which would not otherwise have been available.

> At present he has a party of 70 here, and though it is rather surprising to see them in the woods, I felt very pleased to see them thronging the lawn and avenue field with football and laughter and looking so happy. It was good to see Kilmacurragh providing so much quiet happiness. He tells me that he has been receiving public praise from Alfie Byrne on how excellently he was running it, and Alfie came down himself quite often and knew it well.[69]

This publicity was a welcome antidote to what Charles considered 'spiteful' slanders of Budina emanating from his aunt Irene, who disapproved so strongly of Kilmacurragh having become an hotel.

Charles returned to Haifa briefly in October 1938. Leaving aside the question of war, Charles was sure that he did not want to return to England for work. 'Palestine certainly looks unhealthy', and 'I am still suffering from a bad attack of Wanderlust.' A job in the IPC was a possibility, but not an attractive one. 'I would rather not spend my life in a commercial firm'. He had in fact already left Cook's. A job 'doing something useful, a service to some community' had been one option; another was journalism: 'I know the ordinary journalist's job is lousy, but a journalist in foreign parts may quite easily lead to something, and especially if he is there already. I propose to go to see the *Guardian* when I am again in London.' But, in circumstances of which we know nothing, in mid-1938 Charles had established the Sir Arthur Downes Memorial Library in Haifa. It was a commemoration of a noted figure in the British public health service, who had died that year, aged eighty-six, in Haifa, where he had lived for many years.[70] The library, donated to the public by his widow, consisted of 1400 volumes of his own collection, housed in the British Sailors' Society premises at the Princess Royal Institute, and was opened a year after his death.

---

69. Alfie Byrne (1882–1956), at that time Lord Mayor of Dublin (1930–39) and previously an MP (1915–1918), TD (1922–28) and Senator (1928–31).

70. Sir Arthur Downes (1851–1938) was educated at Shrewsbury, University College London, Aberdeen and Cambridge, where he obtained the diploma in public health in 1877.

Even though its apparently philanthropic basis ('a service to some community' which Charles had sought) may have appealed, the scheme did not succeed, and shortly after the library's opening Charles had, presumably, resigned.

His visit home to Kilmacurragh had probably been spurred on by the question of whether there was a possible alternative lifestyle there for him. It is almost impossible to establish why Charles was so disheartened by his experiences in Palestine, but a letter to his mother some years later, reflecting on a period that had been unhappy for both of them, refers to his growing dissatisfaction with his work at Cook's, but also, after leaving Cook's, to 'my awareness of my false position'. This presumably refers to the attempt to set up the library, since Charles continued: 'I was trying to create what I believed would be an interesting and useful job out of extremely little, being aware that I would not be properly respected by the rest of the community until I had made a proper job of it.' But he also proposed that, with a tax rebate due because Isabel was not living at Grata Quies, he and she could spend the next year touring by car in the Near East. 'We might, when I return, go off for a day or two to Syria and try and see how it worked there, and then if that was successful do more.'

Thus, three months after Charles's Balkan holiday, he and his mother set out in his car, named 'Jane', for the long drive from Haifa to Petra *via* Jerusalem, Jericho and Amman. His record of the journey is an education in the tenuous political situation which continues to persist in the Middle East region. The route took them from Palestine into what was then known as Transjordan and is today the Kingdom of Jordan. It was also a British mandated territory, which had been an emirate since 1921, and would become a kingdom in 1946. Charles had been warned, firstly, that it would be dangerous to travel *via* Amman, and secondly that, by giving a lift to a member of the Transjordan military force, he might well be shot at on the road to Jericho. 'There had been very serious rioting in Amman that very day, and it was a very risky proceeding to go there. [We] had the idea of ringing up Amman. We tried. We asked the exchange how long a call would take to Amman and were told "Oh ages, probably at least three months". We were used to this kind of talk by now, and started happily.'

Having crossed into Transjordan, Charles gave a lift to an Arab policeman who insisted on speaking Arabic even though Charles protested that he did not have the language.

> Every now and then the policeman would say 'shwai' at 20 m.p.h. on the straight, and 'shwai! shwai!' on a corner. I got used to this and was taking no notice, when he suddenly started a whole batch of shwais which I found

meant something, since I came on 20 yards of road that had previously been washed away. I eventually gathered the meaning of the shwais. One meant nothing, two meant an ordinary corner, three meant a bad corner. An unlimited stream meant a major disaster in the road.

This travel diary gives us plentiful indication of Charles's wry humour. Driving from Amman to Madeba, he noted:

It was said to be a five hour trip – distances are measured in Transjordan not in kilometres or miles but in hours: this is very good inasmuch as to say that it is 232 kms from Amman to Ma'an does not convey to the ordinary mortal that it is a journey of seven hours even in a V8; the snag is however that unless you ask a motorist how far a place is you may be told in camel-time, which is not so satisfactory, since apart from the straight conversion it is essential to know whether it is a commercial-vehicle camel or a riding camel, and if so whether at a walk or a trot.

The quality of the roads was extremely variable, and their direction was often problematic:

The following rules govern driving in Transjordan: 1) If there are not more than four different tracks, choose the newest one, or if there are no indications of this, the least used. 2) If there are more than four tracks, but not more than ten, go near and sometimes on the least used. 3) If there are more than ten tracks, strike out in open country, but remember that all thirty tracks may suddenly turn left when you can't see them. 4) When crossing wadis find the largest track, the rest are impossible. 5) When going along wadis, follow the wheel tracks (usually one car's): he got through, you can. When the road has been 'made up' it is not so good, but on the other hand is not liable to crises, sudden wadis, fissures, bushes, boulders etc. When confronted by signposts, use the map and instinct since the signpost has probably been turned round since it was put up.

At some point, Charles transferred from 'Jane' to a horse – 'a lovely white horse called Serda' – and it seems probable that he had left his mother at Amman, since there is no further mention of her on the journey to Petra. At the end of his journey, Charles recorded that 'it was good to be in a land that no one seems to know much about', and certainly his two days spent at Petra were a revelation: the major excavations of the site would not take place for another twenty years, and the Bedouin still lived in many of the caves. Petra is approached through a narrow gorge, the Siq: 'the length, the narrowness, the height and the stillness with which our echoing voices contrasted were very awe-inspiring'. Of Petra, Charles wrote,

It is pleasant to look from bed round one's comfortable cave, see the mountains through the window and the chisel-mark 'decoration' on the walls, and the blackened ceiling, and wonder who and how was in the room before. A disadvantage for seeing Petra is its size: Pompeii, though large is compact, and one can get a good idea of its topography in a short time. Petra on the other hand extends down a number of long valleys, and up mountains, and the mountains being natural are so irregular that it is very difficult till the end of at least two days to get an adequate idea of the geography. A heavily Corinthian façade is dull, and pompous as such whether in Rome, Dresden or Regent St., but when cut out of living rock on gigantic dimensions in an immense mountain of fantastic shape and colour, it is a thing of beauty. There is a strange combination of mystery and lack of it ... The real attraction of Petra I think lies in its natural beauty, and the strangeness of the human structures imposed on this strange and beautiful rock, in its size and feeling of mystery, in the loneliness of the place, and therefore one's feeling that there may be untold things to find, and its strange sanctity which has endured.

Each evening, the visitors sat at the Bedouin camp fire.

Had one a Leica one could have made a very good photograph of these laughing brown faces lit up against the black of their cloaks and the dull red of the rock behind on which the shadow flickered ... They are extremely poor. They are quite different from the Beduin outside and elsewhere, although their faces are Arab types. They themselves believe that they were Jews who got left behind here during the wanderings of the Israelites through the desert, and never got to the promised land. They called themselves the Changed People.

Charles decided to go on to Akaba, on the short stretch of coastline on the gulf of that name, which is the only access to the sea of otherwise land-locked Jordan. At Akaba, the conversation turned to politics. One man

produced his only four words of English – 'English good, Jews ----'. General opinion seemed to be 'Why should the Jews come and make us fight our friend England[?]' Vote of confidence in England as a Mandatory power in general, rhetorical question asking whether some other power would have been better being answered that the French had behaved so badly towards Feisal [the king of Saudi Arabia] and that Italy would be far worse. Throughout the journey the names of Peake Pasha and Glubb Bey were always in people's mouths,[71] in a tone of intense approval and admiration as though they were

---

71. Frederick Peake (1886–1970) was commandant of the Arab Legion (an Arab internal constabulary in Transjordan) which he had helped to set up in 1921; the author of *Transjordan and Its Tribes* (1958), he retired in 1939 and was succeeded by

national heroes or gods. A crowning argument damning the French received wholehearted approval, that whereas in Beyrouth [Beirut] and Damascus there were brothels and in the streets prostitutes, under British rule in Palestine there were none except in Tel Aviv. A sweeping statement, but it went down very well. I suppose that where one may have many wives and one marries young, the prostitute is unnecessary and therefore more to be disapproved of. And so to a comfortable night's sleep.

But Charles's overall impression of life in Palestine was a semi-fictional account of the changing economic and social conditions of the Arabs, which he wrote during his early war days in Kilmacurragh, a 3000–word politically-oriented short story entitled 'New Wine', which Tony Reford encouraged him to publish. Gordon Harbord, the literary and theatrical agent, said it was 'delightfully written' but 'the trouble is that as it disparages England no magazine would entertain it at the moment. They all say, however, that after the war it should be a totally different matter.' He encouraged Charles to write something else, but Charles felt that 'as it was rather in the nature of an inspiration, I doubt if I shall be writing something else for a long time, even had I time for it. However, Bernard Shaw didn't begin till he was forty!' Charles felt that 'New Wine' was 'too good to be put away among relics of failure'. It was an Arab's view of the success of the Jewish settlements in Palestine and of covetable facilities such as cars, books, radio, theatre and cinema. Transported by economic necessity from countryside to town, the young Arab loses everything and his disillusion with the *forces majeures* of international affairs, the British occupation and the Jewish incursion, is complete: 'In the name of God: where is His Mercy, His Compassion?'[72] 'New Wine' was sufficiently well-considered for Peadar O'Donnell to publish it in 1943 in *The Bell*, the influential Irish cultural journal he started in October 1940, in the repressive days of censorship and the 'emergency'. It was, unfortunately, Charles's only sustained contribution to *The Bell*, a vehicle for analysis and commentary on Ireland's artistic and social condition. 'New Wine' was criticized as anti-semitic, and although Charles himself was not at all anti-semitic, his experience in Palestine had left him with a sympathy for the Arabs which could not be shaken. 'It seems that people are so full of the Jews that they won't consider any view of the Jews being out of place in *Palestine*, but will only think such views are anti-Semitism.

Sir John Glubb (1897–1986), who had previously served under him as a Brigadier; author of *The War in the Desert*, Glubb retired from the Arab Legion in 1956.

72. C. Acton, 'New Wine', *The Bell* 6/5 (August 1943), pp. 371–79.

Nobody is fonder of cows than I am, but I should be indignant at the idea of turning them loose in the vegetable garden.'

It is unclear how or when Charles returned to England, or how long he spent in England before reaching Kilmacurragh at the outbreak of war. But his mother remained in Haifa after his departure, before she, in her turn, made her way back to Grata Quies for the duration of the war. Charles's letters to his mother during the years when he was struggling at Kilmacurragh are among the most revealing, not only about their relationship, but also about Charles's views of his own self and his awakening consciousness of what it meant to live in Ireland.

ENDNOTE TO CHAPTER 5: CHARLES'S KNOWLEDGE OF THE BALFOUR DECLARATION

When I fortuitously shared, with some correspondents, Charles's conversation with Michael Weizmann regarding the origins of the Balfour Declaration, extreme doubt was expressed as to the veracity of the account. One referred me to David Fromkin's excellent *The Peace to End all Peace*, where the author says of Chaim Weizmann (p. 285) that 'although he did not know that the Allies were already making plans for the postwar Middle East [he] wanted to secure a commitment from Britain about Palestine while the war was still in progress. As a chemist, he made a significant contribution to the war effort by donating to the government his discovery of a process to extract acetone from maize – acetone being a vital ingredient in the manufacture of explosives.' To this, Fromkin added a footnote: 'Years after the war, Lloyd George – in writing his memoirs – invented the story that he had given the Balfour Declaration in gratitude for Weizmann's invention. Weizmann's important invention was real, but Lloyd Gorge's story was a work of fiction.' Meanwhile Robert Fisk (*The Great War for Civilization* p. 449) states that in his memoirs 'Lloyd George makes scarcely any reference to the Balfour Declaration – and then only to suggest that it was a gesture made to reward the prominent Zionist Chaim Weizmann for his scientific work on acetone.'

The objections raised by my correspondents became somewhat bizarre, one of them suggesting that Charles himself may have invented the story: 'there is no reason to believe that Weizmann's son ever uttered such patently untrue nonsense'; another asserted that, if true, Weizmann's action was anti-semitic, and that if I included Charles's account in this book 'without pointing out that it has no basis in fact then he [Pine] is perpetuating an anti-Semitic smear'.

How the President of the British Zionist Federation (as Weizmann became in February 1917) could be accused of anti-Semitism is unfathomable, even though the alternative suggestion, that as a British civil servant Weizmann would have been acting treasonably by approaching the Germans with his invention, does merit consideration. It has also been suggested that I myself am acting in an anti-Semitic fashion by repeating the story. Since neither I, nor Charles Acton, harbour any anti-Semitic opinions, and since the purpose in relating the episode is to indicate a private (and possibly subliminal) view of the factors influencing the Balfour Declaration, which redounds to the credit of Chaim Weizmann, no anti-Semitic motive may be imputed to either myself or Charles.

Michael Weizmann was seventeen years old when he told his school friend of this episode, which had occurred while he was an infant. It is extremely unlikely that he would have invented it in order to impress his friends, or embellished a series of incidents which, at that time, remained almost completely secret: in my view, the story as related to Charles Acton was true insofar as Michael Weizmann was concerned as its narrator, and had most likely been told to him within the family. Charles, in making it public *via* our radio interviews, was doing nothing more nor less than adding a personal dimension to the origins of one of the most famous (and infamous) documents of the twentieth century, bringing it to life in a compelling way. To suggest that Charles Acton invented this story is absurd. My personal knowledge of my subject convinces me that he would never, under any circumstances, have uttered – let alone invented – such an untruth.

6. *Charles at Kilmacurragh, 1939–44*

Self-discovery

*C*harles officially became the owner of Kilmacurragh at the age of twenty-five, on 26 September 1939 – his mother having handed the property over to him by Deed of Gift – at the same time as he changed his name by deed poll from Ball-Acton to Acton.[1] He said of his heritage, 'I hope that during what period it remains to me, it will not bring the same misfortunes as to my predecessors.' He acknowledged to his mother that, in Palestine, 'I was getting badly on your nerves, but then I was in an unsettled and nervy state and am now my own self.' The new life at Kilmacurragh, whatever it might bring, would be a process of Charles finding his 'own self': it was a process of what he called 'pilgrimage'. The five years of this journey towards himself were to be crucial to Charles's understanding of his own life, of Kilmacurragh, of the world of the arts to which he knew he belonged, and of how and where he might find a place in it.

While there is little surviving correspondence from his time in Palestine, Charles was now pouring out his intimate thoughts to his mother.

> To see one's land that one's ancestors had made, rising once more from a ragged ruin into a piece of land one could be proud of. In spite of my trepida-tion I feel far more of a vocation than I have felt before. When I look around and see these great beautiful trees and all the ditches and drains, and then

---

1. He later wrote 'My surname was Ball-Acton but I subsequently castrated it'. The Deed Poll was executed on 13 September 1939.

go up the hill and look down on it all, I think of Thomas & William & young Thomas and how they planted and drained & ditched and made the land good and beautiful not so much for themselves as for me … And again as I look down from the hill I get smitten with the feeling that it is MINE & yet not so much mine as a trust to hand on, enriched if possible, to other human beings in distant times as in the 18th century they had it in trust & handed it on. Hopelessly sentimental!

He added 'I have no emotions whatsoever about the house.'

He had arrived at Kilmacurragh six days after the declaration of war. Some questions have been asked of those who left England at that time (the Irish pianist Charles Lynch was among them) whether they had genuinely left due to their pacifist beliefs, or simply in order to evade conscription. In Charles's case, there is no doubt as to his sincere views not only on pacifism, but also on what should happen at the end of the war, regardless of who won and who lost. He was a confirmed pacifist, with Richard Gregg's *Power of Non-Violence* (1934) as one of his 'gospels'.

Invasion of Ireland by either side was a possibility. Quoting Eliot's lines from *Murder in the Cathedral* – 'Death will only come when I am worthy, and if I am worthy there is no danger' – Charles added 'It seems to me that to be removed from the fear of or worry about death is a very great freedom, which enables one to live more completely.' On the other hand, 'before pain I feel a coward: I feel I should almost certainly reveal secrets under torture. Will I prove my soul when the time of trial comes? That is what I do not know, and it is my worry and my fear that I may not be able to live up to my principles. I am afraid of being afraid: knowing my own weaknesses.'

The meaning of war: totalitarianism, democracy and neutrality

In 1940 Charles was to write presciently of what would become the 'cold war' between democratic and totalitarian states that followed the Second World War: 'The question of individual nations retaining armaments seems a great difficulty. National sovereignty and national armaments breed ill-will, selfishness, hatred, distrust and militaristic patriotisms. A national armament is a bomb waiting for the fuse to be lit. No, national sovereignty must end: with it therefore, national armies, national customs barriers, and national foreign policies.' His prescience showed through again when he surmised that 'European union, federalism, socialism' would be seen quite differently by the British, the Germans or the Russians. 'Some day perhaps the articulate socialists will realise what the inarticulate know – that the first thing the peoples of the world want is food, shelter, security for his family and the congenial occupation of his waking hours: foreign affairs and political slogans are not half as interesting to the majority as the price of bread.'

Hugh's influence is clear in Charles's remark that 'the incorporation of half Europe with half Asia as one state would be for the tremendous advantage of the majority of people'. Charles foresaw the expansion of the USSR involving

> ten years or more of tyranny. On the asset side there will be the increase in material prosperity and happiness: on the liability side an extinction of freedom and liberty. Considering the present standard of living throughout Europe the majority of the population would be better off. And which is preferable *in the long run*, a decade of material improvement and moral tyranny with the prospect of permanently increased material and cultural prosperity, or a perpetuation of the present anarchy whose destructive effects we have been watching over Europe for the last thirty or more years, in which neither is realised?

Isabel and Charles had different emotions and perceptions about the war. Like many living in England at that time, she believed that it was a 'just' war and that Britain could rightly destroy German civilian lives, not least in retaliation for the destruction of English cities such as Coventry. Charles remonstrated with her: 'When you call upon the deity to bless the bombers, I hope you remember the thousands of innocent people that they will blot out. Whatever the Deity may know concerning the rights and wrongs of the war, it would seem incredible that he would find acceptable prayers for the destruction of 20,000 men women and children in Cologne.'

Charles, for his part, in addition to his pacifism, was apprehensive about the outcome of the war:

> But the worst part of it is the future. The sufferers in Coventry and the sufferers in Cologne will carry the bitterness and hate all their days and hand it on to their children. You know the bitterness and hatred that has been known in Ireland, and I can see here still the devastating results of that remembered hatred: the people have had the bitterness eat into their souls so that to this day they can see no good of any kind in England, and who, though they dislike Naziism, welcome that the country they still cannot help hating is suffering.

Two years later, in January 1943, with no prospect of victory on either side, he wrote: 'This present war is not a war between nations, between rival groups or specifically between Hitler and the rest: it is essentially the so far greatest crisis of an economic and political struggle between different ideas of the organization of the communities – a civil war between capitalism and socialism.' This was followed by a 15–page closely written and closely argued analysis of the development of European society and politics from the middle ages, the Renaissance, the French Revolution, the beginnings of Marxism, the First World War, and the establishment of the USSR.

On the international scene, the current political situation was by no means clear: Charles distrusted British government propaganda: 'I do not know what is lies and what is not. As far as the truth goes, on any contemporary matter, we shall certainly not know it till the war is over, if then.' Charles could be uncannily prescient at times and, at others, very mistaken about the future. He believed, for example, that the future lay in the land rather than in industry. 'Potentially some of the best land in the world, it has not yet been touched hardly' he said of Ireland, and Wicklow in particular. And he discounted the continuation of authoritarianism in Ireland on the grounds that in Spain Franco would 'fall with a somewhat ignominious crash' – Franco's regime would in fact continue for more than thirty years.

Running Kilmacurragh

Charles arrived at Kilmacurragh to discover that his lessee, Charles Budina, was experiencing mixed fortunes as far as business at the hotel was concerned: 'although the bus parties don't care who he is, the people with cars are no longer coming because he is a German ... He therefore is returning to Germany,[2] leaving the business in the hands of his accountant, a man called

2. On his return to Germany, Budina was told that he was not required in a war capacity, and returned to his old trade as a hairdresser in his home town of Kahla. Nevertheless he did subsequently serve as a soldier during the German occupation of Paris, according to his own statement in a broadcast from the Irish section of German radio on New Year's eve, 31 December 1941, which included greetings from Budina to his family in Ireland. According to information received by his wife in mid-1943, he was wounded by shrapnel in Paris, and was transferred to a department plan-ning postwar reconstruction in Russia. David O'Donoghue (*Hitler's Irish Voices*, p. 166) includes a photograph of Budina in military uniform, taken in wartime Berlin, where,

[Dermot or Diarmaid] O'Connor.' Budina left Ireland on 11 September.[3]

Some refugees from Hitler's Germany made the journey in the opposite direction, including a Herr Günther, a former Mayor of Dresden and a director of education in Saxony, who was now living in Ireland, earning a living as a teacher. Charles described Günther as 'entirely Gentile, socialist, anti-Nazi who was in Ireland as a refugee both on account of his own political opinions and for having assisted Jews to escape from Saxony into Czechoslovakia.' Günther was also pursuing a PhD in graphology, in a comparative study of the handwriting of the Irish, English and Germans; he spent Christmas 1939 at Kilmacurragh, when Charles lent him specimens of the handwriting of William and Caroline Acton, Uncle Tom and Janet, Charles's father and uncle and aunt Irene.

Budina had prophetically suggested that Charles, with an eye to taking over the hotel, should learn the business in collaboration with Dermot O'Connor, who would be responsible directly to Budina. It later transpired that Budina and O'Connor had ('owing to the present unfortunate state of affairs' as Budina's solicitor described the 'Emergency') executed a deed of sale whereby O'Connor bought the business (leased from the Actons) for a nominal £100 from Budina, who also gave O'Connor power of attorney. This deed of sale was to cause almost endless, and profound, legal confusion in later years. It was apparently on O'Connor's advice that Budina went back to Germany, leaving his wife and five children, and his sister-in-law, at Kilmacurragh; Charles thought that O'Connor had acted on humanitarian grounds, but, whatever the reason, Mrs Budina was to prove a severe irritant to both Charles and O'Connor in the next few years. The impression had been given that she was a good cook and caterer, which was to turn out to be untrue.

The essential factor binding Charles and Dermot O'Connor together was the need to ensure the continuing success of the business, but Charles was to become increasingly frustrated by O'Connor's prevarication and indecisiveness. 'I have formed the impression that he would require half eternity to make up his mind when he gets to the Pearly Gates whether to accept St Peter's invitation to come in.'

Mark Hull records (*Irish Secrets* p. 136), he was working in a propaganda department of the Wehrmacht. Budina returned to Ireland in May 1947, but as his family, from whom he was now estranged, was living with Alfonso Palčič, and as he could not re-establish himself at Kilmacurragh, he worked at the Grand Hotel, Crosshaven, at Ashford Castle, and the Kildare Street Club in Dublin, dying in early 1954.

3. See endnote to this chapter.

Charles's career as a music critic suggested to many that he was an unpractical man, but in fact, in addition to his interest in natural sciences, he acquired a great deal of practical experience as a farmer and hotelier, for example solving the sluggish water supply to Kilmacurragh (the 8000 gallon tank that had been installed by William Acton II) where the half-mile pipe had become clogged with mud 'where the cows do be thrampling'. Gardening was another area with a steep learning curve: he seems to have assumed that his family's connection with Glasnevin could be extended to cover the subject of vegetables: 'Any particular points I could of course ask Sir Frederick.' On the face of it, it seems preposterous that he would consider it appropriate to ask Moore's advice on the subject of vegetables, but Charles did in fact consult him in early 1940 about the vegetable garden, which had been neglected for the past seven years; Moore passed him on to one of his former pupils, Professor Sherrard at the Agricultural College at Glasnevin, who recommended a recently graduated pupil of his own to undertake an eight-month contract for the work, which would also involve training Charles. Instruction duly took place and Charles learned, among other skills, how to prune his 600 fruit trees. (Later he would win a prize at the RDS for apples grown at Stradbrook.)

In 1940 he recorded

> It is to be hoped that after this season Dermot will find he has sufficient money in hand to [hire] some more labour in the garden, for unless I can have three men there working whole time it is not going to be a success. My six experimental broad beans were doing beautifully until a pigeon had them for supper. The mushrooms are as it were resting. It seems a pity that there is nothing about a rhododendron that one can eat, since they grow and flourish without going wrong.

After Budina's departure, O'Connor took over the running of the hotel, working at his accountancy practice in Dublin during the week and coming to Kilmacurragh at the weekends. Charles kept an alert attention on a situation where he could advise but not insist: when O'Connor redecorated the house, Charles was alarmed at some of the colours chosen, but remarked that 'it shook me. However it is his word that goes.' Charles wrote of O'Connor that

> we are hardly in a position to question his suitability from a practical point of view: he is an old established chartered accountant and professor of accountancy at the National University. Budina has left him his entire interests, including the care of his wife and the education if necessary of his children; unless we know of something wrong with O'Connor which is legally

reasonable, we cannot refuse consent under the agreement [i.e. the power of attorney].

Charles was not only trying to make a success of the farm at Kilmacurragh, but was also taking a hand in the running of the hotel. Christmas 1939 was a busy one for him. Having played badminton in the afternoon, he and the domestic staff had to put out a chimney fire, before the arrival of the house guests and about twenty of the Taylor family for a dance in the ballroom, at which Charles, who considered himself a poor dancer, distinguished himself, taking the floor with Mrs Taylor of whom he said 'We were both incredibly bad, but she certainly enjoyed it immensely.' It was a throwback to the traditional Christmas hospitality to the estate tenants.

'My time has been very full indeed' he wrote to his mother in late 1940; 'there have been a tremendous lot of things to be done in the house, mendings, repairings and so forth: digging: once a week going up to town to bring down supplies, and of course on Sundays dishing out the grub, giving a hand in the bar etc.' Sundays was a favourite day for lunches and tea-dances at Kilmacurragh. Charles was very conscious that the dwindling trade would influence Budina (or O'Connor on his behalf) to relinquish his lease and thus leave Charles tenantless. 'People from Great Britain cannot come: people from the North have difficulty and petrol is very short up there indeed. Casuals again have less money to spend, fewer petrol coupons than they would like and petrol is 2/6 a gallon.' As he wryly observed, 'until the state of petrol next summer is known the future of Kilmacurragh is an enigma.'

Six months later, in mid-1941, he was telling his mother:

> I had a very busy time [at Easter] since not only was I a barmaid but also stoker (it was cold and we had the central heating on), electrician, odd jobs, part receptionist and of course a certain amount of chatting pleasantly to various people. They say, and rightly, never learn in your own hotel – well, I am not: I am learning as Dermot's servant in his. Also I am certainly in bits and pieces acquiring a lot of farming knowledge. So altogether for the immediate future of the next year or two, if Dermot finds himself unable to carry on, I think I could make a better effort than he and very possibly a successful effort, if I could manage to raise some capital.

His conviction that he could do things better than Budina had done, and better than O'Connor was doing, continued right through to the end.

The constant round of duties inside and out did not keep Charles away from his reading, however, and it is noticeable how much contemporary work he devoured. In 1940 he was reading Gerald Heard's *Pain Sex and Time: a new outlook on evolution* published the previous year: 'extremely stimulating'. Also Cyril Connolly's *Enemies of Promise* (1939), and two travel books, Georges Le Fevre's *Eastern Odyssey* (1935), and Peter Fleming's *News from Tartary* (1936). Humbert Wolfe's *Upward Anguish* (1938), Coulson's *Medieval Panorama* (1939), Machiavelli's *The Prince* and T.E. Lawrence's *Letters* (1939) were also on his bookshelf. But he reserved his greatest praise for F.R. Rolfe's *The Desire and Pursuit of the Whole* (1934): 'The character in it is an astonishing queer creature, and the whole thing is very very subjective but it is written with a dry clear style which used every word in its right place and every word the right and exact word.'

The following year he was reading J.R. Colville's *Fool's Pleasure: a leisurely journey down the Danube to the Black Sea, the Greek Islands and Dalmatia* (1935) and Joseph Swire's *Balkan Conspiracy* (1939) on the Macedonian revolutionary movement. He was delighted that his own observations while in Yugoslavia, regarding the relations between Serbs and Croats, were borne out by Swire. And he did not neglect his love of the cinema. When Disney produced *Bambi* in 1943, Charles had reservations, but his deep appreciation of the medium shines through his comments: 'Disney is sufficiently important to be appraised as an artist and not just as a piece of entertainment which does not affect the deeper senses. Consider it in terms of poetry. It is part of the interesting psychological problem of the intensity of the aesthetic sensation.'

A few weeks later Charles saw Disney's *Fantasia* and enjoyed the film, remarking that the audience was prepared to sit through two hours of first rate music. But

> It seemed to me a great pity that at the beginning the commentator actually encouraged a concert audience to make up pictures to abstract music ... For myself and other trained musicians that I have talked about it with, it is extremely difficult to concentrate properly on the music in the presence of extraneous ideas, however much attached they are to the music – the music tends to become a background, and one misses so much of it. [This would be his criterion when judging Seán Ó Riada's *Mise Éire*.] The greatest part of the film, I think, is the Rite of Spring by Stravinsky. I had heard the work a couple of times before, and though I had not been very much satisfied with it before I was very anxious to get to know it better, and see how it developed on closer acquaintance. I had before found it too much a matter of rhythmic sensuality: a powerful stirring of the more primitive emotions. But I found that Disney's treatment of it was really excellent. It made a realisation of the

music in terms of things much deeper and more artistic than the original ballet can have been.

Fifteen years later, reviewing a new print of the film for Radio Éireann, he recalled '*Fantasia* is really a ballet using purely cinematic means, rather than photographing human dancers. Surely this is not only one of the most enjoyable films ever made but a lasting work of art.

Charles also saw the film version of Synge's *Riders to the Sea*. 'I do not remember any film which moved me as much. I was a little frightened when it appeared, since Synge's play is so tremendous and I was afraid it might not be as good; but it was – all except Bartley who was played by an Englishman so that his English words seemed so out of place.'

Modern Ireland – a new society

Charles's letters from wartime Ireland are preoccupied not only with his determination to find a meaningful role for himself in 'the new Ireland' – and preferably one that involved a renewal of his ancestral home – but also with the emergence of modern Ireland, its political and economic stability, and of course with the way the war was developing, not least because of wartime shortages of petrol and foodstuffs which affected the business fortunes of Kilmacurragh Park Hotel.

Charles seems to have had quite a lively time in the hotel.

> I do do quite a lot of conversing with hotel visitors in the evening. It is interesting in many ways, hearing different outlooks. For with the exception of our own class, the visitors cover almost the whole social scale. The modern Ireland is in one sense extremely democratic ... Before the war [Charles is referring to the war of independence] the country was divisible into two classes, really. The English and the Irish. The former, as a ruling force, have disappeared, though they still have a little influence, and are present. The other lot, the Irish, therefore are now in a position of salting out into the social layers ...
> At the moment therefore income is the factor which decides social status. Thus an hotel visitor may have a father who is a labourer, and brother-in-law a small shop keeper, a sister in the sweep,[4] a cousin in the Dáil, and himself in the Civil Service at £500 a year, and another brother director of a factory.

4. The Irish Hospitals Sweepstakes were the principal source of legalized gambling in Ireland until the advent of the National Lottery, and employed a large – mainly female – workforce in its offices at Ballsbridge in Dublin.

Thus between the Anglo Irish and those who are still labourers (or regard themselves as such) there are no rigid social distinctions. It requires constant vigilance on my part to get the right attitude in conversation.

The clientele was indeed a cross-section of the new Irish society; this was exemplified by a full house in late September 1939 which included 'A Mr and Mrs Hall who own a glass bottle factory in Dublin, three typists from Belfast, two middle aged nondescripts from Dublin. None of this bunch can be said to be either county or intellectual, I'm afraid, but still.' In 1941, while advising his mother to come to Kilmacurragh, he cautioned: 'From the point of view of company, they are definitely *not* our sort and would at the least be boring and more likely displeasing & occasionally vulgar. Also, of course, we have no contacts with urban life nearer than a three mile walk to the bus at Deputy's Pass.'

When Dermot O'Connor was contemplating marrying the waitress/chambermaid who had worked previously for his family, Charles was apprehensive:

As far as social class goes, I don't pretend to be able to understand distinctions in this new Ireland. They very definitely exist of course, but at the same time they don't and it is very confusing. All I am reduced to is this fundamental fact that there's US & the rest, but of course the rest regard US as foreigners and so I just act to take everyone at his own valuation. If he does marry Molly & live here, a lot of the regular customers will cease coming since they will feel uncomfortable about treating as the Boss's wife the girl who was the maid.

The need not only to get on well with paying customers was paramount. Charles was at first ambivalent about the way the State was being run, but as the 'Emergency' went on, he warmed to the stability that emanated from de Valera's policy of measured neutrality. Thus in addition to the financial imperatives, and the broader political considerations, there was a sense in all Charles's thoughts about the status of his social class both before and after independence, and the question of whether the polarity of 'us' and 'them' could ever be resolved, especially when one of his deepest convictions related to the difference between the Protestant and the Catholic mindsets.

'County'

A visit from a near neighbour sparked off further feelings about the 'county' people.

I find the parochial insularity of people here so tiresome that I am in continual revolt against it mentally … Ireland may be divided into three different types of people … Catholics, whose church at present combines the worst features of medieval refusal to inquire and of Victorian prudery; church-going Protestants who tend in some way or other towards Irene-ishness;[5] and non-church-going Protestants like us … Of course most of the people coming to the hotel seem to be morons, though every now and then a mind does come. I think that mentally this is as good as any place in the world and better than most.

That he had mixed feelings about the Fianna Fáil government is evident in his faith in Erskine Childers, which may have been due to Childers' class and his proximity as a Wicklow neighbour. Certainly the cronyism on which Charles had commented was exacerbated by his feelings about Éamon de Valera himself:

Unfortunately Dev's position here is thought by many not to be so sound as it has been. Before he came into office he was the living symbol of 1916: now that he has been in office for some time [seven years, in 1939], and the millennium has not yet appeared, he is becoming more a human figure, and the defects, or rather the unsurmounted difficulties met with by his government are meeting much criticism. It appears that at present he is safe enough.[6]

Charles's opinions and hopes were indicative of his feeling that his place was in Ireland and within Irish society. When his mother expressed pro-British feelings which Charles thought to be uncritical, he responded:

I cannot understand how you being an Irish woman can be quite so lyrical over the perfections of the British Empire. As in almost everything there is good and bad and neither entirely overbalances the other. I merely cannot see why, because I have had a British education, speak English and have travelled with a British passport, that I should be expected to think, against the apparent evidence, that because a thing is British and the British say it is the best, it not merely is the best but is almost perfect.

In 1942 his aunt Eva (his mother's sister) wrote to him about 'the distressful state of Ireland in a very lofty tone. Why does she always speak as though

5. Irene held strong anti-Catholic views. On one occasion Charles told his mother 'It is extraordinary still to hear someone say "She's quite a nice woman even though she's a Roman Catholic". So strong is her Anti-RC-ism that she supports the Government in Spain because "it seems a little more Protestant than the other, although I am afraid there are many socialists there".'

6. The Fianna Fáil governments would continue in office until 1948.

she were *not* Irish?' Obviously he had replied in strong tones, for he told his mother 'I am sorry about stirring up Aunt Eva, I did not intend to stir her up: she wrote remarks disparaging our country and our government and I answered in what I thought was a friendly and mild tone of voice that it was not quite as she thought.' Eva apologized: 'My father was born in Ireland, in the North, so I suppose I am an Eirish citizen. But no thank you, I prefer to be British.' Eva had in fact signed the Ulster Covenant in 1912, pledging to keep Ulster within the United Kingdom, and in 1944 she did – too late, it seems – offer to invest £25,000 in the Kilmacurragh farm, following Charles's appeal to every member of his family.

But Charles was not blind to Irish mistakes, however much he wanted to be an Irishman. A year later, in 1943, he wrote:

> Ireland certainly is backward: Ireland seems to have been consistently 20 to 100 years behind the rest of Western Europe, and the present appearances are not much more hopeful: at present the country is apparently trying to combine early nineteenth century private capitalism with many of the more regrettable features of medieval ecclesiasticism. The largest danger in the future is fascism, but it is not immediate. There is hope that occasional efforts, such as the Creamery Movement, Town Planning, and a new Ralahine, will achieve something – in spite of the difficulty and discouragement the lower economic development and the underpopulated virgin character of the land do offer scope. No, compared with England, Ireland is now backward.

At the end of the year (1943) he would return to this topic:

> We are, as you say, a backwards people. It seems to me that as a nation we are, as it were, dreaming. To carry on the metaphor, it is as though in frustration about Partition and the shockingly low standard of living of the people, we were having a Freudian wish-fulfilment dream, that we are living in an entirely imaginary country with a convention and a censorship that prevents us waking up.

Declining fortunes

Politics also had a place in his business interests: in early June 1940 'there was a big party of the South Dublin "Cumann" of Fianna Fáil [at Kilmacurragh].[7] This was of course a very important party for us ... because after all the rumours

---

7. *Cumann*, strictly speaking meaning 'company, association, community', is colloquially used to denote a local branch of a political organization.

that have gone round of alleged connexions between Kilmacurra, Budina and Germany (which are obviously entirely untrue in fact), the presence here of three hundred organizing members of the Government party was excellent advertisement.'

Charles had spent the previous day marking out a Gaelic football pitch for the visitors, and after tea there was a Ceilidhe followed by a speech by Seán Lemass (Minister for Supplies, and a future Taoiseach). 300 had been expected, and 363 turned up, to consume the 250lbs of roast beef which had been prepared. The bar in the house was well patronized.

> 300 people on a hot day seem to be very thirsty, and so I spent nearly all the evening from about 4 till 8 (when the bar closes) therein. At 6.30 they had high tea. For high tea there was also due a party from Dublin of 70. It, without warning, turned up 105. So I went dashing off to Wicklow for some hams. Fortunately I met the butcher on the way and he gave me the key of his shop and his Frig and told me to take any ham I saw. I did, three of them, 25lbs. It was a tremendous dash, and as there is about a mile of the road this side of McCoys Cross that is straight I let the car have it – 80mph.

The following week, after the completion of a service kitchen beside the Pavilion, 400 customers were served.

Despite these large numbers, on 1st October 1940 Charles could write:

> The season is now over. It has unfortunately been a very very bad season …
> For one thing the absence of Bud [Budina] made a difference. His method seems to have been that by overfeeding his guests his peculiar personality did the rest, so that they overlooked the considerable shortcomings of the establishment as an hotel … Again as far as the parties were concerned he had a bad politicians' habit of promising perfection without providing it.

Most of the rising costs could not be passed on to the customer. By December 1940 the financial situation had deteriorated. 'It appears that another year like this last will certainly make it impossible for Dermot to carry on, in which case I should be holding the baby.' The continuing petrol shortage 'means the end of Kilmacurra as an hotel. Unless there is some sudden inrush of petrol, which is extremely improbable, there will be no parties, and very few house guests, so that we lapse now into a farm which takes p.g.s. ['paying guests']'

The petrol shortage had one interesting side-effect as far as Charles's and Brian Boydell's scientific interests were concerned. Not only was Brian Boydell already a notable musician, but, as a scientist, he had a practical bent. Charles's car, 'Jane', guzzled petrol (Carol remembers that 'it would pass everything on the road except a petrol pump', and consumed a gallon every twelve miles), and Brian, as a chemist, constructed a 'gas plant' – as Charles described it, a 'curious thing, consisting of drums and cones in front of her. Not a thing of beauty, but of great use.'

Romance?

When Brian Boydell became, in Charles's opinion, dangerously infatuated with a girl whom Charles considered inappropriate,[8] he expressed his view of his own likelihood of falling in love: 'I certainly hope that I shall never fall into a violent infatuation, mistaking it for enduring love. I regard it as a good sign that I have almost reached 26 without any kind of infatuation at all … when I do find the right girl my love will be a more enduring and real thing because it is not merely a blind passionate explosion.'

A few months later, this was put to the test when Charles was introduced by his artist friend, Tony Reford, to Dorothy Beattie from nearby Knocknamohill, whom he seems to have seriously considered marrying.[9] In early 1940 he told his mother:

> I find that I think I am somewhat in love … At least I think so, though however detached and impersonal my detached self is, there is an emotional self which is not so reasonable; and still being very young, at any rate emotionally, I have no emotional age or experience. My shyness of girls and my preference for things of the mind has had a disillusioning effect on most of them at closer range. By which I mean that at social functions and tea parties, I appeared attractive, but when they made my acquaintance and found firstly that I was inclined to talk highbrow, and secondly that I was green and innocent, they, as it were, departed, putting me down as a cissy and occasionally saying so to mutual acquaintances.

Charles had already mentioned Dorothy to his mother as someone whom he found 'as mentally and intellectually congenial as any man friend'. Later he would write:

> Should this love develop and prove itself permanent and more than boy and girl calf-love, as we are both aware it may be, the question of her family

8. Betty Kinmonth, the dedicatee of his Oboe Quintet (1940).

9. Dorothy Beattie's great-great-grandfather was a Richard Annesley, and thus possibly distantly related to Charles's grandmother Georgina.

may be difficult … It would *not* be a matter of marrying beneath me, as in 'Peer weds shopgirl', since she has the social requirements and education and culture, so that if one did not know that her uncle was Dick Jones of Spring Farm and her father was a tramp skipper one would not suspect it. On the other [hand] incidentally it is pretty unlikely that after this present war the county as such will exist any more.

Charles reassured his mother that 'what must influence our final decision is not how we shall enjoy our honeymoon, but how we should get on thirty years or so after our wedding'. And by the end of 1941 he was able to tell his mother 'As you quite obviously foresaw, Dorothy and I have some time ago decided that she and I were not made for each other. Which is all to the good.' Later (in 1947), Dorothy married Brian Boydell's first cousin, Derek, and she and her husband, and Charles and Carol, became firm friends, regularly dining at the Kildare Street Club (where Derek was honorary secretary). Even in 1943, when he was approaching his twenty-ninth birthday, Charles could write of his emotional, or sexual, immaturity, 'I have a queer kind of a feeling that, of course, when I'm grown up I'll marry and have a family, and all that, but that's all in the future when I'm grown up: and yet in other respects I feel an adult.'

Farming

When it came to the farm, Charles was anxious to ensure that everything was done according to a plan. He needed capital in order to ensure the farm as a working entity.

> This means £6000, which I consider the safe *minimum*. I am at present sounding out the Agricultural Credit Corporation [through Erskine Childers, whose relative, Robert Barton of Annamoe, was its director] and it is possible that they may be prepared to produce up to £2,000 on the title deeds (banks are useless). *IF* it goes through may I borrow £2,000 of your land bonds (with an option of another £1,000) at 4½%? I was wondering if it might be good to ask Eva to lend one or 2 thousand. I am aware of the undesirability of doing business with one's relatives but the whole thing would be presented to her as a cut and dried proposition at 4½ or 5% not asking for a gift or cadging, but as an investment on agreed terms. I gather they have more than they really know what to do with, and Eva has been taking a great interest in my agricultural letters, and I am definitely not asking for any more of her extremely generous assistance, but I do think I am a reasonable speculation.

In 1943 Charles did, in fact, approach every Acton relative of whom he was aware, stating the position regarding possible options for the future of the family home, and soliciting loans which would enable him to secure that future. 'I suggested that if they felt any sentimental attachment to the family seat, or did not wish it to pass out of the hands of the family it depended on them.' Unsurprisingly, very few made any positive response, the most notable exception being Tony Acton, who offered to sell £2,500-worth of stock if the project went ahead. (In the course of tracing his cousins, Charles discovered that one, Georgina Elizabeth, was Mother Superior of an order of Church of Ireland nuns in Dublin's Clyde Lane. Another, Stella Weaver, was the wife of the President of Trinity College, Oxford and an editor of the *Dictionary of National Biography*.)

In thinking about developing the farm, Charles had it in mind to give the farm hands a stake in the business by way of incentive. Given the overtaking of agriculture by industry and the services sector in later decades, his optimism was ill-founded.

> Although the war has produced difficulties, such as artificial manure, diffi-
> culty of getting any imported things, I take it that this country has got such
> a shock that it will not forget the industry in which ½ its population are
> engaged to such an extent again. As far as I can see my farming should start
> firmly founded on local and traditional practices unless you can see that the
> reason behind these practices is either wrong or out of date.

With the background of Thomas II's purchases at local fairs in the 1690s, Charles was following a well-established family tradition: 'I bought 3 heifers in October [1941] two Kerry's and one shorthorn ... They are all due to calve about March and then I shall get myself taught how to milk them, partly to know how to for its own sake, & partly to get to know them better. The short-horn is shy but the two Kerry's are very friendly and I go and stroke them every now & then.' Six months later, he was

> in the throes of calf-rearing. My Kerry (Clairinne) produced her calf on Palm
> Sunday; a nice little heifer calf, with a very dark red coat and a very pretty
> red and white face (her father was a Hereford). Then on Good Friday I was
> surprised to find that the Kerry-Friesian had calved (she was not expected till
> the following week) and here was a fine bull calf with a black Astrakhan coat
> like his mother and his father's white Hereford face. Yesterday afternoon the
> third heifer (shorthorn) calved, unexpectedly, out in the field. Much the best
> place for her in case there were any infection in the yard. He is a most frisky

bull calf. The mothers are all flourishing. Clairinne calved quite suddenly and a day earlier than expected, and you never saw such an expression of surprise and of having no idea what this queer thing at her feet was as she bore on her face. In fact she looked positively relieved when we picked the calf up and took it away.

The German connection

Since 1922, a process of 'reconstruction' of Irish society had been under way. In part this involved repairs to the extensive devastation caused in the war of independence and the civil war, in part a development of infrastructure, of which the Shannon (or Ardnacrusha) hydro-electric scheme, begun in 1925, was the most prominent, the contract for which was awarded to the German company Siemens-Schuckert.[10] Many German scientists, engineers and academics were recruited into crucial public positions as the country adopted industrial and agricultural initiatives and strengthened its cultural institutions. Many of these were associated with the *Auslandsorganisation* (AO) – ostensibly Germany's trade representatives but also a Nazi link with its citizens abroad, which has been described as 'a foreign office on its own'.[11] Most of them left Ireland on 11 September 1939. It would be an exaggeration to say that the execution of their functions in Ireland was infiltrated by Nazism, but their participation in the Nazist celebrations each Christmas identified them as, at the least, sympathizers with Hitler's Reich.

Budina himself appears not to have been a member of the Nazi party, but his pro-Hitler stance made him more than a marginal figure in pre-war German activity in Ireland. The 'German connection' with Kilmacurragh had both a direct, personal dimension – through Budina's role and the general question of German activity in Ireland during this period of neutrality. Charles had experienced Budina's inclination towards Nazism – he referred to Budina 'stuffing Hitler down our throats' – and observed visits to Kilmacurragh of the German envoy, Eduard Hempel and other German officials during the 'Emergency'.

---

10. Mixed reactions to the hydro-electric scheme were dramatized in Denis Johnston's 1931 play, *The Moon in the Yellow River*, where the construction of such a dam by a German company is threatened by IRA sabotage.

11. J.P.Duggan, *Herr Hempel*, p. 9; this biography is largely an expansion of Duggan's previous work, *Neutral Ireland and the Third Reich*.

Charles was, however, *not* aware that Budina had hosted the summer camp of the Hitler Youth in Ireland at Kilmacurragh in 1939.

Budina's wife shared the views of many Germans. As Charles summed it up: 'she did not see what was wrong with Hitler – and she lived through the terrible postwar period – but just as she did not want another Versailles Treaty imposed on Germany. The invasion of Holland shook her faith in Hitler, so that she does not want him to win, though she is very much afraid of what France and Churchill would do to Germany if they win.' On which Charles commented with remarkable foresight: 'Last time the French thought they had crippled Germany so that she could never rise again. Now that the war has really started the tide of hatred is rising, an allied victory will mean presumably the most barbarous treaty. The casualties of the peace may well be as great as those of the war.'

Established in 1933, the Hitler Youth had within two years incorporated 60 per cent of Germans over the age of ten.[12] The Irish branch, numbering perhaps as few as twelve, held a two-week summer camp from 1935 to 1938 at Hampton Hall, in Balbriggan, which was in German ownership. In 1939 the camp took place at Kilmacurragh. Gustav and Ingrid Mahr, children of Adolf Mahr (the head of the AO in Ireland and Director of the National Museum),[13] recorded that it involved night hikes, camp fires with sing-songs, cooking and swimming, and viewing Leni Riefenstahl's film of the 1936 Berlin Olympics. 'The leaders tried to imbibe [imbue?] us with the culture of Nazi Youth of the time. But it was pre-military training in a harmless fashion'.[14]

Kilmacurragh had also been the venue for a previous German tour, when in 1937 the training ship *Schleswig-Holstein* visited Dublin and Adolf Mahr took 300 of its crew to Glendalough, stopping for tea at Kilmacurragh, 'where they danced to music performed by the ship's orchestra'.[15] This was the ship which, on 1 September 1939, fired the first shots of the Second World War when it opened fire 'at near-point-blank range and zero elevation' on the Polish garrison island of Westenplatte, near Danzig/Gdansk.

Eduard Hempel was a completely different character to Mahr. Charles was very conscious of the personal and professional difficulties experienced by Hempel, which have since been discussed by historians of the 'Emergency' – for

12. Information from G. Mullins, *Dublin Nazi No. 1*, pp. 60–62.

13. See the endnote.

14. Mullins, *op. cit.*, p. 61.

15. *Ibid.*, pp. 71–2.

example David O'Donoghue and John P. Duggan.[16] In fact, Charles's knowledge of Budina, and his first-hand experience of Hempel and other Germans visiting Kilmacurragh, enabled him to formulate a viewpoint on Hempel's own ambivalence regarding Nazism, long before the relations of neutral Ireland and the Third Reich became the subject of such extensive research.

In conversation with me, Charles made the extremely valuable point that Hempel, as a career diplomat and, effectively, the ambassador of Nazi Germany, working to foreign minister Ribbentrop, had no alternative but to join the Nazi party. Hempel simply could not have been appointed as Hitler's and Ribbentrop's envoy to Ireland had he not been a member of the Nazi organization, yet for the first two years of his appointment he was dominated by the much more Nazi-oriented Mahr and, after Mahr's departure, by the First Secretary at the Legation, Henning Thomsen. But this did not automatically mean that Hempel was a Nazi sympathizer. (F.H. Boland, at that time assistant secretary at External Affairs, maintained that Hempel 'was never a Nazi'.)[17] If Hempel had been interrogated on the subject of his membership of the party, he would most likely have put forward the same justification as that offered by Adolf Mahr (when the latter was attempting after the war to regain his position at the National Museum): 'I do not and I cannot deny that I thought it my particular duty to join the party and that I honestly believed that it stood for the common good of all Europe. This was an error of judgement.'[18]

Charles maintained – as have subsequent historians – that Hempel's was an unenviable task, in putting forward Germany's wartime interests, not only because of his distaste for, and distrust of, those interests *per se*, but also (and perhaps more importantly) because in wooing de Valera away from neutrality,[19] he was in competition with his American and British counterparts. In correspondence with a writer who maintained that Hempel, as a Nazi, had held secret talks in County Wicklow with the IRA Charles, who vehemently contradicted such a claim, said 'Dr Hempel was, I am convinced, an old-fashioned, career civil service diplomat, caught on the terrible dilemma of his times.

16. O'Donoghue was, however, the only historian to interview Charles Acton personally (2 July 1992), for a book more about Irish people in Germany than about Germans in Ireland.

17. Duggan, *Herr Hempel*, p. 29.

18. Quoted in Mullins, *op. cit.*, p. 194.

19. De Valera held the portfolio of Minister for External Affairs in addition to being Taoiseach.

Loving his country but hating the regime that had taken control of it, he felt that he could do more good in the long run and mitigate the harm of the regime by remaining Minister and pursuing a course of utter correctness, than by resigning and thereby risking the Legation being run by a real Nazi.'

Hempel's wife, however, seems to have had a 'blind spot of "pop star" infatuation for Hitler, which she shared with the majority of German women of the period' who 'saw Hitler as the saviour of Germany. He had solved the unemployment problem, built roads (autobahn) and tamed an inflation which was destroying the family and society. He had given back self-respect to the Fatherland'[20] – an exact echo of what Charles had heard from Bertha von Gietl in Munich.

Neutrality

Hempel's position as the representative of Germany must be seen in the context of the Irish neutrality pragmatically managed by de Valera throughout the war, and so reluctantly admired by Charles. Charles had worked out the complexities of partition as a factor in de Valera's neutrality:

> As far as most of Ireland goes, the thing is not 'ignoring the wrongs of the past' but the wrongs of the present. If there had been an independent 32 county united Ireland in 1938 things might, I won't say would, have been different. But a very large section of Irish opinion feels that for free Ireland openly to have united itself with a government which is oppressing Irishmen in the Six Counties, and with which the nationalists of the Six Counties consider themselves almost or wholly at war would have been a shocking betrayal ... And though the oppression in the Six Counties is a negative affair of a denial of rights, and quite different from the positive oppression and brutality of Nazism, it remains a fact that a large number of people in Ireland cannot see any real difference of principle between Britain and the Six Counties and Germany and Czechoslovakia.

Thirty years later, he would write in *Feasta*

> It is customary to speak of our isolation during the war as a bad thing as something which cut us off from the mainstream of western thought. Contrariwise that isolation and neutrality came very close to making us a nation: it was out of that that our authors became Irish-centred rather than merely regional; that

---

20. Duggan, *Herr Hempel*, p. 224.

the 'Living Art' movement allowed painters to feel that they were not mere provincials; that gradually and slowly and painfully we have bred composers and performers who live and think and work in Ireland as Irishmen and not as people who escape to London or New York as soon as possible.[21]

Charles, as an Irishman, accepted the new state, but was not prepared to live in an inward-looking society; self-reflective, no doubt, but not blinkered, and the need for stimulation from all parts of the world and all creeds ran counter to Sinn Féin's 'Irish-Ireland' philosophy of self-sufficiency in affairs of the mind as well as of the body. While Charles acknowledged that Nazism was 'wrong', he also realized that the prosecution of the war by Britain, which inevitably involved deceit and evasion, was, if not reprehensible, certainly deplorable. In this he no doubt shared W.T. Cosgrave's view: 'Democracy may have as many sins to its credit and may be as faulty a form of government as an autocracy.'[22]

Visions and ambitions for Kilmacurragh

By 1940–41, Dermot O'Connor had already lost £2000 on the Kilmacurragh venture, and had no more capital to invest; he only hung on in the hope of recouping what he had lost so far. Charles, with no capital whatsoever to his credit, nevertheless thought that, given the borrowings he had already discussed with his mother, he could succeed where O'Connor had failed. He made his mother an offer (more of an impassioned plea) to come to Kilmacurragh as manageress:

> The labour involved for you would be mostly of a supervisory nature, giving hands here or there, but not tied to any routine job during normal kitchen working hours. It would be hard work at first [Isabel was sixty-five at the time], and always during the season when there might be up to 25 people staying at a time ... It is important of course to know sufficient about costing and catering ... But I would imagine that the diverse conditions under which your housekeeping has had to operate even in peace time must have made you pretty familiar with that sort of thing.

Charles's hopes were, however, based on wishful feeling. Quite apart from not wanting to be personally involved in the venture, his mother tried

---

21. As in the case of several other contributions to *Feasta* in the 1970s, this appeared in the journal in Irish, having been translated from Charles's original English.

22. Quoted in Wills, *That Neutral Island*, p. 131.

to make it clear that there was no capital available. Charles persisted. The key to his plan was a combination of genteel country-house hotel-cum-farm.

> What would be most attractive would be to have a large enough holding for the bulk of the *routine* work to be delegated and for one to be plan-ning, directing and organizing … For it seems quite plain to me that though farmers know more about *how* to farm than anyone else, they do not know best what kinds of farming and what innovations of modern technique the world is going to require of the land.'

If O'Connor's (or Budina's) tenancy survived until the expiry of the lease in 1944, 'I should have two years to make myself sufficiently cognizant of all farming to be able to do it.'

> In general, I remain convinced that Kilmacurra as an hotel, and Kilmacurra as a farm could pay well, though the difference between balancing out and making a good profit would, it seems obvious, depend on putting into it a good slice of money … since 8 bedrooms is not enough for an hotel. So anyway until 1944 or until the war is over, whichever is the earlier, things are in a state of chassis (as they say) and any year may see Dermot's collapse … All this may be castles in the air.

As he would write to her a year later, when still pleading his cause, 'Before this war you had the knack of making satiety out of nothing – Mrs Budina had the knack of making next to nothing out of lots.'

It almost seems as if Charles took his mother's acquiescence for granted, but he soon discovered that Isabel, despite wavering at first, would not counte-nance such a move. In fact, she attempted the reverse, by suggesting to Charles that he move to Bournemouth to live with her at Grata Quies. Isabel, for her part, had unpleasant memories of living at Kilmacurragh as a young widow, and was therefore equally reluctant to leave Bournemouth. Charles's attempts at reasoning with her were dismally unsuccessful: 'Certainly GQ slightly modi-fied would be a more convenient house than this. Although this could be [a] very lovely house it falls short in several matters.' Any accountant examining the cross-financing or -subsidizing of the two elements would have advised him that it would be a case of robbing Peter to pay Paul to pay Peter *ad infinitum* but Charles did not see it that way: he estimated that with an occupancy of seven people in the house year-round profit of £400 could be generated. The farm had 250 'useful' acres which would yield a profit of £6 per acre (£1500). From this total profit of £1900, overheads of £1000 had to be deducted, and income tax of £200, leaving £700 net 'on which you & I have to live'. However foolhardy and financially misguided Charles may have been, his dedication to the resuscitation of Kilmacurragh is impressive. Nevertheless, he did persist, even going so far as to plan a bedroom wing as an extension, worrying over how it might be done without disturbing the symmetry or the elevation of the existing house.

O'Connor's offer to buy

In October 1941 O'Connor offered to buy a half-share of the entire remaining estate for (on paper) £2000, to form a company to take over the unexpired portion of Budina's lease with an option to renew. The £2000 would represent Charles's share of the company capital. Although O'Connor considered £4000 to be too high a valuation for Kilmacurragh, Charles noted that he had no choice, because it was the stated optional purchase price in the lease.

'At first sight it seems a peculiar proposition', Charles noted, 'since he is offering me a half share in a losing business and at the same time wanting to acquire a half share in the ownership of the land for less than the agreement price and that not for real cash but for the half share of the losing business. In any other man I would be wondering about the honesty of his motives but fortunately Dermot is as honest as the day.'

O'Connor's offer had to be weighed against Charles's vision of the future, both of which appear to have been nearly, if not completely, bizarre in terms of lack of financial sense. After a further four months, in February 1942 O'Connor said that he could not reconcile Charles's plans with 'his [O'Connor's] responsibility (moral not legal) to Budina' – by which he presumably meant that he had an obligation, as attorney, to safeguard Budina's interests. But in a sudden change of direction, O'Connor then proposed to buy the freehold at an agreed figure (less than £4000).

> I asked him what he would then do: answer: that he 'did not want to grow old as a totter', since outdoor occupation had always been his hope. He would sell the office [his accountancy firm], put the proceeds into Kilmacurra, live there and run it. This of course is all very startling. I had no idea this last was in his mind at all. I felt like taking him gently by the hand and saying 'Now, now, my little man, you couldn't make a success of it' and so on. That however I couldn't, though I would have thought it crass folly for him to dispose of his *certain* income in his office and run what is not a *certainty*. Of course I can understand that he would think that if *I* could make a thing go he could.

Charles initially agreed on principle, expecting a maximum valuation of £3000.

> Now if I agree & sell for £3000 what do I do with this 'mess of potage'. Buy a farm? But I do not see myself as what is called a 'working farmer'. The ordinary farm has no room for a steward, and I am not *practically* skilled. Another country house and farm to carry out our intention? Then I would not have the local knowledge of place, neighbours and men to help (apart from the question of having to *buy* one's holding, and one's equipment all out of limited capital).

In fact the professional valuation was £3500–4000: In April 1942 Charles gave O'Connor a three-month ultimatum to make a decision, but in fact the matter would linger on, apparently indefinitely.

One necessity was to remove Mrs Budina from her post in the hotel and, ideally, from Kilmacurragh altogether.

> Bud used to buy as uneconomically as possible from Findlaters (the Dublin variety of Fortnum and Mason). But the biggest trouble of all is that Mrs Budina is hopeless ... We now know that Kilmacurra got its reputation for good food not on her cooking but on her sister-in-law's, who unfortunately drowned herself eighteen months ago:[23] we now understand why Mrs Budina's two sisters went back to Germany in disgust because of her cooking and housekeeping. In contrast to the normal thrifty German housewife she is unbelievably inefficient and uneconomical. Unfortunately last year when Bud left he did not explain the situation to her so that she understood it. She got the idea that being his wife she was the owner and that Dermot was merely looking after the financial side of it. Dermot for his part felt that the poor woman was sufficiently alone, and was not in a position to have news broken to her so soon after parting with her husband did not tell her that financially and legally and every way it was his business and that she and her children were here out of his kindness. The ludicrous part of it is that she herself dislikes the business thoroughly and only takes part because she thinks she ought to and because she thinks it is hers. The relations between her and me were very cordial and very correct until about May, when it seemed that she decided that I was on the premises and a man, and she therefore started becoming amorous. As gently as I could, and certainly without any discourtesy at all, I ignored her advances: I would not be all that of a fool even as an act of charity, apart from anything else. Since when she started a dislike which has grown to hatred for me – Hell hath no fury...

---

23. She was the wife of Charles Budina's brother, Kurt, who at the outbreak of war had returned to Germany with two of their four children.

During the period of these negotiations (1941–42), O'Connor had approached the German Legation, asking for assistance in the maintenance of Mrs Budina and her children. Herr Günther mentioned that Hempel had said he was surprised that O'Connor had supported them for so long. Frau Hempel advised him to send the Legation an ultimatum saying that his support for the Budinas would cease in three weeks' time. Charles wrote that O'Connor had been in contact with the first secretary of the Legation, Henning Thomsen, 'unpleasant, a crook'. O'Connor told him that the Budinas would have to be supported by Germany, as it was likely that the hotel would have to close. In reply, Thomsen said that O'Connor had no authority to close the hotel, as he was merely Budina's representative, with responsibility to maintain Mrs Budina. One of Dublin's most prominent solicitors, Arthur Cox, was engaged by the Legation, ostensibly acting on behalf of the Budinas (Charles very strongly disputed this), and said that the deed of sale into which Budina and O'Connor had entered was no more than a 'fictitious corollary' to the power of attorney. Thomsen stated that he had received instruction from Budina to the effect that he disapproved of the way O'Connor was managing the business, and advising that O'Connor should raise £4,000 in order to buy Charles's interest before disposing of the entire property – again, Charles doubted whether these instructions did in fact emanate from Budina himself, or, even if they did, that Budina would act in such a dishonourable way. He suspected that Thomsen was acting at the behest of Mrs Budina. Charles also thought he detected the hand of a Dublin hairdresser called Palčič 'who has been coming down every weekend for the last ten months, who behaves in the house as though he were her husband, or at least as though she were his mistress (which I don't think she is in spite of appearances) and who is an interfering old faggot anyway.' On which note, Charles decided to suspend any discussions with O'Connor until the situation was resolved. O'Connor did, in fact, close the hotel as a temporary measure at the end of the 1942 season, and Charles went to Dublin to stay with the Boydells.

Life with the Boydells

Brian Boydell had obtained the Mus.Bac. at TCD and was now working for his doctorate. 'Brian, after during the last year, writing one or two slight songs, which though technically better, were musically of a Wilfrid Sanderson type,[24]

---

24. Wilfrid Sanderson (1878–1935) was a church organist and conductor of amateur

is now engaged on a piece for oboe & piano,[25] in which he has returned to the manner of 'Cathleen the daughter of Houlihan' (the first of Boydell's works dedicated to Charles). This is going to be good, I think, since while he has removed many of the technical imperfections of his earlier period he has returned to his earlier manner, which has both feeling and character. Provided he continues to remember that technique is merely a necessary tool and that it is not by itself music the prospect looks good. When I first got to know him, he had never thought of anything but technique, whether in science or in piano playing – so he might then have become either a good player of Liszt and Mendelssohn or a good science don, whereas he has developed, through learning that technique by itself is not enough, into what I hope will be a very good composer. I am also conceited enough to think it was my doing, this awakening. But as his technique in composition improves, I must continue to see to it that he never lets it blind him.' Boydell, for his part, was not at all pleased with Charles's adoption of an almost proprietorial role as his mentor, and recorded that 'he took up an attitude of managing my life for me, with a strangely puritanical outlook which did not suit him. He seemed so satisfied with himself and proceeded to try and dictate to me all my doings.'[26] Nevertheless, the friendship did continue, and the close contact between Charles and Brian was of exceptional importance to Charles's development as a musical commentator.

Now it was Brian's turn to cause Charles some heart-searching in relation to romance.

> There is actually another problem for me: he has got infatuated with a girl, who while pleasant enough is definitely not good enough for him, and who is to boot by birth considerably inferior, though she does not shew it, and also a Catholic … Unfortunately she is not very strong in her church's faith, so that in many respects she agrees with or voices opinions which are far from Catholic, so that he cannot at present see the gulf that must fundamentally exist between their minds. As it is his first love & presumably pretty calfish, I hope it will break off of its own accord, but he is speaking seriously to me of marriage and the infatuation is nearly a year old. With the utmost tact and delicacy I am trying to throw in small occasional spanners, and I am thoroughly aware that I must be very quiet and unrushing.

---

operatic societies; he composed popular ballads such as 'Until', which sold a million copies.

25. The work does not appear in the official catalogue of Boydell's output.

26. I am obliged to Dr. Barra Boydell for this extract from his father's memoirs.

This is another example of Charles's unfortunate manner in 'minding' a friend where no such concern was either invited or required.

'If he cannot be kept out of purgatory, then let him at least go their [*sic*] with a chance of rising out of it, rather than staying there for good, or sinking into Hell. Though I have not been tactless and openly disapproved, I have shewn him that I do not yet approve, and he knows that I am worried, so that gradually it is probable that there is still something left of the enormous influence I used to have and that will gradually leaven his outlook.' At the beginning of 1940 there was some talk of Brian Boydell going to America for further study in composition, which Charles welcomed as a way of separating Brian from his infatuation.

Achill: 'my first visit to the Wesht'

Carraigeaċa Mora, Duaċ, Achill Island

On August 20th [1942] I got a wire from Brian saying 'Come immediately am all alone'. Brian has a cottage here for the two months of his holiday, and the other chap that was to be here with him failed to turn up. Achill is a wonderful place and we have had a few good days so far. It is certainly the real Wesht, even if there is no Irish spoken and the islanders are a people apart, and usually distant in their treatment of foreigners (in the Cornish sense). Fortunately Brian is by now taken for granted almost as one of themselves so that instead of being just treated as a foreigner, I am accepted as being under his wing.

Charles waited until he was back in Kilmacurragh before writing (between 24 September and 5 October) his 50–page chronicle of his two-week holiday on Achill for his mother, finishing it at 'Imaal', the Boydells' house in Rathfarnham. They stayed just outside Dooagh village in a cottage belonging to Stella Frost, whom Charles at that time described as a garden planner and 'most efficient dowser' with 'marked psychic powers'; she was also an accomplished artist who wrote on Mainie Jellett and Evie Hone.[27]

The islanders are very much a separate community, tending to regard even people from other parts of Mayo as foreigners, let alone strangers from the

27. Stella Frost (1890–1962) was born in Birmingham; she had a gardening school in Dublin for many years; exhibited at the Water Colour Society of Ireland, the RHA, and the Exhibition of Living Art. Editor of *A Tribute to Evie Hone and Mainie Jellett* (1957).

east. They may be divided into fishermen & shops and shepherds & others. It is only the first category we came across. They are delightful people: very kindhearted, and neighbourly and generous (probably in business dealings with each other they are as crooked as any others – though this may be too cynical) and have that attitude we used to meet among Arabs not connected with tourists of wanting to be helpful and kind without looking for or accepting any reward. It is very noticeable the natural equality with which one is treated, appearing to come from a real independence. On the one hand there is none of that unpleasant cap-touching smarminess and on the other none of that aggressive 'I'm as good as you, so there' rudeness that comes from an attempt on the part of people who are not independent but try to pretend (mostly to themselves) that they are.'

Charles had his first (unsuccessful) lesson in fishing from the shore, but once out in a currach (or 'corragh' as he spelt it) which he greatly admired for its efficiency as a vessel, he landed a five-pound bream and a dogfish, and on another day conger eels and pollock. 'A corragh is not the unsafe looking thing it appeared from "Man of Aran", but is in fact about the safest thing that floats'.[28] We went down to the rocks to get some sea water to boil the potatoes in – sea water is much better than freshwater and salt. It imparts a delicious taste to them.' Brian, who was an expert cook, provided a dinner of bream and chips, as he did the following day when five mackerel were caught and served to the three Gunning sisters who worked at Major Freyer's boarding house: fried herring, fried mackerel and chips, with sherry, followed by roast lamb, roast potatoes and mint sauce accompanied by a Beaune 1934 – bought from Thea Blackham in Keel – and lastly tinned peaches ('very rare'), soda bread, jam and tea. 'A most enjoyable and extravagant dinner but one is entitled to bust once in a war.'

He and Brian visited Major Freyer (father of their Cambridge contemporary Grattan Freyer) at Corriemore House – 'a peculiar character, an ardent nationalist … It is quite clear from his conversation that he was only a war major, and it is most paradoxical that a socialist, a pacifist and a gentleman should insist on retaining a temporary rank.' Charles was to cross swords with Grattan Freyer many years later on the publication of Freyer's collection of essays on Seán Ó Riada, but at this time he recalled that at Cambridge the son had been 'an ardent Republican almost with New-IRA proclivities' who had nevertheless had difficulty in obtaining an Irish passport due to not having

---

28. *Man of Aran* (1934) directed by Robert Flaherty was a highly stylized film documentary of life on the Aran islands.

spent sufficient time in Ireland.[29] The 'Major' was 'under the impression that he kept a sort of hotel'. 'If one goes and stays there one is there more or less on sufferance, unless the Major regards one as a friend. The Major gets up at 1pm, has lunch at 4pm: dinner at 10.30pm and goes to bed at 4.30am, and likes his visitors to do so too. One is expected also to folk-dance – not as you may suppose Ceilidhe dancing or reels on a half door; but English folk-dancing.'

Brian had warned Charles on no account to mention literature, and in particular poetry, as the Major would then read out all his own poetry, which was 'trite doggerel'.

> Finding the subject turning to folk-dancing, we got in first and taught the Major our Jugoslavian Colo. Then the three Jewish visitors, the Major and Bridie Gunning did a Northumberland sword dance. Whenever I have seen members of the English Folkdance Society folk-dancing, it has always been arty-crafty young women with steelrimmed glasses, straight mouse-coloured hair and buns; and I had always taken a view that on a village green Morris dancing &c. may have been great fun and so forth, but as a thing to revive and do in rooms & things it was pretty daft.

Charles could already see the inevitable commercialization of the West:

> within 9 or 10 years after the war, I am afraid that the tourist trade may have destroyed much of it. There are already portents of doom on the part of one or two who have discovered the fun, power, prestige or what you will to be got from tourists by setting themselves up to act the noble, cultivated, cultured, rude islander, the culture of Ireland, folk-civilization and so forth.

Brian had just completed a work for orchestra, 'so we spent the evening copying parts, a slow job, and talking.'

> This new work is a long way the best that he has written yet: I have of course only heard it on the piano, and, even were it possible to put all the notes onto the piano, one can only get a very small idea of an orchestral work. It is a work that has a complete unity in itself, with nothing that is loose or unnecessary and has a tremendously moving effect on me. Melancholy and desolate: it is strange that most of his work seems to have this quality of desolation: Zeitgeist, or else the phenomenon noticed by John B Yeats that artists

---

29. Charles considered Grattan Freyer during their Cambridge years as 'odd, very "advanced", very left, in literature, politics, art and all, but principally for the sake of being left and advanced', characteristics which he noted among many others, especially products of Gresham's School: 'the results are either dim drips or very eccentric geniuses'.

often present in the works a personality the opposite of that that appears to the world and to themselves. An amateur orchestra in Dublin is starting to rehearse it for performance in January, and it is hoped that the wireless will do it sometime before or after that.[30]

They were joined by Brian's sister Yvonne, who had just gone up to St Hugh's College at Oxford to read music. She played the flute and the viola and was, according to Charles, already composing: 'she certainly has great musical ability.' Like Brian, she was also a visual artist: 'she is a most forceful person – all her thoughts, words and creations have a tremendous power and strength. Her clay models and her painting and drawing have this tremendous strength.' Also, 'Yvonne's arrival had one good effect on our household management; she wanted to wash up after every meal and did.'

One evening the threesome amused themselves by composing 'surrealoids'

poems in which each writes a line in turn; not true surrealism, which is purely automatic, but altering what first comes into one's head to make sound (certainly not sense). It is really a complicated form of 'consequences' and is amusing to the partakers. The result, which should be read with great importance and solemnity, turns out like this:

<u>Crankshafts of history</u> BB, YB, CA

Coughing crab-box maggotina in Honeymuck
Who shuffle mellifluously in tails of eternity
Involving throngs of nonchalant flab-frogs
Cause pain to Punjab Colonials…

Daft, I grant, but amusing to perpetrate.

To which, Charles added several of his own 'pieces of pseudo-Lewis Carroll gibberish', including 'Motet for three carrots' and 'Sonnet to the Gas Company'. He attributed these to his subconscious, and was surprised that the results had both rhyme and metre, of which he was incapable when attempting even doggerel while fully conscious. The composition of 'surrealoids' continued at the Boydells' house in Dublin in 1942–43 and, in addition to the Boydells, Charles and Thurloe Conolly, also saw the participation of Sean O'Faolain and several others.

---

30. This was Boydell's third work for orchestra, a tone poem, *Laïsh* (1942) first performed by the Dublin Orchestral Players (conducted by Havelock Nelson) in 1943. The first orchestral work by Boydell to be performed by the RÉSO ('the wireless') was *Magh Sleacht* op. 29 (1947).

Not all the 'Surrealoids' were quite so disjointed (even though that was one of the structural points of writing them), and one, 'Autumn Leaves' (also dated 1942), by Sean O'Faolain, whom Charles had met in Brian Boydell's company, has a flow and a beat that pushes against the demands (or lack of them) of the 'form', if such it can be called:

> Fine they fling and vacillate: leaves light
> lit. Soapbrown down. The thistle-flabbers.
> Coist. Shim. Soon. Simlake. Streak.
> Gray. Cool. Came. Thwack. Wrack crowds
> finnely when the amber awning crones.

They were also reading Wilenski's influential *Modern Movement in Art* (1927) which was at that stage in its sixth impression. For someone who would be active to a limited extent as a painter, Charles made what may appear to be a surprising admission: 'Originally I quite liked but was not particularly thrilled by pictures. It used to be that I liked the subjects more than the pictures. And a landscape was essentially a representation OF THE LANDSCAPE and seemed to be less exciting than the place had been, having a flatness, an unconnectedness or a secondhandness that other people's snapshots have.' He had admired the Turners in the National Gallery – 'these were *pictures* not representations of something I would rather see itself' – but at school his interest had been ignited by posters:

> here were designs which could be looked at for themselves. And thence I found Van Gogh, Paul Nash, John Nash[31] and found in them the same direct statement of a design: and arrangement of colour and forms that thrilled me. I was thus in the curious position of liking pictures for the abstract compositional quality and somewhat worried intellectually that what I was told was the major point of the picture did not have much effect on me.

---

31. John Nash (1893–1977), younger brother of Paul Nash, had been an official war artist from 1918, and taught at the Ruskin School in Oxford 1924–29 and at the Royal College of Art 1934–40. Although noted for his depictions of war, he was also a subtle painter of landscapes.

The end of Kilmacurragh

From Achill Charles wrote that 'developments are, I think, expected quite definitely at KmaK in the next fortnight, though by now that may seem anticlimactic'; he was right: three months later, at the end of 1942, he was still waiting for clarification: 'If Kilmacurra comes to me under favourable conditions, then I believe I shall be able to do something of good. If Kilmacurra does not come, I am thinking of trying to get a job in some sort of social service – not necessarily a paid job.' 'When it [the war] is over it seems to me possible that I and others like me who think that we have kept fairly clear heads among the rising floods of distortion hatred and lies may be able to be of use in a small way. After the last war, the Society of Friends [Quakers] 'felt impelled' to do some relief work in Germany, Syria & elsewhere.' Charles had already ascertained that the Quakers had a post-war plan as before, and was interested in participating.

> It is extraordinary how reasonable, beautiful and full of lovingkindness the Quaker fundamentals are, and they write of the Crucifixion, Sin, &c without any of that reward & punishment, profit and loss account attitude that makes C of I & RC so impossible. It is splendid the way in which the Quaker fundamentals fit in and integrate with science, arts & psychology without the conflicts that seem inevitable in the ossified dogmas of the other churches.

Later he would be less enamoured of what he came to call 'Quaker arrogance'. His major problem was

> if I could believe in the existence of God... then I feel I could probably go the whole way with the Friends, but so far for me the idea of God is unacceptable – not of course that I am an atheist, since it does not seem that the evidence is sufficiently clear for any reasonable person to maintain with certainty that there is no God. Some day I may come to accept God – certainly Irish Catholicism and Irish Protestantism are most unsuitable environments for any belief in a God.

Charles had in fact shied away from explaining to his closer relatives that he had no faith. His aunts were regularly asking him to lunch, preceded by church, on Sundays: 'apart from the fact that Sunday is usually inconvenient I *don't want* to go to church. I feel that they would be very grieved indeed if they were to hear from my own lips that I don't go to church.' He particularly disliked suburban parish churches: 'the ugliness, the half-heartedness, the tawdriness. Cathedrals, college chapels and at the other end of the scale Kilcandra are different. There feels to be something, even though not enough to make me believe, but the boredom of the parish church[!]'.

He also felt that he was growing away from his aunts in other ways:

> I am always afraid of shocking or offending them, especially Irene ... My not telling them that I don't believe in their religion is not fear of intimidation. It really makes no difference to *me* what they think of me ... But I have a very great liking and respect for Evelyn: she is so very obviously the best of them; and I would be very unwilling indeed to cause her any distress ... Irene of course I am sure disapproves of me fairly thoroughly, though tempering it with the comforting thought that I am her brother's son, and the head of the family. [32]

Irene especially bemoaned and criticized the fact that her family home had become an hotel, where strong liquor was sold.

> I had lunch last Saturday with Irene. I felt that as it was possible that as the freehold of Kilmacurragh might be changing hands it would be kind to her to go and talk to her about it ... She said she did not feel she could give any advice at all – she probably realised in truth that I was unlikely to give any weight to any advice she might produce – and generally made agreeing noises to everything I said. Very good lunch anyway.

But in 1942–3 there was still no hard-and-fast decision on Charles's part that he would have to dispose of Kilmacurragh – in fact, quite the opposite. Charles had offered O'Connor £2000 to buy out the lease and thus regain full control of the property, while O'Connor for his part was offering Charles £3000 to buy out the freehold. Ironically, both had the same idea, of operating farm-cum-hotel as a going concern, and each was convinced that he could do so better than the other.

Knowing that in any case he would not be involved in the management of Kilmacurragh until either O'Connor's lease came to an end or he bought the freehold, Charles occupied himself with finding a job. 'I am going to try to get something which is both congenial and in accordance with my ideals.' He had in fact been offered two positions: as a works chemist, which he considered uncongenial, and as a charcoal burner at a salary of four pounds per week – 'a job with light hours and plenty of spare time, the salary being purely for somebody sufficiently trustworthy'. The idea he had entertained previously, of some form of social work, was now out of the question as he had discovered that it

32. Irene left her estate to Charles Wynne (son of her sister Evelyn) because Charles Acton was, in her opinion, 'not religious' (source: Carol Acton).

would almost inevitably have a 'religious tinge', which was unacceptable. In the meantime he had four calvings to supervise.

There was also the question of Isabel moving to Dublin, which Charles had advocated in a restrained fashion, not wishing to alert his mother to his very real anxiety about her vulnerability on the English south coast. In June 1940 he had written 'You are actually rather safer [in Bournemouth] than you were in Palestine. It is unlikely that any attack would be made on the district between the Square and Parkstone as such ... The chances of your sustaining any injury are enormously more remote where you are than in Haifa.' Now, however, he was anxious that, once the future of Kilmacurragh was resolved, he should see his mother settled in an apartment near to Dublin city. 'My own feelings are very definitely that I want you with me', but he also had to acknowledge that, when they had lived together at Haifa, 'I was horribly cantankerous and disagreeable', and he no doubt feared that that situation might recur if they were to live in close proximity, as indeed it would when they lived in the same house in Dublin after his marriage to Carol.

As the moment of decision drew nearer, Charles's indecision became more acute: 'I feel that my situation is analogous to being adrift on an engine-less steamer.' As neither O'Connor nor Charles wanted to buy out the other, O'Connor now threw in another factor, namely a reversion to his proposal of a partnership between himself and Charles, with O'Connor managing the hotel and Charles as a 'sleeping partner' and Charles running the farm with O'Connor as the sleeper. Charles considered this afresh, but decided that he did not want to work with O'Connor: 'I want to be king of my own dunghill.' And his vision continued to run away with him: 'If I were to be Kilmacurra, my ambition does not stop there. I visualize in my more romantic dreaming, the possibility of gradually getting into a position where I can increase the holding to include three or four hundred acres of adjacent land – Ballybeg, Ballygan-nonbeg, Kilmanogue, Carrigmore, whichever became available' – much of which had of course been in the family estate up to 1916:

and of gradually working up to doing something big and important in that part of the county. If you like, working up to playing a part in the organization of the land in that part of the world as important as the part played genera-tions ago by my ancestors who made the land, but in accordance with the ideas and ideals which should be in operation now. Castles in the air perhaps, but I do feel reluctant to shatter them. Going into Kilmacurra would be definitely committing myself to my final career, or at least, if not for life for at least ten or fifteen years.

Charles really did see himself as a kind of reincarnation of the previous Actons, embodying, rather than merely occupying, their accumulated creation. It was a profoundly Anglo-Irish sentiment, the subjunctive pointing to the ever-present question-mark over place and status, but it also had practical echoes; for example, of Elizabeth Bowen who said of her own family home 'I should, I thought, be able to maintain the place somehow. Had not others done so before me? But I was unable to.'[33] Thus in a sense the second war finished off the disastrous effects wrought on Kilmacurragh and its family by the first.

In June 1943 Charles seems to have made a definite decision to buy out O'Connor's interest for £3000 (of which £2500 would be financed by a mortgage).

> I have been in a state of a mixture of exaltation & excitement and also of cowardice. I broke the news to [Robert] Taylor, who took it calmly and smilingly and wished me luck … If I do make a success of it, my previous life will all have contributed. That I read science and learned the precision of thought of that, and yet did not get a degree which would have taken me to a scientist's job; that I was in Cook's, and not only studied many different sorts of human beings but also learnt a little about business organization; that Cooks took me to Palestine with all the 'broadening of the mind' and experiences of that; that I have taken an intelligent, if often somewhat superficial, interest in almost everything; that I have spent these last four years in the apparently unsatisfactory way I have; all these things I feel contribute to the possibility of my making a success, each in their different way. And of course the greatest thing of all is the influence of my very dear Mummie.

And then came the bombshell. In July 1943, O'Connor discovered that the deed of sale between himself and Budina was inferior in law to the power of attorney and its incumbent responsibilities. This meant that he could not sell to Charles on his own behalf, but only on behalf of Budina, and he was advised by his own solicitor that this could not happen before the following January. Charles, in the meantime, had dispensed with the long-standing services of the family solicitors, Messrs White, and approached Terence de Vere White, who had been articled to White and Meares: 'I have found a chap who I think will

---

33. E. Bowen, *Bowen's Court* p. 458. Cf. G. Lewis, *op. cit*, p.416, who says that by 1939 Edith Somerville 'must have been one of the very last Anglo-Irish to be in a financial position to hold onto family lands, and to have the fervent wish to do so'. But Somerville's attitude was very similar to Tom Acton's: according to her biographer (ibid., p. 362) she was running the farm 'simply for the pleasure of keeping it in the family and giving employment to men they liked and respected'.

be a very good solicitor for us. Terence White. I have met him as a friend of Brian's, and personally he seems excellent. About 30-odd, very pleasant with a brain, an appreciator of modern painting, intelligent though not experienced in music, a socialist, and I am convinced both honest and not stupid.' White was to go on to become a distinguished novelist and literary editor of *The Irish Times*. Now, he was of the opposite opinion, advising that O'Connor could go to court within a fortnight for a declaration that he was, in fact, the owner and had the right to sell, but this was disregarded by O'Connor. Not wishing to wait a further six months, Charles gave O'Connor yet another ultimatum: 'unless the transfer can be arranged by August 16th [that is, one further month] I am no more interested' – although he told his mother that he was in fact prepared to wait until November. To wait until January 1944, however, would mean that he could not begin farming according to his own plan until July, a delay of a whole year. He was prepared to renew O'Connor's lease from August 1944 for three or four years, but only to O'Connor personally, not to him as a representative of Budina or his wife. Charles was extremely apprehensive that Budina might be killed (news having been received that he had been sent to Russia) and that in that case his widow would attempt to gain control of the property.

At the same time, Charles was hoping, somewhat perversely, that O'Connor would be unable to proceed, even though the alternative would realize a lesser sum: the Land Commission was interested in purchasing the grounds (setting no value on the house itself) for the purpose of maintaining the arboretum, in which (according to a letter from Sir Frederick Moore) a daughter of Éamon de Valera had succeeded in interesting her father. This, however, would take at least a year to effect, even with the Commission working at top speed, and in the meantime O'Connor resolved his contractual problems. It would be another twenty years before the Land Commission again evinced interest in the site, and bought it from Dermot O'Connor.

In the middle of all the negotiations and examination of options, Charles (or maybe Isabel) realized that another source of finance was the family trust established after his grandfather's death. It had been worth £41,000 before the first war, had sunk to £36,000 in the early 1920s, and was now back up to approximately £39,000, mostly in government bonds and railway shares. How they can have overlooked the possibility of approaching the trustees to sell what was required to provide Charles with the necessary capital is unclear.

As the discussions continued to go round in meaningless circles, Charles felt apologetic: 'I am very sorry that I am still radiating indecision and confusion.

I feel firmly inside me, that whether it is to be Kilmacurra or not, I shall make my career in some agricultural way.' But once the ultimatum to O'Connor had expired, Charles resigned himself to the end of his visions for Kilmacurragh. Parting with his 'herd' – 'me few bits of cows' – would probably be as great a wrench as parting with the ancestral acres. Many wrote to express sadness at the end of the Acton presence at Kilmacurragh and especially at Charles's lack of success in keeping it going, Sir Frederick Moore particularly regretting the end of an era in which he had been involved since 1875. Charles's cousin Stella Weaver probably expressed Charles's situation best when she said that 'it seems a pity because you do take such a deep interest in farming, & you evidently love land & its ways, & the ways of crops & beasts & are at the same time intellectual in outlook; few men combine these.'

ENDNOTE TO CHAPTER 6: GERMANS IN IRELAND BEFORE 1939 AND THE KILMACURRAGH CONNECTION

The preferred head of the Nazi organization in Ireland (AO) had been Colonel Fritz Brase, who had been recruited to establish and be director of the Army School of Music in 1923, but he had been obliged by his employers to stand aside in favour of Adolf Mahr, recently promoted to the post of Director of the National Museum. The Chairman of Siemens-Schuckert in Ireland, Oswald Müller-Dubow, was deputy leader of the AO. Another German electrical company, AEG, was represented in Ireland by Karl Krause, who was also in the hierarchy of the AO, while Frederick Winckelman, a director of the Irish Glass Bottle company, was 'reputed to be Gauleiter-designate for Ireland' in the event of German occupation.[34] Helmut Clissmann was director of the German Academic Exchange programme, and a link with the German *Abwehr* (intelligence) organization through which links were established with subversive organizations such as the IRA; Clissmann had been openly accused by Peadar O'Donnell of being a German spy. Friedrich Herkner was professor of sculpture at the National College of Art; Heinrich (Harry) Greiner was an engineer who had set up the Solus lightbulb factory in Bray; Otto Reinhard was head of Forestry in the Department of Lands; Heinz Mecking was chief advisor to the Turf Development Board (precursor of Bord na Mona). Duggan puts the number of German professionals working in Ireland at approximately 120 out

---

34. J.P. Duggan, *Herr Hempel*, p. 66

of a total of 500 men, women and children, of whom a quarter (thirty) were members of the Nazi party.[35]

One of the first Germans subject to surveillance by the Irish intelligence services was a Celtic scholar, Hans Hartmann, who came to Ireland in 1937; he stayed for a time at Kilmacurragh, and worked with Mahr at the Museum. He was subsequently a frequent contributor to the *Irland-Redaktion* broadcasting service directed by Mahr from Berlin. He was one of a group of Germans who met socially at the German-owned Red Bank restaurant in Dublin's D'Olier Street, and included Clissmann, now known to have been an active member of the pro-Nazi Germans in Dublin, and who subsequently became a prominent businessman in post-war Ireland. Another Celtic scholar (responsible for recruiting Hartmann to the *Irland-Redaktion*) was Ludwig Mülhausen, who had visited Ireland frequently and extensively in the 1920s and 30s. He had been a member of the Nazi party since 1932, and it was clear to León Ó Broin (later a very eminent and influential Irish civil servant) with whom he shared a room in 1937 in Teelin, County Donegal, that Mülhausen was an extreme Hitlerite.

The chief figure in the German colony was Adolf Mahr, who was, according to his self-description, 'Dublin Nazi No. 1'. Mahr is said to have been anti-Semitic but this was not characteristic of all the Germans or even all the Nazis in Dublin. His son conceded that he might be regarded as a 'desk top war criminal' but was not actively involved in the persecution of the Jews.[36] Moreover, there is evidence from at least one Jewish refugee from Germany that 'although he was fully aware of my Jewish race, he gave me his unreserved assistance and throughout all the following years showed me much kindness and friendship... Dr Mahr had nothing to do with the racial and national hatred, the criminal and inhuman sides of National Socialism'.[37] A striking fact is that the wife of Robert Stumpf (radiologist at Baggot St Hospital and a member of the Nazi party) was Jewish, and even more striking is that the Schubert family, owners of the Red Bank restaurant, had adopted a Jewish child. In July 1938 Mahr was obliged by

---

35. Duggan, *Neutral Ireland*, p. 58; John Carroll (*Ireland in the War Years*) puts the total of the German colony at 400. Mark M. Hull (*Irish Secrets*, p. 29) states that 'by 1939 there were fewer than 200 known German aliens in Ireland, but their numerical inferiority camouflaged both their political impact and their potential utility in information-gathering'; he states (p. 30) that there were approximately thirty members of the Nazi party in Ireland.

36. Cf. G. Mullins, *Dublin Nazi No. 1*, p. 185.

37. *Ibid.*

the Irish government to resign as chief of the AO in Ireland, but it appears that he in fact continued in his self-described role as 'Dublin Nazi No. 1', nor did he resign his membership of the party itself. In February 1939 the Department of External Affairs made it clear that it was untenable for any Irish civil servant – let alone one as eminent as the director of the National Museum – to belong to a political party. Mahr was on holiday in Germany when war broke out, and was unable to return; instead, he took over the *Irland-Redaktion* (Germany's radio station broadcasting to Ireland), where he was joined, among others, by Hans Hartmann and the Irish novelist Francis Stuart.

A curious coincidence of factors ambient to Kilmacurragh and Wicklow came in what seems to have been a query from Isabel to Charles on the subject of Francis Stuart's broadcasts from Berlin on *Irland-Redaktion*: she was presumably enquiring about his connection with County Wicklow, since Charles's reply stated: 'The only Stuart with a castle in Co. Wicklow is a Professor Stuart of Laragh Castle (I don't know the place but "castle" in Ireland often doesn't [mean] much beyond 19th century battlements). I never heard of a poultry farm there, though Barton has (or had) a very big one next door at Annamoe. This Stuart is a professor at Berlin University. His wife is an illegitimate daughter of Maud Gonne MacBride (before she had met MacBride) and a short time back was accused and acquitted of various offences against the state.' In fact, Eduard Hempel, the German Minister, had been friendly with Francis and Iseult Stuart, to whom Charles refers, and had visited them at Laragh, where they did indeed attempt to breed chickens. Stuart had given his address to Hermann Görtz, probably the most notable German spy to arrive in Ireland during the war, and Görtz had been sheltered by Iseult, resulting in her trial and acquittal in the Special Criminal Court in 1940.

John P. Duggan, the most recent biographer of Eduard Hempel, the German Minister in Ireland, has described Hempel as 'a conservative career diplomat' whom 'it is not easy… to pigeon-hole'.[38] His

> 'on the one hand and on the other' style of reporting exasperated, and to some extent, frustrated officials in Berlin… His pedantry, penchant for protocol, conventional correctness and 'keeping himself covered' were crucial factors in enabling de Valera to successfully steer his policy of Neutrality 'with a certain consideration' for a disbelieving, disgruntled and at times, desperate Britain… Being seen to be correct was a task for which Hempel's temperament and training were suited. De Valera pronounced him to have been 'invariably correct'.

---

38. Duggan, *Herr Hempel*, p. xi.

Duggan in fact records that 'Dublin conveyed diplomatically in 1937 they did not want a Nazi as the German representative in Dublin and got Hempel instead'. Nevertheless, Hempel was obliged, on paper at least, to subscribe to the National Socialist *credo*. His muted conduct was in marked contrast to the open Nazism of Mahr.[39]

---

39. Cf. also David O'Donoghue, 'The Nazis in Irish Universities', *History Ireland* September/October 2007.

7. 'An Intelligent Citizen': 1944–1955

Transitus

Between selling Kilmacurragh in 1944 and becoming music critic of *The Irish Times* in 1955, Charles led a life of parallel narratives. On one hand, he continued to develop his intellectual and artistic awareness and to encounter the cultural realities of the new Ireland, especially in the company of Brian Boydell and another Cambridge contemporary, the English artist Anthony Reford; this would hone his aesthetic sensibility and equip him for his eventual career. On another, his – by now – characteristic indecision about earning an income in a suitable employment took him through a variety of potential occupations which could hardly have been more different: working on a history of the Ralahine commune (1944–5), charcoal manufacture (1944–46), trying to start a weekly newsletter for Irish people living abroad (1946–47), market gardening (1947–50), travelling on behalf of the *Encyclopaedia Britannica* (1951–53), and selling equipment for 'tripod harvesting' (1953–55). At the same time, he was also helping to establish the Dublin Orchestral Players, running a series of concerts with his friend John Miley, becoming a founder-member of the Music Association of Ireland, being elected to the board of the Royal Irish Academy of Music, and starting to broadcast on Radio Éireann with some frequency. Underpinning all of these activities and preoccupations were two key factors: a persistent anxiety about the future care of Kilmacurragh, and meeting – and in 1951 marrying – Carol Little.

Although this 'interlude' as we may call it may seem an empty space in Charles's life, its significance as what today would be called a 'learning curve' cannot be exaggerated. In one sense he was, no doubt unconsciously, finding his way through these less than suitable occupations, trying out his personal affinity – or lack of it – with their demands, but, without doubt, moving, as the poet Lawrence Durrell put it, 'through many negatives to what I am'.

In another sense, which we can call the 'spiritual', Charles was approaching an understanding of what he needed in order to *be* someone in the world of the arts, of politics, of Irish society, both as someone versed in the arts and as a commentator on their place in society. This was a further step on what Dorothy Beattie had called his 'pilgrimage'. His experience of music, the visual arts, and the theatre in the 1940s and early 50s was not fortuitous or tangential to the 'real' Charles: it was a plastic and extremely formative immersion, and eventually a revelation to him of what the world was about, and of his place in it. The Dublin Gate Theatre, the White Stag Group, the companionship with Boydell and Reford, with, previously, the Cambridge theatres, the Three Choirs Festival, the operas and art galleries of Munich, all came together like a *mise-en-scène* of his own life.

In employing as the title of this chapter Charles's own description of what he wanted to become, I hope to show that he wished to become not merely a 'useful' citizen by virtue of his new-found intelligence (which was part of his revelation of and to himself) but also a person whose mind and soul were at one with each other and with the world. A letter to Dorothy Beattie provides us with a vital understanding of how Charles saw the earlier part of this crucial experience, while one from Anthony Reford speaks volumes about his spiritual path towards self-fulfilment. Charles told Dorothy, at the time that their relationship was coming to an end, that he had remarked to a thespian friend at Cambridge that 'though we had known each other a longish time, he carried such a thick mask, and lived behind such enormous and impenetrable defences, that I knew as little about his reality as if I hadn't ever met him; to which he answered that he found me also quite incomprehensible, and hadn't the foggiest idea what was the real me.' Charles continued, still, we might think, somewhat bewildered, 'This surprised me immensely since I was up till then and also ever after under the impression that I was an open book for anyone to read, and that being content with what I was I had no need for masks, shells, defences and so forth, and lived on my surface, as it were.' In this explanation, which was deeply linked to his feelings for Dorothy, we can see Charles coming to realize that the complexity and the subcutaneous (or even subconscious) nature of his life was a terrain through which this 'pilgrimage' would take him. If the Cambridge theatre had taught him nothing else, it had imbued in him a knowledge and experience of the layers of meaning and of behaviour that are involved in the creative process and in the living of life.

This interlude between the dramatic acts of life at Kilmacurragh and life at *The Irish Times* must also be seen against the background of the ending of the war, the passing of the Republic of Ireland Act 1948 by the British parliament and the strategic withdrawal of Ireland from the Commonwealth in the creation of the republic. By the time that Éamon de Valera made his much-quoted speech on St. Patrick's Day, 1943, Ireland had already moved considerably from the idyllic freedom and self-sufficiency envisaged during the war of independence, which was to be achieved largely through the redistribution of landholdings such as the Actons'. [1] Central to these political events, as far as the remaining Anglo-Irish were concerned, was the question of whether they any longer had a part to play in the economy – and particularly the incipient industrialization – of Ireland. Everything Charles did after 1939 was an attempt to live by the precepts of Irish independence.

Charles may have listened intently to political gossip and conjecture during his years in the bar at Kilmacurragh, but he was never as sure-footed on political outcomes as he might have wished. In 1946 he told his friend Robert McKeever that 'in spite of the mess, there seems no alternative government: I cannot imagine Fine Gale [*sic*] any better, if they were able to win an election. Clann na Talmhan[2] are fizzling out completely.' In fact, Clann na Talmhan, formed in 1938, was to participate in the next government with Fine Gael, Labour and Clann na Poblachta, in 1948, thus ending sixteen years of domination of the political landscape by de Valera and Fianna Fáil. This was to be a mixed blessing as far as cultural life was concerned, since it saw the departure from office of

---

1. Most critics have mis-read de Valera's speech. He did *not* assert that he envisaged, in 1943, 'a land whose countryside would be bright with cosy homesteads… joyous with the sounds of industry, with the romping of sturdy children…' He in fact said that this had been 'the land we *dreamed* of' – that the rural idyll had certainly been a much wished-for realm of existence but that it was no longer practicable or viable: his own policy of neutrality had inhibited that former dream, by impoverishing the countryside and preventing the growth of industry. His speech was one of regret that the idyll had not been achieved, and that another way had to be found for Ireland to assert itself in the modern world.

2. 'Party of the Land' or Farmers' Party.

P.J. Little (who had done so much to foster the creation of the Radio Éireann symphony and light orchestras at the end of 1947), and the establishment by the incoming coalition government of the Arts Council in 1951 (just before, in its turn, it went out of office); but there was a distinctly negative attitude towards classical music until the return to power of Fianna Fáil and the appointment of Erskine Childers as minister responsible for broadcasting.[3]

The atmosphere remained one of cultural, as well as political and economic, uncertainty and stagnation for the rest of the 1940s and much of the 1950s. The one constant in Charles's otherwise rapidly changing universe was his immersion in the cultural *milieu* of Dublin, in which all his previous pursuits and passions seemed to merge. In Brian Boydell's company he not only developed his appreciation of music-making (especially orchestral) and his understanding of Brian as a composer, but also became aware of the conditions necessary for the management of music-making. With Brian he also encountered the members of the 'White Stag' group of painters – led by Basil Rakoczi and Kenneth Hall – and their multi-talented associates such as Ralph Cusack and Thurloe Conolly. And, from 1939–40 onwards, he witnessed the work of Hilton Edwards and Micheál mac Liammóir at the Gate Theatre, thus deepening the knowledge of Irish drama and theatre business which he had already encountered in the plays of Denis Johnston and Lord Longford at the Cambridge Festival Theatre. That these ever-deepening interests should have been pursued while he was experiencing such a disheartening time in search of a career is the presiding irony of these middle years of his life.

Although Charles did not know it at the time, this interlude of 1944 to 1955 was a crucial period of preparation for the totally unexpected summons he would receive in October 1955 from the editor of *The Irish Times*. If his five years at Kilmacurragh had introduced Charles to the realities of the new Ireland in its emergent – and emergency – condition, and to those of trying to be a gentleman-farmer, the next eleven years were to put a shape on his Kilmacurragh experience and to direct him, however bizarrely and inconsequentially, towards the career and the marriage that would be 'the making of him', as the 'intelligent citizen' he hoped to be.

---

3. Cf. my *Music and Broadcasting* pp. 120–133.

Cultural life

In *That Neutral Island: a Cultural History of Ireland during the Second World War* Clair Wills commented on 'the small gay subculture that grew up around the White Stag Group and Edwards and MacLiammóir at the Gate Theatre'.[4] There was a homosexual nexus between artists and actors, painting and drama, which infused the Dublin arts worlds with their intellectual energy and imagination. Homosexuality was certainly an energizing factor in the arts world, so much so that to describe it as a 'subculture' is perhaps to underplay its significance. The partnership of Edwards and mac Liammóir had been a well-known phenomenon since the Gate opened in 1928, and the two homosexuals openly cohabiting had won the silent respect of Dublin theatregoers. But the homosexuality of Rakoczi and Hall may have been a reason for their being subject to police surveillance after their arrival in Ireland and for friends advising them not to draw attention to themselves. Basil Rakoczi referred to 'the unconscious homosexuality' of his pictures in which, he said, 'I found myself'.[5] This seems to have been particularly true of the pictures he painted in Achill and the Aran islands, where he and Hall frequently visited.

Other associates of the White Stag, such as Ralph Cusack and Thurloe Conolly, were most decidedly uxorious heterosexuals – Cusack, when he left Ireland to live in France, taking with him three female companions (one of them his wife, the cellist Nancy Sinclair) whom he accommodated in separate establishments.[6]

Tony Reford

The reappearance in his life of his Cambridge friend Tony Reford proved to be a valuable link between Charles and the English members of the White Stag Group. 'Ireland is certainly a delightful country and I commence to feel at home' Reford wrote from his apartment in Dublin's Heytesbury Lane, which he seems to have shared with a partner, Philip Seton. Reford was passionate, in much the same way as Charles, about finding himself. He had clearly formed

---

4. *That Neutral Island* p. 287.

5. Quoted in S.B. Kennedy, *The White Stag Group*, p. 29.

6. Source: Carol Acton.

A painting of Kilmacurragh, County Wicklow, after the addition of the wings in 1848.

'Uncle Tom': Thomas Acton (1826–1908) in the grounds of Kilmacurragh.

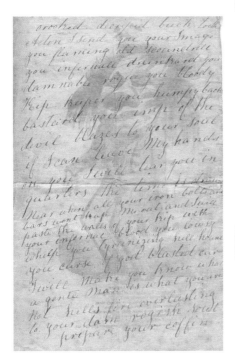

'Curious Valentine': the travails
of landlordism in nineteenth-
century Ireland.

Banks Medal of the Royal
Horticultural Society awarded to
Charles Ball-Acton in 1931.

*Colonel Charles Ball-Acton (1830–97),
Charles's grandfather.*

*Major Reginald Ball-Acton
(1877–1916), Charles's father.*

*Isabel Richmond
(1876–1970) in 1899,
Charles's mother.*

Reggie, Isabel and baby Charles, 1914–15.

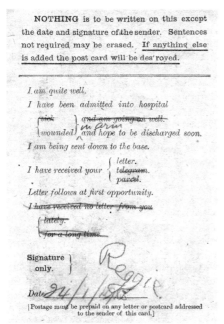

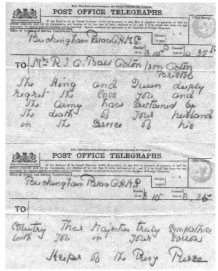

Notification from Reggie that he had been wounded.

Telegram of condolence from the King (George V) and Queen on the death of Reggie.

Charles with Nurse Hallam, 1915–16.

Charles on the steps of Kilmacurragh.

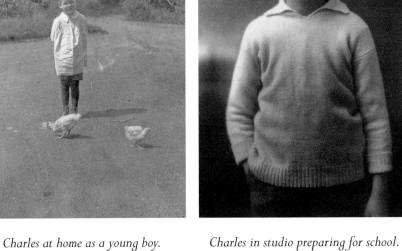

Charles at home as a young boy.   *Charles in studio preparing for school.*

Charles (extreme left) *during Cambridge Rag Week.*

Hugh Digues La Touche (1891–1933),
Charles's stepfather.

Charles, Isabel and Hugh.

Reception at Kilmacurragh for Adolf Mahr and crew of the German
training-ship Schleswig-Holstein, *1937.*

Nazi gathering at Kilmacurragh, summer venue for a Hitler Youth camp,
before Charles's return in September 1939.

Wedding of Charles and Carol, Monkstown Parish Church, 6 March 1951;
from the left, *Frances Little (Carol's sister), Revd Albert Stokes (celebrant),*
Mrs Margaret Jane Little (Carol's mother), Brian Boydell (best man),
Charles, Carol and Isabel Digues La Touche (Charles's mother).

Charles and Polish conductor-composer Andrjez Panufnik at Carrickmines Station, January 1976 (courtesy Camilla Jessel, Panufnik's wife).

Charles and Carol with musician David Carmody, on balcony of the National Concert Hall, Dublin, 1981.

an important attachment to Charles during their years at Cambridge, based on deep respect: 'You are one of the key stones of my sense of proportion. You save me from that complete disintegration of values, which is the result of innumerable, isolated, unrelated experiences. VIVA CHARLES, what an important & indispensable person you are, in the scheme of things.'

Charles clearly relished this companionship, regardless of Reford's sexuality, and we must assume that he was very much moved by his friend's letter. Reford identified Charles's cardinal quest as one for *unity* – 'to be an integral part of society and even help to build it'. The sacrifice of material good for spiritual satisfaction and awareness, to have 'the courage to leave society to its own stupid, material wrangling and to set an example of living for the sake of living. It is those people who will do most ultimately to bring society to its senses.' Marriage, with a recognized place in society, had to be measured against the need for complete independence, but it seems that Reford could see a way forward for Charles as both married and independent, as someone 'integral' to society yet aloof from it.

Already in 1939 at the beginning of Reford's stay in Ireland he had executed illustrations for a story by Brian Sheridan in *Esquire* magazine. Charles recorded that 'The story concerns a Sergeant & three Guards, so that Tony turned up [at Kilmacurragh] on Sunday and asked me to introduce him to the local Sergeant at Redcross & try to get him to sit. The Sergeant & the Wicklow Superintendent both drop in fairly often and of course for policy apart from anything else are always welcome. So I took Tony down & the Sergeant turned up trumps completely, so that Tony sketched everything: all the uniforms, the truncheons, the guardroom table with its ledgers & its packs of cards, even the cell.' The gardaí at Redcross were an important part of life at Kilmacurragh, and Charles was obviously very pleased to have been able to facilitate his friend while at the same time renewing his acquaintance with the local branch of the law.

When, in March 1940, Reford submitted four pictures to the Royal Hibernian Academy (RHA), Charles commented 'the RHA has the same kind of bad reputation as the R[oyal] A[cademy]'. At the RHA, Charles found the pictures by Jack Yeats 'were enormous, and I didn't like them. They were very much impressions, but got with a very painstaking application of small little scraps of various colours: I felt that he would have got what he was after far better if he used fewer colours in large areas. Messy, in fact.'

The White Stag Group

The White Stag Group was a loose association of artists clustered around its two principal – and perhaps strictly speaking, its only – members, the pacifists Basil Rakoczi (who seems to have been half-Hungarian and half-Irish) and Kenneth Hall.[7] Together with other expatriates from Britain and continental Europe, they made Dublin their home for the duration of the war. Their status as non-combatants has never been definitively established. Enrique Juncosa, in his foreword to the catalogue of the 2006 retrospective at IMMA refers to them as 'conscientious objectors'.[8]

The presence of these refugees had a very considerable impact on Irish art and artists. They held their first Dublin exhibition in Rakoczi's flat at 34 Lower Baggot Street,[9] showing work by Rakoczi, Hall, Reford, Nick Nicholls, Georgette Rondel, Mainie Jellett (at that time one of the leading Irish artists) and another friend of Charles, Patricia Wallace, among others.[10] Jellett and Evie Hone had already introduced cubism to the Irish art world, following their study in Paris with André Lhote and Albert Gleizes. Jellett was another Achill-ite, staying with her friend Stella Frost in the same cottage where Charles and Brian holidayed in 1942. Of Jellett, Charles wrote: 'I wonder why one does not hear of her elsewhere: perhaps because she has not exhibited elsewhere: I don't know. She seems to have evolved through cubism to painting abstract designs, but unlike so many of blobby things and peculiarities, the designs are pleasing.' He was meeting members of the White Stag Group on a frequent basis, and getting to know their artistic styles. There was a distinctly abstract character to the few drawings and paintings by Charles that survive

7. Information about the White Stag Group is largely derived from S.B. Kennedy's *Irish Art and Modernism 1880–1950* and his *The White Stag Group*. The group took its name from the family emblem of its patron, Herbrand Ingouville-Williams.

8. S.B. Kennedy, *White Stag Group* p. 6.

9. Later a gallery was established at 30 Upper Mount Street and moved in 1942 to 6 Lower Baggot Street.

10. Patricia Wallace (1912–73), who had studied at the Slade, came from a family which ran the Old Head Hotel in Louisburgh, County Mayo, where Charles stayed several times; she was a scene painter at Jennifer Davidson's Torch Theatre in the mid-1930s and exhibited at the RHA from 1934 and at the Irish Exhibition of Living Art. Her husband, William Griffith, opened the Unicorn Restaurant in Merrion Row where she painted murals.

from this period. The fact that he, as well as Brian Boydell,[11] took lessons from Jellett some time before her early death in 1944 can be seen in the few surviving works of both friends, but he made no mention of it in his letters to his mother because, Carol believed, he did not want her to think that he might be embarking on a career as an artist, however much she may have enjoyed the comments on painting and music during his days in Cambridge and Munich.

The advent of Rakoczi, Hall and their friends certainly provided stimulus and encouragement to Irish artists such as May Guinness, Louis le Brocquy, Ralph Cusack and Thurloe Conolly, and, for a time, Brian Boydell.[12] When, in January 1944, the Group organized an exhibition of 'Subjective Art', warmly endorsed by the eminent British critic Herbert Read, Thurloe Conolly wrote about the nature of subjective art, which he closely identified with surrealism. His own poems, 'The Feather of Death', set by Boydell, were considered by Charles to have been surreal and Charles's unshakeable conviction that all criticism was essentially subjective may well have been influenced by what he saw and heard at this time.

One point on which Charles would have treasured the artistic tenets of the White Stag members was articulated by Herbert Read. In the words of S.B. Kennedy, Read expressed the White Stag philosophy that 'the artist does not merely record what the camera can record [but] it was his job to pierce what he termed "the superficial veil of appearances" to reveal "the inner structure" of things'.[13] This chimed perfectly with what Charles had written to his mother from Munich, and which he had discovered in the work of Paul Nash. Kennedy adds that Thurloe Conolly strove for 'the harnessing of dream images', an orientation he shared with Brian Boydell, and this, too, accords closely with what interested Charles in art at this time.

When Thurloe Conolly had a show in Dublin in 1949, Charles's reaction was immediately positive and excited: 'First impression was of something utterly new, something more new than anything I had come across in painting

---

11. Brian Boydell taught art temporarily at St Columba's College, Rathfarnham, while also working in the family's malting business.

12. Ralph Cusack exhibited in the White Stag exhibitions from 1941; Brian Boydell and Thurloe Conolly from 1943. *Circa* 1943 Boydell wrote to Charles: 'I have just painted my eleventh oil, and therefore only have one more before I complete the quota of a dozen which I set myself. I think many of them are a great improvement on anything before.'

13. Kennedy, *The White Stag Group*, p. 33.

since I began to have sufficient experience to form a critical judgment.' He compared looking at the pictures to the experience of hearing Beethoven's c-sharp minor quartet for the first time.

> There has been all this back to the primitive, back to the child, sort of movement. For me, nearly all unsuccessful since however strongly painters, and particularly sculptors, have wished to regain the freshness, universality and substance of the primitive, they have always taken with them their apparatus of civilization, because they could not help it. In this show I felt that you had had no intention of consciously going primitive, but HAD achieved an ingenuousness, a naiveté. I tend to be excited by the dramatic (?melodramatic) qualities of designs qua designs: thus have I been excited by Jelletts, Pipers,[14] and Paul Nashes. But to me the paintings of Paul Egestorff while very sensitive designs in rare taste do not move me. These paintings of yours are concerned as well as design with something very fundamental, even though I may never understand, just as I doubt whether I shall ever understand why in the Beethoven a-minor quartet the Alla Marcia follows the molto adagio, though I feel that if ever I do understand that I shall get very near to a full understanding of Beethoven.

Many years later, when Charles saw an exhibition of Picasso in Dublin, he wrote to Conolly: 'You and Picasso seem to have similar casts of minds and invention and feeling. So many of the lithographs put me in mind of your drawings at Dugort [in Achill].' He also recalled that 'when Thurloe started, c. 1942, he painted à la Christopher Wood;[15] then à la Piper; then à la Paul Klee; and then, just as he was moving on to being himself, he stopped, more's the pity. A modern polymath, like many another, he took life aisy. And isn't that the way to take it and to Hell with posterity.'

Perhaps the most persuasive statement from a member of the White Stag Group, as far as Charles's later career as a music critic is concerned, was Kenneth Hall's distinction between objective and subjective art:

> The objective element is that which is observed in or drawn from the external world by the artist. The subjective element is that which is contributed by the artist from the depths of his own nature with little or no reference to outside reality.[16]

14. John Piper (1903–1992) was a painter, print-maker and stained glass artist responsible for the windows of the rebuilt Coventry Cathedral after the Second World War.

15. Christopher Wood (1901–1930) was encouraged by Augustus John and influenced by Ben Nicholson. Addicted to opium, he was killed when he fell under a train.

16. Quoted in *The White Stag Group*, p. 37.

Charles was deeply conscious of a 'hidden' or invisible or unspoken Ireland, and in the writing of one associate of the White Stag Group, Herbrand Ingouville-Williams, he may well have found something which provided him with a link between art, life and politics:

> To-day the field of the Unconscious, the conflicts and phantasies engendered within it, the troubling contrast between this almost-unrecognized world and that of surface-appearances, the attempt to resolve the dissonances between these two aspects of the psyche – these would seem to be the trends of the *Zeitgeist* in 1944, which are giving birth to the Subjective Art of our time.[17]

Part of the aesthetic and intellectual excitement of the time must have emanated from the fact that the personalities involved were not only painters, sculptors, musicians and dramatists, but also poets, novelists and philosophers. Rakoczi and Ingouville-Williams were also deeply interested in psychology and psychotherapy and in 1933 had founded the Society for Creative Psychology in London's Fitzrovia, where the White Stag 'group' came into existence two years later.

Ralph Cusack's novel *Cadenza: an excursion* (1958) was a case in point: allegedly a form of autobiography, it is a kaleidoscopic and disjointed ramble through an emotional landscape reminiscent of both Beckett and Flann O'Brien.[18] In a letter to Charles and Carol, he described it as 'an enormous book about Dublin, Here [France], Music, Life in general and death in particular... I think it will finally cause my banning (not to mention its own) from Ireland.'[19]

17. Quoted in ibid., p. 39.

18. It has recently been commended (and described as 'overlooked') by John Wilson Foster in his introduction to *The Cambridge Companion to the Irish Novel* (2006) pp. 17–18. Cusack's talents were not confined to painting and writing, since he also frequented the world of drama as a set designer, working in 1942 with Anne Yeats on *The Strings are False* at the Olympia Theatre and, with her and Thurloe Conolly, on *The House of Cards* (with incidental music by Boydell). At the Gaiety he designed *Saint Joan* the following year and went back to the Olympia for Sean O'Casey's *Red Roses for Me*.

19. In 1962, Cusack told Charles that he had written 75,000 words of a new book which 'will very little resemble *Cadenza*, being a microcosmic image of something like our common (shared) youth in Ireland, England and elsewhere! It is a far more vicious document than *Cadenza* was.' Whether the manuscript was ever completed is unknown. Cusack was unhappy that already one agent had rejected it, and he had lingering regrets over the fact that *Cadenza* had been remaindered that year by Hamish Hamilton at one shilling per copy. Cusack was a cousin of Mainie Jellett, and had lived at Annamoe, in County Wicklow, where he propagated rare bulbs and cultivated

Like Charles himself, Cusack was a godfather to the Boydells' son Barra (b. 1947), although he did not recall the occasion: 'I was nearly always drunk when in Ireland and may have agreed to anything for peace's sake.' Charles and Carol stayed at Speracèdes with the Cusacks in 1954 on their way home from a penurious holiday in Nice (the exchange controls at that time forbade the export of more than £50 in notes, and they succeeded in living on this for a month). The following year Charles agreed to be a trustee of Nancy Cusack-Sinclair's family estate, and the friendship continued until Cusack's death in 1965.[20]

The Gate Theatre

Charles had known of the Dublin Gate Theatre since his Cambridge days, when he acquired a copy of the souvenir catalogue of its first seven years, edited by Bulmer Hobson and largely written by Hilton Edwards. He needed no introduction to modern Irish drama, but his association with friends such as Ralph Cusack gave an extra *frisson* to his playgoing. Beginning in the early 1940s, he often went up to Dublin from Kilmacurragh to see Brian Boydell and his parents, and visited the Gate. It wasn't his first acquaintance with the experimental Gate, which Hilton Edwards and Micheál mac Liammóir had founded in 1928. That had been in September 1939 when he had seen J.B. Priestley's *I Have Been Here Before* and had already formed the impression that Edwards, as an actor, was 'in a different class from the rest'. Then in November 1939 he saw mac Liammóir and Edwards in Auden and Isherwood's *The Ascent of F6*; he and his mother had seen it in London and he regarded Edwards's production as very much superior. Mac Liammóir (whom Charles always considered an inferior actor to his partner, Edwards) was 'quite good, but a bit too theatrical, and a little too much given to the Ivor Novello manner of placing himself so that he looks as beautiful as possible'.

---

jasmine, which was to provide him with a source of income when he emigrated in 1954 to Speracèdes in the south of France.

20. When Charles told Thurloe Conolly this news, he wrote 'I remember him at Skerries, Drumnigh [their house at Portmarnock], and Uplands [Annamoe], tormented, obsessed, sometimes tranquil and happy, sometimes exasperating but almost always lovable. I remember too one week that I spent with Ralph in Kerry. All that week he was quietly gay, happy and utterly serene.'

In January 1940 he was in Dublin, where Brian's mother, Eileen, took him to mac Liammóir's modern-dress *Hamlet*, where he met Prince Alexander Lieven:[21]

> [mac Liammóir] was extremely good, the best I have seen yet, and his careful enunciation and rather too stagy declamation were less in evidence than before. Whoever took Ophelia [Meriel Moore] was really good, especially in the mad scenes, where Ophelia lost none of her attractiveness, and with the madness she portrayed the kind of intelligibleness through it that made one feel there was something there, something to make contact with. In spite of the fact that Horatio, Rosenkranz and Guildenstern and other minor characters were definitely BAD, the whole production had a unity and an understanding that put it far ahead of Gielgud's.[22]

Due to the split in the management of the Gate, two companies had been formed, that of Lord and Lady Longford (Longford Productions) occupying the theatre for six months of each year, and Edwards-mac Liammóir the other six. As a result, Charles saw Longford's production of Flecker's *Don Juan* at the Gate in March 1940, and, a week later, *Peer Gynt*, directed by Edwards, at the Gaiety Theatre to which his company had moved. He found the verse translation of Ibsen lacking in dramatic power, with the result that 'the verse destroyed the possibility of realism in the production', but the original incidental music by Grieg was used, and 'I was very interested to hear the Grieg with the play, after so often hearing it in concert.'

In April 1943 he also saw Sybil Thorndike in *Captain Brassbound's Conversion* and regretted that he had been too sick the previous week to see her in *Ghosts*. 'Not only was she herself so good, but everything was so suitable. So often one comes across a star like that who seems deliberately to pick on a cast that is so bad that the star cannot help shining through as the only person on the stage.'

---

21. Lieven was a cousin of Charles's soon-to-be friend, Nic Couriss.

22. In reviewing the production, David Sears, in the *Irish Independent*, said 'Micheál MacLiammóir would be a great Hamlet if he was dressed as a Chinese Mandarin or a Harlequin, and with that knowledge the Gate ran no risk in their experiment'. John Gielgud played Hamlet from 1930 to 1946. It is quite possible that Charles had seen his performance in 1934.

Music

Ralph Cusack frequently invited friends for evenings of listening to records, thus continuing an education which in Charles's case had blossomed at Cambridge. In December 1942 Cusack invited the internationally celebrated Griller Quartet, who were playing at the RDS, to perform Bloch's string quartet at Drumnigh, his house in Portmarnock – 'a very modern work and of surpassing loveliness and depth', as Charles recorded. 'It was a tremendous experience.' Now, no doubt with the stimulus of living at the Boydells' (he moved temporarily to Rathfarnham, while waiting for the long-drawn-out saga of the sale of Kilmacurragh to be resolved), he began to express opinions which show how deeply he cared about music, especially contemporary work to which Brian was introducing him. (For example, Charles was introduced to the music of the Finnish composer Yrjö Kilpinen [1892–1959] by Brian Boydell, who sang his 'Songs of Death' at a concert in 1946.)[23]

Hearing the Griller Quartet at the RDS introduced Charles to a quartet by Benjamin Britten: 'very thrilling, moving and exciting. It's the first time I have heard any Britten which I have been wanting to hear for a long time, since by all accounts he is *the* coming composer.' As on their previous visit to Dublin, the Grillers also played the Bloch quartet at Cusack's house.

> I went expecting that it might not quite come up to last year's experience, but instead it was more so. After the playing ended there was a long pause before any applause, and then after the whole thirty of us had just about burst ourselves with applause, we all fell into a spontaneous silence. Instead of getting up and gradually going, everyone just found themselves sitting in a curious sort of way.[24]

The Grillers subsequently asked Brian Boydell to write a quartet for them. In 1943 Charles told his mother

> At present Brian is going through a phase of composition that produces either adagia desolata, or presto barbarico.[25] ... he is writing a trio ... a most exacting discipline to make balance, satisfaction and music: there is no chance for broad orchestral effects, or great masses of sound. Which is

23. The recital also included new song cycles by John Beckett and Boydell's own 'Five Joyce Songs' (the accompanist was Joseph Groocock).

24. He had exactly the same sensation in 1969 at the conclusion of the cycle of Beethoven quartets by the Aeolian Quartet at Dublin's Rupert Guinness Hall.

25. The finale of Boydell's oboe quintet (1939–40) was in fact a *presto barbarico*.

one of the reasons why trio and quartet music is the most difficult and most strenuous to listen to. Until last autumn I had never been able to get very great enjoyment out of quartet music for strings, and knew perfectly well that it was lack of experience and lack of practice that held me back: but last autumn with Brian's gramophone and scores, I started: with a Mozart quartet as being the earliest, hearing it five or six times in two days, until I had got thoroughly into the way of listening to it, passing on to an early Beethoven, op. 18 number 3, which is not much more difficult than Mozart, and then taking the plunge into his last quartet, in C sharp minor, op. 132. At a first hearing, even with the score, and a first rate recording, I was lost completely and it just meant nothing. But I persevered, and after the seventh or eighth hearing it began to make a tremendous impression on me; and later I found myself thoroughly in it, and still now feel that it is the most tremendous bit of music I know. He [Beethoven] once said 'Who understands my music is free of the misery of the world'. I think I am beginning to realise what he meant, though I would not be presumptuous enough to say that I understand his music, and am tending to the opinion that hardly anyone has or will.

Charles's involvement as a spectator in the creation of Boydell's string trio allowed him a particularly valuable insight into the process of contemporary composition, and stood him in good stead when he came to discuss new works in his music criticism. The work had evolved over a few months and he had observed its progress, which included a rehearsal in the studio of Louis le Brocquy, 'a charming and well-off artist',[26] attended by Charles, Thurloe Conolly (author of the words of some of Brian's songs), Ralph Cusack and Frederick May – 'a semi-established modern composer whose work the BBC has occasionally done'. Now Brian decided that he wanted a trial performance of the trio coupled with his oboe quintet and some songs, which took place in the Shelbourne Hotel at the end of January 1944, and had all the character of a one-man show, more usually encountered in the careers of painters. Originally intended to be for about twenty friends, the guest list grew to 160. The ballroom of the Shelbourne was hung with pictures by Brian, Conolly and Cusack 'as they were in tune with his music'. The performers were Maurice Sinclair, Carmel Lang, John Mackenzie and Hazel De Courcey (violins), Betty Sullivan (cello; 'Brian and I are both convinced that if she has any luck she will be a famous cellist – already she is extremely accomplished and withal is a musician'), Máire Larchet (viola), Doris Cleary [later Keogh] (flute), and Mary Jones (soprano; a pupil of Brian and soon to be his wife, making her début

26. Boydell believed that le Brocquy deliberately 'kept his distance' from the artists associated with the White Stag group – letter to Charles Acton, NLI.

– Charles thought 'she has a fine voice, and it seems to me that she is a potential [Isobel] Baillie').[27] About Brian and Mary's engagement, he recorded, 'I have announced my approval and benediction – hardly anyone is more critical of a person's proposed bride than his closest friends.'

Charles was very impressed by the words to 'The Feather of Death', songs for baritone (sung by Brian himself) written by Thurloe Conolly: 'They are to some considerable extent surrealist, though not wholly so: and I do not remember before coming across surrealist verse that had any particular significance to me as a whole':[28]

> My body drifts like ash on the singing wind, searching.
> Ravens thread the air with black embroidery
> Like tunnels of glass are the waves on the beach
> But the sea is an ivory breast with foaming nipples.[29]

Of the music itself, Charles said 'I do think he has written something very great. It is immensely moving to me.' At the end of the concert, Boydell asked if anyone wished to hear the trio again, they could do so: about forty people remained, and heard the composer give a short talk on the work, which could be construed as one of the first significant events of modern Irish composition – Charles certainly called it 'a memorable landmark'. It was followed by a party at the Boydells' house, which went on until 6am, attended by the performers, Conolly, and Charles, and consisting of four bottles of Portuguese *vin ordinaire* converted into Glühwein, two pounds of sausages and 'some extraordinarily unsweet and sawdusty cake'.

Music politics

In April 1943, Charles and Brian had attended one of Radio Éireann's subscription concerts at the Mansion House, and the concert signalled the beginning

---

27. Isobel Baillie (1895–1983) was a Scottish soprano who became one of Britain's leading voices, particularly in oratorio; she sang in the first performance of Vaughan Williams's 'Serenade to Music' in 1938.

28. In a letter to Charles of 1992 Boydell states: 'The Feather of Death is very relevant to the period... It is the only overtly surrealist music I ever did.'

29. Conolly said much later that he did not write poetry, but that at that stage in his life he thought he did: Peter Murray, 'A White Stag in France'.

of Charles's interest in the policy of music activity. The letter to his mother is lengthy and detailed, but bears reproduction in its entirety:

> Constant Lambert had come over to conduct, bringing Moura Lympany to play Schumann's piano concerto. Orchestral music in Dublin has a great deal to put up with and struggle against. In the first place there is no concert hall. The largest hall in Dublin is the round room of the Mansion House. The acoustics are bad – various instruments, particularly the brass, suddenly come and hit one having been reflected off part of the round wall, the whole set up is that of an ex tempore amateur concert in the Town Hall, and the room only holds about 400 people, which is much too small. This concert was actually done on Sunday night at the Gaiety, and probably was much more presentable, but most orchestral concerts have to use the Mansion House because the Gaiety is usually doing its own job of being a theatre. Unfortunately we were not in time to get seats for the Gaiety, they sold out within an hour of opening the box office – the Gaiety holds 1400 – and so seeing the demand they put on a repeat at the Mansion House which we were able to get seats for. [30]

The radio authorities were anxious to establish the orchestra outside its normal home in the broadcasting studio, even though the financial constraints were significant, and a series of visiting conductors was considered necessary to raise playing standards, since there were so few Irish conductors able to take command. As Charles commented:

> The second difficulty that has to be struggled with is no real conductor. The orchestra is fundamentally the radio orchestra, who are conducted by Lieutenant Michael Bowles, a young army bandmaster who was seconded some time back to the Radio, and who as well as being young and lacking in experience is having a difficult job to learn the difference between a band and an orchestra. He is trying, however, and is improving, though he will never get very far, not only because his musicianship is not of a very high order – he refuses to let any modern music be performed on the Radio, where unfortunately he is musical director, even if someone else is conducting – but until he takes a course somewhere under a first rate conductor.

Charles was being unduly harsh on Bowles's choice of repertoire, since he did, in fact, introduce a considerable amount of new and contemporary

---

30. The conductor Eimear Ó Broin, then a young student, recalled that Lambert and the orchestra gave a 'stunning' performance of Tchaikovsky's fifth symphony and particularly noted that the programme included Glazunov's tone poem *Stenka Razine*. Michael Bowles, Music Director at Radio Éireann, complained that Lambert, 'an inveterate alcoholic', had 'almost drunk Blackrock dry'.

music to the concerts, if not to the broadcast schedules. But Bowles had no assurance, from one season to the next, that the public concerts would actually be sanctioned; furthermore, these concerts required augmentation of the very small studio orchestra, which meant that wind and brass players had to be hired from the army bands: this increased the musical difficulties, while semi-amateur string players, who might elsewhere provide adequate music-making, but who lowered the standards of the orchestra as a whole, also had to be sought.[31]

> The orchestra itself is in much the same position as the Bournemouth orchestra, that is it is only at its full size for fortnightly symphony concerts, and has to work very hard playing light music and so forth, just as the Bournemouth orchestra was always held back by having to spend most of its time playing trash on the pier. But it has the added disadvantage of not having a Dan Godfrey or a Dick Austin.[32] Also there is the terrible paucity of wind instrumentalists. Even though the Bournemouth instrumentalists have their faults, they are good, certainly up to the standards of any provincial orchestra, and in Britain there are sufficient instrumentalists not only to pick and choose from, but for the practitioners to have round them a tradition of what good playing is. Here unfortunately that is not the case, especially with the brass, who tend to be army brass-bandsmen, who have no idea of musical playing. There is not much incentive for people to take up instruments for the professional orchestra, since the pay is so bad – the pay in nearly all orchestras is shockingly bad, being about the rate of any other form of skilled labour; this is not conducive to musicianship. And there is no wind playing in schools here and so there are next to no amateurs. Everybody learning music here stops dead at the piano and violin: result, there are stacks of amateurs who can play a drawing room piano, and a superfluity of indifferent fiddlers, but no wind, and a high standard of amateur wind playing is almost a necessity for a high standard of professional wind playing.

In future years, Charles would find himself in the thick of debates on music education, having been elected a governor of the Royal Irish Academy of Music in 1954: the differences (again, cultural and social) between the teaching at the RIAM and the Municipal College of Music were very significant, and vested interests prevented the establishment, in their place, of a national conservatoire.

---

31. Cf. my *Music and Broadcasting* pp. 86–95.

32. Sir Daniel Godfrey (1868–1939) founded the Bournemouth Municipal Orchestra in 1893 and conducted it until 1934; Richard Austin (1903–89) was its conductor 1939–47.

It was astonishing the difference a good conductor can make. The performance was up to the standard of Bournemouth when things are going well, or the Palestine orchestra under its own conductors. Tchaikovsky's fifth symphony. I don't care for Tchaikovsky much. I was very very sorry for the poor first bassoon: the bassoon part in the symphony is a very important and prominent one, and very difficult, and he managed it all very very well, until a passage in the scherzo of considerable trickiness and very great prominence. Poor fellow the principle [*sic*] note of the passage would not speak, and the whole little bit was thrown out, and it was very obvious. I did feel sorry for him, since all the rest was so very good, and I am sure he feels that his misfortune was the only thing the audience heard of him. The orchestra throughout played as it has never played before, it was obvious that they got a tremendous stimulus from being under a good conductor, even though he was only here on Saturday and the first concert was on Sunday night. Lambert certainly worked hard: you could see that he was putting everything he had into it, and that it was sheer hard work on his part that achieved the standard.

As a result of attending these concerts with Boydell, Charles developed a sense of what was needed in order to secure more effective planning of concerts on the part of Radio Éireann which was, and remains, the principal source of music-making in Ireland. Five years before the foundation of the Music Association of Ireland (with which he had ambivalent relations), Charles and Brian were voicing their concerns. Brian's was undoubtedly the superior musical intelligence, and the conduit for the larger questions of policy, while Charles's was the practical, stratifying mind which could see the desired results and have a strategy for achieving them. It would be one of the causes of his falling-out with figures such as Olive Smith (one of the founders of the MAI), who had similar objectives but a different view of strategy. In the following we can see how Charles (no doubt to Brian's chagrin) assumed command of the situation:

> At my instigation, Brian and I are carrying on a propaganda campaign, directed principally at Arthur Duff the assistant director of music, and a very fine musician, for the Radio to engage Malcolm Sargent to come over to give a couple of concerts. As we know from Palestine he is the man to make an indifferent orchestra sit up and really put their heart into good playing, and give a magnificent performance. A fortnight of Sargent would do the orchestra more good than anything else.

To further this 'campaign', Charles wrote a lengthy letter to the editor of *The Irish Times*, in reply to the report of a lecture by Arthur Duff and a letter by the minister, P.J. Little.[33] Duff had been reported as saying that 'one of the great difficulties of composers in Ireland was that they never had in music a great brain, a great genius, as they had in poets, writers and novelists'. They also had problems in finding publishers. The 'English school' could be a great example. 'So far as the future of music here was concerned, he felt that they were thinking too much of the Gaelic tunes.'[34] Minister Little wrote to say that he took the opposite view to Duff. 'A country like Ireland should strain every effort to express its own individuality in music. If we are to adopt his advice and follow English models, we cannot expect to be anything but derivative and imitative, and of course, imitation means inferiority.' English music, said Little, was very limited in comparison with that of Russia, Norway, Finland, Hungary, or Czechoslovakia. As far as Irish music was concerned, 'there are Irish songs that rank beside the greatest in the world. There is no poverty here to run away from… I am sure that the best even among British musicians would implore us to be ourselves and to make to international music just that contribution from the riches of Irish tradition, temperament and sentiment that has been made by so many other nations… It is a great and generous objective.'[35]

The occasion of these exchanges gave Charles a perfect opportunity to put down markers which would be his guiding principles for the next forty years; and it also incorporated so many of the arguments to which he would be both witness and participant in the coming decade. It gave him the opportunity to steer a path between Duff and Little which would become the basis of his later discussions with Seán Ó Riada, T.C. Kelly and others in his many columns on the subject in *The Irish Times*. In his letter, he went into considerable detail about the relationship between so-called 'classical' or 'art' music and the folk music of the countries in which it was composed. He underlined the organic connection between the two, the purpose of doing so being to emphasize the unique potential for Irish composers to take possession of their folk heritage and to base their work upon it. He was vehemently opposed to 'arrangements'

---

33. Arthur Duff (1899–1956) was a member of the Army School of Music (1923–31), becoming the first Irish-born bandmaster; he studied composition with Hamilton Harty, and became noted for small-scale compositions of some merit. He worked for Radio Éireann from 1937, becoming Assistant Music Director in 1945. P.J. Little (1884–1963) was Minister for Posts and Telegraphs 1939–48, and retired from politics in 1952.

34. *Irish Times* 31 March 1947.

35. *Ibid.*, 1 April 1947.

of Irish airs as a way of preserving and developing that heritage, however much the result might be pleasing to the ear (Charles called them 'entirely inoffensive'): it did not make music identifiably Irish, because the composers, all classically trained, 'have used the stock clichés of Ravel, Stanford, Mendelssohn... Their traditions do not live *now*. Their language was theirs and not ours.' Radio Éireann was 'encouraging such threadbare forms at the expense of others', by which he meant *original* work. And he voiced the opinion which would bring him into collision with Comhaltas Ceóltoirí Éireann and many of its individual members, that

> composers must be free to use folk material in its genuine form, with its wayward, irregular rhythms, unusual modes and curious accidentals, synthesised with the harmonies, tonalities, polyphonies, forms of living contemporary art-music... If our composers are to produce a great Irish music, let them soak themselves in our folk-songs in their genuine shape, and drink deep of the living modern music... and then they may develop not only a great Irish music, but an advance in the European stream.[36]

This was a remarkable contribution to the debate which was only just beginning on the nature of Irish music, of music in Ireland, and its relation to the music of the European 'mainstream'. It was totally individual, and in its emphasis on authenticity it was characteristic of Charles's own anxiety about roots and origins.

It may have been this letter which elicited the equally characteristic response from Brian Boydell:

> Your observations on the possibility of an Irish school of composition are interesting. I have myself no real desire to draw too much from Irish melody, since I find my style growing towards something which is too remote from folk music to be reconcilable to it. My new ideas, which are beginning to develop, so that I am looking for the right medium for my next work, are more of the Bloch-Prokofieff-Berg type; whether I shall settle down to music of that type or not, I can't tell; but I feel that one can waste a lot of time, which would otherwise be used in reaching forward, by sinking too deep into the modal mud. Folk music is inclined to lead one that way. I find that I am slowly developing a certain type of individual tonal system. I must follow my inclinations, rather than plan away from the emotional element, what my style will become.[37]

36. *Ibid.*, 7 April 1947.

37. This statement, as in the case of similar material relating to Boydell and other composers, is located in the Acton Music Archive, NLI.

Folk music would elicit further negative comments from Boydell in later years, establishing his determination to belong to no 'school' but to be 'his own man' as a composer, a tenet which Charles would, as a matter of principle, totally respect.

Four years later, just before the general election in 1951, Charles wrote directly to P.J. Little, in the hope and expectation that the latter would be returned to his former post as a *responsable* for culture as Minister for Posts and Telegraphs. In the wake of the recent establishment of the Arts Council,[38] Charles was concerned that music would fare poorly as 'the cinderella' of the arts. More importantly, perhaps, was his hope that the Council's budget of £20,000 should be spent not on subsidizing specific arts activities but on producing 'encouragement and advice for people to do things for themselves, rather than bring into being another agency through which money is spent for people in passivity.' Once again, these were policy issues to which he would return on as many occasions as *The Irish Times* would allow him, not least being his opinion, directly expressed to Little, that the radio service (and, with it, the orchestra) should be 'administratively divorced' from the Department and either established as a separate department or as a semi-state company.

Although Charles's relationship with Brian suffered a cooling-off in later years and took on a combative character, the period discussed in this chapter was mostly one in which their friendship developed on musical lines, whatever Boydell may have felt about their personal relationship. Brian was to become severely negative about the role of a music critic and Charles once wryly referred to their collaboration at Cambridge, saying 'I doubt if he remembers that he was one himself, once!' Barra Boydell believes that his father's antipathy to much of what Charles wrote was due to the fact that Charles had no formal training.[39] Charles was no doubt conscious of the fact that he had no formal qualification as a musician, and as late as 1962 was endeavouring, without success and with much frustration, to complete a B.Mus. correspondence course with Durham University. But against that we have to put an alternative fact: that criticism is an essentially subjective art, for which there *can* be no training.

---

38. The Arts Council, sponsored by the coalition government, came into being with the passing of the Arts Act on 8 May 1951; Charles's letter to Little is dated 18 May; the election was held on 30 May and de Valera re-assumed the position of Taoiseach on 13 June. However, Little was not re-appointed to a Cabinet post, but was appointed Chairman of the new Arts Council (1951–56).

39. Communication to the author.

A possible reason for their disagreements and public fights in later years was that each was passionate about the work he was doing and convinced of the need for integrity: as a composer, Brian was totally engrossed in forging a musical personality for himself; as a critic, Charles believed completely in his mission to inform, educate and entertain his readers by working from the highest principles and the standards they imposed. When they clashed, on a matter of opinion, it was inevitable that some level of personal hurt would be inflicted. Brian's widow, Mary, correctly believed that the cooling-off between them had begun as early as the motoring holiday in Yugoslavia, and had continued into the period when Charles – and Thurloe Conolly, soon to marry Brian's sister Yvonne – were living temporarily at 'Imaal'.[40] But it is difficult if not impossible to see any overt coolness, especially since the Yugoslavian trip had been followed by the holiday in Achill and by a general air of collaboration and what one might almost call an 'extended family' centred on the artists, writers and composers among whom Brian and Charles were living throughout this period.[41] While Charles was staying at 'Imaal' in 1943, Brian penned a humorous 'Carte de jour' for 'Mr Chas. Acton, Room 2a, with zinc urinal and roast potatoes, @ 25/– per week', 'many (17) weeks unpaid since November 8th'. While the coolness may have subsisted in Brian's own private feelings, it was nowhere in evidence in Charles's expressions regarding Brian, which were wholly affectionate, admiring and supportive, however irritating or invasive the latter may have found them. Moreover, the decision to ask Charles to be Barra Boydell's godfather in 1947 suggests that, even if there was some distrust or disparity of feeling between Brian and Charles after the Yugoslav trip, the passing of almost ten years had dissipated it.

40. Communication to the author *via* Barra Boydell, who observed that Charles and Conolly 'rather took advantage of Brian's kindness at Imaal, both living there at Brian's expense, without Brian having particularly invited them to stay, nor contributing much to the practical issues of house keeping!' A correspondent informs me that on one occasion at a party at 'Imaal', Charles 'had become rather wild and had kicked his way through an interior wall', causing a very large hole. Barra Poydell is unaware of this incident, and feels that, if it took place at all, it could more likely be attributed to Ralph Cusack.

41. A further indication of the continuing friendship and trust between Charles and Brian is the fact that, while Brian and Mary were in Canada in 1955, where he had been invited as an adjudicator, Charles acted as his *poste restante*.

Ralahine

Despite his growing interest, and involvement, in cultural matters, Charles never lost his interest in rural issues. His passion for the minutiae of country life was not confined to his own ancestral acres, however. In fact, the unfulfilled ambition to rediscover the history of Kilmacurragh and its context was further excited by his discovery of the short-lived commune established in 1831 by John Vandeleur at Ralahine, in County Clare,[42] which caught his attention at the same time that he was parting company with Kilmacurragh.

The Ralahine commune had been organized by Thomas Craig, an English socialist and follower of Robert Owen, whom Vandeleur had invited to Ralahine with the intention of isolating his tenants from the activities of secret societies such as the 'Ribbonmen'. The fact that this self-governing co-operative survived only two years was due not to its inefficacy but to the fact that Vandeleur was bankrupted, and, since it occupied Vandeleur's land, his creditors seized the land and evicted the communards.

Charles was excited by the fact that Ralahine pre-dated the publication of the *Communist Manifesto* by fifteen years; he had discovered, in the RDS library, a copy of Craig's own account of the commune, *An Irish Commune: the history of Ralahine*, originally published in 1882 and republished in 1920 in an edited version, with an introduction (which Charles considered 'irrelevant') by George Russell, the Irish apostle of co-operative farming. Out of the blue, he told his mother 'I have been rearranging the text of the Story of Ralahine'. Charles had become so fascinated by this episode in Irish social and economic history that he had decided to try and interest a publisher in a new edition. He did indeed succeed in interesting a Dundalk publisher in the project, and went so far as to make at least two versions of his 'rearrangement', moving from the RDS copy of the reprint to TCD's copy of the original. As part of his restructuring of the book, Charles meticulously researched the increases in prices of commodities such as hay and barley, potatoes, wool, eggs, butter, mutton, milk, and agricultural wages, and the yields of barley, wheat, turnips, cabbage and mangels per acre from 1760 to the 1940s.

'I know we are an unco-operative nation, but it WORKED' he declared to his mother. 'Not only that, but it was carried out by a young Sassenach who

---

42. By coincidence, the RIAM benefited by a legacy from a member of the Vandeleur family in the 1880s, which was still a matter of importance when Charles joined the Academy's board in the 1950s.

spoke no Irish, in a county that not only is proverbially tough and difficult, but which then was in a state of complete insurgence and Trouble.' The adventurous nature of the undertaking, and the fact that it occurred in an agricultural setting, captured Charles's imagination. The projected edition of Craig's work did not materialize – it was yet another example of Charles thinking ahead of his time, since a new edition did not, in fact, appear until 1983. But it rekindled his interest in his own local history, in which the same factors had been at play as in County Clare: the links between alcoholism and poverty, methods of husbandry and conditions of housing. His difficulty was that there was so little written about 'ordinary' folk: the social and economic history of Ireland in the 1830s was almost unknown, hence the importance, in Charles's eyes, of Craig's narrative.

> I know about the kind of things the ordinary history books are full of: White Boys,[43] crumbling hovels without chimney or window, in which the large family and the livestock lived without furniture. But it is the insignificant little scraps of detail that occasionally turn up that give life to this kind of thing. Some of which are now part of ordinary statistics, and some are the sort of thing that it would never occur to an agricultural writer of those days to mention because he would assume that everyone would know.

Charcoal

In the meantime, Charles needed an income. Despite having the proceeds of the sale of Kilmacurragh, and a continuing small income from his father's estate, Charles was unable to live the life of either a scholar or a gentleman, nor to use his talents to professional advantage. He tried, without success, to interest English journals such as *Tempo*, *Nimbus* and *The Listener* in articles on music, but 'My new about-to-be job with Nic Couriss', was how Charles spoke of the work which was to bring him the lifelong friendship of this remarkable Russian emigré.[44] It was through Brian Boydell that Charles found his first

---

43. A secret society founded in the late 1700s, whose members set out to damage property belonging to the landowners; their name is attributed to the fact that they wore a white shirt over their own clothes.

44. Nicholas Couriss had been born in St. Petersburg in 1896, and during the Russian revolution was a captain in the White Russian army; after its defeat, he emigrated and came to Ireland in 1931, living at Collon, County Louth with his wife Ksana. After the decline in the charcoal business, he took to growing mushrooms commercially, selling

employment after the sale of Kilmacurragh – in the manufacture and sale of charcoal, in a company owned by the Boydell family, which focussed on charcoal as a wartime alternative to petrol, and produced a fuel called 'producer gas'. Charcoal being 'horribly dirty and very bulky', Couriss's company (Oriel Charcoal) would transform it into a dustless fuel.

At first, Charles was unsure if it was the right opening for him, and he let the offer pass. But Nic Couriss made an improved offer: Charles would be 'centred in Dublin and bullying railways and canal companies, going to Rathangan and Mullingar', and contributing capital of £200 which Couriss, as a penniless Russian émigré, did not have. 'I shall be travelling round the country (a tiring but interesting and instructing process – especially when my knowledge of my own country is so slight), I shall be meeting people. As well as being very competent, Nick is as far as trustworthiness goes everything that the expression "officer and gentleman" should mean.' 'Reasonably speaking, it doesn't look like a career with a capital C: and it seems a far cry from agriculture but apart from reason I *feel* that to do this job is the right thing for me to do.' Selling his 'herd' would finance his partnership with Couriss. 'Jane' – his Ford V8 – had to be put back on the road, which entailed a new set of tyres – 'she was hopelessly through the soles of her feet' – so that he could start travelling for Couriss. The business was a success during the war, due to the shortage of other fuels (a great deal of the output was sold to the Post Office for its vans), and Charles established the 'Charcoal Society' as the industry organization; but it declined thereafter, and Charles's involvement effectively ended in 1946, when Couriss declared that if all the company's creditors were to claim what he owed he would be bankrupt. 'I am not going into sentimentalities over our mutual work and its failure. It looked so bright and turned out so dark', he told Charles.[45]

Couriss, his wife Ksana, Charles (and, in later years, Carol) remained close friends, traditionally celebrating Christmas dinner together at Collon, wearing formal evening dress. Before Charles joined Proctors Tripod Harvesting, he tried to influence Couriss in an agency, but this came to nothing: 'I am sorry to

---

as much as 200 lbs per week. He also gave Russian language lessons up to 1960 (when he became very ill), numbering Conor Cruise O'Brien and his wife Máire Mac an Tsaoi among his pupils, and in 1962 translated Arsene Goulevitch's *Czarism and Revolution*. When Ksana died in 1966 he sought ordination as a Russian Orthodox priest, and, as Father Nicholas, despite frail health, ministered to the Orthodox communities in Dublin until his death in 1977.

45. Ironically, the charcoal business was involved in buying timber from The O'Mahony, the Acton family's one-time tenant at Grangecon.

say I was unable to do anything with the tripods' Couriss wrote. 'I covered very many miles and saw about 30–35 people. I did my level best and my damndest and spent many hours honestly trying.' Charles was to renew the offer when he left Proctors, pointing out that the legwork had more or less ceased in favour of mail-order sales, but again Couriss could not be tempted.

During the charcoal years (1944–46), Charles went ahead with plans for Isabel's transfer from Bournemouth to Dublin, and after much searching found furnished rooms with a Mrs Rose ('she CAN COOK') at Alma Road, in the Dublin suburb of Blackrock, from where a tram took twenty-five minutes to central Dublin. The cost for two rooms and full board was £3.5.0. After leaving 'Imaal', due to Brian's insistence that he could not compose if there were anyone else in the house, Charles had had digs at 15 Lower Mount Street, followed by the rooms at Alma Road, but, due to post-war shortages, this was unsatisfactory: digs were uncomfortable: there was no coal for fires, and in town the gas supply – at least in wartime – was limited to six hours per day (6–8 am, 11.30am–1.30pm, and 6–8pm). The major development, after the sale of 'Grata Quies' in 1946–7, was that he and his mother jointly bought Strad-brook House, a large three-storey mansion in Blackrock. Although there is no evidence for this, part of the purchase price supposedly came from the proceeds of selling Kilmacurragh, but definitely some family money (£2200) which had come to Isabel on the death (in 1928) of the widow of Charles's great-uncle William was also involved. Conversion of the house into flats occupied almost three years, during which Charles engaged in small-scale fruit-growing in the large field in the Stradbrook grounds which brought him a prize from the RDS. Isabel occupied the entire ground floor of the house, and the upper storey and basement were let in four units, thus providing Charles with an income during the lean years which came with the end of his involvement in the charcoal business. A digs at Mount Street, followed by the basement in Stradbrook, must have been a huge contrast to the open lands and mansion of Kilmacur-ragh: the extensive horizon which had opened, physically and emotionally, in 1939 was now restricted to suburban living. But although Stradbrook, with its large garden and plentiful fruit trees, was hardly a compensation for the loss of Kilmacurragh, it did constitute a *rus in urbe* that gave him a sense of once more being a 'landowner' with 'tenants'.

A newspaper for expatriates?

In 1946–47 a friend from County Meath, Robert McKeever, was working in Venezuela for a petroleum company, and his letters asked about old friends such as the Boydells, the Courisses, Princes Paul and Alexander Lieven and the fortunes of the Dublin Orchestral Players. Charles, at a loss after the end of the charcoal business, wrote frequently with news of developments in Ireland, and this prompted the idea of publishing a weekly stencilled 'Irish Letter' for Irish subscribers abroad.

Charles's draft prospectus read: 'Clearly there is a definite need for a weekly paper which should as concisely as possible cover the principal events and news of every facet of life at home in Ireland so that all Irish people whether in Britain, America, or anywhere else in the world could keep themselves posted about home life, maintain contact with their roots, and not feel cut off from all their background.' The subscription for six months would be thirteen shillings, for one year £1.5.0, plus postage. A single copy would cost sixpence.

Charles wrote at least nine typewritten editions, just for McKeever, but did not get to the stage where he expected to 'write Saturday, stencil Sunday, print Monday, post Tuesday'. Why the project did not reach that point is not clear from the surviving correspondence.

Acton-Miley concerts

In 1949–50 Charles and his friend John Miley, a chartered accountant and an amateur clarinettist described by Carol as 'of the finest quality',[46] ventured into the business of concert promotion. The original draft of their manifesto, inviting subscribers to their first season, described themselves as 'two young enthusiasts', with the words '(or as they suspect, fools)' deleted. The series, on the four Wednesdays of September 1949, began at Mills' Hall in Dublin's Merrion Row, with a piano recital by the premier Irish pianist at the time, Charles Lynch; baritone Robert Irwin, from a musical Dublin family, at that time making a career for himself in England;[47] and the piano-duo of sisters

---

46. He had applied, unsuccessfully, for a place in the newly constituted RÉSO in 1947.

47. Irwin had toured in Britain in 1939–40 with John McCormack, who had done much to promote him in the USA in previous seasons. He had recently sung Mahler's 'Kindertotenlieder' with the RÉSO under Mosco Carner, and Vaughan Williams'

Joan and Valerie Trimble, also carving out a successful career in England.

Apart from the recitals for members of the RDS, there was little or no regular, sustained chamber music activity in Dublin, so Charles and John Miley were no doubt justified in thinking that a sufficiently attractive programme would draw a subscription audience. This, they considered, was essential, as it would be very unwise indeed to depend on customers paying on the door; pre-sold tickets were priced at four shillings per concert, whereas tickets on the door would cost seven shillings and sixpence. A further anticipated source of income was the fact that the promoters had succeeded in persuading Radio Éireann to take what was then called a 'live relay' of each concert, at a fee of £20 per week. Not only was this a generous gesture of support from Arthur Duff and Fachtna Ó hAnnracháin at RÉ, but the Director of Programmes, Charles Kelly, and the former Minister for Posts and Telegraphs, P.J. Little, purchased season tickets.

The initial response, by 120 subscribers, was not as good as hoped for, and this led to the abandonment of the Gresham Hotel as a venue in favour of a smaller hall. (Mills' Hall held 150.) It also made it clear to Charles and John that they would have to write off their initial investment of £20 in printing and other preliminary costs. In a letter to Radio Éireann, underlining the significance of the radio fee, they emphasized how important it was, in their opinion, to create an audience outside the RDS membership for recitals of this kind.

As soon as the season was under way, thanks to the subscription strategy, Charles and John were sure of almost breaking even on the actual costs associated with each recital, as the hall was full to capacity, and they were sufficiently confident to plan a second series in early 1950, even to the extent of asking the premier London artists' agency Ibbs and Tillett as to the availability of soprano Isobel Baillie. At the conclusion of the series, Charles made a speech to the subscribers, explaining why the subscriptions had been so important to the enterprise:

> We had felt it a great pity that there were so few public recitals in Dublin and so few opportunities for first rate Irish artists in our own country. We were tired of saying 'Somebody should do something about it' and decided to have a go. We knew from other people's experience that to put on a recital in the ordinary way involves a probable loss of up to three figures, which was utterly beyond our possibilities. Had we known last April when we started just how much work was involved we might well have been daunted, but as each new crisis arose we consoled ourselves with the reflection that if it were easy to run recitals in Dublin, we could listen to one every night.

'Five Mystical Songs' with the Culwick Choir.

Thanking Radio Éireann for its support, he said 'We can see nothing but good in the state's patronage of music, provided it is encouraging to artists, enlightened and leads to all of us individual citizens being patrons of music by paying for tickets for concerts.' Unconsciously anticipating his beliefs as a critic in the decades to come, he said: 'There is in fact no more effective advertisement than the critical notice, good or bad: and the critical notice is avowedly the recommendation by the journal to its readers of the merits and faults of the works and performers they may attend.' He concluded 'We hope that you will ascribe any faults of arrangements there may have been to our inexperience.'

In fact, the next undertaking of Acton-Miley was a series of three recitals in January 1950 by Charles Lynch, in which he played major works by Brahms, together with Bax's sonata no. 4 (of which he was the dedicatee), and Rachmaninov's first sonata, of which he had given the European premiere in 1936. The admission price remained attractive: twelve shillings subscription or five shillings for each recital. Hire of McCullough's Steinway was six guineas per week, with Mairtín McCullough giving a 10 per cent discount. The rental of the hall was seven guineas. At the end of the series, Lynch wrote to Charles 'I think that I enjoyed this series of concerts more than any that I have so far given. This is really true, because for the first time for many a long day I was able to choose works and play them simply because I wanted to play them. How seldom this happens!'

This was the end of Charles's collaboration with John Miley, although they remained good friends and corresponded frequently when John and his wife Joan moved abroad in connection with his work. Joan, one of Carol's closest friends, returned to Dublin with her three children in 1962, staying with Charles and Carol at Stradbrook. Charles actively but unsuccessfully promoted John as a candidate for the post of manager of the Belfast Festival.

Dublin Orchestral Players

As part of Charles's initial involvement in music-making and musical politics, he supported the Dublin Orchestral Players, founded by Havelock Nelson in 1940 as an evolution of the former Dublin Junior Orchestra;[48] from 1942 it

---

48. The Dublin Junior Orchestra had been founded in 1939 by Havelock Nelson, D.H. D'Oyly Cooper, Brian Townsend and Constance Harding (who was also responsible for the Musical Arts Society).

was conducted by Brian Boydell (Nelson had left Dublin to work in England as a bacteriologist), and he continued as principal conductor until 1966.[49] He joined the orchestra, not only as a bassoonist, since he had also 'committed myself to play the kitchen, by which is meant bass drum, triangle, cymbal and tambourine'; in the Polovtsian Dances from Borodin's *Prince Igor* 'I have to be hitting everything at the same time'.[50] 'Brian is a delight to play under. A beautifully clear beat, complete control of his orchestra without having to strive for it, and his musicianship, charm and enthusiasm are such as to make one want to do everything one can and put in everything one has got. He reminds me rather of Sargent, and that is praise.'

> The orchestra itself requires somewhat careful handling. The brass are essentially military bandsmen, which is not particularly helpful. The woodwind, except for the first clarinet who is a constable in the detective service, and though extremely efficient is not really a musician, they are enthusiastic. The oboes are rather painful, but then there is an appalling dearth of oboes in Dublin. The strings may in various ways be divided into categories: the real musicians (a small and devoted band of friends, i.e. those who think that the important thing is to gather together once a week to make music); and the professional attitudes, i.e. those whose only idea of playing is to have a concert; or those who play *music* i.e. are prepared to put their head, heart and guts into it; and those with whom it is an 'accomplishment' in the early Victorian sense and who are far too genteel and refaned [*sic*]. The latter we tend to call Rethmanes: the real name of that suburb is Rathmines. Unfortunately the Rethmanes and the 'professional attitudes' are so far in the majority, and this means that Brian has to be pretty tactful and so forth, quite apart from the fact that Dublin music is riddled with catfights. The catfights he can somewhat smooth down; the 'professional attitudes' he can sleuther; but the refinement is the most difficult of all. People who are afraid of using their emotions, or letting themselves go, are almost incapable of playing with exhilaration, or boisterously, or with feeling, or in fact being an orchestral ensemble. These young ladies give one the impression that they badly need waking up and being seduced. That however is neither practical nor desirable.

Charles immediately became involved in matters of orchestral management, having succeeded Michael McMullin as secretary in 1948. Now Boydell wrote to him from Inishere on management issues relating to the balance

---

49. Havelock Nelson would later have a distinguished career at the BBC in Belfast, and as a conductor and composer.

50. Charles continued to play in the DOP up to 1961, when he resigned as a Concert member due to pressure of concert reviewing, but continued as a 'Rehearsal member'.

between amateurs and professionals. It seemed essential to both Charles and Brian that the orchestra, whatever its composition, should be put on as professional lines as possible. As Charles later noted, 'as the orchestra grew and became democratically self-governing, it became desirable to make a fundamental rule that all members play as amateurs' – he meant in the best sense of the word. Although it was self-governing, Boydell's concern over management had to be taken into consideration, especially when one member – the percussionist Val Keogh, later to become manager of the RTÉSO – said that he would not continue to play 'unless the trombones were sacked'.[51]

By 1945 the DOP could claim that, apart from the Radio Éireann orchestra, it was 'the only permanent full concert orchestra' in Leinster, with a strong remit towards education. Not only was it giving more regular concerts than the radio orchestra, which gave it an onus to present instructive programmes, but it now admitted non-playing associate members who could learn from attending rehearsals. It was, essentially, a training orchestra, and, as a young student professional, one of its players was Carol Little, from Clabby, Fivemiletown (near Enniskillen, County Fermanagh, where her father was a Justice of the Peace), who was studying violin at the RIAM with Nancie Lord. She was to become leader in 1955, keeping the position until 1960, besides (from 1956) teaching music and forming a student orchestra at the Hall School in Monkstown. But, more importantly, this was where she met Charles. The fact that he owned a car, which was rare at the time, meant that he was able to offer lifts to and from rehearsals, and three of the people who regularly accepted the offer were Carol, John Miley and Joan McElroy (the latter two soon to be married). As Charles recalled, 'two members [himself and John Miley] went down the hall of the Academy and persuaded two girls to become members there and then – and much later on we married them!'[52]

Carol

After two years of courtship between 1949 and 1950, Charles and Carol realized that the relationship was a serious one. Before he realized that he was in

---

51. Boydell himself held a jaundiced view of musicians, writing to Charles 'the wood wind in Dublin are appalling both as players and people!' and referring to 'the dimness of the average Dublin musician'.

52. In an article on the 25th anniversary of the MAI, *Irish Times* 30 March 1973.

love with Carol, Charles had a deep sense of what he called 'witness' – that she was a soulmate. This was a major development in his way of thinking about women, since, with the exception of his earlier passion for Dorothy Beattie, he had regarded girls as inconsequential, even inconsiderable, as far as conversation was concerned. His men friends were his sole source of stimulating discussion, but now he had discovered in Carol a talented musician and a woman of consequence. With her, he 'found the peace of love, passing understanding' to 'accompany and inspire' him. The biblical reference to 'the peace [of God] that passeth all understanding' was obviously intentional.[53]

Carol (as he told her) 'would be a wonderful companion. And it was a miraculous impossibility seemingly when I also knew I loved you and even more wonderfully impossible that you loved me. For as the years will go by and our love evolves it will be all these other things that it will take to grow with, as a sapling tree takes the sun & the rain and the air & the soil to grow to the great wonderful beech or ilex. But I', he continued – so aware of his personal drawbacks – 'with my caustic irritabilities, my slovenlinesses, my cowardices, my lethargies, my Yahoo-ness, fear that I shall be but a poor ill-favoured thing for you.'

Carol, for her part, was not only in love, but fully confident, as a twenty-three-year-old, that she could cope with Charles's inner anxieties and lack of self-confidence:

> I never thought anyone could write a letter like your first one to me – you should have been a poet. It gave me the greatest delight and joy to read it – the picture it brought most clearly to my mind was of us sitting in 'Jane' at Booterstown, talking about stars and the Sahara and then you reciting the Curlew. Yes, all that long discourse of yours is true – it revolved around the word 'with' and I agree with you wholeheartedly. Thank you, my dear, for saying my mind is alive, quick, clear & interested. Alive & interested, yes; the other two, perhaps. As for your description of yourself – caustic irritability, slovenliness, cowardice, lethargy – just say it again to me in person, if you dare. I now have a one-track mind with the name Charles engraved on it. Charlie, I love you – how often have I said those words since I saw you last – millions of times – I can't even keep them to myself & Frances [her sister] and Mummy are rather awed, I think, that their cool-headed Carol should care so much for anyone.

Mrs Little wrote to Charles: 'How very pleased I am at the prospect of having you for a son-in-law. Since I have met you I feel absolutely convinced

---

53. Philippians ii. 7.

that her happiness and welfare will be safe in your keeping. It is rare to meet a couple who seem so well suited, or as we say in the North, "just made for each other".' On a lighter note, his friend Alec Wallace wrote from Louisburgh 'I envy you the pleasure of having a good fiddler in the family and hope you can persuade her to keep playing in spite of family and household ties. To my mind the only possible improvement I could ask for in Carol is that she should be able to play a harpsichord also.'

Charles's decision to marry Carol caused a serious disturbance in his relations with his mother, which were, in any case, not good. Charles and his mother did not flourish in close proximity and, to the contrary, seemed to get on very well when they were some distance apart. Now, Isabel began a series of manoeuvres which, on the face of it, seemed designed to prevent the marriage. In fact, Isabel and Carol would establish a very workable relationship (Carol recalled that she never had 'mother-in-law' problems), while Charles's relationship with his mother continued unsettled up to her death in 1971. Isabel's strategy was not, in fact, to prevent Charles from marrying, but to re-assert herself as both parent and dependent. To achieve this, she resorted to contradictory notions as the mood took her. Early in the engagement, she claimed that she was 'still young and certainly young in mind, and should go and start a new life' – she even floated the idea that she could re-purchase Grata Quies; or, she 'would go and live near Marcus [Beresford] if Rugby were not such a beastly climate'. This latter ploy was sure to stir Charles's sense of guilt. On the other hand, she 'had hoped for security and contentment for what remained of her life'. This certainly had the effect of unsettling Charles, who worried greatly that, if his mother moved out of Stradbrook, she would be alone and unsupervised – she was now in her seventies. She wanted Charles to 'find the real true love, and not be led astray by the dazzle of lesser lights when he finds the true radiance'.

In what definitely appeared to be Isabel's attempt to convince Charles that Carol was an unsuitable companion, she told her son (as he relayed it to Carol) that 'I was vividly interested in almost every subject (true) that I should be in the end miserable if my wife had not the same far-ranging, vivid curiosity & intellectual interest in everything. Would Carol, she asked, delight to read all the same non-fiction books I get from the library or would I be forced in the end to leave my house to go to Brian & Farrington for mental company[?]'[54] From the Acton side of the family, Charles's aunt Evelyn enquired whether Carol attended church, this presumably being a way of deciding her suitability

---

54. Anthony Farrington was one of the founders of the Music Association of Ireland.

as a wife for Charles, despite his already having explained to his aunt that he himself was no church-goer.

In fact, Charles saw everything in quite the opposite way. By October 1949 he had come to the conclusion that 'Carol's is a mind like mine, alive & quick and clear and interested but while I have allowed mine to wander too much so that it has filled with all sorts of things and failed to acquire enough of any one thing for success, she has the discipline to have confined hers to what was important immediately'. Charles was quite sure that Carol had already improved him. 'You have rejuvenated me, grown me up, but even you won't have turned me into a saint and I am afraid still of the impatiences, tempers, blindnesses, selfishnesses, &c, &c that have always been part of me.' To which Carol responded: 'My dear love, all these things are in everyone – self included – and if they were not we should be saints, not humans. I want you, my love, as a human being, not a saint.'

At the time of Charles's retirement from *The Irish Times*, Gerard Gillen wrote that 'Through the years you have, of course, been supported both personally and professionally by Carol', to which Charles responded: 'I am extremely touched by your perceptive recognition of Carol's part; it certainly is wonderful to be half a team rather than one person, whoever's name appeared at the top.' When, after four-and-a-half years of marriage, the offer of the post at *The Irish Times* was made, the Charles-and-Carol partnership was such that they did think, and speak, with one mind. Charles would write about his relationship with Carol as a critic-colleague, 'our opinions are marvellously unanimous. Nearly always we are together, and we ourselves could not sort out our separate contributions to our ordinary joint notices.' So much so that, after Charles's death, Kevin Myers, then an *Irish Times* columnist, could write: 'He was a deeply emotional man and was not shy about his deep and passionate affections, the greatest of which was for his wife, his companion, his friend, and his love, Carol. Charles & Carol. A single and singular singularity.'[55] To which one might add Thurloe Conolly's comment from 1961: 'what a nice trademark ceeandcee (Charles + Carol) makes: Ɔ+C, consummate charm, courtesy and civility'. Although during their engagement Charles and Carol eagerly discussed possible names for the sons and daughters they might have, the marriage proved to be childless.

Charles's certainty about Carol was one thing; his mother's doubts were another, and a third, basic, factor was his customary relationship with Isabel

55. *Irish Times* 7 May 1999.

which was, in any case, a cause of filial anxiety. In September 1950, after six months of the one-year engagement which had been agreed as a compromise with his mother, Charles wrote to Terence de Vere White of the 'emotional mess with my Mama – objectively I think not much my fault; subjectively I kept on blaming myself. I got engaged with Mum's vigorous disapproval, last March, and for four or five weeks in April and May Mum was ill, so that apart from having hardly any sight of my fiancée I was nursing, cooking, houseminding and everything else, as well as trying to recover from flu myself.' Looking after Isabel had also prevented Charles from visiting the Little family at Clabby, and he began to resent the fact that his sense of duty to Isabel kept him separate from Carol (who was at home, busily studying for her licentiate at the Royal Academy of Music). Isabel's emotional *lien* on Charles was clearly considerable. Many years earlier she had told Hugh Digues La Touche that 'I am always so afraid of tying him too much to my apron strings. If he is so devoted to me, it will be a terrible loss to him when I die – and a boy so absorbed by his mother does not look outward to make his own home & life for himself – but feels he has all he wants already. However, it may ward him past the early shoals of the wrong girl, perhaps, & get him safely on the right one.' Even after twenty years, and especially after the separation of the war years, the apron strings were still affective, and, realizing this, Charles determined that, from that point onwards, his principal affection was to Carol rather than to his mother – a point which Isabel soon came to accept. As Terence White assured him, 'if your mother's objection is simply emotional it will die a natural death. Most only boys have to go through that.'

Isabel, despite her no doubt partly psychosomatic illnesses, had had the sense (or perhaps the courage) to invite Carol to stay with her at Stradbrook in August 1950. It must have been something of an ordeal for both of them. But a breakthrough in the relationship seems to have taken place. Isabel wrote to her friend Faith Bennett, about the lengthy interview, which Faith dutifully reported to Charles: 'Mrs La Touche wrote, that Carol had had the high courage to come & see her & it seemed that there was a character clear-sighted & strong enough to face the issues & not be daunted by them.' Isabel had worried that Carol's reserve in conversation and in company indicated a shallowness, and Carol's mother was also disturbed that her daughter spoke so little about her feelings for Charles. But Carol herself told Charles 'this particular woman has been born with an unusually vivid imagination & a <u>very</u> thin skin and I suspect outward reserve cloaks a very emotional nature.'

This gave Charles confidence to pursue both the engagement and the question of what kind of relationship he might have with his mother after the marriage. 'I am now getting rapidly straightened out and beginning to know where I am going and go there', he told White. 'As you know, the main purpose of this house [Stradbrook] was a home for Mum. When Carol and I marry we don't want Mum becoming a lonely old person far away, and all three are completely agreed that there is no question of the same dwelling.' Isabel had even suggested selling Stradbrook, and buying a two-storey house which they could convert into two flats, but that was out of the question as far as Charles was concerned. In fact, for the first three years of marriage, he and Carol resolutely kept their separate residence at The Hill, Monkstown, only moving in 1954 into a basement flat in Stradbrook when one of the tenants left. They would live at Stradbrook until 1968, when they bought the converted railway station house at Carrickmines, building a studio extension which contained a 'granny flat' for Isabel, which in fact she would never occupy.

Charles did not feel that Stradbrook was his 'home', but he also found it difficult to envisage a situation where he could make a home elsewhere with Carol while also ensuring his mother's comfort and security. Living at Stradbrook would present Carol with 'something pretty terrific in the way of difficulties'. Carol's view was that 'marriage is no bed of roses – it is even more difficult than family life for a time – school or digs all over again, but this time it must be learnt patiently & carefully as it is for life. Rough edges to be knocked off, little faults & big ones to be recognised at least & accepted.'

'As marriage revokes my sensed duty and moral obligation to be company and companion continuously to Mum (who has come to depend on me far too much in this respect) this and my wishes to do so have ended', wrote Charles. The seismic shift in his life which saw his deepest affections transferred to Carol nevertheless did not absolve him from caring about the single parent who had devoted so much of her life, and her own anxieties, to her only son. Charles told Carol:

Thinking about Mum I wonder if it is possible for me ever again to reinstate her as a friend. I do not of course mean by this any reversion to parental relationships, any question of her being fitted into US, but merely whether there is any hope of her ever again becoming as close a friend as Ksana [Couriss] or Brian ... There is a human being who has once been my very close friend who is lonely and old and friendless with all her being wanting friendship (even though she goes the wrong way to get it) and between whom and me there is a wall as thick as the ocean ... I am convinced that provided we have a separate dwelling & keep ourselves to ourselves a bit at the beginning, she has sufficient sense, conscience, will-power & love (& I hope eventually for you too) to avoid completely being the mother-in-law.

The immediate priority for Charles was to find suitable employment with proper pay. He mentioned this to Terence de Vere White:

> I now very strongly and definitely am looking for a job. My qualities are I think unusual: two years of having run a voluntary committee and turned an amateur society (the DOP) from moral and financial near-dissolution to a healthy credit balance and a great pitch of enthusiasm, have confirmed my confidence in being an able, resourceful and diplomatic administrator (which my personal mess had very considerably shaken) even though I am the first to admit that an amateur symphony orchestra of 50 is very small beer. Unfortunately I have no paper qualifications and so forth. Musical administration is my ideal, but as a paying job that obviously does not seem probable in Dublin, and though I would dearly like Ó hAnnracháin's job at the Radio and could do it far better (in spite of what I know to be the peculiar difficulties of it) I have no musical degree, cannot speak Irish and presumably am the wrong religion, even if they wanted a change from Ó hAnnracháin. I do feel I would make a greater success of a job that would fully engage someone of my interests of the intellect or the arts, but of course they are extremely scarce.[56]

White's reply was not encouraging: 'I don't think music in Dublin pays. Frankly I don't believe you'd get into the wireless office. Have you thought of teaching?' Later he told him frankly: 'It is difficult to think of a job that would be suitable for your talents', and suggested the possibility of working in a bookshop.

At the time of their marriage in 1951, Charles's financial position was dire: he had £340 in hand, but no income other than the rent from the tenants at Stradbrook – approximately £650 per year, out of which the upkeep of the premises, and the two gardeners, had to be paid. Isabel had paid £2340 as part-purchase of Stradbrook, and there was some doubt as to whether she expected Charles to repay this sum. She had also lent him £1200 towards the conversion of the house into separate apartments, and she definitely regarded this as a repayable loan. Charles told Carol that he had answered an advertisement for a salesman.[57] The eventual appointment as a representative of

---

56. Charles was being somewhat unfair to Fachtna Ó hAnnracháin as Music Director of Radio Éireann and would, in due course, write fulsomely of Ó hAnnrachain's almost single-handed creation of the Radio Éireann Symphony Orchestra and the development of its repertoire.

57. The first advertisement that Charles answered appeared in *The Irish Times*: 'A

the *Encyclopaedia Britannica* would, however, provide them with the closeness they craved, as Charles, with Carol aboard the 'Jane', travelled the highways and byways of Ireland, and it also gave them exit visas from Dublin and the maternal concerns, sometimes for weeks at a time.

Charles was becoming aware that, at the age of thirty-six, he had achieved little, whereas several of his contemporaries at Rugby and Cambridge were already eminent or in important positions – one an MP, another private secretary to the Prime Minister. 'It was in their personalities. They were the people sufficiently well balanced to use their good brains, sufficiently normal, however odd they might be, to take things for granted, especially their success. Whatever their fears, self-confidence in their ability to do what they were going to do.' Charles was acutely conscious of his own lack of self-confidence (which he was extremely aware of in others), to which he attributed his lack of success in the public world.

> As for me, Mum spent most of my childhood taking it for granted that I was
> an outstanding swan, with the inevitable result of destroying my self-confi-
> dence completely. And I therefore assumed not only that I was a pretty ordi-
> nary goose, but a mere hen. I see now that had I had a normal self-confidence
> I should have shewn great promise & walked into any safe responsible slightly
> cultural job I wanted had I worked for it, & probably become one of the BBC
> young men.

Charles still suffered from a severe deficit of self-confidence and his relationship with his mother was an added hindrance. But, with Carol's help, he was growing in self-confidence – 'it will take a long time to grow out of muddling inefficiency but it is possible that it will have been far better from the point of view of worldly achievement that I should now with you & by you develop my personality & in time take on what I should do.' It would be another five years before that opportunity arose.

The newspapers in February 1951 carried an announcement that the marriage of Charles and Carol 'will take place very quietly in March'. Mrs Little showed scant interest in attending Carol's wedding (Carol's father had died some years previously) and Carol thought that a small gathering would be the most

---

sympathetic hearing from the Sales Manager is assured to a gentleman of refinement – preferably without so-called "personality" – who would be keen to enter the selling world with a publishing house if given a chance. Previous experience is not so important as that the applicant should be over thirty-five years of age, have a sense of adventure and be willing to embark on a new career.'

suitable. In fact the service, in Monkstown parish church on 6 March 1951, was attended by Isabel, Mrs. Little, Frances Little and Brian and Mary Boydell (Brian being both 'best man' and giving away the bride). The marriage was performed by the Revd Albert Stokes. When a marriage with Dorothy Beattie had seemed possible, Charles had said 'Not that I intend a church wedding if I can help it – I do not feel I could expect anyone else to undertake an oath of such awe for me or undertake it myself.' Presumably these earlier reservations had been overcome. The honeymoon did not take place immediately – it was spent in May and June at the Festival of Britain, when they stayed with a London friend, the architect Faith Bennett. They heard the London Mozart Players conducted by Harry Blech, and a season by the LPO, conducted by Sir Adrian Boult, Basil Cameron, Benjamin Britten and Rafael Kubelik, with soloists including Solomon and Benno Moiseiwitsch; both orchestras played at the newly-built Royal Festival Hall, the only festival structure on London's South Bank to survive the return to power of the Conservative government under Winston Churchill two years later.

Encyclopaedia Britannica

Once back from honeymoon, Charles was appointed as a sales representative for the *Encyclopaedia Britannica*. How he achieved the appointment is not known, but it was doomed from the start, despite the fact that he kept at it for two years. There was no salary: reps were paid commission on what they sold, and as Charles frequently said in retrospect, 'I am no salesman'. It was not simply a question of his belief in his abilities so much as a fundamental characteristic flaw – that he could *not* sell. 'A person who *is* a salesman can write his own cheque and sell refrigerators to Greenland', as he once told me. 'But if you are not a salesman, you can't even sell life assurance.' Moreover, Charles always believed that one should approve of the product, and, having read most of the encyclopaedia himself, came to the conclusion that it wasn't terribly good. Ironically, in 1970 Charles was asked to contribute an article to *Britannica* on 'Musical Scales, Modes and the Serial System' – a request that he was happy to decline.

The cost of the encyclopaedia varied according to the binding, the cheapest being a basic cloth binding, costing £40, on which the seller received a commission of £2.10.0; the most expensive being a green, hand-tooled morocco at

£350 – Charles said 'I never even saw one, let alone sold one'. But he did sell a very few at £40 and £80, including one set to the Church of Ireland curate in Swanlinbar: 'I made my presentation, and to my horror the poor little fellow went down on his knees to ask God for guidance as to whether he should buy it or not. Luckily God told him to buy it.'[58]

A great deal of travelling in 'Jane' was involved, and the newlyweds used the job to spend long weeks together on the road, staying, as Carol put it, 'in third-rate, flea-bitten hotels'. It gave Charles an insight into the problems of the Irish catering industry: 'Very many years ago, in a bitter January, I had been driving over snow and black ice for three hours in an unheated car over a distance that should have taken one hour, and arrived at Clones at 6.45 p.m. We stopped at the first hotel and my wife and I staggered in. Could we have some tea and something to eat? No: the dining room closes at 7.' Not only would Charles and Carol write restaurant reviews ('Table for Two') in *The Irish Times*, but Charles, using his nom-de-plume 'Thomas Annesley', would write a regular column, 'Worm's Eye View', for the Irish *Hotel and Catering Review* in the 1970s. In the month of July, Charles recalled, 'I drove 2,600 miles in the County Kerry, and what I don't know about the boreens of County Kerry, not even the Kerrymen know!' At this stage, Charles and Carol frequently visited Kilmacurragh, sitting on Westaston Hill above the house, and agonizing over whether they should buy it back from Dermot O'Connor and try once again to make it a viable business as well as restoring it as the family home.

Shortly afterwards Isabel wrote: 'I want some money badly ... I am beginning to feel overwhelmed like I did at Kilmacurragh. When you come to see me we never seem to settle down to a real business talk, of ways & means. That is why I am writing this – so that you will get it ship shape in your mind & be ready for a business talk & discussion.' This was typical of Isabel's attitude to Charles in the next few years: while she appreciated Carol's support (much more than that of Charles, whom she regarded as dilatory in his filial duties), she resented the fact that Charles had made the decision to devote his life to his wife rather than to his mother; she tried to conceal her feelings, but they were aggravated by her financial worries and her failing health. All her life Isabel had striven to make ends meet financially, and to assure Charles's welfare, and her letters indicate just how much anxiety she carried in the difficult years when she, as did Charles and Carol themselves, had to accustom herself to life in a threesome. Despite the 'terrific wages', Isabel wanted to hire a married chauffeur-gardener with a

---

58. From Charles's interview with me, RTÉ Radio, 1990.

wife as maid, and to accommodate them in one of the flats at Stradbrook. Apart from the two gardeners for whom she had taken responsibility, she had great difficulty in keeping a cook or a companion: Carol reckoned that she hired, and dismissed, as many as thirty-six lady-companions in one year alone.

Charles and Carol had laid down some ground-rules in order to protect their privacy, and on one occasion Isabel had to make peace with her son:

> I gather from Carol that there was a misunderstanding on Sunday – you thought I was <u>com</u>plaining & I thought I was <u>ex</u>plaining. I was apologising for encroaching on your time and being such a burden to you & saying how I couldn't help it & had tried & tried to relieve you of the tiresome duty of caring for your ancient parent. I know it is stupid of me to be afraid to be left alone & I do try to overcome it & it hurts my pride to have to accept from you time which I know you grudge.

Clearly the experience of living at Kilmacurragh after Reggie's death had cut deeply into Isabel's already nervous disposition, but, apart from her obvious distaste for the place, it was only at this stage that she made explicit what had festered in her mind for over thirty years. At the beginning of 1954 she wrote:

> So sorry to have let you see what a state of nerves I was in. It is a throwback to the simply frightful time I had at KmaK, when I went there after your father was killed, & had no money & didn't know what to do. If I get short of money or have bothers of that sort, I get a throwback. Please look on the state I occasionally (<u>very</u> occasionally) get into, as a sort of mental cold in the head & don't hold it against me. I would like you to have a serene & helpful mother, not one who is a trial & nuisance to you … I wish you had known me before 1916, when your father loved me, I must have been much nicer then.

In Charles's correspondence with his friends – Thurloe Conolly and Nic Couriss in particular – there are frequent references to his mother's declining health, her increasing immobility and poor eyesight being the chief causes of her depression, until she left Stradbrook in 1969 for a nursing home where she died in 1971. Chronicling her decline, Charles wrote to Conolly (in 1967) that at 92 she was 'as difficult as ever. Her cook is having her fortnight's holidays so Carol is standing in and this year's 7th companion is about to leave'. At the nursing home, 'run by American Carmelite nuns who mother is convinced are Hebrews', her mind was failing, but 'she is quite clearly happier in herself there than she has been for 30 years'. She died 'after a half year of virtually continuous sleep. And death was so long a-coming although any person had left a long time ago, that no feelings save of relief were involved.'

Broadcasting

Towards the end of this 'interlude', a development in Charles's life indicated that the various strands in his experience might be coming together in a much more positive fashion to point the way forward in his career. In May 1953 he was advised by Brian Boydell (who was to become a frequent contributor to educational programmes on both radio and television) that a new Radio Éireann programme called 'Wednesday Night at Eight' was in the offing, and that he, Charles, could well become a regular contributor. It was to be hosted by Monk Gibbon, at that time a well-established author, known to his friends as 'Bill'.[59] Charles immediately wrote to 'Dear Bill'. His initial enthusiasm led him to suggest that, when Brian Boydell himself was not speaking about music, 'that would be really up my street too – a particular hobby-horse of mine at present is making chamber music in the home, and I would love to produce 5 minutes on that subject' – and it turned out that he would indeed do so. His second suggestion made a more far-reaching claim:

> While it would be presumptuous to hold myself out as a critical expert on other arts, I do find that I have as informed a critical faculty as most of our established critics and suggest therefore that when you are designing a programme and have an exhibition of any sort (including painting) that is worth covering, but have no one else in mind, you let me do it – not as your Critic (capital letter) but as *an intelligent citizen* [my emphasis]. I feel there may be a use in having a general magpie, acting as a citizen of intelligence, to potter stimulatingly on various arts as a contrast to the permanent expert on a single art.

It was a large claim, but the extraordinary breadth of Charles's appreciation of subjects as disparate as local authority housing, furniture auctions, and fine arts did indeed equip him to speak, and to write, with informed opinion even if he usually disclaimed any direct authority. As a result he broadcast not only on musical matters but on a variety of other topics.

The first episode of 'Wednesday Night at Eight' was broadcast on 27 May 1953, chaired by Monk Gibbon and featuring Charles, Ralph Cusack, and Denis Donoghue. The radio producer for the series was Gerard Victory, thus ushering in a strange professional relationship within broadcasting between

---

59. [William] Monk Gibbon (1896–1987) was the author of the autobiographical *The Seals* (1935) and the novel *Mount Ida* (1948); his collected poems had just been published.

Charles, the future music critic of *The Irish Times* and Victory, the future Director of Music at RTÉ. This led to regular appearances by Charles on radio, including a programme called 'Information, Please', and his contributions to 'Film Magazine' in the later 1950s.

The following week, Charles was on the air again, in the company of artist Hilary Heron, sculptor Oisín Kelly, critic Alec Reid and RDS librarian and historian Desmond Clarke. Thereafter, Charles was a regular contributor, on one occasion (nine months before he joined *The Irish Times* and therefore so far unknown as a critic) speaking, with Denis Donoghue (already reviewing for *The Irish Times*), John O'Donovan and Joseph Groocock, on 'The Responsibility of the Music Critic', chaired by Brian Boydell. And, earlier, on 20 January 1954, he had taken part in a panel consisting of architect Michael Scott, Ralph Cusack and Patrick Munden, again chaired by Boydell, on 'The Bowl of Light or, Industrial Taste', and the relevance of public statuary, shortly after the installation on O'Connell Bridge known as the 'Bowl of Light' (nicknamed 'Tomb of the Unknown Gurrier') was thrown into the Liffey. The 'Bowl' surfaced again in Charles's life when, at the end of 1955, he was one of the winners of the *Irish Times* 'Christmas Clerihew Competition' with: 'For putting the hidgeous Trough on the Bridge / The Corporation oughter / Be exported for slaughter'.

Tripod harvesting

In May 1953, Charles, having unsuccessfully applied for jobs at Radio Éireann, Bord Fáilte and several other organizations, was able to abandon the thankless task of not selling encyclopaedias to become Sales Manager of Proctor's Tripod Harvesting (Ireland) Ltd., a subsidiary of a Scottish company selling tripod harvesting equipment which had been incorporated in Ireland in 1950. The Managing Director was Eileen Ware, and it had been through his acquaintance with her that he was appointed, due to his interest and confidence in the product. With his dreary record in touting the *Encyclopaedia Britannica* in the highways and byways of the countryside, why Charles should have considered himself suited to such a position is beyond speculation. Nevertheless, despite ups and downs in his relations with the Proctors, he succeeded in holding the position up to the time that he was appointed to *The Irish Times*.[60]

---

60. Tripod harvesting was pioneered by Alexander Proctor, from Blairgowrie in

As one writer on the subject explained,[61] 'it is an art the real mastery of which requires much time and experience', and this is most probably what attracted Charles to the subject. The fact that he was definitely not a salesman did not interfere with his belief in tripod harvesting, so that he, with the active assistance of the Proctor brothers, was able to instruct the sales representatives whom he employed, and to enable them to travel the countryside with confidence.

At first, Charles employed Seán Fitzmaurice as a sales rep. He had been a farmer himself, and came with a reference from Dr Robert Collis, a paediatrician and playwright. Later, having interviewed eighty-four applicants, he also took on someone whose name, for reasons of confidentiality, cannot be mentioned: this man was in severe financial difficulties which resulted in his wages being diverted to paying his creditors, while his wife and six children lived in dire poverty. The wife succeeded in persuading Charles that a weekly sum should be paid directly to her, having written 'Short of prostitution I can do no more for my family'. Her husband was, however, a very successful salesman and, it was considered more importantly, a first-class demonstrator of the tripod method. Later still, a third rep, Maurice McDonagh was hired. Charles himself was paid £10 per week, plus commission of 6d. per tripod sold. The sales reps received £8 per week, and commission of one penny in the shilling (i.e., 8½ per cent). Based on prior sales, Charles expected that, in 1955, 27,000 tripods could be sold, approximately doubling the figures for 1953 (at that time he had all three reps on the road), although he took the precaution of mentioning that his projections 'are combined of ignorance and

---

Perthshire, from the 1930s, and the company was now run by his sons, Alastair and Herbert. Its purpose was to save hay and corn in uncertain weather conditions, by protecting the crop from the deleterious effects of either sun or rain, curing them slowly through air circulation in ventilated tripod huts in a two- or three-week period, after which the crop is baled, stacked or threshed. Approximately ten tripods were needed per acre, equally suitable for hay, grain, beans or peas, and had a working life of ten years. The equipment was remarkably simple: three poles of seven feet in length, joined at the top with wire, were covered with a wire triangle, to which the crop is attached in quantities up to five hundredweight per tripod. The cost was between nine and ten shillings per tripod, depending on the quantity purchased. The single most likely difficulty in the process is that it differs greatly in method from haystacking, and therefore proved less easy to learn in the case of older farm workers.

61. Captain Deane, Corwen, Denbighshire, in a paper read to the National Power Farming Conference at Cheltenham, February 1954.

guesswork'. At the time that he took on the job, the company was just breaking even, and the prospect was that it would start to repay the Proctors' initial investment of £6000, but Charles warned that as the tripod method became more widespread and appreciated, farmers could start to make their own. Moreover, smaller farms bought less tripods, and the unit cost of these should be increased to cover relatively higher costs of sales. But his greatest worry was that the patent for the tripod method had lapsed, and there was therefore no legal protection for the product.

Charles was so disillusioned by the fact that the Proctor brothers did not respond to his letters in any way that could give him the confidence to manage the business that, after only six months, he applied to Hilton Edwards at the Gate Theatre for a position as business manager, discovering in the process that Edwards's adviser was Dermot O'Connor, the new owner of Kilmacurragh. Edwards did offer him the job, which Charles accepted, subject to clarification as to the hours involved, but, in the interim, changes in the composition of the Gate's board of directors involved a change in the job specification, and, in an atmosphere of uncertainty, Charles withdrew.

In January 1954 he had to report that sales had halted.

> This is a deeply distressing and depressing matter to us. There is no doubt that throughout this country farmers are depressed beyond reason about the last four to five months. It has not really been quite so bad as they make out (naturally) but the farming press do not really help by keeping on talking about floods and disasters. The floods have been very bad, but the trouble has been that (as far as I can see) far too many farmers have persuaded themselves from reading the press and talking with their neighbours that they are in a far worse way than they are.

It was a situation for which his own farming experience, and his nation-wide travels with the *Encyclopaedia*, had prepared him. He urged one of his sales reps: 'Next time you see a flattened field of green oats, find the farmer and SELL him tripods – but choose a larger field rather than a smaller one. But please, go flat out and get me sales during these next three weeks. Be a little less nice. Be a bit more tough.' And, remembering his own sales endeavours, 'After tea is the best selling time in any day.'

After a year as Sales Manager, Charles proposed that his salary should be doubled to £1000 per year, in return for him taking on extra responsibilities as 'General Manager', with the reps taking on winter work in the form of talks to farmers' groups. While the Proctors seem to have been agreeable to the proposal, the company accountant, Micheál Willis Murphy, appears to have poured scorn on Charles's self-acknowledged 'ignorance and guesswork'.

When a meeting took place in mid-1954, it transpired that Charles was very unhappy with the way the parent company was run. He had formed the view that, despite the excellence of the tripod method, the Proctor brothers did not seem to have sufficient confidence in their father's invention, and that, as a result, the company had been set up on ramshackle lines as a 'sideline' to their main business, 'lacking any coherent national direction' and operating one year at a time rather than developing a long-term strategy ... It is the duty of the Company to give its sales manager support, help and co-operation. This has so often been lacking.' There was a lack of liaison with the Scottish operation, and the Proctor brothers seemed to put on the long finger items which Charles felt required urgent attention. He had not even been provided with an office, and had worked from home, firstly at The Hill, Monkstown and, from 1954, at Stradbrook.

It is typical of Charles's frustration that he wrote at such length (ten typed pages) to set out his grievances. So often such lengthy diatribes are ignored by their recipients. It appears, however, that the Proctors were impressed by Charles's arguments and decided to put the company on a better footing. Charles was encouraged: 'All I am wanting is the opportunity to do a really good job of work with a future, to know where I stand, to have the instructions to do it, and to earn my living.'

It may have seemed to Charles that Proctors in Ireland had turned a corner, but by April the following year their resolve had evaporated, not least because further investment in the company was required, and relationships deteriorated again, leading to a showdown in September 1955. Within two months, Charles's professional fortunes had turned the most significant corner of his life, when he received a call from *The Irish Times*. Unfortunately, in his biographical chapter in *The Life and Music of Brian Boydell*, Axel Klein states that Charles's appointment was due to political interference at *The Irish Times* by Erskine Childers, which led to the resignation of Denis Donoghue as music critic.[62] Whatever the truth of the incident relating to Denis Donoghue, it had nothing to do with Charles. In fact Donoghue, who continued to review

---

62. A complaint had allegedly been made about a review by Donoghue of a concert by the RÉSO under Milan Horvat. In Charles's recollection, however, Donoghue resigned after a lengthy criticism of him by Aloys Fleischmann and a subsequent argument with Alec Newman, following which A.J. Potter became the paper's music critic.

for *The Irish Times* as Charles's deputy, was succeeded by A.J. (Archie) Potter, and it was the unfortunate Potter who suffered: he was in Wexford to review the opera festival, and, having consumed a considerable amount of alcohol, made an abusive phone call to the editor, Alec Newman, who promptly gave Potter the sack.[63] The next week, the job was offered to Charles's friend, Joseph Groocock, who did not want it, but recommended Charles, who naturally did. Despite his relative inexperience as a critic, Charles was already well positioned as a commentator on musical affairs and immediately established himself as a writer of both breadth and depth, in one of the most influential columns in Irish journalism.

---

63. Potter was sufficiently forgiven by *The Irish Times* to be able to deputize for Charles at a later stage.

8. The Critic: 1955–1988

Motivation

*W*hen I asked Charles what was his principal motive as a critic, he answered without hesitation: 'a missionary spirit – I go to a concert and if I enjoyed it I would want to tell the whole world how marvellous it was, and if I felt they were making a muck of it I would want to tell the whole world it should be better'.[1] It was not necessarily as 'black and white' as that suggests, but the declaration conveys the deep-seated commitment of a critic who was passionate about his job. Aloys Fleischmann, one of his sparring partners over the decades (with whom he was privately friendly but often disputatious in print) would comment in 1963 that Charles 'is unusual among music critics in that he writes from the heart as well as from the head'.

But Charles's thirty-three year career as a music critic was not merely a matter of attending, and commenting upon, musical performances. Almost immediately after his appointment he was catapulted into the world of cultural politics, and rapidly became a key figure in the ongoing debate about the place of classical music in Irish society. His involvement as a commentator on musical developments, as an instigator of discussion, as a polemicist on behalf of Irish music and musicians, is congruent with the type of contribution to Irish public affairs which, after independence, saw a significant number of Anglo-Irish people participating in cultural, economic, industrial and political

---

1. Quotations from conversations between Charles and myself are taken from three radio interviews on RTÉ Radio FM3 broadcast in 1990.

life, as they attempted to maintain continuity from the old regime to the new. It was Charles's *transitus* across the hyphen, his decision to enter, in what he would call 'a contemporary spirit', into the areas of Irish public life in which he had expertise and personal feeling.

In 1955 the seven-year-old Music Association of Ireland (MAI), with Charles on its Council, was persistently, but not very successfully, arguing the case with government for appropriate facilities for the performance of classical music, for music education and for the building of a national concert hall. While they had found the sympathetic ear of León Ó Broin, Secretary of the Department of Posts and Telegraphs, and his political master Erskine Childers,[2] other politicians and administrators were far less interested in the fate of a musical genre which they regarded as un-Irish, and which, because of the shortage of adequate Irish musicians, required the controversial importation of foreign players. As James Everett TD said in a Dáil debate in 1947, the orchestra existed only 'for the benefit of a few old fogies in Rathmines'.[3] It was against this background of mutual suspicion between social classes and their cultures that Charles took up his critical pen. Thirty years later, he would speak on music in direct contradiction of Everett, and at the same time urging *The Irish Times* not to regard music as a minority interest: 'I do not believe that music (or any or all of the arts) are a little corner tucked away from the rest of life. If we write as though they were, we will have only ourselves to blame if the philistine politicians treat the arts as of no concern.' In this respect, he particularly lauded Childers for having, as minister responsible for broadcasting, supported the RTÉSO's public concerts, and, as President of Ireland (1973–74) having invited Irish musicians to perform at Áras an Uachtaráin – 'something which this present clot [President P.J. Hillery] has stopped'.

In some ways it may seem that Charles had been seduced away from the traditional values of his family. But there were many traits in his role as a critic

---

2. Charles admired Childers enormously; he was Minister with responsibility for the broadcasting orchestras 1951–54 and 1966–69. In 1947–48, León Ó Broin and Fachtna Ó hAnnracháin (as Director of Music at Radio Éireann) had been the main architects of both the R(T)É Symphony Orchestra and the R(T)É Concert Orchestra: see *Music and Broadcasting* pp. 97–163.

3. For a consideration of the early years of the Irish symphony orchestra, see ibid., chapters 2 and 3. Everett, as Minister for Posts and Telegraphs 1948–51, had been obliged to support Radio Éireann's provision of the orchestras. In 1953 he was in opposition, and therefore not constrained by government policy when speaking his mind.

that carry their characteristics. His grandfather had identified two factors restraining him from public discussion: 'dread of cant' and 'the fear of being supposed to set one's self up as better than one's neighbour'. While Charles most decidedly threw himself into the most public of debates, he was also cautious, to the point of diffidence, about making assumptions regarding his status, and willingly apologized whenever he stood to be corrected on a point of fact. And if he was unsure of himself, as he was when RTÉ presented challenging concerts of unfamiliar music (for example, Barraud's first symphony and Hartmann's third symphony in one week in 1959), he could say that the conductor, in this case Tibor Paul, 'has taken us into deep waters and I freely admit to being out of my depth at times'. But his critiques and polemics were noticeably devoid of cant. Above all, the qualities evident in his ancestors were honesty, straightforwardness and commitment, all of which Charles possessed in abundance, as if, as the last of his line, he had a mark to make in his commitment to the new Ireland.

Much in his previous existence seems to have prepared Charles for this new life – and it seems as if his mother's words to his father were equally apt in this context: 'Here you go hunting for employment, when all the time your talent lies buried at your very feet.' His school training as a practical musician, his early appreciation of performance, his exposure to Richard Strauss and Knappertsbusch in Munich, his involvement in the organization of the Dublin Orchestral Players, his friendship with the composer Brian Boydell, his involvement with the fledgling RTÉ, his experience of concert promotion and his marriage to Carol all provided him with a foundation of musical experience. But the other facets of his life up to this point also equipped him for the task of teasing out the psychologies of composers and performers: his questing imagination; his fascination with international politics; his passion for travel and his capacity for bringing his travels to life in his letters; his understanding of what it meant to live in a changing Ireland; his own family's role in relation to its heritage and its future; even his failure at various forms of commercial activity; all these contributed to the making of the most influential and respected music critic in the history of *The Irish Times*.

Above all, perhaps, the close familiarity with artists of all persuasions and disciplines, discussed in the preceding chapter, had given Charles an active appreciation of drama, literature, the plastic arts and music both in performance and composition, so that he would never view musical activity in isolation, but could observe, and comment upon, music as one element in the development of the arts in modern Ireland. Intimate knowledge of artists made him acutely conscious of the need for a vibrant cultural life.[4]

It is frequently stated that one can never observe a situation dispassionately, and that merely to observe inevitably draws one into the situation as a participant. Thus while a single concert review might stand alone as a judgment on a specific evening's music-making, the cumulative weight of such judgments constitutes not only a dossier of, say, the fortunes of the symphony orchestra or of an individual performer, but also a reflection of the critic's personality – his or her musical tastes, knowledge, biases – which in turn makes the critic an integral element in the musical, and wider artistic, environment. Charles's immersion in that environment meant that any single review by him also reflected his absolute participation in the wider scene. So his consistent discussions of the fortunes of the Dublin Grand Opera Society (DGOS), of the Wexford Festival, of the RTÉ orchestras, of Irish composers both individually and collectively, and of emerging performers, made him a leading figure because his columns in *The Irish Times* and elsewhere made these discussions a matter of public interest. One could almost say that he politicized the issues lying behind the everyday, and in the case of RTÉ, it did indeed make policy political.

Life at The Irish Times

Lionel Fleming wrote that *The Irish Times* was a leveller as far as preconceptions and bias were concerned: 'It never occurred to me to ask whether any of my colleagues were Protestant or Catholic, "loyalist" or nationalist, "gentry" or otherwise.'[5] As Conor Brady (editor 1986–2002) recalled, 'There were many aspects of *The Irish Times* organization that evoked its Protestant heritage when I joined in 1969' but 'there was no discernible denominational bias'.[6] 'A great

---

4. The *Irish Times* Features Editors under whom Charles worked were, successively, Jack White (later a senior figure at RTÉ), Donal O'Donovan (later at the Bank of Ireland before becoming a publisher, responsible for the production of *Acton's Music*), Brian Fallon (author of *Irish Art 1830–1990, An Age of Innocence: Irish Culture 1930–1960*, monographs on sculptor Imogen Stuart and his sister-in-law, Nancy Wynne-Jones, and an edition of the poems of his father, Padraic Fallon) and Fergus Linehan (novelist and [with his actress wife Rosaleen] scriptwriter).

5. *Head or Harp* p. 129.

6. C. Brady, *Up with The Times* p. 21.

newspaper... has its own culture. By definition, it must include, among its journalists anyway, the broadest spectrum of talent and ability, of human oddity and frailty... Since its foundation... [it represented] a curious blend of conservative and liberal values.'[7] Nevertheless, there was a general perception of the paper, right up to the 1970s, as a Protestant mouthpiece. In the late 1920s Charles's own stepfather, Hugh Digues La Touche, had said 'the *Irish Times* is deadly dull. Hateful paper. They ought to call it the Anti-Irish Times! They are always picking holes in everything Irish, fouling their own nest.' The idea of the paper as a 'Protestant' mind within a Catholic state persisted, and this suited Charles, because it enabled him to speak his mind rather than to defer to anyone else's point of view. At Charles's retirement, the Dean of St Patrick's Cathedral, Victor Griffin, would write: 'You are a man after my own heart, not afraid of good honest controversy & of saying exactly what you think.' Charles responded 'You are of course right, just as Carol and I immensely admire your courageous flights. You really are worthy to succeed the great Jonathan [Swift]. It is your job to be difficult when you see the need, as it was mine in a much smaller sphere.' It was one of the few instances when a 'Protestant' characteristic was articulated.

When Charles *did* incur the editor's displeasure, this would be made clear to him, but in only a very few instances in his long period of tenure did this arise – most noticeably just before his retirement, when an interview with Michael Dervan, published in *Music Ireland*, was considered to have been 'disloyal' to the paper. It must have come as a shock to both Charles and the editor and features editor of *The Irish Times*, when the latter looked askance at this 1986 interview, shortly before Charles announced his retirement and the appointment of Dervan as his successor.[8] The main thrust of the interview was the poor profile of music in Ireland, and the lack of sufficient promotion of its welfare. Charles said: 'I'm disgruntled beyond words because my paper, which used to be extremely good in this way, is having less and less about music: I'm only writing a third as much as I was four years ago.' So surprised were the then deputy editor, Conor Brady, and features editor Fergus Linehan at this apparent 'disloyalty' to the paper that an explanation was called for: had Charles been misquoted? – no, Charles replied, the report was entirely accurate. 'My loyalty to, and pride in contributing to, the *Irish Times* seems to

7. *Ibid.*, pp. 1, 103.

8. At the time of the interview, Michael Dervan was not aware that he was being considered by Charles as a possible successor.

me instinct in it. There is nothing disloyal about acknowledging the erosion of my international reputation and the paper's world-wide reputation.' His membership of the Critics' Circle was 'a measure of my pride in and loyalty to the *IT*' and that had not diminished over the years. In this conflict of perceptions, Charles's dedication to the well-being of music comes uppermost, and his commitment to the newspaper for which he wrote was a close second. It is no doubt sad that a treasured member of the features pages should have publicly stated a position on which he had remonstrated privately for many years, but I am certain that in Charles's mind there was no conflict between his duty as a polemicist and commentator on one hand and his position as the *Irish Times*'s senior critic on another.[9]

The independence of *The Irish Times* from the prevailing political consensus in the 1950s and onwards was to create an atmosphere in which its contributors could explore the issues of the day with comparative freedom. Founded in 1849 by a supporter of Home Rule, it had become an organ of unionism under the control of the Arnott family, but it had long since ceased to espouse unionism, or to cater almost exclusively to Irish Protestants, whose numbers continued to dwindle. In fact, pursuit of Catholic readers became a commercial imperative, as well as to reflect the *mores* of a changing soiety. This new latitude and inclusiveness applied to the arts as much as to other areas of society. During wartime, the government had – perhaps correctly – viewed the paper under Bertie Smyllie as harbouring pro-British sympathies in an atmosphere of what has been called 'nostalgia for the lost world of British Ireland', and imposed a more rigorous censorship than that experienced by other Irish newspapers. But under Alec Newman (editor from 1954 to 1961 and therefore in place in the year when Charles joined the paper) and his successors, *The Irish Times* became liberal and 'Catholic' in the literal, sense of the word, despite the undeniable fact that its editors were uniformly Protestant in background up to the appointment of Brady in 1986.

The most important element in editorial policy was that of *balance*, so much so that in the 1970s the paper earned the sobriquet of 'the Fenian rag' for its apparent sympathy with republicanism, springing principally from the nationalist leanings of Douglas Gageby, editor 1963–74 and 1977–86. This openness to all persuasions was essential if the paper was to be recognized

9. Conor Brady (personal communication with the author, 2 December 2008): 'I was Deputy Editor to Douglas [Gageby] and I remember there was quite a lot of upset about what he had said in the interview.'

as a 'journal of record'. One of the articles of association of The Irish Times Limited (adopted in 1974) was:

> to publish *The Irish Times* as an independent newspaper primarily concerned with serious issues for the benefit of the community throughout the whole of Ireland, free from any form of personal or party political, commercial, religious or other sectional control.

As an editorial put it at the time, '*The Irish Times* apologizes to no-one.'

The policy of reviewing as many concerts as possible was part of the paper's inclusiveness and its recognition of what was developing in Irish society. (This would only be attenuated in Charles's last years as critic, as Conor Brady and others recognized that it was no longer practical to maintain *The Irish Times* as a journal of record.)[10] At the time of his appointment, Charles's notices of new Irish compositions, emerging Irish performers and developments within R(T)É, and in musical life generally, were a vital part of the paper's reflection on the cultural life of a country which, in the 1950s and into the 1960s, was still emerging from the recession of the years of neutrality, and entering the dangerous years of economic expansion with its social and cultural repercussions.

The mere fact that Charles wrote for *The Irish Times* promoted him immediately into a figure of authority. Many years after his appointment, he would write to Alfred Burrowes, his deputy critic in Belfast, 'before I became the *Irish Times* critic I used to try to put ideas across and all the people said was "That's only Charles talking". Since then they have said "The *Irish Times* says". Same man, same people, mostly the same things.' Whether or not he had any real power, he was perceived, by virtue of his position, as having influence.

It was a point to which he would frequently return. Replying to the Irish composer John Purser, who had stopped short of wishing him 'more power to your pen', Charles disavowed any question of power: 'I agree with you wholeheartedly that no critic should have more *power* to his pen. I should hope that I might have some influence, that people might use me as a whetstone to their own minds, but not only is power in a critic undesirable in itself, but I am always very well aware of the dictum on power made by my very distant

---

10. D. James, *From the Margins to the Centre* p. 219. In Brady's own words: 'I did not believe that there could be such a thing in the late twentieth century as a "newspaper of record"… I preferred the concept of *The Irish Times* as Ireland's "newspaper of reference", the newspaper to which readers will look almost instinctively when important news develops, when significant issues arise in public life or when it is necessary to know what contending ideas are at play': Brady, *op. cit.*, p. 63.

kinsman, the historian' (see above). Later, he was thankful 'that here we have not got a situation like New York's where a Clive Barnes has power. I am quite sure (thank goodness) that I have no power.'[11]

As – originally – 'Music Correspondent', signing himself 'C.A.', and – after ten years – as 'Music Critic' with his own byline, Charles became, first and foremost, a critic and, secondly, a journalist, a skill which came to him more slowly. Although he had written for newspapers from an early age, his conception of what it meant to be a journalist, to *sell newspapers* by the strength of what he had written, to belong to his trade union (he was, unusually, a member of both the NUJ and the Institute of Journalists) was a novel experience that he embraced as he became an honoured member of that profession, receiving after retirement the rarely bestowed honorary life membership of the NUJ. In 1973 he reminded a colleague that 'the reader of a paper who is paying out his hard earned money is our first and last responsibility'.

When Charles was eleven, his headmaster had said that 'he has such a curious way of putting people's "backs up" against him'. Whether liked or not, Charles was respected for the fact that as a journalist responsible for selling newspapers, he spoke his mind. After Charles's retirement, John O'Conor, Director of the RIAM (of which Charles was a governor for forty-five years) wrote that 'Of course he could be infuriating at times but there is nobody who can match his experience, enthusiasm, compassion and exuberance.'

Charles attributed his own arrival at *The Irish Times* to a kind of serendipitous blunder, in that he was offered the position of music critic as a result of a series of accidents. In fact, despite the suspicion and resentment he occasioned in those who had to bear the brunt of his less favourable reviews, Charles was a 'natural' music critic, able to bring to his work 'enthusiasm, compassion and exuberance', even though their negative connotations – dislike, disinterest and boredom – could make his unfavourable reviews appear to be peevish.

Music critics can, of course, be 'trained', but the extent to which a natural ear for music, or a capacity for expressing one's feelings about a performance, can be developed is limited. Charles, like his friends and fellow-critics Desmond Shawe-Taylor[12] and Felix Aprahamian, had a natural aptitude for

---

11. Clive Barnes (b. 1927), drama and opera critic of the *New York Times* (1965–77) and the *New York Post* (1978–); the only other writer outside the UK besides Charles to be invited to join the Critics' Circle (1958) until the election of Freda Pitt (Rome, 1987).

12. Descendant of an Irish landlord prominent in negotiations over land legislation in the nineteenth century.

reaching and expressing his judgments. He regarded Dr Geoffrey Bewley, one of his closest friends in later life, as an excellent critic, even though Geoffrey had no musical training whatsoever, simply because he could express well and cogently a layman's opinion of what he had heard.

A review of a concert was not only a matter of judging whether the performance was 'good' or 'bad', but also a matter of nuance: the structures of musical life and the behaviours of musicians and their facilitators extended far beyond the concert platform and, reading between the lines of the more than 5500 notices penned by Charles in these thirty-three years, one learns to appreciate his concern for those structures and the behaviours that occurred within them. A selected volume of these reviews, edited by Carol's former pupil Gareth Cox, appeared in 1996 as *Acton's Music: reviews of Dublin's musical life 1955–1985*; and all of Charles's output, as published in *The Irish Times*, can now be read in the paper's online archive.[13] In examining his private correspondence it is possible to deepen one's understanding of what concerned him and why it made him the searching and demanding critic that he became.

Moreover, it was not only the 5500 reviews that Charles published which established him as the foremost Irish music critic, but the dossier of what today would be called 'op-ed' articles, features and interviews in *The Irish Times* and other media such as *Hibernia* and *Feasta* (the latter having to be translated into Irish on his behalf) and his broadcasts with Radio Éireann, in the late 1950s and early 1960s in particular, working with producer Edward McSweeney (known professionally as Maxwell Sweeney). These identified him as someone whose opinion was important not merely for the individual concerts which were, for the most part, one-off events, but for the continuing issues that permeated the Irish musical community and Irish culture and cultural politics generally.

It was the function of the music critic or 'correspondent' to attend, and review, concerts in every genre. Thus, at the beginning of his career, the regular diet of Radio Éireann concerts (subscription series at the Olympia or Gaiety Theatres, studio recordings at the Phoenix Hall), recitals for RDS members, the two annual seasons of opera in Dublin and one in Wexford, was supplemented by the celebrity concerts (often at the huge Theatre Royal) by Liberace, Bill Haley and the Comets, or Anna Russell, and visiting orchestras such as the BBCSO, the Vienna Philharmonic or the Boston Symphony (all in

---

13. The title of Cox's selection is somewhat of a misnomer, since Charles's commitment was not merely to Dublin but to *all* musical life in Ireland, including Irish musicians working abroad.

Charles's first year). For many years the *Irish Times* critic was also expected to review ballet, musicals such as *Oklahoma!*, brass bands, jazz, the D'Oyly Carte company in Gilbert and Sullivan, as well as reporting on lectures and musical films, writing book and record reviews and describing new gramophone equipment. Concerts took place not only in the 'regular' venues in Dublin's theatres, but in halls that are now little more than a memory such as the 'Four Provinces' hall (later the 'TV Club' in Harcourt Street), the Philips Hall in Clonskeagh, the Ely Hall (at the rear of the premises of the Knights of St Columbanus in Ely Place), the Aberdeen Hall (the ballroom of the Gresham Hotel) and various venues in Abbey Street where the Feis Ceoil traditionally took place. The variety and suitability of these venues would, of course, fuel the debate on the provision of a concert hall.

Whatever the rates of pay for staff journalists, Charles remained a freelance contributor all his life, paid, initially, at the rate of two guineas for a concert review and four guineas for a fortnightly record review. Record reviews were particularly important, since Charles developed these into 'articles of wider musical interest centred round particular issues' as the editor requested. As time went on, the issues addressed sometimes made one wonder what was the relevance of the particular disc under consideration, as Charles made his text into a pretext for a diatribe.

It was thus a matter of some disenchantment that, however 'at home' Charles felt at *The Irish Times*, he had to struggle regularly to obtain increases in pay (the rates did rise, but slowly) as well as recognition for his role.[14] At first, his average monthly income was approximately £50, or £600 annually, which, although a considerable improvement on his previous income, was hardly a living wage; as he recalled much later, the Features Editor had said, 'But he likes going to concerts, why should we pay him?' In 1968, arguing (unsuccessfully) for an increase in the then rate of £2.12.6d per review, he said 'When Jack White made the original offer, he had no knowledge of whether I would turn out to be a competent critic or not. I hope you [Donal O'Donovan] will agree that my work is sufficient of an asset to the paper for me to be entitled after all these years to the financial equivalent of promotion.' By 1969, he had achieved a monthly retainer of £90, which ameliorated the situation

---

14. Remuneration presumably followed the fortunes of the newspaper as reflected in its circulation: by the end of R.M. Smyllie's editorship (1954) the paper's sales fluctuated between 25,000 and 35,000 copies daily; by 1964 this had stabilized at 35,000; by 1966 it had risen to 50,000, and by 1974 to 69,000.

considerably, and was increased to £150 in 1972, to £190 in 1980 and, eventually, to £330, at which point it represented attendance at all concerts, a weekly record review and compiling the 'Next Week in the Arts' column. And in the 1970s Charles started to receive a car allowance to compensate him for the 10,000 miles that he and Carol drove annually to and from concerts. When he again asked for an increase in 1972, he argued that the rate for a concert notice in London was £12 (more than four times the Dublin rate): 'I am only too well aware that Dublin is not London but I do think I have some definite asset value to the *Irish Times* … While I am a good music critic I am well aware that I am a bad cattle trader.'[15] The retainer, plus fees for extra articles, brought his annual pay to £3870 by the end of 1977, but it was a matter of dismay to him that a senior reporter at that time was paid not less than £5000. It was a shock to his features editor when Charles demonstrated that he worked approximately 2300 hours each year, of which 1000 were 'unsocial', which was considerably more than had been negotiated by the union as a maximum working year. His disillusion was such that, in 1977, he seriously considered moving to Britain, where Shawe-Taylor and Aprahamian were rumoured to be on the verge of retirement from the *Sunday Times*.

A subject which frequently caused Charles to 'squawk', as he put it, was the cutting of his reviews by the sub-editor in order to fit the space available. Anyone who has experienced this knows that it almost infrequently means that the most important part of the text is deleted – not least because it is usually most convenient for the 'sub' to cut the last paragraph of one's piece. The 'squawk' usually took the form of an irate note to the features editor, and was conventionally respected, even though the editor's writ hardly ran at the subs' bench. On one occasion Fergus Linehan had informed the subs that Charles's review of Claudio Arrau was *not* to be cut but he told him 'as you know, they regard the ashes from Jack Lynch's pipe as more important than anything that

---

15. Conor Brady (personal communication to the author, 2 December 2008) writes: 'I was sorry to learn that Charles had a feeling, over such a long time, that his worth was not recognized in terms of his emoluments from the newspaper… Many critics were not paid as well as the organization might have wished. *The Irish Times* was very fortunate in having critics and contributors from many walks of Irish life who were outstanding in their field, but there simply wasn't any way in which the organisation could remunerate them all at a level which would equate to a full salary. Critics and contributors were different from fulltime staffers, in that they were likely to have other, parallel sources of income and their work was part-time.'

might interest you or me'.[16] Despite their agreement with Charles, which was of course part of their own turf war to maintain and expand the arts pages, they still did find him difficult in this regard because his sincerity and persistence both infuriated and won respect. He was a crusader in a land where no one was entirely sure who was the infidel. Sometimes the squawk merited an answer (and often Charles could successfully insist that the deleted part should be published as a Letter to the Editor), and sometimes he was quietly ignored. But the singular point is that, whatever Charles was squawking about, his colleagues recognized that he was totally motivated by what he saw as the course that the paper should be taking, and – despite the irritation he caused – usually he was right. It was only in the last decade of his tenure that his reviews, and those of his colleagues in the arts page, were severely curtailed and he felt increasingly unable to put across his overall message.

On the other hand, not only was Charles taken seriously because he wrote for *The Irish Times*, but he acquired a national significance and, as he frequently asserted, an international reputation – as early as 1962 telling Douglas Gageby that he was regarded as contributing 'some of the best regular musical-journalism in these islands'. It brought Charles a huge correspondence that required him to spend a great deal of time at the typewriter (although Carol undertook much of his typing), conscientiously replying to letters which might be complimentary, abusive, or simply requests for information or advice. Once, the budding playwright Brian Friel (whose *Philadelphia, Here I Come!* had just enjoyed a sustained triumph on Broadway) asked for a recommendation as to which recording of Wagner's 'Ring Cycle' he should buy (adding, as did so many inquirers, 'my wife and I read your column with interest'); less eminent readers of *The Irish Times* wrote in their hundreds over the years with similar requests.

Another constant source of enquiry was schoolchildren writing projects, who thought that, by applying to the music critic of *The Irish Times*, they might be better informed: some wrote politely and – an important point – enclosed a stamped envelope for reply; these, almost invariably, Charles answered carefully and assiduously, especially when he was enthused about the subject, for example on the various arrangements of the national anthem, or the music of Seán Ó Riada. Others were more peremptory, in the vein of 'Please tell me everything I need to know', and these, if they merited a reply at all, were much

---

16. Jack Lynch (1917–99) was a prominent player of Gaelic games; a TD (member of parliament) for Cork 1948–81 and Taoiseach 1966–73 and 1977–79.

more briefly answered. One such began: 'Mr Acton. I am a thesis student of architecture. The subject of my thesis is a college of music. I would be interested in discussing it with you.' This provoked the response:

> You are studying to join a profession which in private practice is very lucrative or in the public service provides a secure job with indexed salary on a generous scale leading to an indexed pension. I am a freelance journalist contributing to this paper with neither a salary nor any pension from it. For your interesting project you wish to make use of either my earning time or my scarce leisure time. I must therefore enquire of you, as a young professional, how many hours of my earning time you wish to have and what fee you are offering.

Apart from financial considerations, there was also the question of whether 'Please tell me…' was a valuable way of undertaking research. But if he was interested in the topic, appreciated the tone of enquiry, and felt that the child deserved a response, Charles could sometimes go to great lengths to give both information and advice. Sometimes a question such as 'what qualifications do I need to become a teacher?' would even provoke an article in *The Irish Times* or *Feasta*.

Quite apart from the authority that Charles acquired, there was a growing sense of him as a musical personality in his own right. In 1966, for example, he was canvassed by Brian Boydell as to whether he was interested in the artistic directorship of the Wexford Festival. 'Actually it is not my cup of tea at all. It needs a specialised enthusiasm for nosing out unknown, but still somewhere performed operas and a detailed experience of as yet unknown singers round the operatic world.' If offered the job he

> would probably refuse because I do not think I would be good at it or could really put my heart into it, or would really want to do it. With a minor European reputation at what I am doing, and the satisfaction of doing something useful well, I have no desire to change except for the one job for which I know I would be more suitable than anyone I can think of, which I am certain badly needs doing by me for a period of two, three or perhaps four years after which there would be someone for whom the machine would be ready and tuned up.

This was clearly a reference to the music directorship of RTÉ, which was then vacant after the departure of Tibor Paul.[17] In 1961 he had in fact been asked if his hat was in the ring for that job, but in such a way that he had had to decline

---

17. And in which Brian Boydell was also deeply involved.

to be considered, after only six years as music critic of *The Irish Times*. Other aspects of his role in music were extremely various: judging at the National Song Contest, and a composers' competition at the Belfast Festival; opening the classical music department at Liam Breen's record shop; and becoming a Vice-President of both the Association for the Promotion of Music in Education and of the RIAM.

It is, in fact, astonishing how many people approached Charles for advice. For example, Mairtín McCullough, proprietor of the music shop established by his father, Denis, asked how he should go about buying a harpsichord for the store. Michael Emmerson wanted to know whether Arthur Rubinstein and Victoria de los Angeles should be promoted in Dublin (and if so, where?). And Niall O'Flynn, PRO of the tobacco company Players-Wills, which presented celebrity recitals in Dublin, enquired who might be worth engaging: in this case Charles warmly endorsed, among others, Miceál O'Rourke ('a deeply poetic player') and cellist Aisling Drury Byrne.

Charles had also become much more politically aware. When, in 1972, a concert promoter wrote to the editor complaining about lack of publicity for an event he was organizing, Charles took up the matter directly with the promoter, John Ruddock, founder of the Limerick Music Association, with whom he was to have a stormy relationship over the decades:

> *The Irish Times* devotes to music a quite remarkable amount of space. At the present time the amount of material crying out to be put into this paper is enormous. The events in the Six Counties are threatening to destroy the social and political fabric of the entire island. The argument for and against entry into the EEC and the change in our constitution is hotting up. I think that we should be thankful for the amount of space that the paper does give to music rather than run any risk of their reducing it.

Charles would not always feel so supportive of editorial policy. At this stage, however, he wanted to ensure that Ruddock, on behalf of his Limerick Music Association, should obtain a reasonable level of publicity by legitimate means: 'I am certainly aware, in spite of everything, just how much valuable work you are doing for music lovers in Limerick … But I am bound to say that a letter like yours undermines a great deal of my advocacy.'

Leaving aside the major positions for which Charles had, at one time or another, been considered or in which he had expressed an interest, his status brought him other associations, some of which were too onerous because they required more time than a freelance writer could afford to devote to them:

membership of an Irish committee of the International Contemporary Music Exchange was one that, after some years of dilatoriness, he realized he should never have accepted in the first place. He told Aloys Fleischmann, its convenor, 'it is all very well for American academics who receive large salaries for short hours to spend their plentiful spare time filling in forms for free, but quite another thing for an Irish freelance writer (whose rates have now jumped up to £20 a thousand words) to use his earning time and earning energies ditto.' His, and Carol's, involvement in the promotion of Irish compositions *via* the Department of Foreign Affairs (also at Fleischmann's behest) was, conversely, an undertaking to which they gave an enormous commitment for several years, despite the low rate of remuneration, until eventually it, too, had to be reined in, due to the disproportionate amount of time it took up.

Whether he approved or not, over the decades a public perception developed that, if Charles Acton could be persuaded to take up a particular cause in *The Irish Times*, it could bring influence to bear in the desired quarters, and might even affect public policy. When, for example, in 1971 he considered that a particular letter-writer had put him in the position of leading the campaign for a national concert hall, Charles retorted characteristically that, if citizens wanted such a hall, they themselves should go about the business of calling on public representatives, rather than expecting the music critic of *The Irish Times* to do so on their behalf. 'Obviously, I cannot start a campaign in the paper (even if I were let do so) to get people to write to Colley [George Colley, TD, Minister for Finance]. If I did and people did write, he would say it was a ready-up; if they didn't, he would say he knew they didn't want a concert hall.' He was only one among several Dublin critics including Fanny Feehan (*Hibernia*), Mary MacGoris (*Irish Independent*) and Robert Johnson (*Irish Press*), but was accused of constituting, with Carol, 'a virtual dictatorship in music criticism'. One correspondent pointed out something which, however eminent and articulate other critics might be, was undoubtedly true of a large proportion of the concert-going public:

> You say that you and your wife do not have an almost exclusive reign in musical criticism in Ireland. I'm afraid that is precisely the case as far as I can judge. Of the many concerts, Feiseanna and other musical occasions I have attended, I have never once heard the performers mention any critique other than the 'Acton' one.

I once heard an elderly lady leaving a concert and saying that she wouldn't make up her mind about it until she had read Charles Acton the next morning.

But the writer was utterly wrong if he thought that either Charles or Carol was expressing anything other than a *personal* opinion. This is exemplified in the choice of deputies for Charles and Carol in Dublin, and to review important concerts in Belfast, Cork, Limerick, and, occasionally, London.[18]

At one time, finding a suitable deputy in London was proving difficult, and Charles approached Thurloe Conolly who, however, declined: 'I would have no respect for a critic so musically illiterate as I discover myself to be more and more as I struggle with music'; even though he thought that if he *could* give reviewing the attention it deserved, 'I should probably enjoy the job and might even come to do it not too badly.' Much more serious were deputies who either failed to deliver copy or were incorrect in what they wrote. In the first case, Daphne Bell, the deputy in Belfast, pleaded the northern troubles as her excuse for not going out at night (she reviewed under the pseudonym 'F.O.', which for her meant 'Find Out', not accepting that it might have other connotations) and she was decommissioned. Belfast was especially important at that time (1972) because, as Charles put it, the Editor, Douglas Gageby, 'a Belfastman, is dedicated to the principle that this is a 32 county newspaper in a 32 county country'. In the second case, getting the correct titles of works performed was essential, as was conformity to house style, and on one occasion Charles had to remonstrate with a deputy who wrote 'Maria Callas is the best Traviata of my experience' since 'In La traviata the heroine is Violetta. Alter "traviata" to "Violetta" or Callas and all Italian readers will read it simply as "Maria Callas is the best whore of my experience".'

Other recognitions also accrued: demand for Charles as a lecturer grew steadily, and came from two principal directions: one was the large number of local gramophone societies around the country, and also the Dublin Gramophone Society for which Charles lectured often (many of these countrywide lectures were given under the *aegis* of Foras Éireann); the other was the Italian Cultural Institute, where for many years he gave lecture-recitals prior to the seasons of Italian opera presented by the DGOS at Dublin's Gaiety Theatre. On

18. Some of the regular deputies engaged by Charles and Carol were: Michael Yeats and Victor Leeson (briefly in the 1960s), Ian Fox (from 1969), David Ledbetter (1973), Michael Dervan (from 1980), Andrew Robinson, James Maguire, Henry Hely-Hutchinson, Barra Boydell, Philip Hollwey and myself (in the 1980s); John Allen, recruited in 1984, continued to review as a deputy for Michael Dervan; Michael Williams, better known as a solicitor and executor of the estates of Micheál mac Liammóir and Hilton Edwards, regularly deputized when Charles and Carol took their summer holiday.

almost all of these different occasions, Carol acted as 'technician', playing the gramophone when each musical example was required. In 1973 Charles was to write 'I am aware that the Foras Éireann fee is still £12.60p all in, which, by this time, is a matter of idealism and little else'. But it was enjoyable work which, for the first time since his encyclopaedia days, brought him around the country: to Thurles, to Naas and Wexford (on the subject 'Modern Music's Not Too Bad'); to the Belfast Festival to debate the topic 'Festivals are Useless'; to Glenstal Abbey, where he took part in a discussion on liturgical music; the extension lecture scheme at UCC; Youghal Arts Society; to Clogher Historical Society in Enniskillen. One of his most popular lectures was 'Beethoven the Liberator', which he first gave in 1963. Some of his lectures were of a directly professional nature, as when in 1976 he spoke to the Association of Teachers of Music in Post-Primary Schools on 'Why do we teach music?' In 1986 he addressed the Culwick Choral Society on the topic 'The Future of Choral Societies'. Charles continued to lecture past his retirement date, right up to 1989 when he spoke to the Irish branch of the European Piano Teachers' Association on 'Irish Pianists', which had been the subject of his essay in the programme of the inaugural Dublin International Piano Competition the previous year.[19] In addition to the incoming invitations to lecture around the country, Charles also actively solicited engagements, just as he sought an entrée into English music publications, and one must assume that, in addition to a 'missionary spirit' to stimulate interest in classical music, there was, at least in the penurious early days, a desire to earn the few extra pounds that accrued after deduction of expenses.[20]

But Charles would not give his services for nothing. When the Dublin Jewish Students' Union told him in 1968 that it never paid a fee to visiting speakers he retorted:

> I have no doubt whatever that your council have found many professional personalities who were delighted to talk to you without charge. That I think is not quite the point at issue. There is a considerable difference between asking, say, a surgeon to present a record programme to your society for nothing and asking him to take out your tonsils for nothing. Were I to accept your invitation

---

19. It was subsequently reprinted (revised and updated) as a chapter in *To Talent Alone* pp. 495–510.

20. In addition to submitting pieces on musical matters, Charles also sent poems, articles and stories to Irish and English magazines, including *Studies* and, under his 'Thomas Annesley' pseudonym, to 'New Irish Writing' edited by David Marcus at the *Irish Press*.

to take out your tonsils I would do it for free. It is unethical to ask any stranger to perform for nothing the expert work from which he earns his living.

And when Peter Beresford Ellis asked him to contribute to a *Dictionary of Irish Mythology* without making any mention of a fee, he wrote:

> You could be surprised at the number of people who expect professional services either for nothing or for very little … A prominent English publisher asked me to write a chapter of 4,000 words on the history of music in Ireland for £45. All too many headmasters invite me to give lectures to their schools, for the honour of their schools in which I have no interest. Magazines in USA, UK and Ireland invite me to write for nothing.

Charles was already appearing in radio programmes with reasonable frequency before his appointment to *The Irish Times*. He was also 'compere' of a series of record recitals of Mozart's music sponsored by the *Radio Review* in 1956 in the 'Little Theatre' in Brown Thomas's department store in Dublin's Grafton Street.

Working with producer Eddie MacSweeney, Charles became a regular contributor to 'Film Magazine' from 1957 until 1960. In June 1958 he spoke on the subject of background music:

> You know the sort of thing. Alan Ladd or whoever it may be, rides out of town into the great outdoors. After hours (or is it weeks) through the track-less waste, he reins up and scans the horizon. Not a soul in sight – not an animal, not a bird, not even an insect. Resting in the saddle, with a far away look in his eye, he muses on the girl he is about to rescue. Does he have peace and solitude for his thoughts? Not a bit of it. A 100–piece orchestra strikes up, and shatters the silence.

In advance of a film to be called *The Magic Flame*, directed by George Cukor, and purporting to be what would today be called a biopic of Franz Liszt (played by Dirk Bogarde),[21] Charles commented on the genre of films about great musicians: 'they are cooked up according to a fairly simple recipe. Take a famous composer; one of his most hackneyed works; and a celebrity performer. Make the performer play the work as sloppily as possible. Take a love-story plot from a school-girls' romantic novel, after first checking that it has no connection with the real life of the composer. Mix well together, adding garrets, an Emperor, starvation, artistic temperament, applause and all the other fixings to taste. Before serving, remove any possible trace of accuracy.'

---

21. The film was eventually released under the title *Song Without End*.

On another, extremely formative, occasion at the beginning of 1960, he was sent by MacSweeney to see George Morrison's film *Mise Éire*, with music by Seán Ó Riada. Charles's response was immediate and compelling:

> *Mise Éire* proves that Ireland has a composer of film music as good as anyone in the world. This warms the critic's heart. For, strange as it may seem, the critic goes to hear new Irish music always hoping to hear something good – or even better than good. He is often disappointed – naturally, because 99% of all music written anywhere, anywhen, is indifferent stuff... In this film, Seán Ó Riada seems to have Mozart's knack of exactly the right notes in exactly the right places – no more, no less. And Gustav Mahler's ability to use strange rich colours with a sparse austerity. His score has the ageless, non-committal quality that distinguishes his folk-song arrangements; an agelessness that lets traditional tunes speak for themselves – out of time, in our time, to us: that can heighten our emotions by removing all trace of sentimentality and artificiality... In Britain, *Henry V* and *Scott of the Antarctic* proved that Walton and Vaughan Williams could only write good music and not good film music. Seán Ó Riada can. Over and over again I had to make an effort if I was to take in this music, so perfectly did it fit the film.

It was a point to which he would repeatedly return, not least in extolling Ó Riada's translation of 'Roisín Dubh' into the symphonic opening sequence, played on the French horn by the RTÉSO's principal horn, Victor Maliř.[22]

The principal perk of Charles's position was the series of invitations that he and Carol received to visit, and write about, foreign festivals. Charles was in Germany in 1963; together with Carol he visited Bayreuth, Salzburg and Glyndebourne in 1959; the festival at Aix-en-Provence (in 1964, 1966 and 1968); Montreux (1964); Rome and Lucerne (1966); Covent Garden for Tippett's *King Priam* in 1967 and *The Ice Break* in 1977; the Edinburgh Festival (and Glyndebourne again) in 1967; Glasgow for Berlioz' *The Trojans* in 1969; the Gaudeamus Foundation at Rotterdam for a conference on 'New Music and its Criticism' (1970); the Prague Spring Festival (in 1968 and 1973); Verona (1974); and in 1984 the recently opened Barbican Centre in London. In Prague, Albert Rosen introduced them to some 'Czech proverbs': 'Conductors are confusèd men', 'We have so many conductors here that we use them to feed pigs' and 'what is organised is done well, but what is not organised is not done'.

---

22. Other approaches by Charles to RTÉ, suggesting (in 1960) that he should host a late-night disc programme, and (in 1963) work as an interviewer in the fledgling television service, were unsuccessful.

The most enjoyable and prestigious of these invitations came in 1973, when Charles and Carol spent a month in the USA as the guests of the State Department, with no obligation to write anything on their return, but simply to see American music-making at first hand. The tour took them to Boston, New York, Washington, San Francisco, Las Vegas and the Grand Canyon. 'Easter weekend among the blacks in Alabama including (Heaven help us) a dawn service. Enormously interesting', as he wrote to Thurloe Conolly. 'And almost immediately on coming home we had an invitation from the French Government to spend 10 days learning about music in France (which, of course, meant 10 days in Paris).' The visit included Charles making two one-hour radio recordings

> on present-day Irish music-making. One of the most hair-raising episodes of my life. From 8pm to 10pm I, who have only basic tourist French, had to cope with [the interviewer] and a recording entirely through the medium, without any word of English or anything else being spoken. [However,] I have since learnt that after subjecting me to that ordeal ORTF mucked up the tapes and never broadcast it.

Another *Irish Times* perk was an internal arrangement whereby contributors were given £30 and sent off to write restaurant reviews, usually in three successive weeks, under the generic title 'Table for Two'. These were, naturally, highly prized by the recipients, and between 1978 and 1985 Charles and Carol succeeded in being sent on twelve occasions, to watering holes such as Paulo Tullio's 'Armstrong's Barn' in County Wicklow; The Grey Door in Upper Pembroke Street; the Rôtisserie at the Royal Hibernian Hotel; White's Hotel in Wexford; and the Park Hotel in Virginia, County Cavan. Charles preferred to write these reviews under his regular pseudonym, 'Thomas Annesley', in order to keep his various writing identities separate, but more often the newspaper insisted that he be identified by his usual by-line. ('Thomas Annesley' usually wrote on social and financial matters, such as capital gains tax, or the demolition by the Electricity Supply Board of Georgian houses in Dublin's Fitzwilliam Street, but he also used his interest in hotels and restaurants to contribute short pieces to the *Hotel and Catering Review*.)

Charles and Carol were superb culinary hosts in their own home at Carrickmines, and appreciated good food and wine in much the same way as they approached the task of reviewing a concert. Two examples from 'Table for Two' are worth quoting: Armstrong's Barn remained almost as good as its reputation; the review was detailed and knowledgeable, encouraging the reader that the venue, near Annamoe, was well worth the detour. But at a subsidiary of

The Grey Door standards were, it seems, non-existent. 'In order to obtain an aperitif, 'I had to invade the kitchen because no one came near us'. Avocado was 'woody and unripe and not helped by a mass of greenery'. Steak was 'rare as requested but woefully tough'. Salad contained 'wedges of unnecessarily green tomatoes with two sticks of tinned asparagus on top'. Service was 'charming and friendly when you could get it – four times during the evening I had to wander into the kitchen to acquire attention, which is deplorable'.

When Eddie Michaels, proprietor of The Trocadero restaurant in Dublin, died in 1980, Charles wrote an 'Appreciation' in *The Irish Times* in which he referred to the 'Troc' as 'a sub-office of *The Irish Times*' and 'virtually a club for performing arts and journalism', where Michaels 'provided pleasant food in a pleasant atmosphere at surprisingly low prices'; if one were 'tired or bruised in spirit… the "Troc" did not just feed the body but gave strange comfort and relaxation to one'.

Another source of well-being came in 1974, when citizens in Kilkenny inaugurated Kilkenny Arts Week. Kilkenny city and county were well known to them, partly through their acquaintance with Hubert and Peggy Butler, who lived at Bennettsbridge and whom Charles and Carol had frequently driven on visits to and from the Courisses at Collon. Later, he was to write that it was 'one of the most exciting experiences of my life, because it brought together in a single tapestry so very many threads of nearly all that I believed in for music and for so many arts'.

The phenomenon of Kilkenny Arts Week (KAW) lay in this concatenation of arts, created by a remarkably vibrant community of musicians, artists, intellectuals, and arts organizers (of whom organist David Lee, painter and VEC teacher George Vaughan and painter and animateur Ramie Leahy were the most prominent); they were centred on the Church of Ireland cathedral of St Canice, the Castle with its Butler Gallery, the Kilkenny Design Workshops, and the hostelry of Kyteler's Inn. As Charles remarked, 'here was a truly amateur (in the word's strict meaning) spirit manifested really professionally'. He and Carol were critics-in-residence, with a very influential round-up of the week's events in *The Irish Times*, but, more importantly, Charles was, quite unofficially, regarded as the 'guru' of KAW. This was reflected in the fact that, for the first few years, he reported on the visual arts exhibitions and literary programme, until his colleague, Brian Fallon, also made his 'annual pilgrimage' to review the art shows, and Elgy Gillespie visited to report on the poetry readings and writers' workshops. Most of the founder members of the committee resigned in 1979,[23] but up to that point, as Charles remarked, the 'striking geographical and architectural unity of the city' combined with many other factors 'to make Kilkenny not only a city of beauty, interest, rare civic spirit and cultural value but fertile ground for arts festivities.' Charles and Carol continued to be associated with KAW while it remained a 'festival of the people', until, as Charles put it, 'the professional begrudgers told them it was "elitist"', and, in order to preserve their summer holidays (KAW took up nine days at the end of August) they began to curtail their involvement from 1979.

A remarkable event, which took place with the full support of *The Irish Times*, came on 20 October 1974, when the Gate Theatre was the venue for Charles's public lecture 'A Critic's Creed'.[24] In this, perhaps ironically, Charles was 'produced' by Hilton Edwards, who had offered him the job of Business Manager at the Gate over twenty years previously. Under Hilton Edwards's direction, Charles delivered his lecture to a discerning, and even daunting, audience of musicians and music managers of all persuasions. It firmly set out the *tenets* of his trade in an utterly idiosyncratic fashion, and quite definitely gave Charles a sense of having established in public what had been present, mostly subliminally, throughout his previous nineteen years as a professional critic. It allowed him to insist that there should be continuity in the relationship between critic and reader, which he called a 'matrix', within which the critic should 'stimulate his readers to do their own thinking'. And it gave him the opportunity for some reasoned chauvinism:

> An Irishman who believes that music is one of the graces of life, part of the whole person's spiritual fulfilments, must hope that the majority of his fellow citizens will eventually come to take pleasure from private music-making and public concerts; that the music in his country shall be as good as in anyone else's (*ceteris paribus*); and that Irish professional musicians of good standard may practise their profession, earn their livings and enjoy public approbation in their own country. It is from this that arises any responsibility he may have to performers, composers, organisers; and such responsibilities are secondary and derivative. And any such responsibility must be exercised within the primary ones. And the critic must try to blend the experience of the present with the hopes of the future.

---

23. Partly as a result of disagreements with the chairman, Rev. Robert Harvey, dean of St Canice's.

24. He had originally given the lecture at UCC in January 1974.

Perhaps the most visible recognition of Charles's acquired status as an authority on music in Ireland came in the mid-1970s, when he was invited to write a booklet, *Irish Music and Musicians*, in the 'Irish Heritage' series published by Messrs Eason's. As Eoin Garrett, reviewing the booklet for *Counterpoint*, remarked, Charles, with only fourteen pages of text, had very little space for a comprehensive account of music in Ireland from earliest times. His only stricture was that the text should not have attempted to encompass the present day, not least because 'Mr Acton's views on the present state of things are well known to his regular readers.' Pruning from an original word-length of 8500 down to 6000 (still much longer than the 4000 initially proposed by the publisher) had meant that much had to be omitted.

When approached by Eason's, Charles had originally proposed two booklets: one on 'art music', the other on traditional music. It was considered difficult to sell both titles, so the entire project had to be covered in one. Ever sensitive to professional rates of pay, he nevertheless accepted the fee of £150, 'the same as 10 days of a civil service messenger'. He was delighted that Eason's agreed to pare down the illustrations rather than insist on the original length of 4000 words, as this still allowed him to indulge in what some editors might have regarded as superfluous material in so short a text: 'I wanted to leave it lively (e.g. [William Vincent] Wallace's extraordinary life) and to do one or two things such as publicise Henry Cowell's passionate conviction that he and his music were essentially Irish'.[25]

The booklet was generally very well received, but a young musicologist named Ann Buckley wrote to Charles expressing the view that 'it is inaccurate in the extreme, and, worse, heavily laced with exaggeration and fantasy'. She even advised that the booklet should be withdrawn, lest it prove 'embarrassing to both you and the publisher'. Four typewritten pages followed, listing 'unsupportable statements' and accusing Charles of 'personality worship'. At first, Charles's reaction was a postcard: 'I have received your letter of July 30th on this afternoon of extreme wetness and darkness. It has entertained both of us greatly and revived our spirits. Many thanks.' But Ann Buckley did not stop there: she wrote also to Harold Clarke, managing director of Eason's, in terms which Charles considered 'defamatory, libellous and actionable', and on which he feared he would have to go to court, if Buckley persisted in the public arena,

---

25. Henry Cowell (1897–1965) was an American composer who was introduced to Irish music by his father. He gave a lecture to the MAI Composers' Group at the RIAM in 1955.

a point which proved unnecessary. He told Harold Clarke 'I believe she is going to Romania on a year's grant from that country. I doubt if anyone in Ireland bar her husband would much care if she does not come back.'

Critical standards and priorities

To be the music critic of The Irish Times was to occupy a position of prestige, both nationally and internationally, which would, in 1970, earn Charles the distinction of being one of the only two persons at that time working outside the United Kingdom to be invited to become a member of the Critics' Circle (founded 1913) – no doubt at the suggestion of his friend Stanley Sadie, at that time chair of the Circle's music section, who told Charles that the election was 'only repairing an absurd, longstanding omission'. The Circle has as its principal aims the promotion of the profession of critic and the preservation of the critic's integrity; thus to be invited is a mark of the high esteem and reputation of the invitee, representing an endorsement not only of the writer's integrity but also of his sense of responsibility and capacity for mature judgment.

One of the most fundamental aspects of Charles's attitude to his profession was his unshakeable devotion to the demands of attending concerts – so much so that, as the number of concerts gradually increased, he wryly commented that his *average* attendance was four or five per week, sometimes as many as seven evenings as well as lunchtime recitals.[26] When George Hodnett ('Hoddie'), the paper's jazz critic, argued that a supervening, political, commitment had prevented him from attending the event for which Charles had marked him, Charles told him: 'One's professional engagements must take precedence over one's private enthusiasms, if one wishes to consider oneself a professional.'

'There is no such thing as an objective value judgment of a performance. All criticism is subjective. All criticism is a matter of opinion and it is for opinion that a critic is paid', Charles wrote to one of his deputies in 1972. As Charles would write very early in his career (and as is evident throughout his lecture 'A Critic's Creed'), 'Criticism is of course a very subjective thing and is always a personal opinion; but I do try to be constructive, to encourage rather than discourage, and to be some help to music and musicians'. In 'A Critic's Creed' Charles would write that 'no one can really get outside his personality';

---

26. In his first year at The Irish Times, Charles reviewed 140 concerts; twenty years later, by the 1970s, his personal annual average had reached over 200, with deputies reviewing a considerable number in addition.

in the same breath he admitted to a dislike of Mascagni and Menotti, and he might as well have added his famously low opinion of the Schumann cello concerto and the Chopin piano concertos ('I've had the experience of playing the bassoon in the Chopin concertos...'): the point being that to review these works involved, as far as possible, putting aside one's personal prejudices.

The critic is also, of course, the arbiter of *fact*: did the performer play the composer's 'repeats'; did the singers carry naked flames on the operatic stage; was the piano a Steinway or a Yamaha; did the players use music or did they play from memory? But the role of the critic is principally as the arbiter of *taste*: was the performance pleasing to the ear; was the operatic *mise-en-scène* pleasing to the eye; did the première performance of this work add significantly to the body of Irish compositions, and should it be heard again; did the critic agree with the level of the audience's applause; did this coming-out recital by a young débutant convince that they are ready for a professional career? Not only was a review subjective, but, allowing for stage nervousness, particularly at a 'coming-out' recital, there was also the question of the performer's health on the night, the critic's own state of mind, and the key factor in critical subjectivity: *intuition*, the means by which messages pass from one hemisphere of the critic's brain to the other.

The question of qualifications has always been much debated. In 1974 a reader wrote to the editor: 'I seem to remember hearing that Mr Acton was neither a singer nor an instrumentalist, nor had he any kind of a musical degree which, one might expect, would qualify him for this job. Be that as it may he has, over the years, done an enormous amount of musical homework and is today widely regarded as an expert in classical music, without playing a note.' Charles saw this as an attack on his professional competence and retorted:

So far from 'without playing a note' I do not remember back to when I started playing the piano. I have played a bassoon and percussion in orchestras in Ireland, England and Palestine. For 45 years I have made chamber music, as the occasion arose, on bassoon, clarinet, piano, harpsichord. I have sung in choirs in Ireland, England, Germany, and Palestine, and have been a member of vocal consorts. I have also played slightly, though without proficiency, cello, recorders, horn and organ and entertained friends and relations with solo singing. In addition to that, a musical degree is a hindrance rather than a qualification for the job of critic on a daily newspaper; and my first stint of criticism was forty years ago. Though I have half a century of very wide and fairly deep experience, I emphatically deny that I am an expert and I see no reason why I should limit my interest to 'classical' music.

A similar occasion arose in 1975 when a Viennese astronomer, working at Dunsink Observatory, referred, in a letter to the editor, to Charles's 'incompetence in matters of music and his breathtaking arrogance. It is quite evident that Charles Acton has his fixed opinion about an artist before the beginning of the recital.' In reply to the astronomer he said 'The only thing I can suggest to you is that you stop reading what I write and take one of the other newspapers as well as *The Irish Times* and read one of my colleagues instead ... I would ask you to consider very earnestly that there may be, running through your letter, a considerable confusion between fact and opinion. As a scientist and astronomer you, quite clearly, would not make any statement about your work that was not rigorously supported by observed fact, inescapable reasoning and/or unimpugnable secondary evidence ... On the other hand you write, in connection with music, "Dezsö Ranki's interpretation was absolutely delightful" in the language of a statement of fact' – a point which the astronomer was unable to refute in subsequent correspondence.

Charles was extremely sensitive to such criticism, so much so that the features editor had on more than one occasion to advise that he should not take a sledgehammer to crack a nut. As a professional reviewer, paid by his editor to make his opinions sufficiently interesting that they would help to sell newspapers, he characteristically took the defensive onto the offensive.

Another dangerfield was the integrity of the critic and his or her motivation in writing any particular review. When a reader said that one of Charles's notices was not only 'foolish' but 'vicious', he retorted:

> To be vicious, there must be an evil motive: not only had I none, but a critic is always disappointed and sad when he finds himself having to express an unfavourable opinion and you may also take it that no critic writing between 200 and 300 notices a year is going to either risk his reputation or be bothered to attack any particular show. You have of course as good a right to your opinion of the show as I have. And I presume that you did enjoy the show and considered it good value for 15/- a head. May I say that I envy you.

The question of integrity could also have political, or at least diplomatic, repercussions: in 1966, the director of the Italian Cultural Institute alleged that both Charles and Carol had personal animosity towards an Italian violinist (or, more particularly, towards his chosen accompanist) who played in Dublin at the Institute's behest.

> It is of course distressing that there are people within the Italian official community who would think that my wife or myself would jeopardise our

integrity, the reputation of the paper we have the honour to write for, our own international reputation and our jobs for any personal matter … In these circumstances, it will have to be considered very deeply whether *The Irish Times* should in future carry any notices of the Institute's events if notices are to be misinterpreted. I very much hope that an unfavourable situation will not arise, since I and the paper are well aware of and grateful for all the good work of the Institute since its foundation.

Fortunately the misunderstanding was resolved, but there was a tendency – perhaps more acute in the case of diplomatic missions – to remonstrate over unfavourable notices as a matter of national pride or prestige, and Charles more than once found it necessary to explain the ethics of reviewing to the representatives of the French, German and Spanish cultural institutes as well as to the Italians; on one occasion he even had to return a bottle of whiskey received from Dr Eugen Vetter of what is today the Goethe Institut,[27] on the grounds that it might be considered to impair his future impartiality.

Writing to a friend in 1961, Charles succinctly reflected on his personal *modus operandi* and the perception of him by his readers: 'I often realize afterwards that I have been too lenient; not yet that I have been too severe. My notices are mildness itself compared with those of my colleagues in other capital cities.' In fact, as his correspondence files indicate, the complaints regarding his notices far outnumbered the commendations, even though the latter were on occasions numerous.

When advising deputies such as Michael Williams and Mark Hely-Hutchinson (a master brewer and later Managing Director of Guinness), he stressed that the primary consideration should be whether or not they, as members of the audience, had *enjoyed* the performance. The essential prerequisite, as far as a critical judgment was concerned, was that the same standards should be applied to all professional performances, with a less stringent standard applying to amateur presentations. As Charles wrote in 1968:

> when people upbraid a critic for not going overboard about something which is only very good, they forget that he, because he attends more events, knows that the very good is far from perfect, and that he must keep his full supply of superlatives available for perfection. And yet when perfection comes his way, the critic feels even more powerless than usual to do justice to it in mere words.

Charles was anxious that his deputies should not carry this critical burden. The biggest critical difficulty was, in fact, not when the performance was bad

---

27. Formerly the German Institute for Cultural Relations.

(since it could be negatively criticized), or when it was ideally pleasing (since it could be praised), but when it left the critic with little or no feeling about its merits, and yet he or she was still expected to pen the same number of words in response as would be necessary for a deplorable or praiseworthy performance.

Living in a relatively small city and within a very close musical community, it was impossible for Charles to maintain his distance from performers. When he heard that one of his London deputies had socialized with an artist immediately after a performance and before writing his review, he was horrified and advised strongly in favour of keeping a critical distance. In Dublin, however, it was near to impossible to remain aloof, and this sometimes made it difficult, if not painful, to write with any objectivity of an artist who might be a personal friend.

When a reader who was also a professional musician complained in a letter to the editor about Charles's 'slaughter' of a coming-out recital, which he considered 'cruel to the point of deserving reprimand', Charles said he admired the 'spirit of kindness and chivalry to a would-be colleague' but denied that there was any danger of what the complainant called 'terrible psycho-logical injuries' to the débutante. While he had previously given favourable notices to this particular singer, he felt that this recital had been too ambitious for a professional debut; he used the following analogy: 'If a promising GP opens a consulting room as a heart specialist, it is as a heart specialist he must be judged and not as a family doctor. So it is no use to recall how charming she had been in other fields. It is not only possible, but often happens, that a really charming drawing-room singer is unsuccessful as a Lieder recitalist.' In the case of this particular singer, Charles went to great lengths in later years to advise on her diction, a recurrent problem for singers, especially when singing in an unfamiliar language.

A further complication of a small music community was that the performer might well be a teacher.

> I have often felt that it is a rather awesome thing to be writing about the performances of people who are teachers. For the sake of faith with the readers (a critic's primary responsibility) I must forget that they are teachers when I am listening to them as performers. And yet I am extremely well aware that everything that I may feel I have to write unfavourable about a teacher's performance may be harming the opinion that his pupils have of him. And it is, obviously, a terrible thing to diminish a teacher in the eyes of his pupils.

Several times, Charles found it painful to have to say that he had not enjoyed a performance by an artist of world calibre. In 1963, for example, a rising star was Luciano Pavarotti, whose voice was giving excitement to talent spotters who gave him his first break at Covent Garden within the year, when he stood in for Giuseppe di Stefano as Rodolfo in Puccini's *La bohème*. But for Charles, hearing him as the Duke in the DGOS production of Verdi's *Rigoletto*, 'he seemed to have a hard, unsympathetic voice of very little variety... uninspiring'. When he heard Elizabeth Schwarzkopf in 1970, he had loved her voice, but the following year he had, painfully, to put his cards on the table: 'There is one task which any critic dreads and seeks ways to avoid. That is having to write that a voice is no longer what it was. While last year my writing could bask in her fabulous artistry, this year I could find no way out of noting that the artistry is no longer wholly supported by the glorious voice itself.'

At times, Charles felt that letters to the editor were so harmful as to amount to malicious defamation, but there was a far greater danger that the subject of a concert notice might bring an action for libel against the critic and the paper.[28] In 1962 a libel action was threatened by Max Thöner, a violinist who had a stormy relationship with the RIAM, where he taught for eight years and conducted the Academy orchestra, besides playing as a member of the RÉSO and giving frequent chamber music recitals. Charles had written that in one of his recitals Thöner had played out of tune, and 'had no idea at all of pre-classical style'. While Thöner's solicitors took the predictable path of demanding an apology, without which their client would be forced to go to court with expert witnesses on his side, Charles mustered evidence from, among others, Gerard Victory (who said he thought Charles had been 'very lenient' to Thöner), Hans Waldemar Rosen (conductor of the RÉ Singers) and Ludwig Bieler, professor of palaeography and Late Latin at UCD and an expert on medieval Irish writing. John O'Donovan, music critic of the *Irish Press*, would testify that 'he has never heard MT without very bad intonation', and would produce unfavourable notices of previous performances by Thöner – which, as Charles observed, 'could show the jury that MT has not considered his reputation damaged by similar notices in the past'. There was, in fact, no action, principally because Thöner's accompanist at the performance in question agreed to give evidence that Thöner had, indeed, played out of tune, that

---

28. Charles himself never had to go into court to defend his writing, although he did appear as an expert witness on behalf of Fanny Feehan when *Hibernia*, for which she wrote, was sued for libel, and lost the case because, in the judge's opinion, 'she strayed outside the limits of fair comment'. Conor Brady (*op. cit.*) has an illuminating chapter on the newspaper's attitude to libel.

he had no idea of pre-classical style, that Thöner had said, before Charles's notice was published, that he intended to bring a libel action, and that he had been told that to do so would be professional suicide. Shortly after this, Thöner gave notice to Radio Éireann and the RIAM and returned to Germany.

An even more distressing episode occurred due to the illness of violinist David Lillis, leader of the RTÉ String Quartet, at the time when he, and the quartet, were experiencing serious personal difficulties. Lillis's illness caused acute disruption in a highly visible and vulnerable musical environment (as I myself was to recognize and have to accommodate when I began work as RTÉ's Concerts Manager in 1974). Reviewing a concert involving Lillis was an extremely sensitive manoeuvre, and this was evident when Charles reviewed a recital by the reconstituted quartet in March 1973.[29] He felt that he could not avoid referring to the fact that Lillis's playing had 'most sadly declined' and that 'his intonation was deplorable'. William Shanahan, a violinist and orchestral colleague of Lillis, wrote to Charles to point out that the review might have caused a personal as well as professional setback: 'over the years I have admired David's talent and his perseverance in reaching a standard beyond most of us, and only too well know how a performance may fail us for reasons outside our control'. Charles's reply is typical of his concern to do justice to a valued member of the music community while at the same time maintaining his integrity as a critic:

> that notice was one of the most difficult that I have ever had to do. What would have been an extremely difficult task at any time was, of course, made all the more difficult by knowing the strain under which David has been living for the past year. Take all these things together and alone and there might have been a case for kicking for touch and saying nothing. But on the other hand was this. I take it that in the strain of the last six months he has allowed his own personal technique to slip very badly indeed. I think it is possible that he will be forced to allow his technique to continue to slip. To a point where he may not be able to pick it up again. You may well say that it is not my job to know that or to think about it when writing a notice. However one is human and cannot help being full of anxiety.

He referred to an earlier recital when he had written that Lillis's intonation had been 'unpleasing and embarrassing' and that was

---

29. Audrey Park (second violin) and her husband Archie Collins (viola) had recently resigned from the quartet and their places had been taken respectively by Eugene Egan and, on a temporary basis, Máire Larchet from the RTÉSO.

the least that I felt I could get away with (from the point of view of the public) and also intended to be notice to David that he must pick up his technique before appearing with the new Quartet. So much for David personally and my distress about his own playing.

If he had been a soloist with no repercussions, the review might have 'let him down gently without too obviously breaking faith with the readers'. But

> the existence of the Quartet is dicey. There is its previous history to think of. There is its future to think of. And, remember, that those performances will be going out on the air sometime. I think there might be a very real danger if David continues to play like that that the Quartet will break up again and not only be even more difficult to re-form but that David will find that through too-long neglect his technique and his playing were such that nobody would play with him and nobody would give him a job as a player. Believe me, if that had been a foreign quartet touring here I would have had no option but to tear its leader into ribbons.[30]

Thus, to sit down at one's typewriter at a desk in *The Irish Times* and compose a review of a single concert or recital was not simply a matter of telling tomorrow's readers what he thought of the recently ended performance, but carried with it a considerable sense of responsibility to the artist, to the music, to that night's audience and to the general readership of the paper. In this particular case, it also involved the baggage of far-reaching consequences for one of the most important, publicly funded, ensembles in the country.

Cultural policy

Leaving aside Charles's regular contact with day-to-day music-making, one major area of his concern was with the policy which lay behind the practice of music of a genre that had no indigenous place in Irish society and received no immediate recognition from its decision-makers. Policy emanated from government, and was manifested through agencies such as Radio Telefís Éireann (which established its symphony and light orchestras in 1947–48), the Arts Council (founded 1951) and the Department of Education, and was debated by voluntary organizations such as the Music Association of Ireland (founded 1948) and Foras Éireann (1949 – an 'umbrella group' of cultural and quasi-cultural

---

30. For an account of the successive RTÉ String Quartets, see *Music and Broadcasting* pp. 403–419.

bodies)[31] – and embodied in other performing organizations (such as the opera companies in Dublin and Wexford) and educational establishments such as the Royal Irish Academy of Music.

Central to this creation and expression of cultural policy, due to its management of the country's two professional orchestras, was RTÉ, and therefore it was the chief focus of Charles's attention. It is possible here to give only a flavour of his concern for the MAI and Ireland's premier music festival, Dublin's Feis Ceoil, but his engagement with RTÉ over a period of over forty years (starting with his criticism concerning the Symphony Orchestra in the late 1940s) demands substantial attention, not least because Charles and RTÉ entered into such a peculiar relationship that was to last throughout his career, and was symbolic of his *transitus* from his family background to his new place in Irish society.

But first, we must examine, briefly, Charles's views on cultural policy and music education in other directions, which focussed very largely on his concern for an appropriate mix of voluntary and professional expertise, and the need to articulate sensible strategies which could be effectively put into operation.

In discussing the Arts Council in 1968 Charles, in pursuit of cultural policy, thought that the founding Act 'has muddled up administration and execution, amateurism and professionalism, the making and deciding about recommendations and the carrying out of them... In the last few years, it seems to have missed so many opportunities, and seems to have developed more into a chequebook than a council' – a reprise of his premonition as expressed in his 1951 letter to P.J. Little (above).

In that same year (1968), Charles would also go so far as to write to Charles Haughey (Minister for Finance) to urge the reconstitution of the Council, on the grounds that 'the existing council seems to me to have shown itself to be well-meaning but essentially out of touch with the musical life of the country, both in the capital and the provinces. In my own work I am continually surprised by what seems to me the extraordinary lack of people with knowledge and enthusiasm over most of the whole range of opera and music, and an equal ignorance about the financial and professional conditions that underlie virtually all performances.'

Five years later, in 1973, the Council was 'giving the same old grants for the same old purposes to the same old bodies... Money is important, but even

---

31. Including the Irish Countrywomens' Association, Macra na Feirme, Conradh na Gaeilge, the Drama Council of Ireland, and the Irish National Teachers' Organisation.

more important than money is imagination and the floating of ideas. It seems such a long time since the Arts Council did anything but freewheel.' But in that year, the Arts Council was indeed reformed, and the young, energetic and iconoclastic Colm Ó Briain was appointed to the directorship, which replaced the part-time post of secretary, held up till then by the Actons' friend Mervyn Wall (the husband of Fanny Feehan). Charles was under consideration for the position of Chairman, and this time he very much wanted the job: he wrote to *Irish Times* colleague John Healy 'I have a conviction that were I to be appointed I could really achieve something and make the Arts Council not merely an arts force but, even, a sociological force around the country. For goodness sake don't tell Douglas [Gageby][32] because I would hate him to get the idea that I am about to go unless I were going.' He had even gone so far as to set out his stall in an article 'The Arts Council and the Coalition' in *The Irish Times* the day before he wrote this letter to Healy, who, he said 'move[s] so assuredly inside the corridors of power' and could therefore put forward Charles's name.[33]

'If you were to implant the odd word in the right place I think that I could do something in that small sphere that would at least fit in with all the things that you have been writing about which have filled us all with so much enthusiasm and hope.' Charles made a formal application, but eventually Professor Geoffrey Hand was appointed.

One effect of the reformation of the Arts Council was to announce a review of the funding of opera, as part of its attempt, as Charles put it, 'to exert some form of influence over the various things which it supports'; on the face of it, the Council's declaration that it would allow no increases in funding to opera 'until effective changes can be made in the organisation of opera in Ireland' was, therefore, encouraging, but Charles was sceptical of what that might achieve, since the Dublin Grand Opera Society (DGOS) was 'apparently a law unto itself' and regarded the Arts Council merely as a cheque book. He was completely correct, if recent attempts by the Arts Council to yet again reorganize provision for opera in Ireland are considered.

One of the problems at the root of the DGOS was its 'pro-am' organization. 'The entire administration of the DGOS is done for love by the enthusiastic management committee and others.' (This was written in 1980, before

---

32. Editor of *The Irish Times* at the time.

33. John Healy (1930–91), wrote the regular column 'Backbencher' for *The Irish Times* and was the author of *Death of an Irish Town* – principally concerned with political commentary and rural society.

the official appointment of an Artistic Director or a Chief Executive.) 'When we quite justifiably damn the DGOS for some of its messes, we easily forget just how many tens of thousands of pounds the unpaid chorus and management are worth. It is, however, no excuse that something bad is being done for love.' Charles's principal complaint, however, was that so many Irish singers, with proven track records in opera houses abroad, were apparently ignored by the DGOS; these included Suzanne Murphy (at Welsh National Opera), Ann Murray (who had sung at Wexford, London, Hamburg, Cologne, and Frankfurt), Thomas Lawlor and Niall Murray – 'if they are good enough for the E[nglish] N[ational] O[pera], Covent Garden, German opera houses, are they not good enough for their own capital?'

At the Wexford Opera Festival, following the retirement of its founder, Dr Tom Walsh, a series of appointments, largely oriented towards Glyndebourne, were put in place, and Charles frequently found fault with the appointees' policies for similar reasons.

One instance must suffice: in the early 1970s, the artistic director at Wexford was Brian Dickie, and Charles's chief criticism was predictable: the virtual exclusion of Irish singers. Dickie's attitude and Charles's were almost complementary: where Charles's chauvinism motivated him to claim precedence for Irish involvement if it was appropriate, Dickie's immersion in the Glyndebourne world made him seem as if he regarded Ireland as a cultural backwater, which he expressed in a reply to some of Charles's criticism:

> You must know very well that I despise neither Ireland nor its press … I know very well too the awards your paper has deservedly won for the excellence it shows in every aspect of its work. What I do not show is an unstinting admiration for everything Irish, because it *is* Irish, but rather hope to judge each and everything without reference to creed or nationality. In this I may well fail, but surely it can hardly be an approach to deplore. I am concerned to help Wexford achieve the best artistic standards under the circumstances, physical and financial which exist.

This did not stop Charles from thinking of Dickie as 'this little pup'.

He hoped that Dickie's successor, Thomson Smillie (who came from Scottish Opera and held the post for eight years) would have a different attitude to Irish singers: 'Heaven forbid that Thomson Smillie should ever engage an inferior Irish artist rather than a really good foreigner but his two predecessors have given the impression of not wanting, or not knowing about, such talent as there is here.'

Side by side with the major opera seasons, Charles also championed local initiatives such as the opera group in Kilrush, County Clare, and Courtney Kenny's opera season in Ballinrobe, County Mayo (these both in the 1960s) and, later, Wicklow Opera Group. He particularly admired, and saluted, the same energy and passion that had made Wexford (and Kilkenny Arts Week) so distinctive and successful: the local effort and determination to achieve 'grand opera' on a shoestring with community involvement in a very small locale.

Music education

Twice, in 1968 and 1982, Charles wrote extensive series of articles about the state of music education. The main thrust of both series was the question of policy – the role of education in music, which in turn looked at the role of music in society.

His implication was that, since at least the Act of Union of 1800, 'classical' music in Ireland diverged from the 'traditional' genre, to the disadvantage of the former, and its place in Irish society became problematic. This constituted yet another instance of the Anglo-Irish mind trying to reconcile its cultural context and its *modus vivendi* with the changing political and social circumstances in which it found itself.

In 1968, Charles deplored the fact that, despite an ambitious programme for music education in primary schools, little was actually being achieved. This was due partly to lack of facilities and equipment, but there was a much larger, conceptual problem:

> the managers and the teachers must arrive at a conviction (and heaven knows how this will be brought about) that the programme is worth implementing, that this is a musical nation which deserves to have its remarkable capacities brought out into the open... Music has always been part of national tradition... We have a nation whose musical contribution to the world is already very large in proportion to our small size without counting the ferocious rural difficulties. We must rethink more or less from scratch exactly how we are going to carry out all these programmes and achieve the object which we have set for ourselves.

The message Charles wanted to convey was that there was insufficient pride and insufficient drive to achieve the potential that was undoubtedly waiting to be realized. This was particularly ironic, given that Ireland was believed to be an inherently musical nation. On one hand, children should be encouraged to enjoy and exploit their musical heritage, and on another it was important to provide adequate training for those children who displayed a strong musical talent and might progress to the professional ranks. Neither of these was available.

In writing about music education and its practical manifestations, such as the various *feiseanna* and the educational work of the MAI, Charles was less concerned with the minutiae of individual performances or competitions, and more concerned with the larger questions of policy. I am convinced that this was almost entirely due to the factors discussed in Chapters 6 and 7 – the way that modern Ireland was evolving as a middle-class, predominantly Roman Catholic, democracy in a new economic climate, and in new relationships to Britain, Europe and America. A cultured landlord in the eighteenth century might be in a position to patronize (in the best sense of the word) a Carolan or a Geminiani; a cultured, landless landlord in the twentieth century had to find another way of contributing to cultural development, without becoming patronizing (in the worst sense of the word).

Charles's famous remark, that the Feis was organized 'by old women of both sexes', merely caricatured what he saw as an inward-looking complacency ('self-righteous certainty') on the part of its committee. 'Its final measure is the encouragement it gives to musical performance', he wrote in 1956, and found it disappointing. Nearly ten years later, he described the Feis as having been 'at one time ... a climax of the Irish musical year and [having] occupied almost too important a place in the calendar'. But 'that is past'. Musical life having grown richer and busier, the Feis had not kept up with the changes. It was 'an old lady wintering in a seaside boarding house, trying to live as much as possible as she did in the past and regretting that the value of her income is steadily declining'.

By 1973, Charles had become as outspoken as it was possible to be: 'The Dublin Feis Ceoil: should it be allowed a peaceful death?... What can be done to give it more life?' If it were to survive – and Charles thought that it should – it required 'root and branch' reform.

Charles's involvement as a governor of the RIAM, from 1954 until his death, was an ambivalent affair, during which he seemed at times to lose his enthusiasm for it as a national institution, and at others to urge it forwards, not least when he, aided by John O'Donovan, pushed forward the idea of a full-time director in addition to the administrative post of secretary. He and

O'Donovan achieved this in 1980–82, with the eventual appointment of Lindsay Armstrong.[34]

But, as he put it to James Wilson who had complained in 1980 of 'the dead hand of the RIAM', 'it is common lore that the Board are a bunch of obstructive, misguided eejits'. It is another instance of many of Charles having no estimation whatever of anyone's social or financial position if they could not make themselves useful in an effective way. He saw 'eejits' everywhere. This caused him to be viewed with caution, if not outright hostility, in many quarters, not least in the MAI, where Edgar Deale, who felt that Charles did not, in fact, have the best interests of the MAI at heart wrote to him: 'I must say that I cannot understand why you want to be on the Council, feeling and acting as you do. If you remain on the Council please be more considerate of the Association and of your colleagues.'

In principle, the social composition of the MAI would have been a natural home for Charles's cultural concerns, but in practice it was not the kind of organization with which he could be comfortable, given the social and political circumstances of the time. 'We were all over-optimistic in thinking that the Department [of Education] was open to reason', Charles wrote in retrospect in 1973. He thought that the MAI had lost sight of its original purpose. 'It was to have been the voice of music. To a large extent it has reneged on being that and has become a minor concert promoting body' and it appeared to have given up its ambitions in respect of a concert hall. 'The MAI was started to be difficult', he said, and, as one of the most 'difficult' lobbyists himself, he well knew what it meant to be persistent in one's probing and cajoling.

In early 1985 Charles pointedly asked George Bannister, the then chairman of the MAI, what the MAI had done as a lobbyist in respect of the crisis within the RTÉ string quartet, RTÉ's music schedules, cuts in the Arts Council's

---

34. Armstrong, who had been the explicit choice of the staff of the RIAM, prevaricated at the end of 1981 about submitting his application for the position (no doubt due to the ill-health from which he was suffering at that time), and in the interim Hugh Maguire expressed an interest in the post, from which he withdrew when it became clear that Armstrong was, in fact, the only candidate – 'he is a person for whom I have respect and who could possibly do the job very well & he would also be cheaper than me!' – Acton Music Archive, NLI. The question of Maguire's remuneration 'has thwarted my return to Ireland, which is something I dearly wish, *still.*' *Ibid.* For a discussion of Maguire's previous interest in the leadership of the RTÉSO, see *Music and Broadcasting* pp. 201–3.

funding, the structure of European Music Year,[35] and the provision of a recital hall at the NCH. He does not seem to have received an answer. His summing up was: 'the sooner the present MAI is dead and a new MAI with its original aims born, the better'. Even though he was coming up to retirement, he told the MAI 'If I get the opportunity to write vigorously in the *IT* on this subject I will! Because it does seem to be literally YEARS since I heard any word of the council making any squawk at all about any of the disasters that are happening to music.'

A concert hall?

Quite apart from the support which he gave as a member of the MAI to its campaign for a concert hall in Dublin, Charles was able, through the columns of *The Irish Times*, to conduct his own campaign, by means of letters, feature articles, concert reviews (especially during the MAI's Beethoven festival and other concerts in the 1960s to raise funds for a hall) and even record reviews. As early as 1956 he was writing to the editor on the subject, but the real momentum for a definite project came after the assassination of John F. Kennedy in November 1963, when the government announced that a 'Kennedy Hall' would be built to commemorate him. The site chosen initially was the army barracks in Beggar's Bush, between Sandymount and Ballsbridge, but this was abandoned in favour of a hall in the Phoenix Park. In 1967, when it seemed that the project had ground to a halt, Charles was able to write an 'op-ed' piece which was, in some ways, typical of an Anglo-Irish view that the Irish were unfit for self-government, although many angry Irish people might well share such an opinion: 'The secretiveness and silence in high places is characteristic of our Government departments. The ineptitude and stupidity with which they throttle and kill public approval of their good doings by refusing to allow the public to know what is happening, induce a sort of hopeless, numbed despair in those of us who want to cheer and encourage.' That *The Irish Times* would countenance such a denunciation is indicative not so much of the paper's own political leanings as of its faith in Charles to articulate a personal view of public policy that was also in the public interest.

---

35. 1985 was internationally designated European Music Year, marking the tercentenaries of Bach, Handel and Scarlatti.

Charles was vehemently opposed to the Phoenix Park proposal, and favoured the site of the Model Schools in Marlborough Street (in the mistaken belief that the Department of Education was about to move from Tyrone House to the UCD premises in Earlsfort Terrace), since it was close to almost all bus routes passing through O'Connell Street and the chief cultural centres of the Abbey and Gate theatres, besides the nearby cinemas. He felt that the Phoenix Park concept, despite its greenfield advantages, smacked of elitism, whereas the hall should be available to all – a point he would vigorously insist upon when he saw the artist's impressions of the hall that would eventually evolve from the Great Hall of UCD.

> We do not want to plan concerts for those devoted souls who will make pilgrimage to music, but for those who are coming into the city after their tea for their evening's entertainment… Music is certainly an art, but primarily an entertainment. We want a concert hall not for worship but for pleasure. It is very hard for those of us whose lives are concerned with music to keep in our mind that it is a part of show business: but we must, if we are not to betray the very art we are trying to foster.

Charles's championing of the Marlborough Street site brought him a stern letter from Brian O'Nolan (who signed himself in this letter as such and also as 'M. na G' [Myles na gCopaleen]).

> Dear Acton, I find your suggestion about the Model Schools site preposterous. It is bad enough to have this steaming slum area within half a minute's walk from O'Connell Street but to plonk a new opera house down opposite the abominable Pro-Cathedral would seem not far from offer of insult to Kennedy's memory. Slum areas cannot be treated or dealt with by improved patching but must be wiped out in toto. Congestion and filth is of the essence of this area.

He went on to express the same feelings as Charles regarding both the government and the need for a strong public will:

> If immediately after Kennedy's death the Plain People of Ireland had been asked to subscribe from their own pockets to erect a fitting memorial, I'm certain one £million would have rolled in within a few weeks. What is styled our Government is an assortment of peasants and uneducated shopboys and the head of the 'Arts Council' is a member of that lodge of wine-bibbing pietistic toadies, the Irish Jesuits.[36] You will find that the prime qualification of the hall will be that it shall be suitable for the holding of Feeny Fayl[37]

36. The Chairman of the Arts Council was Fr Donal O'Sullivan, SJ.

37. A reference to the Fianna Fáil political party.

conventions and hooleys. The day is lost once the politician swine are in command. Cf. Abbey Theatre.[38]

Eventually the government abandoned plans for the 'Kennedy Hall' and, instead, committed itself to the redevelopment of the Great Hall of UCD, causing a storm of protest from those who had, in many cases, spent decades campaigning for a purpose-built facility. Charles was asked to write a leader for *The Irish Times* which was not, in fact, published, perhaps because the language he used (he referred to the previous government's 'dishonest silence') would have been unacceptable in an editorial. 'If we could be sure that this Government will not buy any more white-elephant jets at £20m, or spend £7m a year on jobs for the Irish-speaking boys to achieve just nothing whatever in saving the language, and if the [hall] could only be built with state funds, there might, possibly, be a case for a slice off the loaf being better than no bread.'[39]

Charles had expressed the hope that he would live to see the opening of a national concert hall, and when the 'slice off the loaf' came into existence in 1980 he was, of course, still working and greeted the hall with all the enthusiasm that he could muster.

Radio Telefís Éireann

From its inception in 1924–26, RTÉ (as it would become) had to find its way in a climate of uncertainty and instability. Whether 'classical' music had any place in the radio schedules was open to question, since many who had supported

---

38. An example of how strongly Brian O'Nolan could express his opinions beyond the columns of *The Irish Times*.

39. Many, including Dónall Ó Móráin (Chairman of the RTÉ Authority 1970–72 and director of Gael Linn), believed that the public exchequer could not, in addition to construction costs, bear the annual burden of a loss-making concert hall, but Charles urged that a concert hall *complex*, incorporating not only a symphony hall but also conference facilities, would be a profitable, revenue-gathering attraction: 'If everybody had called this a congress hall (with music as a by-product) people would have thought of it as part of the tourist industry and not as Culture or Art. Unfortunately this is another bit of public climate that we have inherited from the 19th century British establishment and cannot grow out of' (Acton to Ó Móráin, 2 September 1977 – Acton Music Archive, NLI). He continued to believe that conversion of the Great Hall of UCD 'could not possibly be a potential moneymaker' with the result that 'the climate of opinion will remain (quite unjustly) that the performing arts should be discouraged' (*ibid.*).

the war of independence from Britain wanted an 'Irish-Ireland', self-sufficient and free of external influence; classical music, as taught and practised by Irish, Anglo-Irish and immigrant teachers and practitioners, could be regarded as anathema to the sense of an Irish identity which looked to indigenous cultural genres to create self-awareness and self-confidence.

Charles regarded the radio station as a prime example of the State's evolution of a policy in relation to music and to culture in general. He was most insistent that the two roles of music critic and music journalist should be embodied by the same individual, in order that the *context* of music-making and its hinterland of policy should provide the writer with an ongoing point of view. To separate the functions would be to confine the critic to individual performances and thus limit his capacity for commentary on that context, and this characterized his writing (both public and private) on all aspects of musical life.

Radio Éireann itself was, and is to this day, the single largest employer of musicians in Ireland and the single largest source of 'live' and broadcast music. Charles, with his responsibility to share his views on cultural policy with his readers, probed beyond the mere pleasures or disappointments of any single concert by the RÉSO or the RÉLO, the RÉ choral groups or the Cork-based RÉ String Quartet, to discover what the policy might be which determined the repertoire, the choice of artists and the arrangements for both 'live' concerts and recorded output.

When Charles formed the view that such policy was not in the best interests of either the musicians, their concert audiences or the radio listeners, he found ways of saying so, sometimes by way of a feature article, sometimes in a record review, sometimes by an 'open letter' to the chairman of the broadcasting authority, and always by means of persistent correspondence directly with the people responsible.

The principal conductors of the RTÉSO during Charles's time as chief critic were Milan Horvat (1953–58), Tibor Paul (1961–67), Albert Rosen (1968–81, during the last two years of which he shared the principal conductorship with Colman Pearce), Colman Pearce (in his own right, 1981–83) and Bryden Thomson (1984–87). Behind the scenes were the successive directors of music Fachtna Ó hAnnracháin (1947–61), Tibor Paul (1962–66, while also occupying the principal conductorship), Gerard Victory (1966–82) and John Kinsella (1983–88, with the reduced title of Head of Music). These would be the chief figures on whom Charles would focus his critical spectacles, and to whose reputations as artists and administrators his commentary would be addressed. As a private letter-writer to any of these, Charles was unfailingly courteous and mild-mannered, but in the columns of *The Irish Times* he spoke his mind with as much vigour as he considered the occasion warranted.

There is no denying the fact that Charles could be very personal in criticism, especially of bureaucrats, and Gerard Victory and Louis McRedmond (Head of Information) certainly received more than their fair share of exposure on Charles's pillory, as exemplars of RTÉ's reticence and apparent lack of policy. One of his articles (in 1967) concluded with an exhortation to C.S. Andrews, the then chairman of the RTÉ Authority: 'Is it not time you and your colleagues did more to satisfy the cultural needs of the Irish listener instead of trying to find means of betraying them?' That was probably the most vehement and accusatory language he ever adopted, but, in all his addresses to RTÉ, Charles never relaxed the determined assault on what he perceived as its failure to safeguard and promote its musicians. Later, in 1979, when invited to contribute his views to the RTÉ-published *Irish Broadcasting Review*, he accused the organization of 'debauching a nation's musical taste' by a 'pervasive musical education' based on pop music. His chief anxieties were: lack of programme planning for the Symphony Orchestra, the relative absence of serious music from the airwaves, the almost complete absence of the Symphony Orchestra from the television screen, and failure to give adequate support to the RTÉ Singers and String Quartet.

The distrust between Charles and RTÉ worked both ways. After Charles's retirement I recorded three conversations with him concerning his career, which were broadcast on RTÉ FM3 in 1990 as interval talks during symphony concerts, as a result of which he heard that an RTÉ radio producer had said it was 'a disgrace' that someone who had been critical of RTÉ, who was 'no friend of this institution', should have been accorded such a distinction. Charles wrote to the producer in question: 'I was always, from the 1940s, a friend of your institution. But, being a friend of your institution imposes a duty on a critic of making honest comments and trying to persuade its powers-that-be to do even better. I laboured long in the vineyard to help RÉ/RTÉ, especially at times when others were taking very dim views. You may not have liked what I wrote for a third of a century, but it is possible that you may find that others may write less sympathetically about RTÉ and the NSO.'

The single greatest obstacle to the emergence of the original Radio Éireann Symphony Orchestra into today's National Symphony Orchestra was the fact that it was conceived principally as a studio orchestra broadcasting on radio, rather than a symphony orchestra whose work was also recorded for broadcasting. The second greatest obstacle, at the time of its inception and up to the early 1960s, was that its administration was part of the Department of Posts and Telegraphs, which in turn was dominated by the Department of Finance. Despite the heroic efforts of the Secretary of the Department, León Ó Broin, and the Director of Music, Fachtna Ó hAnnracháin, constraints on the development of the RÉSO were severe. In 1958, ten years after its formation, and at the point where Milan Horvat's tenure came to an end, Charles took the opportunity of a stocktaking article 'The RÉ Orchestra: Present and Future'; as the relative newcomer to music criticism, it marked the first of many occasions when he would survey the imbalance between artistic ambition and administrative restraint, and, naturally, Charles vigorously promoted the first and castigated the second. The following sentence makes it clear to those reading between the lines that he was fully aware of the difficulties faced by Ó Broin and Ó hAnnracháin: 'we may assume... that Radio Éireann is more fully aware of all its problems than anyone else, and there is no doubt that it continually surmounts difficulties of which outsiders are unaware.' At that point, there had been a coalition government from 1948 to 1951 and another from 1954 to 1957, in which the ministers responsible for broadcasting had been far less favourable towards the orchestra than had been those in the Fianna Fáil administrations. Thus Charles wrote: 'the orchestra is constantly under the critical gaze of the public, quite apart from politicians looking for targets and internal bureaucrats striving to prevent it from emerging from the studio'. He pinpointed the paucity of music education for the fact that the orchestra was predominantly staffed by foreign players (a hot political issue at the time)[40] but commended the adventurous nature of the programming – a subject to which he would repeatedly return over the years. Working with too many conductors made the orchestra unstable in performance and prevented it from developing a 'corporate personality'. And the link with the DGOS, for whom the orchestra worked for a quarter of the professional year, meant that RÉ, the DGOS, and the general question of opera performance became inextricably linked to those of artistic policy, administration and finance.[41]

In 1961, at the end of Fachtna Ó hAnnracháin's term as Music Director, Charles could write that 'Radio Éireann and Fachtna Ó hAnnracháin... have

---

40. Cf. *Music and Broadcasting*, pp. 104–107.

41. For a discussion of RTÉ's relationship with the DGOS, see *Music and Broadcasting* pp. 338–370.

created an audience in Dublin that desires the interesting and not the pot-boilers'. But by 1965 he would be disenchanted with the choice of reper-toire. Tibor Paul *did* introduce new and unfamiliar works, but seemed less interested in Irish compositions, and his programming was, in general, less adventurous. Charles frequently reminded his readers that the BBC, before the advent of William Glock as its controller of the Third Programme in 1959, had sent representatives to Dublin to enquire how Radio Éireann succeeded in sustaining such interesting programming.

Concurrently, he noted a rise in the standard of the orchestra. When the Hallé, under Barbirolli, played Schubert's 'Great' C major symphony in Dublin during the 1959 music festival, he thought that the work would have been 'beyond the present RÉSO'. Ten days later, 'I have to take back those words', having heard Jean Meylan conduct the same work with the RÉSO, reflecting a considerable improvement in both technique and interpretation over recent performances. 'The RÉSO showed itself on a par with the Hallé.' It would always be a great source of pride and joy to Charles that the Irish orchestra was, at least for its size and resources, as good as one of the better known, international, orchestras, and generally at least as good as the regional British orchestras.

I have written elsewhere about the restructuring that took place in the Music Department under Ed Roth (Director-General) and Tibor Paul as a result of the so-called 'Willoughby Report'.[42] Charles had been one of the prominent people in Irish musical life who had been invited to meet George Willoughby (seconded from the BBC as a consultant to RTÉ), and had shrewdly told Roth that Willoughby 'may not be very familiar with the differences between the attitudes of the ordinary Irish public to traditional music, light music, ballad songs, sound-radio methods of production, and in a different scale to serious music programmes.' It could therefore be assumed that, as in so many other areas, Charles was familiar with what was envisaged, which included the sidelining of Dermot O'Hara and Eimear Ó Broin as conductors with the RTÉLO. Charles's private letter to Ed Roth of September 1961 is utterly characteristic:

> A very disquieting but persistent rumour is circulating that you are about to dismiss Dermot O'Hara and to import a London band leader;[43] and it is said that in these ten months you have not been able to find time to interview

---

42. See *Music and Broadcasting* pp. 422–5.

43. This was a reference to Frank Chacksfield, who effectively replaced both Dermot O'Hara and Eimear Ó Broin as staff conductors of the RTÉLO.

Mr O'Hara or to find out his views about his ability to transform his present general purpose light orchestra into whatever you want it to be. As Dermot O'Hara and his RÉLO are popular in the country it would help me very much indeed to be able to contradict these rumours if the occasion arises.

This is an excellent example of three of Charles's enduring qualities: firstly, as a journalist, his 'nose' for a potential story; secondly, his feeling that he had a role to play in cultural politics; and thirdly, his personal affection for Dermot O'Hara, of whom he would later write: 'he was a brilliant musician of immense range and deep sensitivity… remembered for his infinite and unpublicised kindnesses'.

Charles considered that RTÉ's chief problem with regard to radio broadcasting (he, like so many, despaired of any adequate provision of music on television) was lack of confidence in itself. This problem is hardly surprising, given that RTÉ is a public service broadcaster which relies increasingly on advertising for the greater part of its income, which has traditionally been subject to direct or indirect control by government, and which must satisfy many different and disparate audiences. But Charles saw the problem more concretely. In 1976 he said that 'RÉ's music broadcasting has been planned (if that is the word) on the assumption that nobody much wants to listen to the RTÉSO, the RTÉ Singers or the RTÉ Quartet… Accordingly, there appears to be no planning of music broadcasting that covers the whole spectrum continuously from encouraging the newcomer gradually to come to, for example, the rigours of "Composers' Rostrum".'

Lack of pride on the part of RTÉ in its performing groups, as Charles perceived it, lay behind the lack of information. In 1978, when the RTÉSO went to the German city of Mainz to give a single concert in a prestigious series of visiting orchestras, Charles's frustration at the lack of information from RTÉ caused him to pen one of the most succinct appraisals of the way that the orchestra, and the organization, were perceived; he sent it to Louis McRedmond, Head of Information:

> It is a fact that the orchestra as a whole and the musical public do feel that RTÉ either does not appreciate its orchestra or (which comes to the same thing) allows it and the public to think they under-appreciate it – as compared with other organisations elsewhere in the world. I have already heard reports of Mainz being a very exciting event for the orchestra and for the audience. For a nation who always tends to deprecate our best endeavours, the fact that our orchestra was invited as being the equal of the Bamberger and the Mozarteum is something which, I think, should have been publicised.

When Tibor Paul was appointed Principal Conductor, RTÉ was undecided as to how the position of Director of Music should be filled, vacant after the resignation of Fachtna Ó hAnnracháin.[44] Charles had learned that Archie Potter was a potential applicant, as was Brian Boydell. It was something of a shock to Charles that Ed Roth (the Director-General) wrote to ask if he were interested in the post, but he wrote in such a way as to make it clear that an application from Charles would not be welcome. Charles took the opportunity of recommending Potter who 'has marked administrative ability with a really wide range of knowledge and sympathy with all sorts of music'.

Although Charles had a very great respect for Tibor Paul as a *musician*, especially in the romantic repertoire, he developed a serious disapproval of his behaviour as a *conductor* which very much coincided with that of the musicians who played under him. This was intimately bound up with the fact that Paul was also Director of Music, which led increasingly to administrative and personnel difficulties. When it appeared that RTÉ was moving towards decommissioning Paul from his administrative post, Charles wrote to a friend that 'it is hard to believe that Tibor Paul will be allowed to make a hames of our music as director much longer. It is a story long enough to make a book out of.' One episode in such a 'book' would have been the incident when Paul allegedly commissioned work from Irish composers for the RTÉSO concert in London: it appears that no such commissions were offered, and Charles told a correspondent who was involved in the dispute, 'one cannot accept the accuracy of anything Tibor Paul says or writes unless it is corroborated by someone else'.

Charles also took the step of writing to Fachtna Ó hAnnracháin (who had become RTÉ's Legal Officer) to recommend his old friend John Miley who, with his wife Joan, was returning to Ireland from Jamaica. 'It would be hard to find anyone anywhere near as good as him to be Director of Music ... He would be able to bring your old department back to where you left it and go on from there.'

As Tibor Paul's tenure was drawing to a close, Charles took the opportunity to write three articles on 'RTÉ and Irish Musical Life' in *The Irish Times*. Although he had been music critic of the paper for eleven years at this stage, and had written hundreds of reviews and feature articles, it was his first major commentary on RTÉ's policy. The importance of these articles is that there was no other sustained public forum for criticism of such issues.

---

44. There remains some confusion as to the order of events at that time.

In these articles, Charles set down markers for the contributions he would make to the public debate on the status and future of music and broadcasting which produced similar series in 1974 and 1979–81: the chief issue being the relationship between artistic policy and financial and personnel management.

Nowhere was this more evident than in Paul's dealings with the RTÉ String Quartet. Charles's papers reveal a fully documented dossier including a chronology of the quartet's relationship with both Paul and his deputy, Gerard Victory, and a fourteen-page statement by the quartet, prepared on their behalf by a leading Cork solicitor, Gerald Goldberg. Basing his arguments on the facts contained in these documents, Charles was anxious to use the columns of *The Irish Times* to expose Radio Éireann's – and particularly Paul's – shortcomings in dealing with musicians who were, he thought, on the brink of becoming a world-class ensemble. His reason for doing so was that the *débâcle* was 'a matter of public interest' – the *raison d'être* of any intervention on his part in *The Irish Times*. Charles's view was that

> there is a cast-iron case for getting sense into the music department – either privately through talking to various people, or if that does not work out, then publicly. In the latter event again [there are] alternatives – either by presenting a statement of the case simultaneously to the DG, the Authority and to members of the Oireachtas and the Minister; or by a newspaper splash after the manner of one of the *Sunday Times* 'Insight' pieces. I have learnt in dealing with these people that one not only wants a strong case, but the whole suit of trumps up one's sleeve in the form of documentation in order to avoid every risk of the other side making a totally false assertion which one cannot undermine without actual documents.

The dossier makes it very clear that he had the necessary evidence, and he even went so far as to ask the quartet members to swear an affidavit as to the truth of the matter, which they considered to constitute severe and undue media pressure from Charles and *The Irish Times*. In the outcome, it was only due to the delicacy that the quartet members believed was required, in order to safeguard their professional future, that a major public discussion was averted.

When Paul was removed from the administrative post, Charles – perhaps unwisely began to mention the 'fear' that members of the orchestra had experienced, and how the atmosphere had improved considerably since his departure. In reply to one correspondent, he stated that 'fairly early in his position as principal conductor Tibor Paul himself told me that an orchestra must be made always to fear its conductor. He made no secret to other people that he considered fear a necessary tool in a conductor's kit.' As far as musical direction is concerned, Charles's view was the exact opposite: 'an orchestra cannot... play well for a conductor whom they do not respect as musician and man. No conductor ever got good results by slave-driving or fear.' It seemed that the personal regard and, indeed, friendship which had existed between the two men had evaporated, and that Charles was now laying down markers for his replacement. When Aloys Fleischmann remonstrated that Tibor Paul had not received due credit for the improvement in the standard of the RTÉSO, Charles responded by neatly underlining the dichotomy in Paul's dual position: 'there is much evidence that the great improvement made by the conductor was very greatly retarded by the music director'.

Charles was concerned that any debate about the status of the RÉSO should not obscure the need to consider the breadth of functions of the Director of Music. He believed that 'we have a flowering of musical talent that in after years may be likened to the literary harvest of the early years of this century' – and he had given plentiful evidence of this in his praise of up-and-coming performers. He did not think in 1966 that the RÉSO should be 'hived off' from the music department (although he would come round to that view twenty years later). But above all, he warned of the danger if 'gulfs should be fixed between traditional music and light music and "serious" music... There has in the past been far too great a tendency everywhere to think of music as divided up into separate compartments, instead of being (as it is) a continuous field, each part of which shades into each other part.' He wanted Paul's successor to 'make its traditional music programmes of headline interest', including television exposure, 'giving our musical heritage a real shot in the arm'. Commending the RTÉ Singers and String Quartet, looking for an improved RÉLO, fearing 'a constant stream of pop', demanding more jazz, he summed up the incoming Music Director's task as 'to fight the corner of the music department in the allocation of new programme schedules', especially as far as television was concerned; and to improve the music department's communication with the public.

This period saw the early stages of a debate about the ultimate fate of the Symphony Orchestra, and in 1971 Charles wrote to Donall Ó Moráin, the then chairman of the RTÉ Authority, with a curious piece of musical gossip:

At a recent party the British Ambassador [Sir John Peck] started talking about orchestras in Ireland as though he were deliberately flying a kite or wanted the thing passed on unofficially. He said it seemed such a pity to have an inadequate orchestra in Belfast [the Ulster Orchestra] and this excellent one in

Dublin that is always said to be on the verge of financial trouble. Wouldn't it be a good thing to have a single, highly paid orchestra for the whole country that would circulate through Dublin, Belfast, Cork and Derry? Whether the whole idea is a good thing or not, I don't know whether anybody would be particularly keen on the idea of British subvention, however large, to what is our own national orchestra. However, I thought it a good thing to pass the idea on to you.

There does not appear to have been any response from Ó Moráin, but it is worth noting that, while the idea was before its time, it contained the seeds of cross-border co-operation; and it is indicative of the high esteem in which Charles was held by someone as senior as Peck (with whom he was friendly) that he should be approached in a semi-official capacity to act as a conduit in this regard.

The prospects of the RTÉSO had in fact improved significantly with the appointment of Albert Rosen as Principal Conductor in 1968. He was clearly a superb music-maker in the style of *mittelEurop*, but, due partly to his background and experience in Prague,[45] and partly to his reluctance to conceive of overall themes for concert seasons, he had limitations as far as a sense of artistic direction was concerned. This provoked Charles in March 1974 to publish a three-part article in *The Irish Times*, 'What Can Be Done With The RTÉSO?', based on interviews with Gerard Victory and Proinnsías Ó Duinn, whose champion (as Rosen's potential successor) he appeared to be: he put forward Ó Duinn (who had made his début with the RTÉSO in 1962) as a conductor with experience of orchestra-building from his four years of 'virtually creating the National Orchestra of Ecuador' or, as Ó Duinn himself put it, 'trying to find out how a successful orchestra works, what makes it work, and how to get the best from an orchestra'.[46] He said that he did not see why his views

---

45. At the time of his appointment to RTÉ, Rosen (1924–97) was Director of the Smetana Opera Theatre and resident conductor of the Prague National Opera.

46. *Irish Times* 19 March 1974. When Ó Duinn returned to Ireland from Ecuador in 1971, Charles wrote of his first concert: 'Quite clearly, Mr Ó Duinn had authority. He knew what he was doing and knew what he wanted – and got it with clarity and no fuss. He had the air of being willing to, and knowing that he could, trust his players as artists without unnecessary and annoying detailed gestures'. In 1973, he wrote: 'Proinnsías Ó Duinn has of course a rather special understanding of strings: he can mould phrases so that the speed fits the players' breathing and bow length like a glove; this knack or skill makes it very rewarding and satisfying to play with and for him. Add to that the ability to play a romantic work such as the Sibelius [second symphony] with

'should antagonise anybody', although in fact those same views, expressed in the context of an extensive article in what RTÉ would have regarded as the hostile environment of *The Irish Times*, probably did more than anything else to withhold from Ó Duinn the principal conductorship of the RTÉSO.

Charles's articles, and his interview with Ó Duinn, were based on the assertion that 'for some time critics and public have been anxious about the RTÉ Symphony Orchestra, since many of its performances seem to be sub-standard'. Led by Charles, Ó Duinn committed the cardinal sin, in RTÉ-speak, of agreeing that 'the good of the orchestra is being offered up to the organisation mind… We should get out from under the heels of people with civil service minds and then we will have a chance.'

Ó Duinn then pushed the conversation towards the seminal point: 'the function of an orchestra in society'. He believed 'that it's a luxury for a country like this to maintain an orchestra solely for the purpose of broadcasting… I don't see any attempt by RTÉ to get the public interested in its orchestra or to get them accorded the dignity and reputation that they should have.'

The difficulty of making anything other than minor changes to the organization and operation of the orchestra was made clear in Gerard Victory's response that 'RTÉ is not a package of self-contained entities. The orchestra (and all that belongs to it) is a part of quite a large public service organisation, with its grades and privileges and rules'. Such a statement typifies both the advantages and the disadvantages of the orchestra's – and the Music Department's – position. As I know, having worked for twenty-five years in both the Music and Public Affairs departments, the Music Department, as a concert-giving organization, was constrained by its sister departments which were not ancillary but superior: Finance, Personnel and of course Radio Programmes, within which it was located and through whose hierarchies any proposed change must be shepherded. Victory himself, while a man of immense creativity, artistry and imagination, was not, as an employee of RTÉ, a 'self-contained entity' but a bureaucrat who had to speak the language of his opposite numbers and to elicit the sympathy of his superiors for the fortunes not only of the two orchestras and their cadre of conductors, arrangers and administrators, but also the musicians outside RTÉ who depended on the organization for employment as

---

such musical feeling that one wanted to sing the tune with him'. Charles's successor. Michael Dervan, would also appear to be a champion of Ó Duinn's conducting skills: in 1990 he wrote (*Irish Times* 16 March 1990) 'he is still one of the most inspirational conductors working regularly with any Irish orchestra'.

either orchestral or chamber players or as soloists, and the music-loving public attending their concerts or receiving their broadcasts in their homes. This was anathema to Charles, and it is quite possible that his lack of sympathy for RTÉ, and for Victory himself, was due to his poor perception of the bureaucratic circumstances within which Victory and others were obliged to function.

The major positive points in Victory's interview were his acknowledgement that the Symphony Orchestra should undertake more international touring (which would in fact be achieved two years later with its first European tour): he also hoped to see more experimental music 'not only in the contemporary music festival (which has been very successful)', and 'a proper hall which is absolutely essential'.

If Ó Duinn's anxieties were energetic and radical, and Victory's response appears lacklustre and institutional, it can be explained, as Charles put it, as the difference 'between the idealist on the outside who feels he can see what must be done, and the man in the hot seat who has to cope'.[47] That difference is essentially an artistic-versus-pragmatic gap.

But Charles did not let it rest there: he also characterized Ó Duinn as a practising musician with administrative experience and Victory as 'something of an outsider to an orchestra's problems in spite of being a composer and having done a certain amount of conducting'. He hoped that 'Mr Rosen might now take a stronger line with Dr Victory and demand that more be accorded to the orchestra… Certainly some of the red tape surrounding all RTÉ's decisions might well be thrown away.' But Rosen was also an arch-pragmatist, knowing, from his background in dealing with the *apparatchiks* in Prague, exactly what could be achieved by the art of the possible. While he was without doubt one of the finest musicians ever to work with the orchestra over extended periods, he was not one to rock the boat in administrative matters.

Charles's conclusion was that 'The National Song Contest is regarded as something of national television importance and the RTÉSO is regarded as the Cinderella of the entire broadcasting organization. Is it not high time that somebody in the organisation took his responsibility for this fine body of musicians reasonably seriously?'

In 1981, Charles still felt that the orchestra's stability was again endangered not only by its own performing difficulties, but also by the continuing lack of a long-term strategy on the part of management: he asked 'Will RTÉ's top administration now give Dr Gerard Victory and his music department whatever is

47. *Irish Times* 21 March 1974.

needed to work out a real new policy, to carry it out and to organise a real, continuing organization able to plan everything ahead and put through its plans, in place of the hand-to-mouth life that seems characteristic of nearly all its radio and television work?' By now, this had become such a hobby-horse that Charles's persistent repetition of such questions cut no ice whatever within RTÉ. Nevertheless, Charles became the first critic to ask publicly: 'Has the time now come to extract them [the RTÉSO] from RTÉ administratively?'

With Victory's retirement in 1982, Charles hoped that 'that sensitive musician and fine composer, John Kinsella' would succeed him, but warned that 'he will face a lot of problems', urging, quite impossibly, that the new director must extend his area of influence to all radio activity and to television.

Five months later, Charles was announcing 'Succession Problems', since no procedure had been put in place for selecting Victory's successor.

> It is now, in mid-1982, that the RTÉ Music Director and the RTÉSO principal conductor-designate [Bryden Thomson would become principal conductor at the end of 1983] must get down to the planning board. It is *now* that programmes, soloists, guest conductors must be planned... At the end of the first and therefore tentative and experimental year of the National Concert Hall, it looks as if the topmost brass of RTÉ could not care less about this crucial job at the most important time for Irish music during this century.

After another two months, in the continued absence of any announcement regarding the filling of the vacant post, Charles had written to the Director-General (now George Waters, the former Director of Engineering) and had received the reply that 'We propose to advertise for a new Head of our Music Department as soon as our income permits. When that will be I am not in a position to say.' A further two months went by, and in December 1982 Charles was addressing an open letter to Fred O'Donovan, Chairman of the RTÉ Authority:

> For half a year, John Kinsella, as Deputy Director, has been carrying on, but, at a time when far-reaching plans are being made and policies laid down for the next five years or more, a deputy must be reluctant to arrogate the prospective powers of his future principal and therefore leave the latter powerless to put forward his own policies and ideas. You could, Fred, suggest, perhaps, to George Waters that if there is no need to have a Director of Music, there is no need to have a Director-General and that he might retire leaving the station in the hands of the deputy DG... The single most important musical job in our whole island is the Director of Music of RTÉ. It is he who will plan for the next quinquennium, if not the next decade, what the various groups of RTÉ musicianers will be doing; what the punters will want to listen to; what

Irish composers will compose... Dear Fred, please do not let the present vacuum persist.

When Kinsella was, eventually, appointed to the diminished post of 'Head of Music', Charles exhorted him to push for the inclusion of the RTÉSO on the television screen – perhaps not being aware that the post was specific to the Radio Division and had no remit in television: it was simply a fact that Kinsella had no authority to do what was being asked of him. He further urged him to devise planned concert seasons with musical excitement such as he had witnessed in the 1950s and '60s – a development which indeed bore fruit with Bryden Thomson's inspired symphonic cycles of Bruckner, Nielsen and Sibelius. But at the time of Kinsella's appointment, Charles asked one of his deputy critics, James Maguire, to interview Kinsella; Carol told me that he took the decision not to undertake such an important interview himself so that there should be no evidence of personal bias, since he was convinced from the outset that Kinsella 'was not up to the job' – a realization that very soon came to Kinsella himself, and contributed to his early retirement where he could engage more fully in his true vocation, that of a composer, undisturbed by the wheels of the RTÉ bureaucracy, which had treated him most cavalierly.

Over the years, Charles became acutely conscious of the workings of this bureaucratic mind, and in particular he realized that representations on his own part, or on that of anyone who could be regarded as an interested party, carried far less weight than those of 'ordinary' citizens. When, therefore, RTÉ threatened, as a cost-cutting measure, to reduce the number of its regional concerts, Charles urged Aloys Fleischmann (of UCC and the Cork Orchestral Society) to 'persuade everyone you know in Cork to write to the Authority and protest at the cut down and to write to the Editor of their ordinary daily newspaper in the same vein.' It was advice which he would give to Fleischmann, and many other concert promoters, again and again. Another correspondent was advised:

> 50 letters to the Chairman of the Authority, spread over 2 or 3 months asking for your idea to be put into operation are 100 times as effective as anything I can write. According to an extremely experienced editor, what one of his own contributors wrote was simply a matter or personal opinion, but if he got 20 letters over a few weeks advocating one thing he could not help feeling that that was the voice of the people of Ireland.

Charles attacked RTÉ's programming policy in explicit terms in December 1979, referring to 'the triumph of RTÉ's apparent intentions to debauch the musical taste of the nation'. This, he considered, was due to a *trahison des clercs* on the part of the heads of the station, most of whom have high tastes themselves, but personal convictions that the People have not or are incapable of having; to a similar *trahison* on the part of advertising people who will say, of course they love Schoenberg, but no one else does; and to a succession of bright, more or less young middle-aged producers and personalities of good education in most other fields who suffer from musical illiteracy and subnormal musical education.

Two years later, insisting that 'taste is formed by exposure', he was again asserting that 'the high-ups in RTÉ are either genuinely ignorant of the facts or totally indifferent to their cultural responsibilities, even to those spelt out in the Broadcasting Acts'. It was a fruitless, self-appointed task to beleaguer RTÉ on behalf of either the musicians or the audiences, and one wonders why Charles continued to persevere in this quixotic vein.

Performers and performances

From his very first *Irish Times* review, published on 7 November 1955, Charles displayed a level of confidence and critical maturity which was surprising in one who had previously published very little in this genre. While his frequent attendance at concerts and his practical experience as a member of the DOP had given him a deep insight into the ways in which a performance could succeed or fail, he had not been required to put his views before the public in the critical vein expected of the music correspondent of *The Irish Times*.

Charles was a tireless and persistent champion of Irish performers, particularly of young, emerging, artists: 'I want Irish artists to be Irish' he fulminated. Readers of *The Irish Times* would have been unaware of the chauvinistic way in which Charles insisted that the 'What's On' column listed performances abroad by Irish artists. His point was that a performance *anywhere* by an Irish artist was a matter of public importance (and, in those days, of public record), and an appearance by, say, Peter Sweeney in an organ festival in Barcelona deserved to be brought to the attention of his readers, as a matter of national pride.

However, Charles's championing may not have been especially evident to those who were unfortunate enough to receive unfavourable reviews. It gave Charles no pleasure or satisfaction to have to tell a débutant (and the readers of *The Irish Times*) that he or she was not yet prepared for a professional career. To use a cliché, he implicitly felt that 'this hurts me more than it hurts you'

– the point being that he had no wish to send a budding musician back to their studies unless it was, in his opinion, absolutely necessary in order to save them (and the paying public) from later disillusion and disappointment. Charles's reviews of student concerts, for example at the RIAM or the College of Music, or at the annual Feis Ceoil in Dublin, were, mostly, encouraging. He might pass over student blemishes in looking for the positive qualities to be praised. However, once the student had crossed the threshold onto the professional stage, different criteria applied, the most stringent of which was the question of taking the public's money in exchange for a professional performance. Of course, a débutant would lack experience, but the most important quality in a young performer was self-confidence, the ability not only to present the music to the audience but also to project a sense of musicianship in an authoritative way that would be gradually enhanced as the career progressed.

Charles's chauvinism in this respect sometimes sent him over the top. When, in 1979, Miranda Guinness (Lady Iveagh) allegedly said that 'it is such an exciting abnormality to get a good concert' in Ireland, Charles penned a diatribe that assessed both the problems associated with experiencing a 'good concert' and the opportunities and energies of Irish *and* foreign performers, referring obliquely, and perhaps impolitely and impertinently, to the support for music in Dublin, Belfast and Wexford by 'her husband's company' and saying that her lack of awareness of what is going on here was 'breathtaking'. And he listed about fifty events during the year which he regarded as having been of top quality.

In the 1950s and 1960s a new generation of musicians emerged at the RIAM and the College of Music (more particularly at the former), among whom were violinists Audrey Park (later leader of the RTÉLO and NSO), David Lillis (leader of the RTÉ String Quartet and RTÉSO), Mary Gallagher (founder-leader of NICO) and Maeve Broderick (professor at the RIAM); singer and harpist Grainne ní Éigeartaigh, the singer Austin Gaffney, and pianists Anthony Hughes (better known as an academic) and Seóirse Bodley (better known as a composer). Charles followed and encouraged their progress keenly, in particular drawing public attention to the performances of Mary Gallagher and Anthony Hughes,[48] the latter at a very young age succeeding John F. Larchet as professor of music at University College, Dublin. He was a remarkably fine pianist (especially in Mozart) who gave a début recital at the RDS in February

---

48. For reviews of Mary Gallagher's performances, see *Music and Broadcasting*, p. 177, note 55.

1956. Hughes had studied piano at the RIAM with Dina Copeman before going to the Vienna Academy of Music for three years' further study with Bruno Seidlhofer. In his *Irish Times* review, pointing out that an RDS début was the Irish equivalent of a Wigmore Hall recital in London, Charles mentioned that, prior to going to Vienna, Hughes 'possessed a formidable technique but had not awakened to the feeling of music'; now, 'he is aware of the feeling of the music, but is afraid to give way to it'. His review, characteristically, ended: 'If I have pointed more to matters for improvement than to good points, it is because the latter are obvious. So much was there, so much skill, so much knowledge, so much command of the instrument, so much of the essential of the solo artist. The rest will come when Anthony Hughes takes the brake off his emotions and lets them appear too.'

It is clear from the letter which Charles sent privately to Anthony Hughes the next day that he urgently felt the need to expand on this review in order to give Hughes as much positive direction as possible. It also gives us a clear picture of the factors influencing Charles's assessment of a developing talent and, perhaps more importantly, his sense of his personal responsibility towards his subject:

> Comment on your recital yesterday is taking this form because I have been getting more & more anxious about you, and this seems the most helpful way to do it. Up to now, while I have not praised you insincerely, I have withheld or softened blame, waiting for you to establish yourself fully. But you do not seem to do so. Your performances have shown you as full of authoritative erudition and thoughtfulness. The price of artistry is constant vigilance. For all your knowledge, you do not give the impression of feeling the music. Music, as an art, combines the brain, the mind, the emotions, the heart, and the revelation of the spirit of God. Have you the last three? I find it hard to believe that you have not, but they never show. Please remember that you must express your feelings and you must have the feeling to express. This is a plea to come to terms with yourself as a concert pianist.

Many young performers would reject such advice as an unwarranted intrusion into their professional lives; others would acknowledge Charles's wisdom and concern, even though they might question his authority for making such comments. There is no record in this instance of Anthony Hughes having responded to Charles's letter.

The problem, which Charles saw in so many performers, was that the player did not convey the *musicality* of the music, however much he or she may have felt it within; and it was a difficulty, or inhibition, that Charles also detected in the conducting of Eimear Ó Broin and Colman Pearce, that the music seemed to stop at their fingertips, and was not transmitted to the members of the orchestra sufficiently to convince them of the musical excitement. In the latter's case, study abroad had, in Charles's opinion, effected a considerable improvement in Pearce's skill as a conductor,[49] but he stirred up a storm of protest in 1959 when he said that Ó Broin did not 'show any signs of development after several years as assistant conductor'. His sustained view of Ó Broin over many years was expressed in this review: 'he does not seem able to call forth any adequate response from the RÉSO ... one feels that Mr Ó Broin's great gifts lie in the field of research and musicology rather than on the rostrum.' An unpublished memorandum by Charles observed that the actual effect of his programmes was 'extremely dull', due mainly to 'absence of nuance'. He did not want to copy his colleagues and write notices of 'gentle meaningless faint praise', but to express his actual impression of each concert. This, however, was a thankless task: 'it is pointless and disheartening to tear strips off him every time' (especially when Charles acknowledged that Ó Broin was at that time 'the only Irish orchestra conductor in the field'). 'I am still hoping for an occasion when I can honestly praise him' – and this would, indeed, occur more than once in future years – but 'there is the lamentable possibility of his becoming the permanent conductor [of the RTÉSO]. If this did happen, it will be the end of any hope of a permanent orchestra of moderate standard in Ireland'. Charles believed, at this crucial juncture in the orchestra's development, that regular work with top-class conductors was the only way forward.

Clearly, Charles was passionate, and he wanted to experience the passion in others. Several times in his career his reviews recorded that he had left a concert with tears in his eyes, which one might say was, for him, the ultimate accolade of a performance. When Stephen Bishop-Kovacevich played Beethoven's 'Emperor' concerto with the RTÉSO under Colman Pearce in 1983, Charles wrote 'either I was in a highly emotional state last night or the RTÉSO concert at the National Concert Hall was a most unusually fine musical experience. I prefer to believe the latter.' Having, exceptionally, employed all the superlatives he could muster to salute the piano soloist, he concluded 'If I were to die now, this concert would be a satisfying *Nunc dimittis* and it is certainly the finest thing that I have heard from Colman Pearce.'

Charles and Carol developed the habit very early on of leaving a concert immediately – one might almost say abruptly – once applause had started, in

---

49. Cf. *Music and Broadcasting* Ch. 6.

order to avoid queues at the exit, and to get to the *Irish Times* office in time to hand in copy (he would frequently say that 'I'm not paid to listen to encores'). Dublin being a small community, it was not difficult to guess, from their body language as they left the hall, what tone the next morning's review might take. Seldom were the tears in evidence. A contented smile usually indicated the gestation of a favourable notice; a tight-lipped, grumpy expression suggested the opposite. Charles quickly developed a close critical bond between himself and Carol, going so far as to say that a review that carried his own byline belonged just as much to Carol. In matters of string technique he deferred to her almost exclusively, and, on the increasingly frequent occasions when there were two – or even three – concerts on the same evening, Carol, who operated the deputy list, would try to ensure that she was with Charles if a significant string work was involved. Carol herself was, perhaps, the stricter and less forgiving element in the partnership, and her own notices read more sternly. As a duo, however, Charles's search for passion and Carol's for accuracy melded into the notices that appeared the following morning; as their occasional deputy, I was in a position to observe their discussions – often protracted and always anxious – in the arts-and-features room of *The Irish Times* which led to a notice that both felt did justice to the performance.

In order to give some indication of the support that Charles gave, especially behind the scenes, to Irish artists, it is necessary to be highly selective. One could simply catalogue the names of the many players, singers and conductors whose careers he championed, on and off the page, but I would like to highlight a smaller, representative, number of musicians, whose careers Charles was able to observe over a sustained period. In each case, a particular aspect of Charles's concern for the musician's well-being and potential career is demonstrated. In doing so, it is difficult to achieve balance, as it might seem that he had nothing but good to say of the young people in whom he was particularly interested. It was a point on which he had reservations about Gareth Cox's selection of his reviews for *Acton's Music*; Cox had been given *carte blanche* in the matter of editorial selection, and both Charles and Carol felt that the resulting volume gave the impression that most of his reviews were favourable. Unlike the tenor of almost all of Charles's 5500 reviews, the selection was bland, or, as Carol put it, 'like an egg without salt'.

CHARLES LYNCH

The exception to the younger generations of musicians mentioned here is the senior figure of pianist Charles Lynch (1906–84). Lynch had enjoyed what one might call a spectacular career in London in the 1930s, associating with Rachmaninov, Moiseiwitsch, Arnold Bax, and Beatrice Harrison; his return to Ireland in the war years had led to the eclipse of his career in England, but he entered fully into the musical life of his native Ireland (as we have seen, Charles and John Miley promoted him in 1949–50), with regular concerto appearances with the RÉSO and conducting engagements with the DGOS. Charles knew that Lynch was remarkably adept at modern music, as well as being a fine interpreter of the impressionist French composers, but he also knew that he was lazy and prevaricated to the *n*th degree, mainly because he had a phenomenal capacity for sight-reading. While he utterly respected Lynch's reputation and his particular musical affinities, Charles observed him in mid-career with a mixture of tact and affection, not at all deaf to the imperfections that might show themselves when Lynch (probably due to financial necessity) was playing a work not truly suited to his repertoire. Perhaps because he knew Lynch so well, Charles was able to play a form of cat-and-mouse in his reviews, making subtle allusions to the more dubious elements in his music-making and far more encoded than a straightforward notice of a less eminent or a more junior musician.

It was perhaps the monolithic nature of Lynch's character that most impressed Charles. He did on one occasion translate this into physical terms, describing his approach to the keyboard as: 'a large man in white tie and tails makes his immensely stately way onto the platform with all the inevitability of a great liner coming into dock'. Thus when, in 1968, Lynch gave two recitals in which he played most of Debussy's solo music, or, in 1971, all the transcriptions by Liszt of the nine Beethoven symphonies (in a series of four recitals), Charles greeted the achievements as major milestones placed in Dublin's musical calendar by 'a musician with a remarkable knowledge and strong intellect'. The result (in Debussy) was 'a performance full of thought': exactly what that thought consisted of, and what it led to, was not defined – it was Lynch's intellect *per se* that commanded respect and attention, and here Charles was able to shelter whatever reservations he might have about what he actually heard. When Lynch gave a Wigmore Hall recital in 1968, Charles wrote privately to William Mann (critic of the London *Times*, who occasionally deputized for Charles in London) that Lynch was 'our one undoubted celebrity pianist, regarded with affection and admiration by the uninstructed Irish public, and with affection and gross exasperation by the Irish musical world'. He recalled that at one of the Acton-Miley concerts in 1950, Lynch had played the Berg sonata at sight, 'admittedly with shall we say certain aleatory additions. I attribute part of my white hairs to this event.' Due to the laziness which his sight-reading ability induced, Lynch's performances 'range from the nearly inspired to the damn well slapdash'.

Another milestone came in 1972 with Lynch's recording, by the newly-established and short-lived New Irish Recording Company, of a volume of solo piano works by Irish composers. Bestowing the accolade of 'our one undoubted national celebrity pianist', Charles succeeded in lauding the appearance of the disc without making any judgment on the playing. When he wrote a profile of Lynch shortly before his seventieth birthday, Charles charted the achievements of 'a legend', for whom, at this time, life was not as full as he might have wished it. 'One cannot ask such an artist about the things that went wrong, the misfortunes and disappointments.' He recorded 'great if slightly quizzical affection for a remarkable and important figure'.

GERALDINE O'GRADY

One of the most distinguished violinists to emerge from Ireland in the 1950s and '60s was Geraldine O'Grady (b. 1932), who studied with Jean Fournier at the Paris Conservatoire (where she was awarded a *premier prix*) and led the RÉSO from March 1960 to the end of 1963.[50] She enjoyed a successful career as a recitalist (less so as a concerto player) and spent a great deal of her later life touring outside Ireland with her principal accompanist, Havelock Nelson. Charles's review of her first concert after her return from Paris, in 1956, is typical of what he would write of many an aspiring player who displayed obvious potential: 'Such a first recital is a more than ordinary ordeal, before so many people eagerly hoping that the departed cygnet has returned as a swan. Miss O'Grady shows every sign of turning out one of our few real swans.[51] The technique she now has. The musicianship and feeling which she always had have not been submerged by the necessary concentration on technique.'

---

50. Geraldine O'Grady was never officially appointed as Leader of the orchestra: see *Music and Broadcasting* pp. 204–5.

51. In 'A Critic's Creed' Charles would also say that 'we certainly have at least two Irish organisations presenting concerts who sometimes seem to think that all British geese are swans and Irish swans all geese.'

And Charles came round to what would become one of his recurring themes: 'it would be pleasing if the RDS were to offer her an engagement next season' – which she achieved two years later.

In 1958, O'Grady played the Beethoven concerto (under Carlo Zecchi) with mixed feelings on Charles's part, although his overall impression was 'a performance in which I revelled', and a milestone in O'Grady's career.[52] Her RDS recital caused Charles to remark that she was 'only the second young Irish artist to have given a recital at the RDS within the last 15 years or so'. It was another occasion for serious assessment: 'it must have been of far greater significance [for O'Grady] than to the foreign artists we usually hear there. She knows that they are birds of passage, of less intrinsic interest to the audience than she is. She knows (and so do we in the audience) that her stature as a player has finally come to the bar of Irish opinion, and that, to satisfy her audience there, she must emerge among the top performers and not merely as one of the ruck. Yesterday she passed this arduous test admirably.'

In the meantime, however, Charles felt it necessary, as a member of the RDS, to point out to its music committee that 'the Society should seem to be friendly and encouraging rather than aloof and over formal'. In the case of young Irish artists 'is it not worth a bit of extra trouble in letter writing to give them the impression that our Society with its prestige and eminence regards their struggles with sympathy rather than indifference[?]' As an indication of Charles's support for young Irish musicians, we might mention that, as early as the end of 1950, Charles had felt very strongly that the RDS was too far oriented towards foreign musicians, to the neglect of Irish – and particularly young Irish – players and singers, and that they should not have to apply to the RDS for engagements, but should be offered them by a more enlightened music committee of the Society. The RDS had initiated many activities in its 200 years that had eventually taken on a life of their own (the College of Art, the National Museum, National Library and the Botanic Gardens) and he couldn't see why it should not 'take a bold initiative in the musical field'. He put forward the notion that the Society should appoint a person at a salary of £500 and with a budget of £600, for the purpose of nurturing Irish performers. (One would not have to look far to see whom he thought might fit the job, at a time when his own fortunes were in a

---

52. Carol's own notes of this performance indicate the difference in emphasis between herself and Charles, and the way in which they would work together to establish a fair and acceptable review; Carol's summing up was: 'Poised, good girl, tough work, more experience needed. Necessary fire & feeling there, but subdued by cautiousness.'

poor state and he was on the verge of marrying.) Well-intentioned intervention on Charles's part on behalf of an individual performer might well have an effect opposite to that intended – not to mention the possible embarrassment caused to the person thus highlighted, and this form of advocacy may not have been as valuable – and certainly not as tactful – as Charles expected.

In 1962 Charles was asked for assistance by the RTÉ String Quartet who 'wrote to them [RDS] two years ago; beyond a printed acknowledgement, we heard nothing further – as I'm sure you'll understand, one doesn't wish to ask twice. There would seem to be a certain prejudice in that body against artists resident in Ireland. In our case it is resulting in the ironic situation in which we are undertaking our first continental tour without having been heard at the leading chamber music organisation in the country.'[53]

PROINNSÍAS Ó DUINN

On 31 May 1963, Charles addressed the following letter to the Director of Broadcasting at Reykjavik, Iceland:

> Dear Sir, A visitor here from Iceland has just told me that you are about to make an appointment of a conductor of your orchestra. I am hoping that a young conductor here, Proinnsías Ó Duinn, will be applying to you for the position and I am taking the liberty of writing to you to recommend him most warmly. As the senior music critic of the leading Irish newspaper I am convinced by his performances that he has real ability as a conductor. You may well wonder why he would be considering conducting abroad if he has such ability, and the reason is that the limited number of conducting positions here are filled for the next few years. I should add that he does not know that I am writing to you, although I have urged him strongly to apply to you himself. Yours faithfully...

Proinnsías Ó Duinn (b. 1941) was at that time twenty-two years old, and struggling to establish himself as a conductor, with, as Charles had pointed out, little hope of making a career in RTÉ. He was also a budding composer (he had been awarded an Arts Council scholarship to encourage his compositional interests, and studied with Hendrik Andriessen in Holland) and an accomplished cellist who played in a quartet organized by Carol.[54] He did apply to

---

53. The writer of the letter was the quartet's leader, Roger Raphael.

54. Proinnsías Ó Duinn's compositions at that time included a clarinet sonata (1957), a horn sonata (1958) and a string quartet (1962); these were followed by his Symphony

Reykjavik, and was given a trial period of three months at the end of 1963, after which he was invited for a return visit a year later. At that stage, Charles, ever suspicious of Tibor Paul's role as Director of Music at RTÉ, told Paul that

> I am worried about Proinnsías Ó Duinn. You told me that you were giving him adequate work. This in fact appears to be, in three years, three studio engagements with the RÉSO, only two of them before audience or critics; a weekly television concert with the RÉLO on a week to week contract, terminable at the end of each recording. That, you will agree, is not enough to enable anyone to arrange his life. Unemployment at a week's notice is hardly adequate, and light music only is hardly fair. As Director of Music you should surely be fostering a real talent such as his. As things are now, I believe that he feels (and I for one think he is right judging by the past two years) that he will receive neither encouragement, nor fostering, nor his deserts as an Irish musician from his own public broadcasting service. I understand that he feels that he will be forced into emigration at the end of this year. If he is forced to emigrate (or is let do so) there will be a considerable body of public opinion that will blame Radio Éireann in general and you as Director of Music in particular for losing to our country (which can ill afford the loss) a conductor of very great potential. It may well be that his present promise may never be fulfilled, but I (and many others) feel that you have a duty to us to let this be discovered here as an alternative to forcing him to develop and achieve fame in the service of other nations, while we have no one adequate.

Paul refused to be told what to do:

> It is a matter of policy of the organisation not to be influenced by any individual or group with regard to the engagements offered to artists. It has been amply demonstrated in the past that the policy of Radio Éireann, and my own personal objective, has always been to work for the retention of Irish musicians at home and to encourage wherever possible the return of Irish musicians from abroad. However, Radio Éireann can hardly be expected to maintain on its limited resources every musician in the country or because of the impossibility of such an undertaking be accounted responsible for the emigration of a particular person or persons.

Paul said nothing whatever about the particular qualities of Ó Duinn; this was disingenuous of him, and indicative of what Charles would later call his 'pathological jealousy'. Charles, needless to say, did not let the matter rest there: he

---

(1968/9). The other members of Carol's quartet were Joan Miley (violin) and Kathleen Green (viola).

would have realized that Paul was not prepared to discuss Ó Duinn's merits or otherwise, and reiterated 'Because I am anxious about the possibly permanent loss to the country of the only young native conductor yet to appear capable of eventually succeeding you, it is unfair of you to write as though I were expecting Radio Éireann to "maintain every musician in the country".'

As we have seen, Ó Duinn was involved in a discussion about the RTÉSO in 1974, which damaged his chances of being engaged as its conductor. Before that, however, when Tibor Paul had left RTÉ and had been succeeded as Director of Music by Gerard Victory, Charles continued to push Ó Duinn forward: in 1968 he told him: 'It seems more than likely that if you were to write and say that you hope to be [in Ireland] during the next season or so and would like to be invited to conduct the RTÉSO, an invitation might well turn up. Dates and times and so on being as they are, it is possible that they would in the first instance only offer you one or two Xavier Hall Fridays.'[55]

After Iceland, Ó Duinn, with a wife and young family, worked as a session musician in New York, before his appointment as Principal Conductor of the Symphony Orchestra of Ecuador (1966–69) where he also lectured at the University of Quito, and later at the University of Cauca in Colombia. He returned to Ireland in 1974 as RTÉ's Choral Conductor for four years, and his talent as an orchestral conductor was demonstrated extensively during his twenty-four years as Principal Conductor of the RTÉ Concert Orchestra, 1978–2002.

BERNADETTE GREEVY

At the same time as he was endeavouring to secure work for Proinnsías Ó Duinn, Charles was giving advice to the rising star Bernadette Greevy (1940–2008), at that time a contralto (she later developed her voice to mezzo-soprano) who was to achieve world renown with works such as Elgar's *Sea Pictures* and the *Kindertotenlieder* and *Lieder eines fahrenden Gesellen* of Mahler. At that time, however (1962), the twenty-two-year-old was inexperienced and anxious to learn. When Charles thought he might have to decline an invitation to review her recital at the beginning of 1962, Greevy wrote that 'I shall greatly miss your valued counsel which means so very much to me. Whenever my performances please you I know I have sung well.' She was very much under Charles and Carol's wing at that stage, dining at Stradbrook and being

---

55. The RTÉSO's home was in Dublin's St Francis Xavier Hall, where it gave a weekly 'Studio Concert' to an invited audience on Fridays.

introduced to her influential elders such as Tibor Paul – and in this case, with positive effect, since Paul gave her her 'Prom' début that year, and would engage her to sing *Kindertotenlieder* with the RTÉSO in their London concert of 1966.

On that occasion in 1962 Greevy, accompanied by Jeannie Reddin, sang in aid of the concert hall fund fostered by the MAI. (This was the reason why Charles expected that he could not attend, as the MAI had a policy of offering only one ticket per critic, which it was *his* policy not to accept; clearly the MAI changed its mind on this occasion.)[56] Charles did print his 'valued counsel' but, because he gave the recital a mixed review – praising her sincerity, musicality, voice and 'beautiful line', but having reservations about the suitability of the repertoire, including the daunting 'Four Serious Songs' of Brahms – he wrote to her personally the next morning (as he had to Anthony Hughes): 'I very much hope that you have not found the notice too severe. Anyway if you are what I think you are, you have a far clearer idea of the state of that Brahms than you needed to read in the notice! The next few paragraphs are going to read uncomfortably perhaps but you will see that they are not really too hard. Anyway, fasten your seat belt.' And he went on to analyze the recital in far greater detail than would have been possible in the space allowed by *The Irish Times*. Mentioning the encores, he advised, 'you have something to learn of the timing of encores. Nearly everyone is far too quick with them. It can do nothing but good to you to return once, twice, thrice (according to the mechanics of the hall) before bringing your first encore, and thereby making the audience feel that it is a concession graciously awarded and not a routine procedure. If by now you are in tears, take heart: there would be no point in saying all this to someone who was not very well worthwhile and in sight of something very near the top. After all, it is not usual for any professional critic to launch into hundreds of guineas worth (or more or less!) of unsolicited free criticism for second-rate singers or poor artists.' To which Greevy replied:

> Far from being in any way offended I am deeply grateful to you for your candour and interest. I have studied your comments most carefully, and there is no doubt whatsoever that your advice will be of tremendous assistance to me in preparing for similar recitals in the future. I want you to know

---

56. As did Wexford Opera, which also attempted to restrict critics to a single seat: 'Carol and I are very fond of each other, but to have both of us in one Theatre Royal seat does seem to have its practical difficulties' – Acton to Nicky Furlong, 16 November 1977 (Acton Music Archive, NLI).

once again how deeply I appreciate your interest and concern for me. I shall continue to strive for improvement and shall dare to continue to look to you for the most sincere, learned and constructive critiques that an artist can ever hope to receive.

Much later (1976) Charles would write of Greevy as 'a Brahms and Mahler singer second to none in the world'.[57]

JOHN O'CONOR

Without a doubt, the most significant of the younger generation of players to engage Charles's and Carol's attention and affection, and the one musician to whom they felt closest during his growing years, was pianist John O'Conor (b. 1947), and for several reasons: firstly, he demonstrated considerable potential when he first came to critical attention in his teens; secondly, when he won the Beethoven Competition in Vienna in 1973, while studying there with Dieter Weber (on an Austrian government scholarship), Charles realized that Ireland had a pianist of world class, at least equal in status to Charles Lynch, and therefore someone deserving of professional as well as personal support; and thirdly, a strong bond of loyalty developed between Charles and Carol and O'Conor and his wife Mary. In later years, Charles was – initially, at any rate – delighted when, in 1994, O'Conor, who had been teaching at the RIAM since his return from Vienna, was appointed its Director.

O'Conor first came to Charles's attention at the age of eighteen in 1965, in a student concert at the College of Music, and received a non-committal notice, especially as far as Beethoven's 'Moonlight' sonata was concerned. Charles was to observe over the years that 'technical prowess was a long way behind musical intention', and, when O'Conor went to Vienna to study in 1971, he hoped that technical problems could be overcome. But when O'Conor gave his coming-out recital in 1968, Charles had already welcomed 'a mature, convincing performance', particularly liking the approach to Beethoven's 'Appassionata' sonata – and thus signalling O'Conor's deep appreciation of Beethoven which has marked him out internationally. The outcome of the début was a relief to Charles for, as he wrote privately some years later, despite his 'obvious musicality', his 'interpretative feeling was hampered by severe technical problems. I was dreading his Coming Out recital (as he

---

57. In the same breath he signalled the rising star of Suzanne Murphy as 'a world opera singer in the future'.

himself knows by now) because, judging by his public work up to then, he simply had no prospects of being a competent recitalist. To my great surprise and unbounded pleasure he played unprecedently [*sic*] well and showed that he could be a real performer.' He was also relieved to discover that O'Conor was not 'stuck among the classics' when he gave the first public performance (in 1970) of Seóirse Bodley's sonata. A year previously, O'Conor had asked Charles for a reference for a position at the College of Music, in response to which Charles wrote to the Principal, Dr J.J. O'Reilly, 'I know that he already likes teaching and feels that he has a gift for it. I have long admired his all-round devotion to music and his versatile abilities. His vivid enthusiasm is surely something of incalculable value, not only to himself but to all with whom he comes in contact.'

After the Beethoven prize, Charles immediately suggested that O'Conor acquire a London agent (he suggested Michael Emmerson, formerly at the Belfast Festival) and gave him every encouragement to foster his career. O'Conor in fact put himself on the books of the (then) leading London agents, Ibbs and Tillett, and the following year we find Charles writing to his London deputy, Marèse Murphy, 'Sorry to learn that the O'Conors are being persuaded by Ibbs and Tillett to settle in London. I think it will be a very great mistake for them indeed, and will only make John seem to be chasing Philip Martin.' Martin – O'Conor's exact contemporary – was busily making a career for himself in Britain, but Charles's overriding worry was not that they might become small fishes in a big pond, but that they might leave their Irishness behind and become assimilated into English cultural life, as Martin to a certain degree, and répétiteur Courtney Kenny (with a family background in Ball-inrobe, County Mayo) to a much greater degree, had done. To O'Conor he wrote, many years later,

> I have tried so hard to persuade Irish musicians, including yourself, to bypass the neighbouring island. Thank God you went to Vienna, and not to London. It dismayed me that, after Vienna, you tried London. Thank God you discovered the wit to leave London. When Irish musicians leave Ireland, as they should for experience, I want them to go anywhere but Britain. In Britain they will only sink into the British musical pool, will be Britons. I want Irish artists to be Irish – which they may in France, Austria, Germany, Italy.

On occasions Charles noticed faults in O'Conor's playing. Once he spoke of 'a surprising number of small fluffs, especially in a pianist not given to fluffs', and worried that O'Conor's 'air of technical cautionness', suggesting that he was not entirely on top of the music, indicated that 'he may not yet have come to terms with exactly the demands and standards of the league in which he now is'. By 1978, however, Charles was still championing O'Conor, pointing out that he had been selected, in a cadre that included Alfred Brendel, to mark the Beethoven bi-centenary with a concerto performance with the Vienna Philharmonic. He particularly commended O'Conor's 'special harmonic sense that makes one hear more deeply into the pattern and shape of the music than usual, and an intellectual understanding of the thought of the composer, especially that of Beethoven'. These are qualities – particularly the latter – which continue to make O'Conor's performances of Beethoven events of magisterial as well as lyrical intensity, and which marked him at such a young age as a mature interpreter of Beethoven belying his own actual years.

But one of the most *angst*-ridden and prolonged responses to one of Charles's reviews – and one which would mark the beginning of Charles's gradual disenchantment with O'Conor – came in 1984 when Charles reviewed a recital by Barry Douglas, a young pianist from Belfast who was to win the Tchaikovsky Competition in Moscow two years later. Charles had called him 'perhaps the most outstanding pianist to have come out of Ireland in my listening lifetime and perhaps the finest we have heard in the National Concert Hall'. O'Conor professed himself to be 'devastated' by this commendation and wrote to Charles to express his feelings at 'the hurt that you have done me'; Charles's review of Douglas had 'shattered' O'Conor's confidence and self-respect. 'Suddenly I'm second best because if one uses the superlative to describe one person then nobody else can occupy that position.' Charles was 'therefore dismiss[ing] apart from myself Mícheál [O'Rourke], Philip [Martin], Charles Lynch, Hugh Tinney and a host of others. I know you use the word "perhaps" but the effect of reading your review is that he is – you feel it to be a certainty.' The devastation was such that 'I have thought of slapping your face, of never speaking to you again, of hating you forever but yet I can never stop loving you for the help you gave me. Yet you have cast me into such a despair that I can hardly deal with it … They say the pen is mightier than the sword. I can now believe it. If the sword had penetrated as deeply as your pen has I'd be dead now and wouldn't have to worry at all.'

In reply, Charles said that he was 'complimented and honoured' by O'Conor's letter, and that he was 'deeply distressed' that his review of Douglas should have had such an effect. His response indicates that he realized that to a certain extent he had been unwise to employ the superlative of which

O'Conor complained, but his diplomatic answer made it clear that O'Conor had over-reacted to the encomium of a potential rival, and it also indicated that Charles could not apologize in any way for expressing his sincere opinion. He said that he had attended Douglas's recital with some scepticism, on the basis of what he had heard about Douglas (he had not yet heard him play), but 'within the first few bars of [Beethoven's sonata] op. 110, I knew that here was something remarkable'. It 'just overwhelmed me. I do not know whether that performance was a flash in the pan or a measure of his capability. All I know is that I was a wet emotional rag by the end and have never heard a performance so deeply Beethoven since Denis Matthews at the RDS (if then) or Solomon at the Queen's Hall. I could not help it: there it was.' This cannot have helped to assuage O'Conor, since apart from Charles's review could also be read as displacing O'Conor as an interpreter of Beethoven, on which he had built his international reputation. 'When you were 24 [the same age as Douglas in 1984], I do not think that you could have played either Op. 110 or Pictures [Mussorgsky's 'Pictures at an Exhibition'] like that. But you have grown all the time since ... You have your own niche and fame in the world already and it is growing ... But last Thursday was for me an overwhelming experience, no matter what he does.'

Quite apart from this exchange (there seems to have been no further reply by O'Conor to Charles), in his professional, rather than personal, judgment, Charles was beginning to realize that O'Conor's occasional lack of preparation was due to the fact that he was taking on too many commitments. Returning from Vienna, O'Conor was appointed to the staff of the RIAM, and this development eventually led to his appointment as Director, and at this point Charles and others (including myself) began to be anxious that O'Conor was spreading himself too thinly: he was effectively head of the RIAM's piano school, founder (in 1988) and artistic director of the Dublin International Piano Competition, a member of juries in several other international competitions, and a busy recording artist.

Two years after Charles's initial salutation to John O'Conor, Mičeál O'Rourke (b. 1948) gave an all-Chopin recital at the RDS, and he could rejoice again:

> Within his very first two chords I knew that this was going to be a special recital. Everything was exactly felt, as in the spirit of the composer. Rhythmically, everything flowed as one's breath and senses knew it had to flow. Those who can convey Chopin's poetry sometimes play without power as

though frailly. There should be nothing frail about him, and there was not about Mr O'Rourke, for all the exquisite sensitivity and the infinite singing of the soft melodies.

O'Rourke's presentation of the second Chopin sonata was 'about the most impressive and revealing performance I have ever heard. I found myself thinking of the succession of Cortot, Arthur Rubinstein and O'Rourke. We are a very small country, and it is really extraordinary that at the present time we should have two young pianists of world class.' Again, he immediately set about using his international contacts to try and boost O'Rourke's career.

Readers' responses

One of the greatest bugbears in the wake of any of Charles's reviews was the likelihood that his written opinion would be challenged by concertgoers who thought his review too harsh or too lenient. On many occasions, the Editor of *The Irish Times* would receive fulminations that he declined to print, but that were forwarded to Charles for his information. Invariably, he responded privately to these letters, because he saw it as part of his responsibility. As he said at the opening of 'A Critic's Creed', 'Every now and then a critic is attacked from various directions for what he has written. This is as it should be. It is his function to sit in judgment on others, and it would be neither fair nor natural for others to refrain from judging him.' If Charles was the 'high court', letters to the Editor were appeals to the 'supreme court' against his judgment. When he was berated for being too lenient, he would say: 'If a critic had to mention all the faults of each performance his notices would be uniformly depressing and distressing, and would thoroughly defeat their own object.'

An early example of how a critic's opinion can differ from that of other members of the audience came in August 1956 when Charles reviewed the Boston Symphony Orchestra under Charles Munch. He had scant praise for what he called 'probably the most efficient musical machine that we have heard here'. Where the BBCSO under Malcolm Sargent, four months previously, had shown themselves to be 'very slick indeed but with little soul', the Boston orchestra, under Charles Munch, 'proved to be even slicker, with virtually no soul'. The review was typical of Charles's response to music-making: 'Technique is but the means, and not the end, of expression.' The playing lacked 'feeling, depth and love' and Charles professed himself to having been 'bored'. [58] But Edgar Deale of the MAI, using the occasion to push forward the demand for an acoustically acceptable concert hall, thought that the playing (of the strings at least) 'approached the regions of genius'. Another letter came privately from John Ruddock: he had heard the Boston orchestra in Edinburgh and asserted:

> I heard 3 successive concerts by the BSO in the Usher Hall and I have never heard three better concerts. In the last 10 years or so, I have heard about 150 symphony concerts by first class orchestras. The playing of the Boston orchestra was a revelation to me, and, I am certain, to 99% of the Usher Hall audience. You should have heard its superlative performance of Don Juan. I hope you will have an opportunity of reading some of the Edinburgh reviews. You will then understand perhaps my perplexity!

Of the Bostonians' concerts in Edinburgh, one was conducted by Pierre Monteux and received favourable reviews: it was Munch who displeased the critics. [59] One did not need the agreement of one's fellow critics, but in the case of such eminent colleagues it was reassuring. (Of one English-based critic, Kaikhosru Sorabji, Charles said 'I shall be seriously worried if I ever agree with him'.) [60]

When Charles's review of pianist Craig Sheppard at Wexford referred to his having perhaps been distracted by 'a coughing child in the front of the audience, clearly too small to have been subjected to such a grown-up programme', the child's mother remonstrated, firstly, that other members of the audience had not been distracted by the child and, secondly, 'children are never, ever, too young to be "subjected", as you call it, to grown-up performances. Children will

---

58. Charles later had to record that 'I did not know that his [Munch's] wife had died the day before' – see 'A Critic's Creed'.

59. As a critic, Charles need not have worried: he had indeed seen the reviews from Edinburgh, and pointed out to Ruddock that 'the *Times* spoke of lack of delicacy, lack of subtlety and complete absence of finer shades'. Peter Heyworth, in the *Observer*, even though he acknowledged the orchestra's 'wonderful freshness, zest and confidence', deplored the trumpets who 'raise their bells aloft with the uninhibited fervour of a Louis Armstrong and with a strident, rasping shriek, more reminiscent of a fire alarm than a musical instrument, mercilessly hack their way through the most opulent score' (*Observer* 2 September 1956). The *doyen* of critics, Ernest Newman, in the *Sunday Times*, also acknowledged that there had been a 'manifest contradiction' between the rapturous applause and his own opinion: 'I have never heard worse performances of the Haydn symphony in B flat major, the Strauss "Don Juan" and "L'Apprenti Sorcier"; all were excessively and meaninglessly noisy.' (*Sunday Times* 2 September 1956)

60. Kaikhosru Sorabji, born Leon Dudley, 1892–1988, composer and music critic.

absorb at any level if interested and if given the chance. I regret the cough. You should regret your comments on age.' Charles replied:

> I would not trust your neighbours' disclaimers. People tend to be polite (or perhaps one should say cowardly) when directly asked and I think also nearly everybody feels in awe of 'Suffer little children'. All coughs are distracting and have an extraordinarily high intensity of sound. I was very sorry for your son. How strongly I agree with you about giving children the opportunity of hearing proper music instead of training them up to think that pop is the right thing. But it does seem to me important to remember that a child's time scale and ability to concentrate attention are normally limited. Children must no more be played down to than talked down to.

One writer, living in 'Valhalla', Letterkenny, asked 'Are you like Caesar's wife, above reproach? I have a right to express my opinion. Your inability to accept graciously any personal criticism only shows your lack of breeding and integrity. PS have you no sense of humour?'

When the young and rapidly rising Anthony Goldstone played at the RDS at very short notice after the advertised pianist had fallen sick, Charles acknowledged his artistry but, characteristically, questioned whether Goldstone's heart was in the music: 'Mr Goldstone showed himself a celebrity pianist of unquestionable ability in complete command of his instrument and of his music. And yet I missed all sense of poetry, of real love for the music he was playing.' Goldstone, in a letter to Charles, considered that this 'casts serious doubt on my integrity' – it had hurt him 'most deeply'. He felt that his love of the music must have been evident to the audience 'for their response was very warm and enthusiastic'. Charles's response was to argue that artists do, unfortunately, suffer from time to time from the repetitiveness of a restricted repertoire, but he was glad to have Goldstone's assurance that he did, indeed, love his music.

A Dublin audience was certainly not the barometer by which Charles measured his own response to a performance, and when, in 1976, Lionel Rogg (perhaps at that time the world's leading organist) played in an international series at Dún Laoghaire, Charles had not enjoyed the recital, despite the applause which, Rogg considered, was indicative of the success of his playing. 'It is certainly no part of a critic's function to refer to an ordinary amount of applause', Charles wrote in reply to Rogg's private letter, disputing Rogg's assertion that the applause displayed 'extraordinary enthusiasm'. Rogg felt that 'a critic should have at least enough culture, musical taste, and understanding of the art of performance, to avoid "matter-of-fact" description' – if Charles had not appreciated the rare quality of Rogg's communication with the audience, 'you are the poor one'.

A more serious matter arose in 1978, when the New Irish Chamber Orchestra, on the eve of a tour of the USA, seemed, to Charles, to be losing its original standards. Formed in 1970, the orchestra had toured to Russia and China and was about to give an all-Bach 'Prom' under John Beckett at the Albert Hall, London. The manager of NICO, Lindsay Armstrong, suggested to Charles that his recent comments on the orchestra were causing 'some distress and a great deal of puzzlement... We cannot complain about a bad notice if, in your view, we played badly on the night, but to return twice to the same subject, when it was scarcely relevant, is certainly hurtful to us and could be damaging and destructive.' Armstrong adamantly denied that standards were slipping or that concerts were under-rehearsed (one of Charles's criticisms). As one might expect, Charles's *apologia* was his over-riding concern for the perception of NICO and of Irish musicianship generally.

> NICO *must* do bloody well in North America. In general, orchestras (large and small) do not play as well on tour as they do at home. NICO has got unlimited prospects but only if it plays as magnificently as you and I know that it has done and, I hope, still can. That is exactly why I *must* help it to get back to its true form. There is no reason why NICO should not be as good as any of the world's well known chamber orchestras. In your early days you seemed all set to be among the world's leading chamber orchestras. During the last two years you certainly have not been. But you must not go to North America without being..

At one stage, in 1964–5, Charles had to admit that his confidence was being drained by attacks from readers. In a private letter to his own Editor, he asked 'is the purpose of publishing these denigrations to destroy my own small store of confidence in my ability to serve you or to undermine your readers' respect for my work and your sagacity in engaging a critic?' Finding this letter on his desk, Brian Fallon told Charles 'the attacks made on you from time to time are a sort of compliment – the inevitable corollary of trying to apply critical standards which are not purely parochial. In a town like this, standards like that are impossible to maintain without treading on people's tocs. But what of that? As long as the paper backs you, go ahead.'

Composers and composition

In an article on 'Contemporary Irish Music' written for publication by the Department of External (later Foreign) Affairs in 1968, Charles dealt at the outset with the reasons for the paucity of Irish compositions of merit in the nineteenth and early twentieth centuries, pointing to the predominantly literary nature of the Celtic Revival.[61] He also dealt diplomatically with two figures widely regarded as excellent miniaturists when he wrote 'in spite of the craftsmanship of the late Dr John F. Larchet and the delicate and beautifully wrought charm of the late Arthur Duff's small output, it is only within the last quarter of a century that new music has come to be written in Ireland, by composers who are conscious of belonging to an independent sovereign community and who are writing music that is ready to take its place in the repertoires of the world'.[62]

When Charles's *Irish Music and Musicians* appeared in 1978, he had more than one occasion to express his regrets that the restrictions on space had forced him to omit many important personalities. When a member of the Larchet family mentioned that John F. Larchet did not appear in the booklet, Charles, although regretting the fact, justified it on the grounds that 'the isolation of the war forced us to be ourselves and not provincials', and that the five composers he *had* mentioned, while some of them had been taught initially by Larchet, had gone on to study with five 'world-famous composers, only one of whom was native of these islands.[63] Please be completely assured that the omission of your father does not indicate any failure to appreciate the massive part that he played in Irish music.' He also explained to one of the composers whom he had been forced to omit (and who had written to him that 'you are grossly unfair in omitting any mention whatever of Potter, Victory and Wilson'), that 'I worried about Fleischmann, Victory, Potter, Boydell, Wilson, [Roger] Doyle, [David]

---

61. This was followed much later by a detailed study of the subject by Harry White: *The Keeper's Recital*.

62. In 1956, for example, reviewing J.J. O'Reilly's tone-poem 'Oluf', he was at pains to find the positive qualities of the work, writing that it was 'not perhaps very original – it would make excellent folk music – it is adroitly put together in a Romantic way by a writer thoroughly versed in the technique of orchestration'.

63. Frederick May studied with Egon Wellesz, Seóirse Bodley with Johann Nepomuk David, Frank Corcoran with Boris Blacher, Brian Boydell with Vaughan Williams and Seán Ó Riada (allegedly) with Frank Martin..

Byers, [Howard] Ferguson, [Redmond] Friel, [Elisabeth] Maconchy, Kinsella and more besides. I tried to get them all into a paragraph, then into a couple of sentences, but by that time I had become quite unintelligible by compression.' The two composers to receive more than a one-word mention were Seán Ó Riada and Seóirse Bodley, and Charles's *apologia* concluded 'I have instanced and contrasted these two composers in a way that is not only unfair to them, but grossly so to all our other composers who are so vigorously working.'

The purpose of the article on 'Contemporary Irish Music' for *Ireland Today*, the Department's information bulletin, was to draw attention to the work of the Department's Cultural Relations Committee in promoting Irish composition, a scheme administered by Carol Acton (although he did not mention her by name), aided and abetted behind the scenes by Charles himself, and by Bill Kane, librarian of the RTÉSO. The composers actively supported by the scheme at that time were Seóirse Bodley (lecturing in music at University College, Dublin), Brian Boydell (Professor of Music at TCD), Aloys Fleischmann (Professor of Music at University College, Cork), Gerard Victory (Director of Music at RTÉ), James Wilson, an independent composer, Seán Ó Riada (lecturing at UCC) and – surprisingly perhaps for readers today – Proinnsías Ó Duinn, at that time permanent conductor of the Ecuador National Symphony. It is worth noting that Wilson was the only composer mentioned who had no other means of support.

The most significant points of contact between Charles and Irish composers were the four interviews which he conducted with A. J. (Archie) Potter, Seóirse Bodley, Brian Boydell and Seán Ó Riada, published in consecutive issues of *Éire-Ireland* in 1970–71. These, for differing reasons, were, in Charles's opinion, the composers most relevant to the development of music in Ireland: his old friend Boydell – to whom, of them all, he was undoubtedly the closest – because he admitted to no explicit 'Irishness' in his music; Bodley, because he represented a younger generation and was attempting to explore Irishness in the light of his training in serial technique in Germany; Potter, a northern Protestant, because he was providing a vigorous repertoire of both 'serious' and light music in several genres; and Ó Riada, who also became a close friend, because Charles, like many others at that time, thought that he might develop a thoroughly European palette of Irish music, based on the slim evidence of his 'Nomos' compositions up to that time. He much later told Harry White that he had also realized that a fifth interview was required, with Gerard Victory, but 'I quailed at Victory because of his incredible flow of words'. Others whom he admired included Frederick May – at least as important as Boydell – but sadly May's persistent ill-health had brought his career to a halt; the Englishman Raymond Warren, during his years as professor at Queen's University, Belfast (Charles was to write an influential essay on Warren in *The Musical Times* in 1969); and the prolific Victory, successor to Tibor Paul as Director of Music at RTÉ, who was demonstrating a facility for orchestral and vocal music in particular.

The attention to the development of composition in Ireland came second only to Charles's nurturing of performance talent. Sometimes they coalesced, as with the performances by Bernadette Greevy of Ó Riada's 'Hölderlin Songs' or by Herbert Moulton of his 'Nomos 2'. Very occasionally, performer and composer were one and the same, as when Philip Martin played his own work – either his piano concerto or in accompaniment to songs he wrote for his wife, Penelope Price-Jones. But the general course of new works from Irish composers took two directions: work for the RTÉ performing groups (the RTÉLO, the RTÉ Singers and, less frequently, for the RTÉSO), and works for amateur or semi-professional chamber groups such as the Dublin Orchestral Players, NICO or smaller, often *ad hoc*, ensembles of various sizes. The opportunity to compose for full orchestra was a comparative rarity, although the number of first performances of Irish compositions by the RTÉSO was by no means as small as many people believed, as I have demonstrated in *Music and Broadcasting*, and certainly not a diminution from earlier decades.[64]

A challenge to the critic was to give a balanced, informed review immediately after the first hearing of a new work; Charles, as often as possible, solicited scores of such works from their composers, which allowed him to study them in advance as well as to have them to hand during the performance. Back in 1943, with only the experience of Vaughan Williams's *The Poisoned Kiss* under his critical belt, he had foreseen this difficulty when writing to his friend, the composer Diccon Shaw: 'the music critic is expected to write a reasoned appreciation of a new work within a couple of hours of a first hearing, often with no chance to read the score. I do not see how anybody can, on a single hearing, assess the merits of a new work of any importance unless it is written in a manner that is so completely familiar that there is no difficulty.' Nevertheless, 'a critic that won't write an assessment of a new work under these conditions is no good to an editor.' This helps to explain why Charles so often adopted the 'kick-for-touch' approach when he felt out of his depth.

---

64. See Table M (1959–1968), Table R (1969–1978) and Table V (1979–1988) in *Music and Broadcasting* for performances in the core period of Charles's tenure.

One of the tragedies of the fate of composition was the ill-health of Frederick May, who wrote a pathetic note to Charles some time in the 1960s, drawing attention to 'some very severe ear trouble which has prevented me from completing anything on an extended scale lately, although I <u>have</u> tried very hard. It has been a great worry to have had to confine oneself to arrangements and that kind of thing, but I'm in hopes that something can be done to improve the situation.' To Joan Trimble, Charles wrote that 'Fred had a very real talent, but an undisciplined one. He was someone for whom everything went wrong, always. Like Seán Ó Riada, in his different way, he staked out his claim to be a great Irish composer, but wouldn't really work at it.' Nevertheless Charles had already written, in 1958, that May's '"Songs from Prison" is without any doubt, the outstanding Irish composition of our times: full of strength and feeling; written with assurance and complete command of all the resources used. But its very greatness underlines one's regret that Frederick May seems to be a composer no longer.'[65] And of May's other masterpiece, his string quartet, he would write 'I feel this must be the most sheerly beautiful piece of music to have been written in Ireland since the composition of the great songs... music of melodiousness, of long, loving, cherished melodies... music of an infinite beauty.'

It was no rarity for Charles to write privately to composers to propose some possible outlet for their music, in the same way as he tried to suggest performance opportunities for singers and players. In this he had the advantage that, on the nomination of Aloys Fleischmann, he and Carol were retained by the Cultural Relations Committee (CRC) of the Department of Foreign Affairs to promulgate the work of Irish composers in the international arena, and to nominate scores to be published. Thus at the end of 1965 we find Charles writing a 'round robin' to Boydell, Bodley, Victory, Ó Riada and

---

65. The world (and broadcast) première of 'Songs from Prison' was given by the BBC in 1943. Its first professional performance in Ireland was by the RÉSO in 1946, followed by performances in 1953 with Michael O'Higgins under Milan Horvat and in 1958, by Knut Erman, with the RÉSO under Eimear Ó Broin. At the time of its composition, in 1941, Brian Boydell had written to Charles: 'Fred May played over his latest work to me the other day. It is a long work for baritone and orchestra – a setting of some German poems, which Nigel Heseltine has translated. To my mind, this work is far in advance of many semi-famous composers in England today. It is so much more sincere and original than Moeran, Brittain [sic] Bridge Bliss or any of that lot – but Fred has no strings to pull. I am sure that he will do very well indeed as soon as he gets a reasonable hearing.'

Potter concerning an inquiry he had received from a record company, asking for suggestions for songs by Irish composers which they might record. In fact, Charles spent a great deal of his working time beating on the doors of record companies in what he saw as an off-stage function of the music critic of *The Irish Times* – sustaining and developing the health of music in Ireland and of Irish music abroad. Another example came shortly after Ó Riada's early death in 1971, when Charles, partly wearing his CRC hat and partly out of loyalty to Ó Riada, urged Garech Browne of Claddagh Records to issue a record of Ó Riada's songs. That same year, the New Irish Recording Company came into existence, with recordings by Gerard Gillen (organ), Edward Beckett (flute) and Charles Lynch (piano), and several others in preparation. Charles told the CRC 'we think we have the possibility of a real breakthrough. For just about the first time a music LP has been made of Irish artists that did not require much expenditure.' He wrote at length, urging the CRC to support the initiative, and also to support, by way of guaranteed purchase, publication of the scores by McCullough-Pigott Ltd. It remains regrettable that this laudable recording enterprise was so short-lived.

Publication by a commercial publisher, preferably one noted for sustained music publishing, was seen as a prerequisite for gaining any serious attention or recognition of Irish compositions abroad. In a lengthy joint memorandum by Charles and Carol to the CRC, it was stressed that, in the absence of an Irish publishing house or a cultural foundation such as the Gaudcamus in Holland, it was inevitable to look abroad, Britain and the USA being the most likely outlets. Carol had tried to interest the London firm of Novello in undertaking publication, subsidized by the CRC, but the sample scores sent to them were considered uninteresting. The Actons glumly observed that the only Irish composer with a real chance of obtaining performances abroad was Gerard Victory, because, in his position as Director of Music at RTÉ, 'he has so many contacts abroad and is able to offer reciprocity'. The conclusion in the present circumstances was that 'none of our works *on its own* is yet able to demand attention'. The prospect seemed to them that 'if the Committee is concerned only with this scheme (as far as music is concerned) then there is no point in further activity'.

The Actons' suggestion, of a more comprehensive scheme, adequately funded, was far ahead of its time, anticipating, as it did, the establishment of a separate department for the arts (which was achieved by the Fianna Fáil-Labour coalition government in 1993), and a body expressly charged with promoting Irish arts abroad (Culture Ireland was established for this purpose in 2005). Charles's principal contribution to the document was:

> Felix Aprahamian[66] told me that, as a London critic, he was totally unaware that we had a sizable musical life here until two events: the first was the visit of the RTÉSO to London [1966] and Charles Lynch's relatively recent Wigmore Hall recital [1970] where he brought works by Victory and Wilson. As Aprahamian pointed out, neither performances nor music were any better than anybody else's, but it was exciting to know that we had serious performers and that we had serious composers.

Charles felt that in addition to promoting individual performers, 'Irish weeks' should be organized, but here again he was ahead of his time: it would not be until 1980 that a major Irish festival, 'A Sense of Ireland', would take place in London.[67]

By early 1972, Charles and Carol had decided to step down from the administration of the CRC scheme. The first reason was that 'while we feel that we have put in more time and energy and effort than corresponds strictly to our honorarium [£75 per year], we are not able to put into it the amount of time that is required to make a thoroughly good job of it.' Certainly, from the extant files, the amount of correspondence involved was enormous, and the mental energy required to try to persuade publishers and concert promoters in Europe and America to take an interest in Irish compositions must have been draining. Even by using personal contacts such as Eoin McKiernan,[68] the uphill struggle to convince the leaders in these larger centres to take Irish work seriously had not paid off in terms of the effort invested.

The second reason for their withdrawal was what they perceived as institutional moribundity in the civil service. Although their correspondence with the Department had always been polite and helpful, Charles and Carol clearly suffered from frustration at the slowness with which the departmental wheels turned, and they now expressed this in their letter to Aloys Fleischmann, chair of the music sub-committee of the CRC:

---

66. Music critic of *The Sunday Times* 1948–89.

67. In March 2008, on foot of a discussion as to whether Irish composers were receiving adequate attention from *The Irish Times*, a letter to the Editor proposed regular promotional concerts by Irish composers in London and elsewhere in Britain – suggesting that recognition of them by British critics and audiences continues to be limited.

68. Principal of the Irish American Cultural Institute and publisher of *Éire-Ireland*.

The consistent failure over years to keep us informed, let us know about dates of meetings have been deeply discouraging. There is no fun in trying to do a job of work of any sort and so often find that the basic information which should have come to one from the Department percolates too late from totally outside parties. Such things as discovering that it takes a whole week for the Department to put a score and a gramophone record into the post is all part of our general sense of frustration.

In addition to his and Carol's work with the CRC, Charles also cultivated his own contacts on behalf of Irish composers: thus after a visit to Berlin in 1963 he asked Ó Riada whether he could send any of his scores, such as 'Hercules Dux Ferrariae' or the 'Nomos 4', to a radio station there. Later, in 1971, after meeting Gérard Souzay after his Dublin recital, he sent the singer a collection of Irish works, including Boydell's 'Five Joyce Songs', Raymond Warren's settings of Yeats, and Victory's of Shakespeare. When the scores were returned with the comment 'unfortunately he has little time at present to learn contemporary music', Charles's typical response was 'Why ask for them then!?'

A growing frustration on Charles's part was his difficulty in understanding why *young* Irish composers seemed so reluctant to promote their work by what he regarded as effective means. The formation of the Association of Young Irish Composers was particularly annoying to him, as was the corralling of their new works at the Twentieth-Century Festival into a Sunday afternoon concert, as if they were a by-product of the Festival and a mere adjunct to the main items and personalities of the week. He felt that separation from the already established organizations, such as the 'composers' group' of the MAI, was unnecessary and possibly divisive, even though it might serve to highlight the youth of its members and a new energy in their work.

> Inherently it obviously seems to be an excellent idea. But, even so, I feel that there is a certain artistic irresponsibility as well. More power to them for wanting to do their own thing, for wanting to cash in on the very real interest in the achievements of the young. But is there not a reciprocal responsibility towards their art, if only put at its lowest, to safeguard the future professional possibilities of the art and of the group? There seems to be a sort of isolationism, a tendency to regard themselves as an island, when no man is an island, let alone when no composer is an island.

Charles was astonished that none of the new group had any knowledge of the Gaudeamus Foundation which existed specifically to foster new music, and, having twice invited several of them to Carrickmines for a conversation, greatly saddened that some of them felt that there was a bias against the younger generation on the part of the more established composers in the MAI. (This may well have been a strong motivating factor in the establishment of the AYIC, given that one of them, Raymond Deane, subsequently told Charles that 'we are trying to break down no doors (as yet). What we are doing is opening new doors which are complementary to those which already exist, and of which there are too few for all concerned'.)

By 1975, Charles's view of the younger generation of composers had settled: he regarded Frank Corcoran (born 1944), Raymond Deane (b. 1953), Derek Ball (b. 1949), Brian Beckett (b. 1950), John Gibson (b. 1951), Jane O'Leary (b. 1946) and Roger Doyle (b. 1949) as the most noticeable. It is surprising that Charles omitted from this list (requested by his boss at *The Irish Times,* Brian Fallon) the name of John Buckley (born 1951), given that he thought highly of Buckley's work and welcomed the award to Buckley of the Arts Council's Macaulay scholarship in 1978, advising him also to contact the Gaudeamus Foundation. He subsequently maintained friendly contact with Buckley, whom he rightly regarded as one of Ireland's up-and-coming composers. Less surprising are his personal comments on the characters and abilities of the individual composers – most of them unprintable even today – which indicate that he had little faith in the ability of many of them to graduate to the level of attainment of some of their seniors. Corcoran, O'Leary, Doyle and Deane have become substantial figures in the compositional landscape, as has Buckley, but, as with Charles's list in 1969, several of the others – Beckett and Gibson in particular – have effectively abandoned composition as a career.[69]

When Archie Potter's second symphony, commissioned by the Irish American Cultural Institute, received its belated and posthumous premiere in 1983, Charles wrote to the Institute's president, Eoin McKiernan, that if ever another commission were to be offered, Buckley should be considered: 'to my mind he is a real musician, a composer who can write music that is enjoyable, that is NOT drearily old-fashioned and that is not tediously avant-garde.' When Charles retired, in 1986, Buckley wrote to him: 'I am very grateful for your support and promotion of contemporary Irish music in general, and in

---

69. Derek Ball, having taken up the profession of psychiatric medicine, appears to have written nothing between 1973 and 1982, but has become a prolific composer since his retirement, with 100 works to his credit from 2004 to 2007/8 (source: Contemporary Music Centre, Dublin).

particular for all the encouragement you have given me over the years since 1971, when I put my first tentative notes on paper' – to which Charles replied 'Your own music always does sound as if you wanted it to be enjoyed – as well as being individual and sincere.' Letters of thanks like Buckley's were not 'toadying' to an influential critic, but genuine expressions of gratitude for positive advice and support, often over a sustained period: people who knew Charles well and enjoyed his confidence, support and approval were fully aware of the kindnesses which he could undertake on their behalf, and it was those to whom he had spoken his mind in a less than admiring or positive way who perceived him as a menace, especially if they belonged to a 'special interest' group or clique, and resented his presence in the pages of The Irish Times.

Éire-Ireland interviews

The four Éire-Ireland interviews with the leading composers owed their origin to a suggestion by Colette Redmond, formerly a violist with the DOP and now editor of Guinness's house journal, The Harp, where they first appeared in abbreviated form. Their significance lies in the fact that the four composers were encouraged by Charles to make major statements about their own work and about their views of composition in Ireland generally. It should immediately be pointed out that in 1958 Radio Éireann had broadcast short statements by seventeen composers in a series entitled 'Composers at Work', in one of which John F. Larchet (whom Charles regarded as a slight composer of an old-fashioned school) spoke ominously of 'the great Irish composer for whom we are all waiting'.[70] This established a messianic sense of aspiration and anticipation which was still very much evident twelve years later when Charles conducted his interviews. For example, Bodley was perhaps only half joking when he wrote to Charles in 1974: 'all I have to do now is to write the "great Irish music" that everybody keeps talking about, and I will have filled another gap in Irish life!!!' Significantly, Charles's interviews came almost half-way between the 1958 radio series and another, in 1988, 'Composers in Conversation' with Dermot Rattigan. The first series demonstrated an almost universal preoccupation with the question of Irishness in music, whereas the later series was marked by the almost complete absence of the topic, at least explicitly.[71]

---

70. The texts of these statements are printed in Music and Broadcasting, pp. 219–38.

71. Ibid., pp. 274–87.

Of Potter, born in Belfast's Falls Road, Charles wrote – somewhat surprisingly, perhaps – that 'in many ways he can already be regarded as our leading composer', because he 'is probably a more truly Irish composer in a basic, historical, realistic way than if he had been born and bred in the Aran Islands. When he wants to, he can know and use all the strands that make up the nation's music and he can see it with that startling clear realism which has always gone along beside the dewy-eyed romanticism which is the other yarn in our national fabric.' (Charles was here no doubt thinking of Larchet, Harty and Stanford.)

Charles had an abiding affection and admiration for most of Potter's output (he especially relished the 'Concertino Benino' written for the RTÉLO's first trumpet, Benny MacNeill), but he was deeply impressed by his 'Sinfonia de Profundis', premiered in 1969, when he wrote of an 'overwhelming musical experience [after which] words seem even more inadequate and harder to find than usual… A major national event'. It was particularly impressive, beside any question of its craftsmanship and musical inspiration, for the fact that it represented the composer's thanksgiving for his release from alcoholism. There is little question that 'Sinfonia de Profundis' retains its distinction as one of the most, if not *the* most, important full-scale symphonic works by any Irish composer.

Potter himself said that 'being Irish does not consist of arranging folk tunes or doing music that happens to have bits and pieces of folk tunes in it or even giving it Irish-sounding titles. In other words, being Irish does not mean doing what Dvořák did. Being Irish means you produce Irish music, just as being Irish means that you produce Irish literature.' The interview merits reading in its entirety,[72] as does the original transcript,[73] since both Charles and Carol felt that it was 'one of the most extraordinary documents that either of us have come across'.

In his interview, Seóirse Bodley spoke of his early work, 'Music for Strings', as

> trying to develop something out from the field of Irish music. Not actually developing the ornamentation of traditional music which of course is so bound up with the actual method of performance as to be almost unusable but with the sort of basic line – it's a sort of technical problem. The idea was to use some of the modal characteristics of Irish melody combined with certain notes foreign to this… I was trying to expand the Irish idiom, if you like.

---

72. *Éire-Ireland* 5 / 2, 1970.

73. Acton Music Archive (NLI).

Charles asked if Bodley was likely to attempt any analysis of 'what makes Irish traditional music, particularly the slow air, tick' and when Bodley answered that he hoped to do so, Charles pursued this by asking 'is that going to influence or have any effect upon the music you are going to write?', to which the answer was, 'No, I suppose in a sense it already has had some effect on music that I've written because there is this funny sort of sense about the slow air in particular with a sort of timelessness, which is a thing that I've been rather involved in in recent years.' One easily gets the impression that it was Charles's anxiety about the 'Irishness' of Irish music that impelled him to press Bodley, and later, much more strongly, Ó Riada, on the topic. As with Potter, Bodley affirmed 'You don't get up one morning and say today is my day to be an Irish composer. You just are what you are.'[74] But he also acknowledged that there were issues in Irish composition: 'You have the confusion of the whole question of the Irish music thing. I mean traditional music. Many people feel what a nice thing it would be if we could have our national composers writing in a national idiom. And it is all very nice if you never actually have come to grips with the real practical problems of the situation and the problems of such things as the feeling that, say, the rhythmical pattern used in so much of the older type of classical music in general had been worn out. And when you had to come to grips with the new rhythmic situation then how are you relative to Irish music?'

In order to give adequate consideration to Charles's interview with Brian Boydell, it is necessary to reveal a much earlier commentary by Charles on one of Boydell's comparatively youthful works (he was forty-two when it was written): on 18 January 1959 Charles had reviewed Boydell's new work 'Ceol Cas Corach', played by the RÉSO under visiting conductor Maurice Miles. Charles had, understandably, followed the development of his old friend and travelling companion very closely. Now he wrote that 'the big defect of this short work is that it is an excellent aperitif for a meal that never comes: several times it was about to say something important, but it never did. According to the programme, Mr. Boydell regards it as "impetuous, disturbing music" and refers to Cas Corach's overpowering and spell-binding effect on his hearers. All this is over-statement.'[75]

---

74. The quotations in these interviews are extracted from the exact transcriptions (Acton Music Archive, NLI), made by Carol Acton from the Stanacord tapes and therefore differ from the interviews as published in *Éire-Ireland*.

75. In Celtic mythology, Cas Corach was a harper in the Tuatha Dé Danann whose playing distracted werewolf-like creatures intent on killing sheep. This was not the

Shortly afterwards, Charles suffered the same type of anxiety as he had in the case of Anthony Hughes's RDS début, but in this instance the stakes were much higher because Brian was his close friend and confidant, and their discussions of music, and of Brian's own ambitions as a composer, had been a central element in their friendship. Charles wrote a private letter to Brian in an attempt to supplement his printed argument. While members of the Boydell family believe that there had already been a cooling-off between the two friends over the past few years, I am certain that this letter was the cause of the rift that held them apart up to the point when Charles successfully interviewed Brian for *Éire-Ireland* eleven years later.

In his letter, Charles wrote:

Ever since listening to Ceol Cas Corach and finding it necessary to write a nasty notice of it, I have been worrying – not lest you should feel umbrageous because I know that you wouldn't at sincere comment – but because it brought up a long latent worry about where your writing is going. I have hesitated about this lest it might only be hurting you with what is already tormenting you – but I am going ahead in case some part of it might become a seed for a much better crystal of your own – and the problem of your music is getting in the way of writing for the I.T. about other people's music. So forgiveness in advance, please! To start with Ceol C.C., my impressions are of course only one individual's opinion and that from a first hearing. But I doubt whether anyone else in the Gaiety would care much if they never heard it again – or whether anyone felt that repeated hearings would really tell them anything more about it.[76] Ceol C C only brought to a head a latent nagging anxiety. You should soon be approaching a creative peak and writing significant, memorable, enduring and assured music in quantity. And yet I feel you are still experimenting in means: and this has been going on too long. Even the Megalithics [Boydell's *Megalithic Ritual Dances* op. 39, 1956] had this. Most ballet & incidental music by everyone is pretty dim, so I do not think much importance should be attached to the slightness of the Moon and Etain [Charles is referring to Boydell's ballet suites *The Buried Moon* op. 32a (1949) and *The Wooing of Etain* opp. 37a and b (1954), both premiered by the DOP]. But even so the fun of playing and hearing them is rather slight.

---

first time that Charles had written publicly about what he regarded as his friend's musical *stasis*: in 1957 he had said of Boydell's 'Meditation and Fugue' 'I fear that his writing will tend to be a collection of aphorisms rather than a connected story. These are harsh words, I am afraid, about a work that I did find extremely interesting and want to hear again'.

76. It was in fact performed again by the RÉSO six months later, in July 1959.

I wish I knew the [violin] concerto better because without it any consideration of the total oeuvre is rather pointless. The 1st Qtet we play fairly often on the gramophone.[77] I enjoy it and am much moved by it at each hearing. But taken all round (and leaving the concerto in the air) the 1st Qtet is the only work I can think of that is really significant. This is a hard saying, but I think true. Why?

It was most certainly 'a hard saying' and must have cost Charles dearly. To have ignored *In Memoriam Mahatma Gandhi* (1948) and dismissed *Megalithic Ritual Dances* among Boydell's orchestral works to date was a severe and hardly sustainable judgment, as was his setting aside of the violin concerto, considered by many as ranking with May's string quartet and Potter's *Sinfonia de Profundis* as the three most important compositions of twentieth-century Ireland.[78] But, reading his reviews on new works by Boydell in the 1950s, it is clear that Charles thought his friend was lacking in new musical ideas, while steadily improving his technical control of his material. It is typical of Charles's professionalism that, although the incident separated him from Brian for some time, it was simply a fact of life that his criticism had brought it about: it wasn't anything he could have averted if he was to do his job and speak his mind, however painful that might be. To have, effectively, lost his oldest remaining male friend by doing so may have been unwise on a personal basis, even though the letter was replete with personal concern, but it was necessary on the basis of a critic writing to a composer.

Nevertheless, he did not leave the matter there. The letter continued with some practical suggestions:

Are you writing enough? I do not mean have you enough commissions, enough first performances, but just the writing itself. The possibility of setting yourself a stint of an hour a day five days every week of writing, irrespective of commissions, inspirations, &c. True it is awfully difficult, especially with a living to earn, & the exhaustion of adjudicating &c.? The possibility of studies. i.e. to set yourself to write as pure exercises 15 minute fugues, using whatever contrapuntal rules you like (or evolve), "classical symphonies" à la Prokofiev – a song a day, &c. Why not (even pseudonymously) get into R.É's folk song arrangement for the L[ight] O[rchestra] racket – or of course original pieces in that medium. Someone, I forget who, was talking about John Reidy [Seán

---

77. Boydell's first string quartet, op. 31 (1949) had been recorded by the Benthien Quartet on the Deutsche Gramophon label.

78. Apart from the 'Shielmartin Suite' of 1958/9, Boydell wrote no more orchestral music until the very important *Symphonic Inscapes* of 1968, and little of major consequence after that until his final work, *Masai Mara* in 1988.

Ó Riada] the other day and wondering had he had any opportunity of studying with a master. Whoever it was made the point that, with very few exceptions, composers have found intimate study with an eminent, if not great, composer or teacher vital: not for the sake of technical matters, but for the intimate mental contact – even conflict. Come to think of it, your only *continual* contact with a master was during your year at the College [RCM] and then really only in stated lessons. It may seem impertinent, but it might create just that release and opening of the gates, to go to someone. The summer months – May to September – might be enough and would not take away from the main earning period of lectures & Feiseanna. I would avoid England – partly absence of masters, partly it is not far enough away in ideas. Walton in Italy might be all right. Stravinsky, Werner Egk or even Orff suggest themselves. Hindemith is too arid and I expect the wrong direction. Frank Martin. Or is Kilpinen too old & too Straussian? Henry Cowell. Someone of that calibre. There is a possibility that some change in direction is needed. What about writing an opera? Don't look so startled! It could be a fascinating and valu-able exercise in limitations. Go next year to one of the Wexford operas and see the atmosphere, limits and spirit of a Wexford production. Then find a subject, not too distressing and even if tragic with a good deal of humour as well. John O'Donovan might be an admirable librettist. Cast for (say) Dermot Troy, Ronnie [Veronica] Dunne, a chorus of 24 and the augmented RELO. Finally, all this may be terribly trite, obvious or ridiculous as you read it. But it is sincerely thought out. And it is not kind to think these comments without passing them on. And there is no point in being a critic, however poor, without trying to be constructive & helpful, even if it is no help.

Given Charles's advice to essay an opera (which Boydell never did), it is ironic that in his *Éire-Ireland* interview he asked: 'have you any hankering after stage music, opera?' – to which the reply was completely negative: 'I am less inter-ested in opera than in any other musical media. Less interested because I find that the mixed media become more and more difficult to manage.' This exchange did not appear in the published version of the interview.

It is unclear how Charles persuaded Boydell to agree to the interview for *Harp* and *Éire-Ireland*, given the coolness which his (apparently unanswered) letter occasioned, but one can only surmise that Boydell considered the inter-view sufficiently important to set aside their personal differences. (It is very significant that Charles asked Boydell to verify the transcript before publica-tion, a step he had never taken before, and almost never since. As Carol wrote to Eoin McKiernan, 'Charles was so anxious to produce a result which would not offend Boydell.')

Boydell's personal honesty, and his aversion to any sort of clique or band-wagon, came out strongly in the interview: 'I feel very strongly about creative activity, that one should be absolutely honest and write what one feels, rather than what one feels one ought to do.' The principal concern was that the music should give pleasure and be considered beautiful (he thought in 1970 that his third quartet was his most successful from the point of view of both beauty and honesty). 'I see the job of a composer as very much an idealistic job, that one is doing some kind of service… that one adds to shall we say the cultural heritage of one's area.' But this did not necessarily lead him into any nationalistic endeavour to write 'Irish' music, and his main concern was to write the music that he personally wanted to write. The invitation from RTÉ to write for the 1966 commemoration of the Easter Rising had resulted in his cantata 'A Terrible Beauty is Born' (the title came from Yeats's poem 'Easter, 1916'):

> That interested me enormously because first of all I was excited by the fact that I was offered a commission at all, being a Protestant and Anglo-Irish composer, and a pacifist to boot … But that challenge in itself excited me enormously. Because of two things. First of all in order to try and get over a point of view, this is quite extra-musical if you like. There is the point of view that what we should be doing in the 50th anniversary of 1916 is not waving flags about the past but thinking about what we should do for the country for the future, in fact the pacifist idea. The constructive pacifist idea. And the second thing was knowing that one was writing a piece of music which was for a particular occasion and there was a problem here of writing something which would appeal on that particular occasion without playing down.

When the cantata was performed on 11 April 1966, Charles wrote that it was 'the culmination of so much that he has previously written… many previous ideas seemed here to find their meaningful expression'.

Passing on to 'the history of the contemporary movement in music in this country', as Boydell put it, he felt that

> naturally being a young country there was an accent on what almost became Chauvinism and there was a period during which contemporary Irish composers were expected to write things which were specifically Irish. I'd go as far as a thing which caused quite a lot of amusement, I used the phrase 'the plastic shamrock'. What I mean is stuff turned out for the unthinking particularly American public.[79] This is things that are written into the Irish jig and all the rest of it quite regardless of the fact that the Irish jig is not Irish anyway.

79. As *Éire-Ireland* enjoyed a large circulation in Irish-America, the words 'particularly American' were cut from the transcript.

The conversation continued:

CA: Hear, hear.

BB: This sort of stuff, this pseudo Irish flavour music. If you look at the composers in the late forties you will find that we were more or less divided into two camps. There were those people who were following what I might call the Stanford Anglo-Irish tradition in which Irish folksongs were married in a curious bastard type of marriage to Brahmsian Teutonic text book harmony –

CA: Larchet and Duff in fact?

BB: No quote, no quote. In fact some of them did it extremely well. Again there were those of us who wrote in a more international idiom… The creative artist, if he is worth his salt, should be a man of a certain extra-sensibility. By living in a community and by living in a country with certain types of scenery, certain types of traditions, certain types of atmosphere, so that it affects his creative personality. The important thing is that if one is writing absolutely honestly then the things that one has absorbed by being part of a community will come out in one's writing. And surely it is better to use a reasonably international language so that one can make a contribution from one's own corner of the world to the international language of music, rather than, shall we say, taking the short cut… There are certain types of folksong in this country which attract me enormously. I'm not one of these people who is sold enormously on folksong, I don't go and dig it as they say. On the other hand I have found I think that's partly a reaction because it was used so much as a nationalistic flag… But I'm aware of being extremely moved by some of the most beautiful of Irish melodies, particularly when performed in a really genuine way… The great songs. I mean jigs and reels bore me to tears, absolutely to tears – can't stand them. I mean the extraordinary thing that happened after the performance of my 2nd quartet, an ardent nationalist (Fachtna [Ó hAnnracháin]) came up to me and said "Oh I was fascinated to hear that you used such and such a folk song, quoting the Irish title, in your string quartet". I'd never heard the damn thing. The point is that one absorbs certain turns of phrase which are in the national music which go into one's bones and come out the other way.

As far as the difficulties facing Irish composers were concerned, Boydell thought that the opportunity for performance of new works was a considerable advantage, but the disadvantage was the lack of a publishing house or commercial recording facilities with universal distribution. It was something that he had tried to initiate through his membership of the Arts Council, without success. 'It's just that people don't know about us.'

Charles's final major contribution to *Éire-Ireland* was his interview with Seán Ó Riada, published in the Spring 1971 issue, a few months before Ó Riada's death in October. His first involvement with Ó Riada had been in 1960, when the latter had broadcast a Thomas Davis Lecture on Radio Éireann on 'Irish Traditional Art-Music', and Charles had been so excited by the lecture ('a wonderful breath of fresh air through a smoky fog') that he responded to it with a lengthy set of comments, hoping (without success) that Ó Riada's script and his own commentary might be published side-by-side in a journal such as *Studies*. Characteristically, he made the point that his questions about the lecture 'derive from my ignorance and desire to have knowledge comprehensively recorded'. He had also published an article entitled 'Seán Ó Riada: the next phase' in 1967, discussed below.

The publication of the interview is complicated by three factors. The first is that Charles and Ó Riada were friends, and at one stage near neighbours when the Ó Riadas lived near Carrickmines, at Galloping Green: unlike Charles's friendship with Brian Boydell, his relationship with Ó Riada was almost entirely to do with the latter's musical tastes, beliefs and ambitions. From quite different backgrounds, they had moved towards one another across the terrain of Irish music, stimulated by the topic of Arab music as a source of *sean-nós* and by the concern for Irish music-making which Ó Riada had made evident in his 1962 radio series *Our Musical Heritage*.[80] Charles undoubtedly respected the depth and breadth of Ó Riada's erudition and linguistic skills, and regarded him as quintessentially both an Irishman and a European. Together they discussed in detail Ó Riada's plans for a series of 'Nomoi',[81] several of which remained incomplete or unwritten at his death, which allowed Charles to appreciate to the fullest extent his friend's capacity to write Irish music in a European vein, including his 'Hölderlin Songs' (written in 1964 *in memoriam* Aloys G. Fleischmann).[82]

The second factor – chronological – is that, in July 1971 Charles harshly reviewed a concert given by Ó Riada which he criticized as insufficiently professional. This led to an exchange, firstly in the form of Ó Riada's 'Open Letter to

---

80. For a discussion of this series, see *Music and Broadcasting* pp. 260–72.

81. Ó Riada's extant 'Nomoi' are: 'Nomos 1' (also known as *Hercules Dux Ferrariae*), 'Nomos 2', for baritone, chorus and orchestra, 'Nomos 4' (a piano concerto) and 'Nomos 6' for full orchestra; numbers 3, 5 and 7 (the latter conceived as a violin concerto) were never completed. Ó Riada adopted the word 'Nomos' to indicate 'a composition strictly following the laws [*nomoi*] of classical aesthetics'.

82. That is, the father of composer and professor Aloys Fleischmann.

Charles Acton', published in *The Irish Times* on 27 July, in which he referred to Charles's successive reviews as the work of 'a sort of well-meaning uncle'; and Charles's response, 'A Reply to Seán Ó Riada' which appeared on 2 August, ending with the words: 'I write this in deep sincerity and true friendship, and cherishing the privilege of being regarded by you as your friend'. Neither was aware that Ó Riada would be dead, at the age of forty, in two months' time, and Charles deeply regretted the severity of his remarks, so much so that he was outraged when they were republished by his old Cambridge contemporary, Grattan Freyer, in the commemorative volume *The Achievement of Seán Ó Riada: Integrating Tradition* that Freyer co-edited with Bernard Harris in 1981. There is something quite extraordinary in two friends addressing each other 'privately and publicly', as they put it, at such length through the columns of *The Irish Times*, thus creating a new impetus to the discussion of the future of Irish composition.

But the third factor is the question in Charles's mind of the status and motivation of Ó Riada as a composer, and Charles's *angst* for his friend's career, which he exhibited in quite a different way from those who believed – and perhaps still believe – that Ó Riada was 'the great Irish composer for whom we are all waiting' and whose early death deprived Irish music of that messianic possibility.

In 'Seán Ó Riada: the next phase', Charles had explicitly discussed the composer as a potential, anticipated, *great* composer with a capacity for 'pure, creative, fantastic art'. He mentioned Ó Riada's use of 'Róisín Dubh' (or 'Dark Rosaleen') in his music for George Morrison's film *Mise Éire* as inspirational for a generation discovering Irish traditional music for the first time. He discussed the creation of Ó Riada's group Ceoltóirí Cualann to perform traditional music in an authentic manner far removed from the ubiquitous ceílí band. And he concluded that 'Much of Ó Riada's most significant work was composed, or at least had its origins, in a period round 1956–57. The last decade may have been a consolidation of that period, combined with the absorption of further raw material. I believe that he has all the elements now for a new creative outburst in a few years' time', but hoped that Ó Riada would 'renounce' the 'musical distractions that can so easily surround him'.

The *Éire-Ireland* interview had been intended as the first, rather than the last, of the series, but had been delayed by Ó Riada's suffering from jaundice. This in itself suggests that Charles continued to think of Ó Riada as embodying the future leadership of Irish composition, and the interview began with Charles's preface that, with the appearance of the record 'Vertical Man' from

Claddagh Records, the composer might have reached 'a new turning point'. By this time, Ceoltóirí Cualann had just been disbanded – to Charles's surprise and disappointment, because he had hoped that it would continue to 'create a form of music using traditional means and international means too – primarily contrapuntal – to arrive at a new form of musical art which was a development from traditional music but was different from traditional music'.

Here, he was on difficult ground, since Ó Riada, firstly, wanted to work with local communities in developing forms of folk Mass and folk opera, and, secondly, rejected the concept of 'art music' as being relevant to music in Ireland. Charles agreed that it was a 'beastly word' but could find no other to define the topic under discussion: he wanted to engage Ó Riada on the subject of the inherent music of a people as the basis for the development of an 'art music' such as Ó Riada was teaching at University College, Cork. But Ó Riada would not be drawn, and rejected the discussion because, as he put it, 'we are all two people. There is a rational man and there is the instinctive man... The rational side of me can cope with European music. The instinctive side of me is involved in traditional music because I am first and foremost, more than most Irish composers I would say, involved in traditional music from my early youth.' He refused to consider where his instinct might take him in the future, and he denied that it might be, as Charles put it to him, 'taking an easy way out'.

Throughout the interview, one senses Charles's frustration at his inability to persuade Ó Riada to engage on the subject of 'art music', and senses also his bewilderment at his friend's determined immersion in his work in his home village of Coolea. Where he had been able to 'push' Brian Boydell into a discussion of Irishness in his composition, now he could find no way to discuss the Europeanness of Ó Riada's work. There is even a sense that, towards the end of the interview, Charles began to hector Ó Riada about what he – Charles – considered to be the other's responsibility to the musical development of his country: 'something which you should really be doing... Is it right that you should be doing what you want to do rather than a person of your talents doing something of longer lasting capability for the country?' Much later, Charles would tell Harry White that Ó Riada 'was apt to move always where the wind listed, and I for one would never blame him for that', but this was easier to say with hindsight, whereas at the time of the interview he felt strongly that he *could* blame, or at least chastise, Ó Riada for 'doing what he wanted to do'.

This provocation succeeded in stirring an irate and slightly arrogant Ó Riada: 'I think I have changed the face of Irish music already. I have changed it in terms of orchestra and I have changed it in terms of traditional music. And I feel that I am entitled to do what I want to do and I believe that what I want to do is the right thing, therefore it's what I should do.' The interview ended – and had, perhaps, begun – in a stalemate. The problem of Seán Ó Riada was Charles's – and most other people's – inability to understand the man, which is almost without question because the preconception of him as *the* 'great composer' cannot be reconciled with the extraordinarily disparate elements in Ó Riada's life and imagination. Perhaps when he came to consider the work of the only-forty-year-old Ó Riada, Charles recognized in his subject the series of discontinuities that had made such a mosaic of his own life. In the enigma of Ó Riada he saw the enigma of himself.

But at the root of Charles Acton was his determination that – to adapt his expression about Irish performers – 'Irish composers should be Irish'. He was so exercised by his own need to be Irish (and to prove his Irishness) that he expected it, unquestionably, from others.

In Ó Riada's 'open letter' he suggested that 'selling himself cheaply' amounted to an accusation of 'prostitution' and stated bluntly: 'You are not entitled to lecture me on my duty, Charles, and you shouldn't have called me a prostitute.' He went on to establish his (famously) fundamental point about the dichotomy within Irish music-making: 'there are in this small island two nations: the Irish (or Gaelic) nation and the Pale'. The latter 'has about the same relevance for the Irish nation as would have a column about bee-keeping in a tricyclist's monthly journal'. Clearly, whatever he may have thought of Charles's interest in, and concern for, Irish music, he regarded him as a product of the Pale and therefore incapable of appreciating Irish music 'in its proper context'. 'In the heel of the hunt, you are a foreigner; but you are welcome to become one of the natives, should you wish to do so.' Did Charles recall the 'you are no Irishman' delivered to him at Kilmacurragh? And did he feel any more confident now, having been explicitly called 'a foreigner' in what he thought of as his own land, that he could ever become a 'native'? I doubt it, since he did not attempt a response to the label of 'foreigner'.

When Ó Riada died two months later, Charles's view remained unchanged: 'As a composer [he] had immense promise to be, possibly, our first great composer. The width of his activity, his zest for actual life threatened the realisation of this promise, a continued anxiety to many of his friends.' Privately, he wrote (to someone who criticized his obituary of Ó Riada) what few appreciated at the time, but which has become much more widely recognized in recent years:

Seán Ó Riada was a great man, a great musician, a greatly creative man. But his creativity went more into his living than into his writing. One cannot call a man a great composer unless he has composed greatly. I still believe that Seán had it in him to be a great composer. Our grief is that he did not make this potential a reality. It is essential to separate the person and his influence on the one hand from his actual continually usable achievement on the other. It is still justified to say that Seán should have been our Grieg, our Sibelius. It is our tragedy that he did not live to be. I do not think that a critic's obituary assessment of a composer however well-loved should be a mere panegyric.

Charles consistently made the point that a comparison with Duparc was valid: that, on the evidence of Duparc's slim output of songs, he could have been a great composer, and since Ó Riada's work was at least as impressive as Duparc's, he, too, was potentially, but not actually, great. (Charles said much the same of the piano concertante work 'Nomos 4', when first performed by Charles Lynch and the RÉSO in 1959, that 'it says a great deal for John Reidy[83] that his new "Nomos" can follow Hindemith and completely hold its own.')

Charles's public and private expressions on Ó Riada exemplify his capacity for diplomatic and balanced, positive critical comment in one sphere and outspoken, radical remarks in another. Thus, while giving his honest opinion of Ó Riada (in relation to his 1971 concert), his sense of the critic's responsibility to both subject and reader would not allow him to say exactly what was in his own, private, mind. Several years later, in 1978, he discovered from Aloys Fleischmann that Ó Riada's alleged study with Frank Martin during his time in Paris was a myth, and he wrote to Fleischmann 'his talk about Frank Martin was another part of his myth-making. I shall soon get to a point where I shall become convinced that Seán was a self-generated mirage or a total work of fiction.'

'Classical', 'traditional' and 'national' music

Charles's abiding concern for the health and status of Irish traditional – or folk – music probably stemmed from three causes: firstly, his sense of Irishness, and his cultural origins and education in musical genres distant from Irish music; secondly, he had a deep-seated belief that there were no unsurmountable borders between different musical genres, and that those who attempted to

---

83. Ó Riada used the English form of his name during the early part of his career.

police such borders were doing a disservice to whatever cultures they believed they were protecting; and thirdly, his long-held belief that there was a definite link between the Arab music he had heard in Palestine and that of *sean-nós* encouraged him to develop his theory in the company of musicians such as Seán Ó Riada and musicologists such as Joan Rimmer. But these beliefs and aspirations led him into some violent controversies in which his concern for what he saw as 'Irishness' in Irish music-making was obscured by his proselytism and the vigour of his critical expressions.

Behind all the discussions which he conducted in the columns of *The Irish Times*, *Feasta*, *Éire-Ireland* and elsewhere, and in his private correspondence, was a nagging question: what is '*national*' music? The European mainstream of 'classical' music was not generic to Ireland, nor was it cognate with indigenous Irish forms of music. The romantic, melodic music of Brahms and Tchaikovsky was foreign to Ireland, and its supporters ran the risk of being regarded themselves as foreigners, or un-Irish, because the cultural tradition to which their education brought them closest was *not* an innately Irish cultural tradition.

Charles, as an Anglo-Irishman, would have felt this acutely as he endeavoured to find his way culturally as well as socially. As music critic of *The Irish Times* his conscience – or at least his sense of responsibility – would have insisted that he try to understand Irish 'traditional' music; luckily for him, his exposure to Arab music had tempered the musical education he had received at school and which he had developed at university. Now, his search for a cultural homeland made him both Irish and European, while his interest in the music of Ireland became both a passion and a crusade.

However, this was made more difficult by two factors: on one hand Charles, as a purist who was anxious to discover the inalienable or irreducible roots of Irish music, rapidly came to the conclusion that the 'arrangements' of such music, while undeniably popularizing it from the time of Moore's Melodies, were, as he put it, 'prostituting' and 'degrading' the original; on another hand, he was attempting to establish dialogue with aficionados who were unable to reach any consensus among themselves, each of whom regarded himself as the custodian of whatever authenticity there might be. As his *Irish Times* colleague Bill Meek would remark in connection with Irish dancing, 'dissent would appear to be almost inevitable when people associate with the purpose of collectively cultivating some or other creative urge or skill'. This would prove to be particularly true of one of the self-appointed custodians of the traditions, Comhaltas Ceoltóirí Éireann (CCÉ), with whose members Charles would frequently cross swords, and whom he would accuse of establishing an institution of 'illiberal dictatorship'. It put him in the difficult position of appearing as the custodian of the custodians – a theorist who disdained much of what the performers put before the public.

Charles's principal concern with regard to our knowledge of Irish music was to discover its origins and its performance styles, and he distinguished this from modern-day performance where he saw considerable scope for discrimination. The fact that Irish 'traditional' music had survived longer, and in a better state of preservation, than folk musics elsewhere in Europe came almost second to his devout wish to connect the various strata and facets of the music with those other musics. Thus in 1974 in *Éire-Ireland* he wrote of the need for research to establish whether there was a connection of 'the elbow-blown pipe' with the European bagpipe, of vocal music with the medieval songs of the troubadours, and of the 'traditional fiddle' with the Cremona technique brought to Ireland by Geminiani.[84] It was Charles's conviction that Irish music and pre-classical music had a common source: 'I believe it to be possible that we may yet rediscover from the vestiges [of high art] that we have a reasonable approximation to medieval bardic music. If that happens, we shall have, perhaps, something equivalent to the art of the troubadours.'

It was equally Charles's concern that all types of music emanating from Irish sources should be regarded as 'Irish music', and not alone the genre of folk music. Charles insisted that music written by Irish composers, in whatever genre, was 'native' and merited discussion, if possible in the same frame of reference. Writing in 1975 of Frederick May's string quartet, he intuited that many might not regard it as 'the native music of Ireland' but 'I do, and I regard it as an Irish achievement, as a beautiful piece of Irish art and something which I wish with all my heart that the traditional musicians would know and love as I love a superb performance of one of the great songs.'

If there was a difficulty in appreciating the need to go back to roots, it lay in the nineteenth-century collection of folk music by antiquarians such as George Petrie, when, as Charles put it, 'the uncouth or barbarous qualities that reflected the lack of education of the rustics to whom it belonged' were removed in

---

84. Francesco Geminiani, who died in Dublin in 1762, is widely believed to have introduced the Italianate style of violin playing to Ireland, and to have met and influenced the harper Turlough Carolan (1670–1738). Charles published his opinion on this stylistic connection in *Éire-Ireland*, telling Joan Rimmer 'fortunately I have no scholarly reputation to lose!'

order to make it 'fit for polite, highly educated ears'; 'it must be remembered that the very words "polite", "civilised", "urbane" mean specifically those qualities which derive from people coming together into cities and towns and developing aesthetic and material conditions then impossible for the rustics'. This once again underlines what Charles had meant when he wrote to his mother 'the remains of my real history are at Kilmacurra'. It was 'the remains' or, as he called them, the surviving 'vestiges' of Irish traditional music that he felt 'in my heart' to be the 'real history' of the new Ireland as it had been of the old, and if he could encourage contemporary composers to embrace that heritage, while making themselves thoroughly European, he would do so.

In 1968 Charles endeavoured to explain the difference between continental Europe and Ireland in musical terms, with an accent on the complexity and uniqueness of the latter: 'In Ireland things have a tendency to look not quite the same as they do elsewhere. Some people say the reason is ethnic, but I think we can put it down to a combination of geography and history. Thus, folk music, traditional music, popular music and art music are apt to take on particular connotations with us.' This was not the case, for example, in Germany, where 'they have light and serious, good and bad art music. The borderlines between each are impossible to draw and there is a virtually complete musical spectrum. The completeness and inseparability in the spectrum is a reflection of a complete historical continuity and, at nearly all times, artistic creation and folk life were only separated by barriers of class or of those between town and country.' In Ireland, the situation was quite different: 'Far too often in Ireland we hear traditionalists, members of CCÉ and people on Radio Éireann using the expression "Irish music" to distinguish our traditional music from that being composed for international forces by such as Seán Ó Riada or Seóirse Bodley: such a use of "German music" to distinguish between an Alpine band and Beethoven would be totally devoid of meaning to any German.' Charles's argument was that a lack of interest in music on the part of the Anglo-Irish in general, and the literary community in particular, led to an almost complete absence of nineteenth- and early twentieth-century Irish composers, while 'our many 18th century composers are all very minor figures whose music is graceful but insubstantial'.

> The situation is now very different. We have a number of native composers turning out music equal to that of their contemporaries all round Europe. We may not yet have produced our Sibelius or our Smetana and our present composers are not in the forefront of the world's fame, but as long as anybody

can describe Seán Ó Riada's Ceoltóirí Chualann as 'Irish music' to the exclusion of his 'Hercules Dux Ferrariae' for string orchestra, then limits are being set to the musical march of the nation.

Charles felt that unconsidered performance and the 'adulteration' of the genre was irresponsible, if the 'essence of our traditional music' was to be discovered.

> Here is something of enormous beauty which can all too easily be lost: and something which may have in it details of medieval and continental European practice or truly ancient Celtic significance. Do not let us risk losing either the beauty itself or things of which we may yet be unaware by careless disregard, as we are losing the history and beauty of the city of Dublin by careless development and are in danger of losing a mine of archaeological knowledge of medieval and Viking times by building new offices for Dublin Corporation without proper archaeological investigation of the oldest part of Dublin city.[85]

Charles recognized that there was a case to be made for the development of Irish fiddling, singing and dancing – he enjoyed the original *Riverdance*, for example – but he had specific reservations.

> As folk music evolves continuously with its folk, so it can be claimed that those who play Irish traditional music in modern vernacular are only carrying on an age-old process. Many able practitioners of traditional music, especially the young and adventurous, feel very strongly that this indigenous music is not just a relic, not a museum piece, but something which must be allowed to live and develop with its own creative life. And that was the vision of Seán Ó Riada, when starting the Ceoltóirí Chualann, that he could develop from traditional instruments and styles an art music based upon them. Alas that he did not. There could be a hope that Paddy Moloney and his Chieftains could do just that, but in spite of his brilliant and imaginative technique, and his knowledge and experience, I doubt if he has either the composer's equipment or the composer's (as opposed to the performer's) creative gift. And, certainly, when he incorporates a harmonically played harp or an orchestrally played oboe the result to me is like finding a spoonful of strawberry jam in the middle of a smoked salmon sandwich.

The debate in 1972 on whether or not Ireland should enter the (then) European Economic Community provided Charles with an opportunity to join

---

85. This was written at the time (1975) when the Civic Offices were about to be built at Wood Quay, believed to have been the site of the earliest Viking settlement in Dublin, and thus the origin of the city itself.

a discussion of Irish music with that of national identity within Europe. As a confirmed European, Charles saw Irish accession to the EEC as an opportunity to develop, rather than to inhibit, a sense of Irish identity. He believed that a major factor in preserving Irish culture was the nature of rural life: in continental Europe life was urban rather than rural, and folk music had provided the basis for the development of art music. British rule in Ireland, and the educational and social contexts which it provided, had inhibited a similar process.

Charles, with remarkable foresight, saw accession to Europe as 'the greatest opportunity for developing our national identity since 1916', but that 'we can only do it with our own efforts, our own cooperation, our own trust and belief in ourselves. There is no reason for anybody else to do it for us and if we fail to do it ourselves then there will be no point in our whingeing.'

Equally presciently, he wrote

> There is the possibility that our membership of the European Community may show us just to what an extent our ordinary lives are English in fact. We may, perhaps, import from the continent new ideas which will not submerge those which are truly native but merely dilute the Englishness of our life. If we were to become European and not solely English in our day-to-day life, we might then develop the things which are left which are Irish: we might then realise that our language is a cultural heritage and not a badge of bigotry, we might shake off our sense of inferiority which stops us from asserting our faith in ourselves. We might start realising that the Protestant Orangemen of the east of the Bann are more Irish than Mr John Stevenson.[86]

He went on to make an impassioned plea (the cliché is entirely deserved) for performance on RTÉ of work by living Irish composers; for the engagement of Irish performers rather than foreigners, if Irish artists of suitable standard were available; for the recording and sale of Irish music; for the promotion of music education; for the inauguration of the proposed Kennedy concert hall as 'the *national* focus of all sorts of Irish music'; above all,

> in terms of music at least (and I believe in terms of virtually everything else in our life that is worth working for) our country may now take her place among the nations of the world if we have the genuine pride to do so, and if we recognise that the effort of supporting and paying for the good things that we have can bring us a national prestige in the European Community

---

86. Charles was referring obliquely to the English-born Seán Mac Stiofáin [né John Edward Drayton Stephenson], 1928–2001, at that time chief of staff of the Provisional IRA.

that will make and keep us truly a nation and not just a region. If the Dutch had as little pride in their achievements as we have, and if they did as little to help their own as we do, they would merely be a water-logged rural slum speaking a dialect of German and washed away at every high tide. We have qualities and products and cultural treasures to bring to Europe and to assert in Europe if only we would say Yes in our hearts.

Despite his consistent promotion of Europeanism as a way of life and thought, Charles recognized that 'the preservation, and evolution and life of our traditional music is independent of whether or not we voted for the Community. Nobody is going to invade our traditional music from the continent or anywhere else, except ourselves.'

It was ironic that Charles had so little of the Irish language; despite many attempts, he told Fachtna Ó hAnnracháin that 'I regret that education abroad deprived me of the Irish language, and there has never since been time or energy' to learn it. In June 1972 he would write: 'It may be said ill to behove a critic who has to be translated into Irish to refer to the language, however much he may deeply regret that he cannot write in it.' This was written towards the end of the period when he was writing for *Feasta*. Indeed, some of his most important contributions to the debate appeared, in translation from his original, in *Feasta*, an Irish-language cultural journal (literally 'henceforth' or 'the future'), published since 1948, to which he contributed fifty monthly articles from 1968 to 1972.[87] It was particularly ironic since he was convinced that the fortunes of Irish traditional music were inextricably bound with those of the Irish language.

Charles recorded that 'I grew up (as did most others) with an idea of Irish folk music being Moore's Melodies and ceilidhe dancing' – and no doubt, if they had any feelings at all about music, his grandparents and great-grandparents would have experienced the sentimentality which Charles had come to abhor. However, he had lived in Palestine in the 1930s, and

> little though I knew of Arab music I could hear that this Beduin music was different. They were singing long ballads (perhaps equivalent of our aislings) – the words, I was told, were by 10th or 9th century poets of the Bagdad caliphate. When I was back living in Ireland, sometime in the 1940s I heard on RÉ Tom Collins, the then white-haired leader of the violas of the RÉ

---

87. The extracts from his articles in *Feasta* quoted in this chapter are taken from the original, English-language, typescripts in the Acton Music Archive (NLI) and have never previously been published in English.

orchestra, play (quite solo) what must have been a *sean-nós* tune with all its pulseless rhythm and full, differing decoration each time, and knew immediately that I was hearing not only something totally different from 'folk' and dance music of the Irish urban world, but the same *sort* of music that I had heard in the desert. Shortly after that I heard my first flamenco and read that flamenco was but a debased form of *cante jondo*[88] which dated back to the Moorish times in Iberia. I put it to Seán [Ó Riada] that the legends were right and that the music had travelled from the Arab lands, and across North Africa and Galicia. Bless his heart, Seán took the idea up enthusiastically – though he took it too far claiming to have found artefacts in Morocco cognate with Irish early medieval art.[89]

This had a direct bearing on Charles's difficult relationship with CCÉ, which had begun in 1959 when he heard his first CCÉ concert on the fringes of the Wexford Festival and reviewed it in a notice which the *Irish Times* sub-editor headed 'Damage to folk music tradition'. 'An Comhaltas should learn what genuine traditional music is. The ground between *sean-nós* and Gems from Ireland on Blackpool pier is treacherous.' He thought that if this presentation by Comhaltas was typical of its regular concerts, 'they are in danger of destroying Irish traditional music'. At that stage, a vice-president of CCÉ, clearly recognizing that such a voice within *The Irish Times* should, if possible, be accommodated, or at least appeased, invited Charles to meet for discussion. Nothing came of this for some time.

Yet eventually, in early 1969, Charles was invited to speak at a forum held by CCÉ, at which he urged that

> musically speaking, the departures from tradition which are popular now are as destructive and as irrelevant as anything Moore's melodies, or symphonically arranged Irish rhapsodies, or a Victorian 'Emerald Gems from Old Erin' could do. But while we can now see and deplore those three sorts of example from the past, we cannot so easily see that what we want to do at the present

---

88. *Cante jondo*: literally 'deep song', the vocal style of flamenco, native to Andalusia, which had been celebrated by Federico Garcia Lorca in 'Poema del Cante Jondo' (1921); Manuel da Falla called it 'the only song on our continent that has been conserved in its pure form'.

89. In a letter to Harry White (Acton Music Archive, NLI). Charles had previously claimed this contribution to Ó Riada's ideas in a letter to the Editor of *The Irish Times*, 29 July 1981. The idea was also taken up by film-maker Bob Quinn, in his television series *Atlantean* (1984/1998) and subsequent book (1986; second edition as *The Atlantean Irish* 2005).

time is the same thing. If we allow the tradition to be altered during our days, our successors may be deprived not only of their heritage but of an enormous amount of information about the nation's remote past.

At the start of the 1970s Charles had slightly mellowed, to the point where he could remind his readers that CCÉ acted 'from good motives' but that their action was also based on 'fundamental ignorance' which had resulted in the 'residue' of authentic music being permeated 'by totally foreign commercial idioms... It was presumably bound to happen, but it is all the sadder for having been fostered by an allegedly preservationist movement.' Privately, in a letter to a member of Comhaltas, Charles wrote 'it is this continual arrogance about conserving the best and at the same time playing the worst that makes one despair'.

After 1972, when he stopped writing for *Feasta*, Charles's periodical writings on Irish traditional music, and its relation to 'classical' composition by Irish composers, appeared principally in *Éire-Ireland*.[90] In many issues of the quarterly magazine he drew attention to what he saw as the vagaries of the fate of Irish traditional music. He had CCÉ in mind once again when he wrote that 'unless the guardians of [traditional music] realise what they are doing and have been doing over the past couple of decades, Irish traditional music as we have known it for centuries will be dead in another decade or two.' Charles saw the folk music tradition in Ireland as superior to and separate from the various traditions of Europe: 'even though a great many folk tunes survive in Germany, Italy, France and so on, 500 years of fertilising art music has left art music and traditional music so intertwined in western Europe that most of the blood has been drained from the latter.'

Charles was afraid that the continuation of the Victorian fashion for making drawing-room material out of Irish ballads would impoverish the tradition. This caused him severe critical difficulty when a performer whose work he admired in one genre undertook a programme in another genre which Charles considered did not suit him or her. This was particularly upsetting when the production in question was a gramophone record, since Charles made it a point to badger record companies to record and promote Irish music and musicians. When, in 1968, Veronica Dunne recorded 'An Album of Irish Love Songs' with Eric Hinds and Havelock Nelson, Charles's *Irish Times* review was headed 'In

---

90. Charles contributed approximately thirty articles to *Éire-Ireland*, on all aspects of music in Ireland, from the issue of Spring 1967 until the Summer issue of 1975, when he requested remuneration at his professional rate, which the editor, Eoin McKiernan, felt unable to pay.

the Wrong Field': besides his judgment that 'the whole thing is redolent of an English drawingroom with a background of an Irish grandmother', he felt that Dunne's exceptional skills as a singer in opera and oratorio did not extend to music such as 'She Moved Thro' the Fair', 'B for Barney' or 'Danny Boy'. Privately, he wrote 'I would much prefer not to write about it, but readers would take a very dim view of me if I did not, and therefore I think I have to.' It was a striking example of the critic not wishing to make a harsh judgement of a musician whom he otherwise thoroughly admired, but being obliged to keep faith with his principal public – his readers.

A similar and distressing episode arose in the case of tenor Frank Patterson, who had recorded an album entitled 'The Voice of Erin'. Charles had praised Patterson's earlier recordings of Purcell, Berlioz and Beethoven, but felt that the promotion of this record as 'authentically Irish' or 'ethnic' was misleading; on a later occasion the inference that Patterson was taking the wrong route professionally by recording 'Irish' songs would lead to open debate between critic and artist. 'John McCormack earned an enormous amount of money for his records of the "Mother machree" type but it is his "Dalla sua pace" and his "Il mio tesoro" [both from Mozart's *Don Giovanni*] and so on which keep alive his deserved international fame and which shed reflected lustre upon our country.' But while John McCormack could succeed in wearing two hats – as a balladeer and as an operatic tenor – Charles felt that, in the 1970s, that dual role was no longer valid. 'Mr. Patterson must consider very carefully whether it is possible nowadays under the same name to lead the sort of Jekyll and Hyde existence that was possible to a McCormack... I doubt if you can succeed in being both a sentimental "Irish tenor" and a serious artist. And Mr. Patterson's potential as a serious artist is far too great for him to jeopardise it.' It was an unfortunate example of Charles hectoring an Irishman on the subject of an Irishness that was open to debate. To suggest that the dual roles were a 'Jekyll and Hyde' activity was, in my own view, a most lamentable lapse on Charles's part, and I well recall Frank Patterson's heartfelt rebuttal of the idea that, by recording Irish popular material, he was either doing something 'unworthy' (to use Charles's word) or damaging his reputation as a 'serious' artist.

In 1973 Charles found himself in *Éire-Ireland* referring to another, similar, Patterson disc, 'My Dear Native Land'. He quoted Patterson's riposte to the review of the previous record: 'As long as I have the voice that God gave me and as long as there are Irish people and people of other nationalities who wish to hear me sing Irish songs, I will continue to sing them.' This brought Charles to the nub of his problem: 'This poor adjective "Irish" seems to give a lot of trouble.' (He had previously dubbed the record 'Oirish' and said: 'if this is authentic, I am a gamelan'.)[91] He was worried that, on one side, 'the gaelgóirí tend to arrogate the expression "Irish music" and "Irish song" to traditional music in a real or debased *sean-nós*, to the exclusion of Irish composers', and on another side Patterson was using the same word to describe 'Anglo-German-type arrangements and frankly popular songs like "The Rose of Tralee", to the exclusion of any Irish composer since the last century'. Charles continued to feel that, while no one could or should tell Patterson what to sing, or how to make money to support his family, it was untenable for the artist to pursue both types of music. Sentimentality was, basically, damaging to Irishness, and this deeply held conviction overrode his admiration for Patterson as a voice or as a person, as it overrode any individual presentation of what he might consider 'sentimental'. As he wrote to a private correspondent, 'perhaps we tend to feel a little sensitive about this sort of performance, since, like the stage-Irishman, it has spread far and wide in the past so that far too many people in Great Britain and the USA think that that sort of thing is true Irish traditional music'.

By 1979, Charles had reconsidered his verdict on Patterson, in an article entitled 'The Two Worlds of Frank Patterson' (he may not have been responsible for the headline), in which he congratulated the singer for 'straddl[ing] the musical divide'. It had been an unfortunate series of episodes, not least because Charles himself tried so hard to convince readers that there was, in fact, no such 'divide', that *all* music was part of a continuum, from the most rustic to the most rarefied, and I think that he realized that in this instance his attack – or at least the vehemence of his attack – on Patterson had been a mistake.

In January 1958, Charles's palpable excitement at the appearance of six 78rpm records of Irish folk music from Gael-Linn was due to the fact that 'until this month there was not a gramophone record of genuine Irish folk music on ordinary sale in Ireland. It is almost too fantastic for belief. The fact represents an unanswerable indictment of our loud-mouthed pseudo-patriots, of our national genius for hypocrisy, of the emptiness of the Gaelic revival.' While he had reservations about some of the performers, Charles's overall verdict was that it was a first-class production, technically flawless, attractively packaged and 'thoroughly genuine'. This was not least important because 'genuine folk music is dying, as surely as is the Gaeltacht and perhaps the reason is the same. Up to right now, our folk music has been made by and for people living in a

---

91. An oriental orchestra of percussion instruments.

climate of manual or pastoral work. Up to now it has survived by personal transmission. The people and the climate are changing, whatever the politicians may say. Therefore we must save its remnants by the recording microphone.' This was the first year of the *Programme for Economic Expansion* of Seán Lemass's government, based on T.K. Whitaker's *Economic Development*, introduced in May, so that four months previously Charles had been exceptionally prescient of the changes about to affect rural life, the heartland of traditional music. The Gael-Linn records remained for a considerable time the only ones produced in Ireland, although at the end of the year Charles would be reviewing some American imports and castigating 'the Department of Education, the Gaelic League and half a century of politicians' for neglecting 'the fundamental musical expression of the nation for the last 300 or thousand years'.

Charles wanted field recordings to be made of surviving traditional playing styles, such as that of Pádraig O'Keeffe of Sliabh Luchra, so that there might be 'sufficient body of recording and commentary with which to preserve the tradition that we have inherited so that it can be picked up again'. O'Keeffe's playing was, in Charles's mind, linked to the style of Geminiani, and thus was a vital link to the roots of traditional fiddling. It was therefore appropriate that his concern was recognized by Con Houlihan, who wrote in 2007 that O'Keeffe 'had the compensation of knowing that some good judges appreciated him', and mentioned in the one breath Charles, Séamus Ennis, Ciarán Mac Mathúna, Seán MacRéamoinn and Aindreas Ó Gallchoir.[92]

Charles in fact enjoyed an affectionate friendship with piper and music collector Séamus Ennis (1919–82), with whom he had a regular correspondence towards the end of the latter's life, including, unsuccessfully, forwarding Ennis's poem 'An Odium' (written on New Year's Day 1975) – a 'spiteful revenge on bad weather too long endured' as Ennis put it – to the Literary Editor of *The Irish Times* for possible publication. It was typical of Charles that, when Ennis wrote to him concerning a review Charles had written of Tommy Potts's fiddling, he should regard it as 'an honour' to receive the letter, in which Ennis discussed the question of pitch. 'I really do feel very much complimented that you should have read what I wrote.' And when Tommy Potts himself wrote to thank Charles for his review, the letter began 'For the happiness and encouragement your review of my record gave me I did thank God and now I wish to thank you as His instrument. Your appraisal was so searching as to cause me to

---

92. *Sunday Independent* 26 August 2007; I am indebted to Patricia Kavanagh for drawing this to my attention.

weep in – I hope – unselfish joy.' Charles in his reply said 'your kind letter leaves me not just grateful but awed. Please allow me to assure you from the bottom of my heart that any thanks which are due for your record are to you and your outstanding artistry. All I can do is to express a little of my appreciation for it.' I once wrote that, in 'Ó Riada's Farewell' (his posthumously issued record of harpsichord arrangements), the musician was reaching out to touch the hand of Carolan, one of the last great harpists. In this brief exchange between Charles, Ennis and Potts I can detect a similar sense of connection; I think that Charles's enthusiasm was due to the fact that for once he recognized that he was in the company of a truly great musician in the tradition with which he wanted so much to be connected.

The culmination of Charles's involvement in the discussion of Irish traditional music came in early 1973, when, as senior critic, he persuaded *The Irish Times* to publish a six-part series on the subject, representing a spectrum of viewpoints, and prompted by the success of Eigse na Trinóide organized by TCD's Cumann Gaelach. The series is indicative not only of the strength of feelings on the topic, but of the diplomatic way in which Charles's chosen experts – Bill Meek, Breandán Breathnach, David Hammond, Ciarán Mac Mathúna and Seán Mac Réamoinn – negotiated their differences, with a summing up by Charles himself.

Charles's introduction would have been familiar to *Irish Times* readers by this time: 'Irish traditional music is in greater health and greater danger than perhaps at any time in the last two centuries'. Meek, writing on singing, had the same view: 'the whole aura of modern multinational uniculture is threatening. And yet the traditional instrumental life-force is remarkably buoyant.' He supported Charles's often-expressed conviction that *sean-nós* should never be subjected to accompaniment, and believed that 'if *sean-nós* is eventually destined for the archives, surely much of its beauty and *starkness* can be passed on to a younger generation and be meaningful to them'.

Breathnach made the valuable point that dance music (on which he was an expert) had depended for its social meaning on open-air dances, which had been closed down by the war of independence and the civil war, and on country-house dances which had succumbed to 'the social changes in the thirties' (even though dances of a sort had been held in Kilmacurragh during the war). What was now required was 'a sustained, intelligently planned presentation of the music to the public such as only a national radio and television service can provide', and he looked 'in vain' for RTÉ to fill such a need.

In a moving survey of the traditions (he necessarily emphasized the plural) of music in Northern Ireland, David Hammond, a folklorist, identified them as 'the by-products of environment and inheritance and consequent poverty and bad communications. They were the ideas of an underground movement, a subterranean culture, not necessarily subversive, considered unimportant by the ruling classes.' Acknowledging the separation of Catholic and Protestant traditions, Hammond nevertheless saw the similarities between them: 'these spiritual subscriptions transcend mere politics for they involve race-memories, the notions of heritage, hero-figures and pride in the past... Handy labels like Planter and Gael are not sufficient to encompass all the joys, the sorrows, the vigour of the inhabitants of this corner of the island.' He, too, expected urban society to obscure these energies, and that archival existence might be the most likely way of ensuring some kind of survival.

Ciarán Mac Mathúna had already spent years collecting and broadcasting traditional music, and could legitimately be regarded as representative of RTÉ practice, if not of policy, and thus a target for Breandán Breathnach's criticism. So it is ironic that he specifically mentioned Breathnach as someone whose seriousness of intent might diminish the enjoyment of performance. He felt that, despite the incursions of other musical genres, traditional music, with the possible exception of *sean-nós*, was in a healthy state because of its enjoyment by younger performers and audiences. In response to Breathnach he defended his employers:

> RTÉ, God bless it, is expected to save our language, save our music, save our morals, save our souls. One can say with justification and humility that the great revival of interest in our traditional music over the last 20 years is largely due to RTÉ programmes. I hate to be the one to say this, but I assure you that I am not blowing my own trumpet. RTÉ was recording and feeding back Irish traditional music to its listeners before I came on the scene and would have continued to do so if I were never there.[93]

Seán Mac Réamoinn's piece was a sustained plea for pluralism, for the recognition that 'culture' is an all-embracing term and not a means of dividing one set of practices from another. It was a European argument, sustained by what Mac Réamoinn knew as an Irishman, and therefore accorded closely with Charles's own views or beliefs. 'It is in the nature of things that all the public arts, among which I count our music, must live in a relationship of

---

93. For a brief discussion of RTÉ's treatment of traditional music, see *Music and Broadcasting* pp. 316–330.

tension with society.' (It was a point that he would argue passionately when he came to write the 'Foreword' to Grattan Freyer's and Bernard Harris's *The Achievement of Seán Ó Riada*.) The revival of folk music over the past twenty years 'has been one of the great social phenomena of our time, and it has played its part in changing the shape and mood and texture, as well as the sound, of Irish life'. Mac Réamoinn pinpointed the Irish language as 'the heart of the matter, the key to the whole problem, the very pith and marrow of the tradition'. The social decline of the Gaeltachtaí would, in perhaps two generations, lead to a cultural tragedy, with the erosion or death of the culture which the language was expected to sustain. One can see, given such an argument, why Charles had, apparently, abandoned his wartime dismissal of the importance of the language revival, in his recognition that Irishness did, indeed, depend, if only in part, on the survival of the Irish language – why else would he have decided to have his articles translated for publication in *Feasta*?

It seems from Charles's own article, summing up the series, that he felt more optimistic than previously on at least one aspect of the subject: the existence of research as a tool to the understanding of what the music was, and what it was about. The fact that an Anglo-Irishman, writing in a newspaper that was still widely regarded as an 'ascendancy' or 'west-Brit' mouthpiece, should have decided to commission such a series of articles, and should have persuaded such compelling authorities to contribute to it, two of whom – Meek and Hammond – came from Presbyterian backgrounds, was remarkable. Bill Meek had written that he was ill-equipped to appreciate *sean-nós*: 'I was born in the wrong place at the wrong time.' Charles wrote to him: 'So too was I' and immediately followed it with the *apologia* 'But this very fact, of having found this heritage from that "wrong" environment permits us, perhaps, to see it and a lot of other things with even greater clarity because we can, perhaps, see these things more in the round.' The double use of 'perhaps' should alert us to the fact that that sense of a 'wrong' environment made the entry into another environment, culturally, socially or politically, always tentative, always provisional, always searching, always negotiable.

And this consideration of Charles's passion for traditional music must end with the fact that, in 1986, he was the recipient of the first 'Seán O'Boyle Award', commemorating the folklorist, antiquarian and author of *Ogham: the Poet's Secret*. Although he had never met O'Boyle, Charles said that 'in correspondence he was extremely civil to me', to which David Hammond, one of the award committee,[94] responded that O'Boyle 'often spoke of you with admiration and a genuine feeling of kinship'. It might have been expected that the inaugural recipient of such a trophy would be someone deeply connected with the practice of traditional music – someone from CCÉ, perhaps, or a figure directly involved in research. It may be that the presentation to Charles was made in order not to give undue prominence to any single person among players or scholars in a world where, as we have seen in the words of Bill Meek, dissent was almost inevitable, but in Charles, who had gained the respect of *gaelgoirí* such as Donall Ó Moráin and Brian Mac Aonghusa, the O'Boyle family had identified someone from outside the tradition who nevertheless had given it service.

---

94. The other members of the committee were Ciarán Mac Mathúna and Proinsias Ó Conluain. The award was made each year for five years. It consisted of a small sculpture by Clíodna Cussen.

Epilogue

'Valete'

*I*n mid-1986, at the age of seventy-two, Charles took the decision to retire. Writing to his features editor, Fergus Linehan, he thought that the newspaper needed 'a fresh campaigner'. 'For a decade and more I have been looking for someone with a similar commitment to music and the *IT*.' Knowing that he could not nominate his successor, he nevertheless had 'taken the liberty of consulting Michael Dervan. Thank goodness he seemed pleased by the idea.' Dervan had been deputizing for Charles, had been music critic of the *Sunday Tribune* and had edited *Soundpost* and *Music Ireland*, if controversially, with aplomb.

> I think he has the commitment, the knowledge, the ability to write English (God knows that is in increasingly short supply), the independence of cliques, the impartiality, the determination to be his own man in expressing his opinion and the care for meticulous accuracy that are needed (and which I claim to have exercised). I think that this should provide you with at least as good a critic as you have had in me; the minimum of worry to you; the best service to the readers and the probability that the *IT* may go on leading in this art.

As a job specification for what he had been doing during the past thirty-one years, it could hardly have been bettered, and the word *commitment* leaps off the page as the defining quality, which without a doubt Dervan possessed.

It was only when I came to read through Charles's papers that I discovered that, to use his own words, he and Carol had 'agonised' over the choice of successor between Dervan and myself, with Dervan winning by 'a short head'.

This came as a shock to me, since I had only deputized for Charles on a very few occasions, whereas Dervan had not only written much more frequently for *The Irish Times* but was editor of *Music Ireland*, occupying a far more important position than I in the world of musical politics.

Not everyone was happy when Dervan's appointment was announced. One correspondent thought, 'It will take a long time for your successor to fit into your shoes', but Charles did not agree: 'I do not think it will take Michael Dervan any time to adjust my shoes to him. I think he has done it already and am thrilled that he has taken it on.' His old friend Norris Davidson told him, 'In RTÉ the opinion was that one could contentedly agree or disagree with you but that your successor is actually offensive in himself as well as in his writing.' Naturally, Charles could hardly allow this to stand. 'Carol and I certainly do not find him offensive in himself, and, in fact, I am overjoyed that, when I approached him, he was willing to take on the job, and, then, that the paper was willing to accept my recommendation of him.' To John Ruddock, who had also expressed some reservations about Dervan's appointment, Charles wrote, 'I think that he is the only and ideal person. He is very shy indeed, but otherwise he is as opinionated, idealistic (and perhaps as temperamental?) as you and I are – which is saying a lot. I can only hope that Michael will be able to fight for music better than I have been able to do.'

Linehan's initial reaction to Charles's letter of resignation was

> one of sadness – *The Irish Times* without Charles Acton as Music Critic will be a lesser newspaper. You know that whatever differences we may have had – and I think they have always been minor ones – I have always had the greatest respect and affection for you, both as a man and as a writer. Be certain that your place is assured in the history of music in Ireland, and that as a journalist you set headlines of commitment, honesty and good judgment for us all to follow.

He accepted Charles's recommendation about a successor.

It is clear from Charles's disappointment at the reduction of arts coverage that this was a major factor in his decision:[1] the memos between himself and Linehan during the last few months of his tenure consisted largely of bickering about cuts in his notices due to lack of space, and his frustration was mounting. As he wrote to one well-wisher, 'The *IT* has, during the last year, become increasingly hard to work in'; and to another 'What is sad is that I would not have had the sense to do so [i.e. to resign] if things had not got very sad in the

---

1. See the comments by Conor Brady in the endnote to this Epilogue.

paper' – a point on which it seems Fergus Linehan was tacitly in agreement.[2] In addition, Charles's attempts to secure what he regarded as proper levels of pay for his time, his reputation and his seniority had continually met with severe resistance from management, on the grounds that he was a 'contributor', rather than 'staff', and therefore regarded as a casual. As early as 1975 he had told Linehan that the newspaper's 'treatment of me has turned my pride in writing for the *IT* and my enthusiastic loyalty into bitterness and frustration'.

But there were other reasons: just as the space was shrinking, more and more concerts were being staged. As he wrote to a former London deputy, Marèse Murphy (and, in similar vein, to many others), 'increasing amounts of music have made it all seem like a treadmill that I really want to get off'. But there were compensations: 'We notice that on Tuesday 18th [November] the Vienna Boys Choir will be in the NCH. One of the pleasures of retirement will be not having to hear them ever again – even for money.' He might also have mentioned the innumerable presentations of *Messiah* that occurred in the approach to Christmas. (James Wilson had once mischievously written one December, 'There are 198 Messiahs on at present – I must go to one some time', and Michael Garvey, inviting Charles to attend a performance by RTÉ of the oratorio, said with tongue in cheek, 'I dare say you will feel obliged in your capacity to suffer yet again through this immortal work.') The huge increase in the number of concerts in Dublin every year (partly due to the availability of the NCH) meant that not only did Charles himself have to review at least 200 events in most years, but the proliferation also meant that it was not always possible for Carol to accompany him, as she had to review another concert herself, and without this support he felt increasingly at a loss. From the start, in 1955/56, attendance, and all the concomitant tasks such as the record reviews and the colossal correspondence that Charles took upon himself, plus the committees on which he found himself placed, had created a daily grind that inhibited their social life, which had to be built around the concert schedule. In 1970–71 he had worked 2200 hours, and had written

2. This sense of restriction was not unique to *The Irish Times*: in 1988, when Brian Mac Aonghusa retired as Controller of Radio at RTÉ, he wrote to Charles, 'I greatly fear that RTÉ, quite unnecessarily in my view, has begun the process of diluting the high standards and quality of public service broadcasting in the face of emerging commercial competition. Radio 1's quite distinctive service of quality has nothing to fear from commercial radio in my view, but there are those now in command who believe that it will be necessary to move "a little downmarket" in order to survive.' (Acton Music Archive, NLI)

85,000 words in concert notices and a further 60,000 in record reviews, for a remuneration of just over £4000 – hardly enough on which to live. Exceptionally sociable as a couple, enjoying both entertaining at home in Carrickmines and visiting friends, Charles and Carol nevertheless found it a rare luxury to spend an evening relaxing by their fireside.

Charles continued to review for a further two years, acting as a deputy for Michael Dervan. But it was at this valedictory point that, as he put it, he could read his own obituary during his lifetime, in the many plaudits that he received from Gerard Victory, John O'Conor, Bryden Thomson, Michael Dervan, and Fergus Linehan, in a special page of *The Irish Times*. After the news had broken, Fred O'Donovan who, as chairman of both the NCH and RTÉ, had been on the receiving end of several of Charles's op-ed pieces, wrote: 'You were the only critic (Carol also) who spoke without fear or favouritism and made us all look in the mirror. You dragged the music profession by the scruff of the neck into some semblance of professionalism.' Fachtna Ó hAnnracháin, now in retirement, recalled the early years: 'From the time our paths first crossed I believe we recognised in each other a burning desire to advance the cause of music in this country. We were both young at the time but, considering the challenges confronting us, I do not believe that youth was a disadvantage', to which Charles replied, 'What you write kindly of youthfulness I take to mean a missionary spirit, an enthusiasm, a desire to make things better (even better). Perhaps life was a little simpler in our younger days.' He referred to Fachtna's exit from the position of Music Director and the appointment of Tibor Paul, speaking of Paul's 'pathological jealousy': 'my depression about music on RTÉ stems still from that.' Not everyone was so complimentary to Charles. On his last night as music critic of *The Irish Times*, a member of the RTÉSO spoke to him in the foyer of the NCH with what Charles considered to be 'hurtful, offensive and ungracious remarks' – he was deeply upset.

Charles wrote a 'valediction' for *The Irish Times*. 'I used to tell our Arts and Studies Editor that, as Ernest Newman went on writing for *The Sunday Times* until he was 95, I intended to go on infesting him until that age. However, at only 72, and after about a third of a century writing for this paper, I have decided to bow out (mostly) for various good reasons.' One reason was that he expected his successor, Michael Dervan, to carry on in the tradition he had established – a wish that was not fulfilled to his satisfaction. At the farewell dinner given to Charles and Carol by *The Irish Times* Charles offered 'belated apologies for thirty-one years of being troublesome. I hope that you will find

Michael Dervan just as uncomfortable.' In his 'Valete' he said that he hoped that Dervan would continue his, and the paper's, tradition 'opinionatedly and idealistically as I have, but in a new contemporary spirit'.

Retirement

Apart from the two years in 1986–88 when he continued to write for *The Irish Times*, Charles's years of retirement were in marked contrast to the hectic, and constant, daily schedule of record reviewing, answering correspondents, and – usually around 6pm – setting off with Carol for a concert, writing his review at a typewriter in the newspaper office between 10 and 11pm, and, quite frequently, taking supper afterwards at a favourite hostelry such as 'The Troc' or the 'Rôtisserie' at the Royal Hibernian Hotel. Now, with few exceptions, life's duties were negligible and Charles was able to devote himself to reading that was not connected with criticism (the collected edition of Trollope was a special treat) and to living a quiet, uninterrupted existence.

He continued as a governor of the RIAM, where he doggedly pursued occasional inefficiencies, in particular urging his colleagues to have closer and more informed contact with the teaching staff. In 1990 he received the rarely bestowed honorary fellowship (in the company of Walter Beckett, Brian Boydell, Aloys Fleischmann, Anthony Hughes and Gerard Victory) and in 1995 a special presentation was made to mark the fact that he had been a governor for over forty years – the presentation consisted of a glass sculpture by Killian Schürmann, son of his friends Werner and Gerda Schürmann. It was only when ill-health prevented him from attending the necessary quota of meetings that he agreed to relinquish his cherished position as a governor representing the Coulson Endowment and to become a Vice-President.

In 2001–2, two years after Charles's death, I suggested to Carol that she and Charles should be commemorated in the RIAM by something rather better than a competition silver cup. My thoughts were on the subject of enabling students to use the summer months to further their experience through study abroad. Charles and Carol's own holiday opportunities in the 1950s and '60s had been limited by the restrictions on the amount of currency that could be taken out of the (then) sterling area. And at that same time so many students could not take up places to study abroad for want of funds. So the 'Charles and Carol Acton Travel Bursary' was put in place, for which students on the second and third years of the RIAM's BA in performance degree could compete. For six years, until Carol decided that her sponsorship could be more suitably employed elsewhere, outstanding young players and singers strove for the valuable award, with each year the first place going to a candidate who would undoubtedly benefit from a planned season of study with either a specific teacher or at one of the highly prized summer academies. Several of those winners are now launched on international careers, including the inaugural winner, Kate Hearne, whose virtuosity with the baroque recorder has earned her further prizes and already a stellar reputation.

Ill-health was also the chief factor in Charles's reluctance in 1995–6 to co-edit, with me, the official history of the Academy. Luckily I was able to persuade him to undertake this from his armchair, and *To Talent Alone* coincided with the RIAM's sesquicentenary in 1998. Charles's chief contribution (besides the revision of his own essay on Irish pianists) was to check the material in every chapter to ensure that it reflected, accurately and fairly, the recorded minutes and to fill in the gaps in those minutes from his own personal files and from his memories of the institution and its various personalities over a period of almost fifty years. An additional attribute of his co-editing was the fact that he was able to view the evolution of the Academy with the eye of someone who had seen it, as in the conditions of his own life, emerge from an 'Ascendancy' standpoint into one gaining increasing acceptance from successive Ministers for Education. It also gave him the chance of renewing his old acquaintance with Joan Trimble, whose family had been associated with the Academy almost since its foundation; with her he compared notes on each chapter as it was drafted, resulting in notable additions, corrections and new insights. Unfortunately Charles was not well enough to attend the launch of the book in Iveagh House at the end of 1998.

In 1997 I asked Charles if he would contribute a Thomas Davis Lecture to a series that I was co-ordinating for RTÉ Radio (also to mark the RIAM's anniversary), but his increasing incapacity for sustained writing obliged him to decline, and Carol's much wished-for project of a ghosted autobiography also failed to materialize.

A late anxiety came to Charles and Carol in the likelihood that their converted railway house would be required for compulsory purchase as the Luas tramline was being built, largely over the old railway line from Harcourt Street to Bray *via* Foxrock and Carrickmines. Typically, Charles sought to establish whether or not this was actually the case, persistently attempting to inquire what the timescale might be, and plaintively asking if he might be permitted to live out his remaining years at home – to which bureaucracy refused to give him any satisfactory answer.

On the other hand, his faith in the State received a welcome boost when, in 1996, the arboretum at Kilmacurragh was finally taken into complete State ownership under the custody of the Botanic Gardens, a project which had had Charles's, and his family's, strong support since the 1920s. This was one of the few developments which cheered Charles in his declining years, since it was a recognition of his family's contribution to Irish (arbori)culture which could now be preserved and extended. The announcement, by Síle de Valera (Minister for Arts, Heritage, Gaeltacht and the Islands, and daughter of Charles's old friend Terry de Valera), acknowledged the Actons' long-standing commitment to the arboretum and was a culmination of her own grandfather's interest in the property as an internationally recognized scientific facility.

The major disappointment of Charles's retirement was the fact that his 'heir apparent', Michael Dervan, had not lived up to expectations in continuing that contribution in the same spirit. As Carol told me, he quickly became very sorry about the appointment, 'and knew that he had made a big mistake'. The chief cause of the disappointment was expressed in Charles's letter to Dervan in 1990, when he felt that Dervan was doing less than he might to probe the administrative difficulties surrounding the financial cuts caused by the Broadcasting Act of 1990, which severely inhibited RTÉ's financial position, causing it to disband the RTÉ Chamber Choir and curtail the RTÉ String Quartet:

> You are a critic with a job to express opinions and to *care*. It seems to me that the job of the senior music critic of the country's one really important paper is to CARE about music and support the good efforts of all the others who care and work. I know that you do care. After all, *your* opinion is important, if only you would express it. We have the radio critic, a leader-writer, sundry writers of Letters to the Editor all writing [on these subjects], but not the one person whose opinion really matters, the music critic of the *IT*.

Believing that Dervan undoubtedly possessed the opinions and idealism that he sought in his successor, Charles nevertheless regretted that, as he put it to Linehan, Dervan was not displaying the fighting spirit that he himself had put into the job. There was no passion, and too much clinical dissection. He himself, as he said in his 'Valete' piece, wanted to be remembered as having 'tried to help as many people as possible to have the chance to hear as much music as possible, to enjoy it and love it … and to that end he did his damnedest to encourage Irish musicians of all good sorts'.

Ill-health was due partly to a faulty valve in his heart which had developed in the last couple of years of his life, which his physician said would have been operable in a younger man, but inadvisable for one in his eighties. It was also due in part to a condition at first considered to be pernicious anaemia, which led to Charles's rapidly dwindling energies. He lived, however, to contribute to a television documentary (directed in 1996 by Ann Makower) on the life and work of Brian Boydell.

From late 1998 Charles's health rapidly declined and he died on 22 April 1999, just three days short of his eighty-fifth birthday. By his express wish, there was no announcement of his death until after his burial in the family vault at Dunganstown, at which he was attended by Carol, Joan Miley and myself, and the celebrant, his distant cousin, Canon Billy Wynne. Immediately after the funeral, I telephoned Conor Brady, recently appointed Editor of *The Irish Times*, whose reaction was one of dismay and evident grief, which is typical of the way in which Charles, like most contributors to the paper, was regarded. Not only was his death a front-page item the following morning, but three days later half of the Arts and Studies page was dedicated to 'Remembering Charles'. Michael Dervan's summing up was perceptive and straightforward: 'His writing style inclined towards the polemic... You name it, he fought about it.' Fergus Linehan's tribute was as eloquent as Conor Brady's grief: 'With his devoted wife Carol at his side, he presided (and the word is not excessive) over a period in which classical music in Ireland grew from a marginal, semi-amateur activity to a fully-grown, vital art form.'

But Kevin Myers (already quoted in Chapter 7), in his customary style, captured the subject of Charles's temperament more pungently:

> He was in himself simply a man of enormous courtesy and grave attentive-ness. Manners were not an adornment to his daily intercourse; they were what made that intercourse possible... He was a deeply emotional man and was not shy about his deep and passionate affections... He was a perpetual little boy, with all the expansive exuberance, mischievous joy and simple, unvarnished emotions of such a creature.

Probably Charles's greatest difficulty, evident since childhood, was his 'little boy' impatience, particularly with organizations that did not seem, to him, to be living up to their potential, or fulfilling their appointed functions. Displays of impatience and frustration, bordering often on anger, were occasioned by what he saw as institutional paralysis. In the case of official bodies such as RTÉ and its political masters in the Department of Posts and Telegraphs, Charles's expressions of annoyance could easily be construed as Anglo-Irish irritation at the operations of 'native' administration which, in the common cliché, showed the Irish to be 'unfit for self-government'. But it also manifested itself in what many regarded as the last bastion of Anglo-Irishness, the Royal Dublin Society, the 'misguided eejits' at the RIAM and the MAI, which had begun as almost exclusively a gathering of people from Anglo-Irish backgrounds. Even at *The Irish Times*, the frustrations we have noticed could be considerable, and Charles's 'squawk' at unfair treatment did not always receive the appreciation he thought it deserved: on more than one occasion his arts editor (in this case Brian Fallon) had to write: 'Really, will you ever learn? You have an apparently infinite capacity for being your own worst – or rather only – enemy.' This, as Charles once reminded Billy Wynne, was 'The classic conjugation: I am firm minded. Thou art obstinate. He is pig-headed.'

Charles was many times embattled as both a public and a private writer, because he saw polemics as his way of bringing issues to the fore and creating public debate. But, as an Anglo-Irishman, was he also embittered? Because he enjoyed influence but not power, and authority without a mandate, his diatribes could place him at the centre of a storm of his own making with no safety net other than the discretion of his editor. He was always ready for the fight, but was it the 'last stand' of one of the last of the Anglo-Irish, or the, perhaps painful, emergence of a new type of Irishman, as described in the opening chapter, and which was extremely unusual among the Anglo-Irish? So many of Charles's 'crusades' – reiterating the *raison d'être* of the MAI, artistic policies and standards at the DGOS, the direction of 'Irish' composition and the future well-being of 'traditional' music, the adequate support by RTÉ of its performing groups – were either lost battles before he embarked on them, or concepts far ahead of their time. Were they also the 'crusades' of the Anglo-Irishman, attempting to put right what he saw as the improprieties or simple mistakes of a cultural system that was less than pluralist?

In my own view, Charles displayed his innate characteristic as far as his place in Ireland was concerned in two expressions. The first was when he told Tommy Potts that he was 'awed' to have received a letter of thanks from the traditional fiddler. The second was when he wrote about Ireland's entry into Europe, 'if only we would say Yes in our hearts'.

The disillusion that Charles experienced in his last year as principal critic may have stemmed from the fact that the newspaper itself might be changing from the institution which had supported and nurtured his talent, into a more popular organ. Up to that point, Charles had been thoroughly 'contemporary', but perhaps, even if he had decided to out-do Ernest Newman, he would have found it increasingly difficult to deal with new work practices and changing editorial styles. But in his three decades, he had created a culture of awareness among his readers and an awareness of culture, especially in its political dimension, and this was not only consonant with the prevailing house style of *The Irish Times* but also with the role of self-discovery of the Anglo-Irish in the new Ireland.

ENDNOTE TO EPILOGUE BY CONOR BRADY
(EDITOR, *THE IRISH TIMES*, 1986–2002)

There may be a perception among critics and journalists who report the arts that they are often invisible to the editor of *The Irish Times*. But I don't think this is confined to the arts area. Other specialized areas, such as sports, finance and foreign news will often express a similar sense of being distant from the editorial core of the newspaper.

I think some of this may be due to the fact that successive editors – and I can certainly say that this was so in my tenure – tended to take the view that if you put the right people in place, you then let them get on with it. A chief editor is likely to be a 'generalist' rather than a 'specialist'. An arts editor, by contrast or a front-line critic, must have a deep knowledge of his or her subject or subjects.

I took the view that it was important to put my confidence in the judgment of departmental editors like Brian Fallon, Caroline Walsh, Fergus Linehan, John Banville *et.al.*

My principal job as editor was to ensure they had sufficient resources to do theirs as well as might reasonably be possible. One had to ensure they got sufficient space in the newspaper columns. They needed good production and sub-editing staff. They needed adequate budgets to hire and pay their critics. The chief editor's job is not to second-guess specialist editors or critics.

I was fortunate in that my editorship, after a 'lean' start in the period 1986–90, coincided with the strengthening of the Irish economy. I was able to expand the size of the newspaper and make additional pages available for coverage of arts and culture. We put in additional pages for books, music, theatre, cinema, radio and television.

Some critics may have felt upset that with this additional space, their own particular specialization or area of expertise was not proportionately expanded. But my priority was to enable the newspaper to broaden its range of coverage. So we expanded books coverage to take in many *genres* of writing that *The Irish Times* had not addressed before. We did the same with theatre, expanding to cover productions outside of the capital. We did the same with music, providing additional critical coverage of pop, jazz, country and so on.

Yet there are occasions when a chief editor has to ask a departmental editor or a critic to consider or examine a particular trend, or perhaps even an individual notice or review. Sometimes a critic or a reviewer may cross the line between fair judgment and bias. Sometimes what may appear to the critic or the departmental editor to be appropriate criticism may appear as irrationality or vindictiveness to somebody who is that little bit removed from the 'front line'.

There were such occasions in my editorship. *Irish Times* critics right across the arts spectrum were highly regarded and their approval – or otherwise – of an artist's work could be very important to his or her success. I was constantly being told by people in the performing arts that our critics were too demanding or too perfectionist and that this was discouraging to aspiring performers. I was told that some regular reviewers on the books pages were pursuing various personal agendas. I would estimate that I ignored 99 per cent of these but there were times when I would have raised an issue with the departmental editor.

There were also occasions when I would nudge a departmental editor to have a look at a particular artist or performer or production. An editor has to be very careful not to be seen to nominate 'favourites'. But I recall asking one editor to reconsider his adjudication that Roddy Doyle would 'never come to anything' and another to think again when he expressed the view that reviewing a concert by a young band called U2 would not be a sensible use of space.

Appendix

Tenants on the Acton Estates, from earliest records to 1917

*T*his appendix is intended as an approximate guide to the tenants holding land either by lease or yearly tenure. As there are several sources providing overlapping information, the identities of some individuals are unclear. In the case of families with a long association with the Acton estate (Bolton, Byrne, Hudson, Keegan, Taylor etc.) as much ancillary information as possible has been included.

The denomination of the 'land held' does not indicate that the tenant held the entire townland, but that a portion of the area was occupied; wherever known, the amount of the holding is listed. Portions of townlands such as Macreddin, Ballygannon-more and -beg, Rahavil, etc., would have been held by several tenants simultaneously.

Sources: rent books from 1700; Dunganstown Parish Tithe Register (pre-1869); some records kept by Col William Acton MP and some by his son Thomas Acton; Janet Acton's diaries; also diary of Grace Ball-Acton, 1913–14.

'TA' indicates Thomas Acton.

Dates of death and ages at death are mostly taken from Dunganstown burial records compiled by Stanley Lane-Poole in 1908 and are indicated as: (Dunganstown).

The locations are: Ballygannon-more and -beg; Bellpark; Clohernagh; Cunniamstown 'big' and 'little'; Kilcandra; Kilmacurragh (East and West) *also known as* Westaston; Kilmacrea Upper and Lower; Kilmanoge; Kilnamanagh-more and -beg; Macreddin (East and West); Oghill; Rahavil; Templelyon; Togher; Tullylusk.

The dating of tenancies (whether yearly or by lease) has been established as far as possible, given that documents relating to a single portion of the estate, or to a single tenancy, may provide different forms of information.

Griffith's Valuation, conducted in County Wicklow by Richard Griffith firstly in 1843 and updated in 1851, was largely published in 1854, as far as the Acton tenancies were concerned. Where *Griffith* lists a tenancy that is not referenced in the estate records, it must be assumed that this indicates a missing estate document. These data are inserted in italics. Some tenancies recorded in the Acton estate records within these dates do not appear in *Griffith's Valuation*. No immediate explanation of such an omission by Griffith is available. Inclusion of each tenancy in *Griffith* is signalled by 'GV'. Where a variant on the surname as it appears in the estate records is given in *Griffith*, it is indicated.

As far as can be established, the total number of individual tenancies was 157, with the following dates of commencement. It should be noted that 1851 was the year in which Thomas Acton took over the management of the estate from his incapacitated father, and 1854 the year in which he inherited. The years of the 'Great Famine' were 1845–48. The tenancies for the years 1848–49 have been amalgamated, as there is considerable lack of clarity as to when some of these commenced.

Year	number of tenancies	Year	number of tenancies	Year	number of tenancies	Year	number of tenancies
1719	1	1805	2	1825	2	1855	1
1745	1	1806	1	1829	2	1857	2
1776	2	1808	1	1830	1	1859	3
1787	1	1809	3	1834	1	1869	10
1789	1	1814	1	1836	4	1877	1
1790	1	1815	1	1837	7	1878	1
1795	1	1819	5	1838	3	1881	1
1798	1	1820	2	1847	1	1882	1
1800	6	1822	3	1848/9	42	1883	2
1801	9	1823	1	1850	1	1888	12
1804	1	1824	1	1854	2	1891	1
						1898	1
						1916	9

In all cases, rent stated was the annual rent

HOL indicates that the tenancy was for House, Office, Lands; where acreage alone is stated, the tenancy related to land only.

P denotes Protestant

	Land held	Earliest dates for land-holding recorded, and date of termination of tenancy where known
ANNESLY, James	Kilmanoge a lease for life or 31 years at annual rent of £56	1801 (died 1832)

A Miss Annesly [or Annesley] was the teacher at Kilcandra School for many years in the late nineteenth century; salary £10.

A Richard Annesley held 48 acres at Rahavil in 1812; his tenant was William RIDER; his land was bordered by Joseph REVELLE and Peter BLAKE.

| BLAKE, George | Rahavil
HOL, 56 acres; [rent 1849 = £94]
GV records land also held at Templelyon, jointly with James RYDER | 1848–9 GV |

| BLAKE, Peter | sold his interest in 70 acres at Rahavil for £63 to Jane LAUGHLIN | |

BOLTON

The Bolton family figures very largely in the Acton history, as tenants and as employees/servants. Alexander Bolton was employed as a labourer 1782–1821 at £3, £4, £5 per year, employed at Cronroe, Westaston until at least 1820. John Bolton, woodranger/gamekeeper, was executed by the United Irishmen in 1798 (as discussed in Ch. 2).

A Fanny Bolton was housemaid 1834; later Selina Bolton 1843–4.

Mary Bolton was employed as a servant, from 1815 till 1821 at £4, when it seemed she then became Mrs Acton's maid.

A Christian Bolton married Catherine Redmond in 1798; she had been employed as a servant 1790–98 and remained in employment until 1821. Examples of the copper-plate writing exercises of Catherine and Christian Bolton are contained in a manuscript book (Acton Estate Archive).

| BOLTON, Alexander | A house and small garden
Rent £3 | 1830   P |

BOLTON, James   Tullylusk   1888

BOLTON, John (GV)   Tullylusk
House and garden, 10 perches

BOLTON, Joseph   Ballygannonmore   1849 GV
HOL, 14 acres
d. 1880; rent (1849) £10.9.0

BOLTON, Lawrence   Cunniamstown 'big'   1849 GV
HOL, 53 acres, rent £24.9.0
This may relate to the land he acquired from Thomas Bolton
in 1816 (see below); Lawrence died 1862
Son of Thomas Bolton (below)

BOLTON, Samuel   Tullylusk   c. 1840–50 GV
House and garden, 1 rood, 25 perches

BOLTON, Thomas   Cunniamstown   1801–1816
31 acres at £25 – interest passed to Lawrence Bolton
in 1816; he died 1824.

BOLTON, Thomas   Ballygannon   1825
Listed as a carpenter; rent £11.

BOLTON, Thomas   Cunniamstown   1859
Father of Lawrence Bolton (above)

BOLTON, William   Cunniamstown   1795
A lease of 25 acres @ £20; possibly the land which passed to
Thomas Bolton in 1801.

BOLTON, William   Tullylusk and Cunniamstown   1869
d. 1874; on his death, he being the last life in the lease, this
land was let to David HUDSON.
In 1873 Wm Bolton had asked permission to transfer his
interest but Thomas Acton refused.
In 1940 William BOLTON had held land at Kilcandra since at least 1925
In 1941 a Rosa Bolton was still living on the Kilmacurragh estate

BOOTH, William   ?   1847
Rent of £26, interest taken over 1850 by James BRYANS

BOWES, James   Kilmanoge   1808 GV (Bowe)
      Held from Acton, Truell and reps. of Lord Holmes
      HOL, 112 acres
James Bowes was William Acton's agent; TA was his executor
      Bowes took over this land from ? DOYLE and was granted
      extra land at Kilmanoge in 1845.
      Rent paid in 1849 = £62.11.0
      TA wrote (18.3.1869): 'James Bowes by will left all his
      money to his son William who has since died intestate.
      The estate divided between his grandchildren (children of
      his daughter Jane), surname Bady [? Bodley?]'
A Sarah Bowes was employed 'to attend children' 1830–34 at annual wage of £8.

BOYNE, John   Macreddin   1838
      Rent £7

BRADSHAW   **P**
The Bradshaw family was a long-standing tenant on Acton lands
A James Bradshaw d. 1793, age 58 (Dunganstown)

BRADSHAW, Peter   Ballygannonmore   1848 GV
      HOL, 58 acres
      Rent £46.10.8
      His interest was purchased from William BRADSHAW by
      TA in 1898 for £150. *See* MALONE, Jack

BRADSHAW, Richard   Ballygannonbeg   1849–1898 GV
      Held from Acton, Truell and reps. of Lord Holmes
      42 statute acres @ £36
      Rent @ Kilmanogue in 1849 = £28
      He held 212 acres in 1887, rent £36, which he applied to
      have reduced
See also HUDSON, John

BRADSHAW, Robin   Kilnamanagh   1776
      Lease for 3 lives, @ £73. This passed in 1828 to the
      representatives of ? Bradshaw and in 1835 to John Buckley
      who surrendered his interest in 1846, the land being sold
      at auction for £300.

BRENNAN, Edward   Tullylusk   1888

BRENNAN, John   Kilcandra   1877
A field behind the schoolhouse; succeeded on his death
by Edward BRENNAN
GV also records land held at Tullylusk: house and garden, 10 perches

BRYAN, Andrew   Kilcandra   1815
7 acres with house @ £9; he died 1838 –
see Alexander HILL jr.

BRYANS, James   Cunniamstown 'big'   1850 GV (Brien)
13 acres
Took over interest of William BOOTH
GV also records land held at Tullylusk: HOL, 20 acres

BRIEN / BRYANS, John   *GV records land held at Westaston Hill – house only*

BRIEN / BRYANS, William   *GV records a holding of a house and garden at Kilnamanaghbeg*

BURKITT, Robert   Kilnamanaghbeg   1849
Rent £103.16.10
Looked for fixed rent 1891; died; land passes to
'Miss Burkitt'; sold 1892.
See Ch. 2 for Burkitt's involvement with TA

BYRNE
The surname Byrne is very common in this area of County Wicklow; it is impossible
to state accurately which of the following were related to the dispossessed Byrne
family, at this time in Cronybyrne.

BYRNE, Catherine   *GV records land held at Cunniamstown 'big': HOL 51 acres*

BYRNE, Edward   Ballynacooly   1789
41 acres leased for 21 years @ £55; extended for a
further 10 years @ £60.

BYRNE, Edward   Kilmanoge   1801
House and land @ £5.10.0; died 1858; interest acquired
by Andrew HYLAND

BYRNE, Edward   ?   1849
Rent £89.11.0

BYRNE, Mrs E   Cunniamstown   1849
Rent £28.8.4

BYRNE, J   Coolbeg and Cunniamstown   1869–

BYRNE(S), John   Rahavil   1916

BYRNE, Martin   Cunniamstown   1719
These lands were held by James Byrne from 1886
Rent in 1801 was £16

BYRNE, Michael   Cunniamstown   1801 GV
HOL, 2 acres, rent £24
also held land at Ballygannon

BYRNE, Michael   Macreddin   1838
Rent £4.12.0; he died 1865 aged c. 90
TA's household notes record that Michael Byrne worked at
Kilmacurragh 1852–63 but 'Put Michael Byrne out of
house; he is to get two pounds a month on good behaviour
and one penny a week for taking care of house and field
at Round Mount. House had better be pulled down on his
death lest his heirs give trouble.'

BYRNE, Owen   Coolbeg   1883
land later held by William Byrne, nephew of Owen Byrne
1884
He also held land at Kilcandra and Ballygannon

BYRNE, Patrick   ?   1800
House and garden and 2 cows

BYRNE, Peter   Westaston Hill   1849 GV
House and offices only; rent £7; he surrendered his holding
in 1857 to Thomas COONEY and 'got possession of a house
nearer Rathdrum built 1856–7 as tenant at tenpence a week'.

BYRNE, Terence   Coolbeg
d. 1874
He also leased part of Ballygannonbeg (59 acres) for 3 lives
at a rent of £67

BYRNE, William   Kilmacrea   1848–1916* GV
and later his reps.   75 acres, rent £95.3.6; later acquired a further 46 acres;
                         in 1882 under the Land Act he was granted a rent reduction
                         to £70.
                         He died Dec. 1880.
                         *GV records 9 acres at Kilmacrea Lower and 74 acres at Kilmacrea
                         Upper – HOL*
                         * See endnote by Lewis Kemmis
                         GV also records House only held at Kilnamanaghbeg

BYRNE, Winifred   Ballygannonbeg   1809
                        c. 20 acres with John QUIN, in a lease for 3 lives @ £39;
                        interest passed to Richard WILLIAMS in 1823.
Janet Acton's diary: Timothy Byrne d. June 1891 'a good honest man son-in-law of
old Michael Doyle'.

CAHILL, Thomas   GV records land held at Kilmacrea Upper – house and land, 3 acres

CARROLL, Alexander   ?   ?   **P**
                        There had been an Alexander Carroll as a tenant of Acton
                        since the early seventeenth century.

CARROLL, Henry   Baltinglass

CHAMNEY, Christopher   Cunniamstown   1819   **P**
                        paid rent to 1847

CHAMNEY, Edward (son of Christopher Chamney)   1849
                        Lease for 1 life 1819; 45 acres; rent £57
                        Rent £47.13.8

CHAMNEY, Mary   GV records land held at Cunniamstown 'little' – HOL, 74 acres

CHAMNEY, Thomas   Ballygannonmore   1849 GV
                        28 acres, rent £32
                        *GV also records land held at Cunniamstown 'big' – 10 acres –
                        and at Cunniamstown 'little' – HOL 15 acres*

CHAMNEY, William   Ballygannonmore   1819
A Joseph Chamney was a captain, and a Thomas Chamney was a lieutenant, in the
Coollattin militia in the aftermath of the 1798 Rebellion.

CLANCY, John   Macreddin   1916

COONEY
The Cooney family had a long association with Kilmacurragh   **P**

COONEY, Edward   Ballynaskea   1869–1916
                     Thomas Acton purchased his interest for £500 in 1882–3;
                     when he died in 1890 the land came into TA's possession.
[he was gamekeeper/woodranger at a salary of £20]
[described by TA in 1866 as 'my steward', as was his father, Thomas Cooney who d.
1892 age 83 or 84 (Dunganstown)*
In 1864 Edward Cooney took possession of 'Keegan's farm' from William STEDMAN

COONEY, Henry   Ballynaskea   1857–
He worked at Kilmacurragh 1857–63.

*COONEY, Thomas   *GV records holding at Kilcandra — house and garden, 1 rood*
                     10 perches.

DAVIS, John   Kilcandra   1814
                     7 acres with house @ £9

DOYLE, Edward   TA offered to sell him Bellpark for £5,400 in 1884

DOYLE, John   Macreddin West   1836–1916 GV
                     HOL 20 acres, rent £13.10.0
                     later Michael Doyle [also held land with James O'KEEFFE
                     at Macreddin from 1887]
                     GV also records land held at Macreddin East, jointly with
                     MERNAGH, Judith

DOYLE, Martin   Kilmacurragh East   1849 GV
                     HOL, 137 acres, for use as dairy; rent £178.5.10
                     Gave up possession in 1881 to George LATIMER

DOYLE, Michael   Kilmacurra and Kilmanogue   1854
[d.1890]   also Cunniamstown   1888

DOYLE, William   Kilmanoge   1804
                     Rent £9
For 'DOYLE, Michael, sr and jr', *see* endnote by Lewis Kemmis.

DUFFY, Michael   *GV records land held at Tullylusk — house and garden, 10 perches*

EVANS, Richard   Ballinaskea   1888

EVANS, Mary Ann   1898–1916
                          18 acres @ £35 for grazing & despasturage for cattle & sheep

FARRAR, Benjamin   Cunniamstown and Kilcandra   1829–1883
                          [and his nephew Bryan] Rent paid in 1849 = £59.18.2
                          78 acres from 1827 @ rent of £58; 155 acres in 1887 –
                          rent £75.18.2 – reduced in 1902 by 10% – *see* endnote
                          by Lewis Kemmis
                          Benjamin Farrar was son of Joseph Farrar

FARRAR, John   Cunniamstown   1888

FARRELL
The Farrells were also a numerous family with long association with the Acton estate.

FARRELL, Bryan   Cloghernagh   1869–1883

FARRELL, George   Cloghernagh   1869–1883

FARRELL, John   Cunniamstown   1801?
                          90 acres @ £54

FARRELL, Mrs Mary   Cloghernagh   1837–49
                          Rent in 1836 was £16; in 1849 was £22; repossessed 1901

FARRELL, Matthew   Cunniamstown   1819
                          Lease for 1 life on 24 acres @ £31

FARRELL, Michael   Cloghernagh   1849–1883 GV
                          HOL, 910 acres, rent £44; held jointly with Michael FARRELL
                          jnr and Bryan FARRELL
                          In 1887 Michael Farrell had 940 acres, rent £170; land
                          described as 'rough & wet', suitable for 500 sheep,
                          300 cattle; 15 acres arable, 15 acres pasture.

FARRELL, Patrick   Ballygannonmore   1849/54
                          51 acres; rent £52.12.2

FARRELL, William   Cunniamstown   1800?
Rent £6
GV also records land held at Tullylusk – HOL, 7 acres

FAWCETT   **P**
The Fawcett family were spoken of as being loyalist and living at Rathdrum in 1798

FAWCETT, Anthony &   Ballygannonbeg   1809
William   Lease for 3 lives; 65 acres @ £79; in 1899 the cost
of re-roofing the house was £18.14.0

FAWCETT, Richard   Ballygannonbeg   1822
A lease was granted in 1859
TA purchased his interest in 1880 for £500

FAWCETT, William   Ballygannonbeg   1849 GV (Faucett)
HOL 112 acres + 88 acres, rent £114.10.2
d. 1865 age 85.

FITZGERALD, Thomas   *GV records a holding – house and office only – at Westaston Hill*

FLEMING, Michael   Macreddin West   1837 GV
HOL, 20 acres
later acted as the rep. of M. DOYLE
Rent paid in 1849 = £26.2.2
in possession until at least 1859
GV also records land held at Macreddin East, jointly with
MERNAGH, Judith
Also a Patrick Fleming d. May 1895 (Dunganstown)
1897, *note* in Janet Acton's diary: 'The Flemings poor aunt died a few days after arrival
from America, had lived for 35 years with a Bishop & his wife in America'.

FORBES, James   'Miller's Garden' in Dublin   1848
Rent £129 [land unidentified]

FORD, Matthew   Ballyherra (?)   1849
Rent £5
GV also records land held at Macreddin West – House, offices and
garden, 20 perches

FORD, Michael   ?   1849
Rent £15.4.0

FORD, Richard   Macreddin   1836
         Rent £16

FORD, William   ?   1849
         Rent £8

FORDE, James   *GV records land held at Macreddin West — HOL — 17 acres and*
         jointly at Macreddin East with MERNAGH, Judith

FORTUNE, John   Kilmacurra West   1849, GV
         HOL, 101 acres, rent £119
         Also held land at Ballygannonbeg (1883–85?)

FORTUNE, Walter   Kilmacurragh (part of) 1837
         For dairy; rent £123.

FRANKLIN, Robert   ?   1820
         2 acres; rent £1.13.0

GRACE, Thomas   Cunniamstown   1801
         Rent £17
         Having surrendered his interest, he acted as agent for
         Christopher CHAMNEY in 1819
         Lease for 1 life on 32 acres at Cunniamstown, rent £40.

GREGORY, John,   Tullylusk   1888
reps. of

HANLY, John   Cunniamstown   ?

HARRINGTON, Henry Grangecon*   1822
         Lease renewable for ever, rent £241
         * see note re Pierce MAHONY

HILL, Alexander*   Kilcandra   1849   **P**
         Rent £18
         Also Tullylusk   c. 1850 GV
         HOL, 21 acres

HILL, Alexander jr.   Ballygannon   1837
         11 acres Irish; rent £14; he also had a lease on 14 acres,
         previously held by the late Andrew BRYAN @ £18

HILL, Mrs Alexander   Tullylusk   1849
                                      Rent £23.13.9
                                      Note on estate accounts: 'Mrs Alexander Hill got possession
of Michael Byrne's field at £2 1866 and 7 acres statute
1866 from late Wm Farrell... 1867 Mrs Hill got
possession of 5 acres statute late Ben Farrar'

HILL, Anne   *GV records land held at Macreddin West — HOL, 60 acres*

HILL, John   Macreddin   1834
Lease on 1 life; 33 acres in 1837
Mrs John Hill in 1834 had a lease for 21 years on the life
of William Carter then aged one year, son of William
Carter of Sheana in Australia, thirty three acres; rent
originally £21.13.0.
TA asked for ejectment proceedings against 'Hill of
Macreddin' 1876

HILL, Richard   Tullylusk   1916   **P**
Also a Sarah Hill; also a Richard Hill d. 1803 age 25; also William Hill, d. 1813 age
70 (Dunganstown)
**see* endnote by Lewis Kemmis *re* Alexander Hill

HUDSON   **P**
The Hudson family had a long association with the Acton estate

HUDSON, Benjamin   Tullylusk   1883
1882: TA writes that the father of Benjamin Thomas
Hudson of Kilcandra Tullylusk was undertenant to Edward
PITTS whose lease expired in 1860; TA then let land to
William Hudson father of applicant

HUDSON, David   Tullylusk   1829– d. 1874 **GV**
27 acres, rent paid in 1849 = £21.19.8
Cunniamstown
HOL, 30 acres, rent £43.19.4
David Hudson also held lands at:
                               Bolagh   1838
16 acres Irish, 26 acres statute; rent £24
In 1865 TA's agent McDermott acquired possession and
some of these lands were leased to Robert KEEGAN

HUDSON, John   Kilnamanaghbeg (HOL, 98 acres), Tullylusk
         and Cunniamstown   1849 GV
         Rent £91.8.9
         In 1876 TA served notice to quit on John Hudson and
         widow of David Hudson in respect of William Bolton's
         farm at Cunniamstown

John Hudson also held lands at:
         Ballygannonbeg   1822 GV
         Held from Acton, Truell and reps. of Lord Holmes
         HOL, '2/3 of 38 acres' on estate papers, – lease for 21 years;
         he was still in occupation in 1849 @ rent of £30; *but GV*
         records holding of 83 acres
         Note on estate accounts: 'Capt Truell and Alfred MacDermott
         got possession of above farm from David Hudson, J Hudson
         having left [in] 1864. Richard Bradshaw got possession in
         consequence of letter from Capt Truell 1864'.

HUDSON, Mrs Margaret Tullylusk   1857–
(successor to William Hudson)

HUDSON, Thomas   Bolagh   1805
         9 acres; lease for life or 21 years; rent up to 1807 £9,
         increasing to £11.5.0 in 1809 and thereafter £14.5.0.
Thomas Hudson also held lands at:
         Kilnamanaghbeg   ?
         124 acres; under the Land Act 1881 rent of £168 was reduced
         to £142; TA purchased his interest for £199 in 1883;
         rent was further reduced in 1902 by 10%. *See* endnote
         by Lewis Kemmis.
HUDSON, William   Kilmanogue   1849 GV
         15 acres, rent £18.18.6; d. 1867 age 77.
         GV also records land held at Tullylusk (from Acton and Edward
         PITTS) – HOL, 64 acres
Hudson, another J., d. 1856, in service with Kilmacurragh since 1848; also a
Mrs Hudson @ Kilcandra died 1898; Michael Hudson wrote to William Acton,
1834, in relation to a collection for the 'Patriotic Fund'; another Thomas Hudson
of Kilcandra d. 1834 age 73; a Sarah Hudson d. 1824 age 64 (Dunganstown).

HYLAND, Andrew   Togher [The Togher]   1859
(as executor of John Byrne deceased; Hyland was a named life in Byrne's lease and
was Byrne's executor) *See* endnote by Lewis Kemmis.

JENKINSON, George   Kilcandra and Tullylusk   1878–89
note on estate accounts by TA: '1878 in presence of
Thomas Cooney and Woolahan caretaker I let George
Jenkinson into possession... Jenkinson gave up
possession 1889.'

JENKINSON, John   Kilcandra   1800
7 acres with house; rent £5.10.0
TA bought his interest (when?) for £189.

In 1830 William Acton, William Henn, Joseph Leigh and Mary Leigh leased 17 acres
at Bolagh to John Jenkinson; rent £26.16.5.
An Elizabeth Jenkinson was employed at some time before 1832 and returned to
employment 1832–35.

JOHNSON, William   Kilcandra   1805
lease on 49 acres, for the lives of Joseph REVELL son of
John REVELL, James Critchly son of Joseph Critchly
publican and Neptune Blood son of George Blood; rent £73.

JONES, Charles   Kilmacurragh and Ballybeg   1800
150 acres @ £113; land eventually passed to a member
of the SHARPE family.

KEEGAN   **P**
The Keegan family were both tenants and house servants of the Actons.
Robert Keegan (d. 1899) was Groom 1848–52, Coachman 1853–1883; married Mary
Hamilton, a Kilmacurragh servant. John Keegan worked as a gardener 1850–57.
1866 Janet Acton recorded 'Mr Keegan's good & excellent wife died'; he died 6 weeks
later.
Andrew Keegan, assistant in stable 1838–48 (?), married a Cooney 1850; became
woodman; 'had to discharge him for incessant drunkenness for years'.
Thomas Keegan had worked at Kilmacurragh before emigrating to America in 1848
– see Ch. 2.
A Robert Keegan was a neighbour to Charles Acton in 1942.

KEEGAN, Robert   Kilmanogue   1869–1904
when purchased by Widow Keegan; in 1887, 38 acres
@ £50; rent reduced in 1887; in 1904, 115 acres, rent £150
– reduced in 1902 by 10%. See endnote by Lewis Kemmis.
See also HUDSON, David

KEEGAN, William   Kilmacurragh West   c. 1850
                         House and Office

LATIMER, George   Kilmacuragh (part of)   1881
                         in succession to Martin DOYLE

LAUGHLIN, Jane   Rahavil   ?
                         Acquired interest in 79 acres from Peter BLAKE
                         Built a house there in 1901 at a cost of £900
                         She sold her interest (date unknown) to Loughlin Kinsella

LINEHAN, Timothy   Togher   1916

LOUGHLIN, Dennis   Bellpark   1848

McDANIELS,   Cunniamstown   1801 [?]
Alexander   rent £13

McDANIELS, Thomas   Kilcandra and Ballygannon   ?
                         Rent £25

MAHONY, David   Grangecon*   1849–1916
                         Rent £223.10.0; later fee farm grant @ £200
                         *In GV, all lands at Grangecon were leased by members
                         of the Mahony/O'Mahony family, but the estate papers
                         unequivocally record this tenancy; see Ch. 2 for rent
                         demands by TA from Pierce (O')Mahony.

MALONE, Anna   Ballygannon   1800
                         'Widow of Michael Malone'
                         Rent £23

MALONE, Edward   Ballygannonbeg   1819
                         Lease for 1 life; 28 acres; rent £40
                         Son of Anna MALONE

MALONE, Jack   ?   1820
                         12 acres; rent £10; surrendered in 1843 and let to
                         Peter BRADSHAW

MALONE, James   Ballygannon   1798
                         Rent £10

MALONE, *Patrick*   *GV records land held at Tullylusk — HOL, 4 acres*

MALONE, *Thomas*   *GV records land held at Ballygannonmore — HOL, 42 acres*

MALONE, William   Ballygannonmore   1800
                        Rent £31

MANL(E)Y, John   Kilcandra and Cunniamstown 'big' 1849 GV
                        HOL, 52 acres, rent £26.15.0
                        See endnote by Lewis Kemmis

MANNING, Anthony   Macreddin West   prior to 1855 GV
                        HOL, 14 acres
                        Formerly held by Matthew FORD
                        Note on estate accounts: 'James Bowes sent to demand
                        possession for non-payment of rent; the house of Anthony
                        Manning was pulled down 1855, field at other side of road
                        let to Mrs Hill'.

MATES, William   Bell Park   1916

MEADE, *Matthew*   *GV records house land held at Ballygannonmore — 77 acres*

MEREDITH, Samuel   Ballykerrig   1916

MERNAGH, Chas   Macreddin   1849
                        Rent paid in 1836 = £29.10.0; 1849 = £35.19.6
                        When Mernagh died, — Kavanagh married the widow —
                        he was put out 1876?
                        A John Mernagh was a prominent rebel in, and after, the
                        1798 Rebellion; he was a native of Glenmalure, but his
                        uncle, Thomas, lived at Macreddin; it is not impossible that
                        they were connected with Charles Mernagh (above); John
                        Mernagh was eventually captured and deported.

MERNAGH, *Judith*   *GV records land held (jointly with William STRAHAN, Michael*
                        FLEMING, James FORDE, Hugh SMITH, John DOYLE) at
                        Macreddin East— described as 'mountain' — 336 acres
                        GV also records land held at Macreddin West — HOL and pound,
                        20 acres

MULLENS, Thomas   ?   1849–61
Land passed into possession of John HUDSON; rent £75.

MURPHY, Andrew   ?   1837
5 acres @ £8

MURPHY, Dorothy   Ballygannon   1801
Sister of Patrick MALONE, mother of Matthew MURPHY
Rent £7

MURPHY, Matthew   Cunniamstown and Ballygannon 1819
Lease for 1 life; 32 acres; rent £44

O'KEEFFE, Mary   Macreddin   1916
[previously James O'Keeffe: *see* endnote by Lewis Kemmis

PERRY, Henry   ?   1849
Rent £35.10.3
Note on estate accounts by TA: 'I was compelled to sell above
for £885 i.e. 26 years purchase'.

PERRY, James   Kilcandra   1859–1883
and later his reps.

PHILLIPS, William   ?   1849
Rent £16

PIERCE, George   Cunniamstown   1849 GV
[or PEARCE]   HOL, 40 acres, rent £22.16.0; reduced in 1902 by 10%:
see endnote by Lewis Kemmis
Later Edward Pierse/Pierce   1916

PITTS, Abraham   Kilcandra and Tullylusk   1869   **P**
In 1874 TA remonstrates with Abraham Pitts about the
condition of the farm both in his tenancy and that of
his father

PITTS, Edward   Kilcandra and Bolagh   1787
Lease for lives of his wife Elinor and daughter Mary.
Rent up to 1791 £41 and thereafter £62; rent paid in
1849 = £60.4.0; lease expired 1860 when Edward Pitts
died; some of this land had been let to William HUDSON

QUIN, John   Ballygannonbeg   1809–23
                   Joint lessee with Winifred BYRNE

REGAN, Dennis   Kilmacurragh   1801
                   House and meadow; 16 acres; rent £16.

REVELL *or* REVILL   **P**
John Revell of Ballymoney (Co. Wicklow) d. 1740 age 75; another John Revell
d. 1767, age 76; Henry Revell d. 1759; Jane Revell d. 1814 age 80; Mary Revell
d. 1840, age 78; Elizabeth Revell d. 1777, age 74; William Revell d. 1799, age 84
(Dunganstown)

REVELL, John   Ballykerrig and Ballynacooly   1745
                   Lease for lives renewable for ever; rent £18 and 2 pullets
                   An agent (in business with Matthew Byrne) at Redcross.

REVELL, John   Ballykerrig   1790
                   Lease for lives of Henry John and James Revill; 43 acres;
                   rent £50.

REVELL, John   Ballykerrig   1849
                   (d. 1867, age 72) and later his reps.; rent £105.16.8.

A William Revell held 210 acres at Kilmacurra Lower (rent £27.13.10) on a lease
dating from 1752 by Thomas Smyth to John Revell, renewed by William Acton in
1845 for the lives of John Revell, Henry Revell and HRH the Prince of Wales.
Lt. John Revell was in the Wicklow Town Cavalry in 1798, was considered an
extremist and 'one of the greatest enemies of William Byrne of Ballymanus'.

RICHARDSON, Thomas Ballykerrig   before 1882–1915   **P**
                   44 acres, rent £89, reduced by arbitration 1882 to £73.
                   See endnote by Lewis Kemmis
A Frances Richardson was employed as Mrs Acton's personal maid 1791–93.

RINGWOOD, J P   Kilcandra   1891

RUSSELL,   ?   1849
James Forbes (?)   Rent £129.4.8

RYDER   **P**
John Ryder d. 1760, age 75; another John Ryder d. 1840, age 42; William Ryder
d. 1767, age 52; Catherine Ryder d. 1771 age 48 (Dunganstown)

RYDER, James   Rahavil   1825- at least 1886 GV
HOL, 80 acres
Held land with Peter BLAKE; rent paid in 1849 =
£193.16.6.
GV also records land held at Templelyon, 46 acres, held jointly
with George BLAKE

RYDER, William   Rahavil   at least 1888
reduction in rent by 10%, 1902: *see* endnote by Lewis
Kemmis.
Also held lands at Templelyon Upper and Oghill 1888–1901
109 acres; rent £124.
The tenancy was eventually bought by Dennis BYRNE on
the death of William Ryder's widow

SHARPE
A Robert Sharpe was elected a member of the inaugural board of guardians of the
Rathdrum Union in 1839.

SHARPE, Mrs   ?   1849
Rent £331.4.2

SHARPE, Robert   Coolbeg   1824
                                                  139 acres; £347
He also held land at Kilmacurragh from 1848: note on
estate accounts by TA in 1860: 'I got rid of him and let
land to John Hudson of Kilnamanagh.'

SHARPE, Thomas   Ballynaskea   at least 1837,
when original lease expired
Thomas Sharpe died 1875, when his holding was let for
1 life to Thomas Kinch of Springfield, Co. Wicklow

SHEANE, Archibald   Cunniamstown   1916   **P**

SHEANE, Samuel   Tullylusk   1916
William Sheane d. 1897 age 49 (Dunganstown)

SHEPHERD   **P**
John Shepherd d. 1732, age 73; Mary Shepherd d. 1737, age 79; Margaret Shepherd
d. 1803, age 39; James Shepherd 'of Sheep Hill' d. 1847, age 76; John Shepherd 'of
Sheep Hill' d. 1850, age 75; John Shepherd 'of Sheep Hill' d. 1829, age 29; Elizabeth

Shepherd (Mrs. F. Wright) d. 1839, age 27; Henry Shepherd 'of Oatlands' d. 1908 (Dunganstown).

SHEPHERD, Henry	*GV (SHEPPARD) records land held at Kilnamanaghbeg — 2 acres*	

SHEPHERD, William   ?   1849
Rent £2

SMOLLEN, Thomas   Kilnamanaghbeg   1849 GV (Smullen)
HOL, 100 acres, rent £64.11.6

SMYTH, Hugh   Macreddin   1849 GV   **P**
or SMITH   rent £13.5.6; held jointly with MERNAGH, Judith
note on estate accounts by TA: 'without my leave let eleven
acres Irish to John Byrne of Cronawinna keeping one field'.

SMYTH, James   Macreddin   1837
Rent £7.12.0.
Robert Smyth d. 1823, age 26 (Dunganstown)

STEDMAN, William   Ballynaskea   1854?
Land previously held by COONEY; lease 1858 for 21 years,
rent £165
A Stedman was temporarily agent for the Acton Estate
in the 1920s.

STRAHAN, John   Macreddin   1836
Lease for 1 life; rent £35

STRAHAN, William   Macreddin West   1836–1916 GV
and later his reps.   HOL, 21 acres, rent paid in 1849 = £41.3.2; lease in 1836
for 21 years on the life of his son (also William) then aged
4; obtained a judicial lease in 1898 @ £74, reduced in 1902
by 10 per cent: *see* endnote by Lewis Kemmis.
see also MERNAGH, Judith for joint holding of 64 acres at
Macreddin East

TAYLOR   **P**
The Taylor family was the closest in association with the Actons of Kilmacurragh for most of the history of the estate, with members of the family still living and working on the estate in the 1940s. James Taylor worked as a groom 1852–63.

TAYLOR, Anne   *GV records land held at Ballygannonmore – 13 acres, and at*
                      Kilcandra – HOL, forge and garden, 1 acre, 3 roods and 20 perches

TAYLOR, Benjamin   *GV records land held at Cunniamstown 'big' – HOL, 127 acres*

TAYLOR,   Kilnamanaghbeg   1857
Bentinck[?]

TAYLOR, John   Kilnamanaghbeg   1776
                      Lease for 3 lives; 90 acres; rent £47.

TAYLOR, Richard   Kilcandra   ?
                      House with 7 acres; rent £5.10.0.

TAYLOR, William   Ballygannonmore and Kilcandra 1869–1916*
Blacksmith; TA's note: 'forge given up 1881 to be occupied as my servant'; d. 1894.
Janet Acton's diary, 20 August 1886: 'Our good & faithful Taylor laid in his last earthly
resting place d. 10 August serving us 32 years' – it is unclear to which member of the
family this refers.
*See endnote by Lewis Kemmis.
1942 Violet TAYLOR married Fred Newton
1942 her sister Rita TAYLOR about to marry Victor FARRER

THOMAS, John   Tullylusk and Bolagh   1806–57
                      Lease for life or 31 years; 36 acres; rent £43.

TINDALL, Samuel   Kilcandra   ?
                      Blacksmith's forge, slated house and 1 acre, with 14 acres
                      at Ballygannon; rent £12.
                      GV (Tyndall) also records house only held at Tullylusk

WILLIAMS, Richard   Ballygannonbeg   1823
                      acquired interest of Winifred BYRNE and John QUIN

WINDER, Henry   Kilcandra   1849 GV   **P**
                      HOL, 81 acres
                      Had a lease for 1 life (of Edward Winder who was aged
                      45 or 50 in 1870); rent £70.
                      Also held Bellpark   1849 GV
                      118 acres, rent £136.4.0

WINDER, Martin   Bell Park   1869, evicted 1883
& reps of M. Winder   Kilcandra
[but also 1898, TA notes 'The Winders evicted for debts about £200 to miller & grocer]

WINDER, Thomas   Kilcandra   1869–1916
1872 Jeremiah Winder was the eldest son; Martin Winder next (Bellpark)
A Charlotte Winder died 1898; a Robert Winder d. 1832, age 62 (Dunganstown)

WOLOHAN, James   Cunniamstown   1888
This was the name of a Kilmacurragh gardener c. 1908 (see Ch. 2).
Also Hugh Woolaghan, mason, 'notorious killer', member of Cavalry in 1798, court-martialled; a spy in United Irishmen.

YORKE, John   Macreddin   1837–59
                     Rent £5

ENDNOTE

In 1902 Lewis (or Louis) Kemmis, who had succeeded Alfred MacDermott as the Actons' agent, and was a member of the landed family at Ballinacor, listed the remaining tenants on the Kilmacurragh lands, categorizing their current status: William Strahan (Macreddin), Thomas Hudson (Kilnamanaghbeg), Andrew Hyland (Togher), George Pearce (Cunniamstown), Benjamin Farrar (Cunniamstown and Kilcandra), William Ryder (Rahavil) and the widow Keegan at Kilmanogue, had all agreed to a renewal of their leases at a 10 per cent rent reduction. The leases of Mary Ann Evans (Ballinaskea), Loughlin Kinsella (land unknown), James O'Keeffe (Macreddin), Michael Doyle senior and junior (both of Macreddin) were due to expire shortly, and they could apply to court for similar reductions, as could Mrs William Taylor (Ballygannonmore and Kilcandra) and Alexander Hill (Kilcandra and Macreddin) who were on yearly tenancies. Thomas Winder (Kilcandra) had already obtained a judicial lease, and the leases of John Manley (Kilcandra and Cunniamstown), William Byrne (Kilmacrea), Thomas Hudson (in respect of his land at Tullylusk) and Thomas Richardson (Ballykerrig) would not expire for periods of one to six years. The list noted that John Hudson, with holdings at Kilnamanaghbeg, Tullylusk and Cunniamstown, 'is not to be offered an agreement out of court'.

Bibliography

I. PRIMARY SOURCES: MANUSCRIPTS AND TYPESCRIPTS

Thomas Acton II, manuscript notebook, 1694–1700 (Acton Family Archive)

Thomas Acton II, Thomas Acton III, household account book 1701–57 (Wicklow County Archive)

Thomas Acton III, William Acton III and Caroline Acton, household accounts 1781–1840s (2 volumes) (Wicklow County Archive)

Thomas Acton III, William Acton III, estate rent books 1780s-1850s (Wicklow County Archive)

Voting record of 1832 General Election, County Wicklow (Wicklow County Archive)

Janet Acton, household accounts from 1854– (Acton Family Archive)

Correspondence from William Molesworth Cole Acton, 1854, from the Crimea (National Museum of Ireland)

Charles Ball-Acton, diaries 1861– (4 volumes) (National Museum of Ireland)

Janet Acton et al., 'The Kilmacurragh Book', c. 1885– (Acton Family Archive)

Thomas Acton IV, correspondence books (3 volumes) (Wicklow County Archive)

Correspondence to and from Thomas Acton IV concerning plants and trees, including letters from Sir Frederick Moore (Botanic Gardens – Kilmacurragh Arboretum, County Wicklow)

Irene Ball-Acton, manuscript entries in 'The Field Botanist's Diary' (1910, 4th edn.), recording .... plants identified on parts of the Acton estate, and ... in other parts of County Wicklow in 1911 (Wicklow County Archive)

Letters to and from Charles and Carol Acton: Elizabeth Barrett; Charles Beresford,

Marcus and Patricia Beresford; Brian, Mary, Barra and Cormac Boydell; Thurloe and Maria Conolly; Nic and Ksana Couriss; Ralph and Nancy Cusack; Heinz and Alice Hammerschlag; John and Joan Miley; Proinnsías Ó Duinn; Gráinne Yeats (Acton Family Archive)

Letters from Charles Acton to Carol Acton (Acton Family Archive)

Charles Acton, collected reviews, 1955–89 (21 volumes) (NLI Music Collection)

Charles Acton, correspondence files 1960–95 (10 volumes) (NLI Music Collection)

2. SECONDARY SOURCES

Family history and local history

Bence-Jones, Mark, 'The Changing Picture of the Irish Landed Gentry' in L.G. Pine, op. cit.

—, A Guide to Irish Country Houses (London: Constable, 1990).

Bowen, Elizabeth, Bowen's Court and Seven Winters: memories of a Dublin childhood with an introduction by Hermione Lee (London: Virago, 1984).

Corlett, Christiaan and Medlycott, John (eds.), The Ordnance Survey Letters: Wicklow (Roundwood and District Historical and Folklore Society, 2001).

Flynn, Arthur, A History of County Wicklow (Dublin: Gill and Macmillan, 2003).

Foster, R.F., Charles Stewart Parnell: the man and his family (Harvester Press/ Humanities Press, 1976).

Hannigan, Ken, 'The Barndarrig Band: life and death in an East Wicklow village of the 1890s', Journal of Wicklow Historical Society 1995.

—, 'A Miscellany of Murder: violent death in County Wicklow in the nineteenth century', Journal of Wicklow Historical Society 1/7.

Hannigan, Ken, and Nolan, William (eds.), Wicklow: History & Society: interdisciplinary essays on the history of an Irish county (Dublin: Geography Publications, 1994).

Heavener, Robert, Credo: Dunganstown: an age-old Irish parish with a living message for everyman today (Jordanstown: Cromlech Books, 1993).

Hope Simpson, J.B., Rugby since Arnold: a history of Rugby School since 1842 (London: Macmillan, 1967).

O'Donnell, Ruán, The Rebellion in Wicklow 1798 (Dublin: Irish Academic Press, 1998).

O'Donnell, Ruán, Aftermath: post-Rebellion insurgency in Wicklow 1799–1803 (Dublin: Irish Academic Press, 2000).

Pine, L.G. (ed.), Burke's Landed Gentry of Ireland 4th edition (London, 1958).

Prunty, Jacinta, Maps and Map-Making in Local History (Dublin: Four Courts Press, 2004).

Ronan, Rev Myles, Ancient Churches of the Deanery of Wicklow (1938).

Slater, Eamonn, 'Contested terrain: differing interpretations of County Wicklow's landscape', Irish Journal of Sociology 3 (1993).

Wallace, Valerie, *Mrs Alexander: a life of the hymn-writer Cecil Frances Alexander 1818–1895* (Dublin: Lilliput Press, 1995).

White, Brian, *The County Wicklow Database 432AD to 2006AD* (Dublin: Nonsuch Publishing, 2006).

Irish political, social and economic history

Becker, Bernard H., *Disturbed Ireland: being the letters written during the winter of 1880–81* (London: Macmillan, 1881).

Bolger, Dermot, *The Family on Paradise Pier* (London: Fourth Estate, 2005).

Bowen, Elizabeth, *The Last September* (London: Vintage, 1998).

Bull, Philip, *Land, Politics and Nationalism: a study of the Irish Land Question* (Dublin: Gill and Macmillan, 1996).

Butler, Hubert, *Escape from the Anthill* (Gigginstown: Lilliput Press, 1985).

Craig, Edward Thomas, *The Irish Land and Labour Question: illustrated in the history of Ralahine and co-operative farming* (Manchester: Trübner, 1882).

—, *An Irish Commune: the history of Ralahine,* introduction by George Russell (Dublin: Lester, 1920).

Curtis Jr, L. Perry, *Apes and Angels: the Irishman in Victorian Caricature* (Washington: Smithsonian Institution Press, 2nd edn. 1997).

Davitt, Michael, *The Fall of Feudalism in Ireland* (London: Harper and brothers, 1904).

Donnelly, James S. Jr, *Landlord and Tenant in Nineteenth-Century Ireland* (Dublin: Gill and Macmillan, 1973).

Dooley, Terence, *The Big Houses and Landed Estates of Ireland: a research guide* (Dublin: Four Courts Press, 2007).

Drudy, P.J. (ed.), *Ireland: Land, Politics and People* (Cambridge: Cambridge University Press, 1982).

Dun, Finlay, *Landlords and Tenants in Ireland* (London: Longmans Green, 1881).

Feingold, William L., *The Revolt of the Tenantry: the transformation of local government in Ireland 1872–1886* (Boston: Northeastern University Press, 1984).

Foster, R.F., *Modern Ireland 1600–1972* (London: Penguin, 1988).

Guinnane, T.W. and Miller, R., 'The limits to land reform: the Land Acts in Ireland 1870–1909', *Economic Development and Cultural Change* 45 (1997).

King, Carla (ed.), *Famine, Land and Culture in Ireland* (Dublin: University College Dublin Press, 2000).

Lewis, Gifford, *Edith Somerville: a biography* (Dublin: Four Courts Press, 2005).

McCarthy, Róisín, 'The Landlords' Defences: Organised landowner counteraction to agrarian agitation, land reform and the Home Rule movement 1879–1914', BA dissertation, UCC, 2004.

McDowell, R.B. (ed.), *Social Life in Ireland 1800–45* (Dublin: Colm Ó Lochlainn, 1957).

—, *Crisis and Decline: the fate of the Southern Unionists* (Dublin: Lilliput Press, 1997).

Moran, D.P., *The Philosophy of Irish Ireland* (1905; reprinted with an introduction by Patrick Maume, University College Dublin Press, 2006).

Norton, Desmond, *Landlords, Tenants, Famine: the business of an Irish Land Agency in the 1840s* (Dublin: UCD Press, 2006).

Paul-Dubois, L., *Contemporary Ireland* with an introduction by T.M. Kettle (Dublin: Maunsel, 1911).

Robertson, Nora, *Crowned Harp: memories of the last years of the Crown in Ireland* (Dublin: Allen Figgis, 1960).

Robinson, Lennox, *Bryan Cooper* (London: Constable, 1931).

Solow, Barbara Lewis, *The Land Question and the Irish Economy 1870–1903* (Cambridge, Mass.: Harvard University Press, 1971).

Somerville, E. Œ., and Ross, Martin, *French Leave* (London: Heinemann, 1928).

Thomson, David and McGusty, Moyra (eds.), *The Irish Journals of Elizabeth Smith 1840–1850* (Oxford: Oxford University Press, 1980).

Ussher, Arland, *The Face and Mind of Ireland* (London: Gollancz, 1949).

Vaughan, W.E., *Landlords and Tenants in Ireland 1848–1904* (Economic and Social History Society of Ireland, 1984).

Whyte, J.H., 'Landlord influences at elections in Ireland 1760–1885', *English Historical Review* 80 (1965).

First World War

Brice, Beatrix, *The Battle Book of Ypres* (London: John Murray, 1927/1987).

Dunn, J.C., *The War the Infantry Knew 1914–1919* (London: Abacus, 1994).

Fisk, Robert, *The Great War for Civilisation: the conquest of the Middle East* (London: Fourth Estate, 2005/2006).

Fromkin, David, *A Peace to End All Peace: the fall of the Ottoman Empire and the creation of the modern Middle East* (London: André Deutsch, 1989).

Groom, Winston, *A Storm in Flanders: the Ypres Salient 1914–1918: tragedy and triumph on the western front* (New York: Atlantic Monthly Press, 2002).

MacGill, Patrick, *The Great Push: an episode of the Great War* (Edinburgh: Birlinn, 2000).

Terraine, John, *The Great War* (Ware: Wordsworth, 1997).

Warner, Philip, *The Battle of Loos* (Ware: Wordsworth, 2000).

Ireland in the Second World War / 'Emergency'

Carroll, Joseph T., *Ireland in the War Years 1939–1945* (Newton Abbot: David and Charles, 1975).

Duggan, John P., *Herr Hempel at the German Legation in Dublin 1937–1945* (Dublin: Irish Academic Press, 2003).

—, *Neutral Ireland and the Third Reich* (Dublin: Lilliput Press, 1989).

Girvin, Brian, *The Emergency: neutral Ireland 1939–45* (London: Macmillan, 2006).

Hull, Mark M., *Irish Secrets: German Espionage in Ireland 1939–1945* (Dublin: Irish Academic Press, 2003).

Kershaw, Ian, *Hitler 1889–1936: Hubris* (London: Allen lane, 1998).

Mullins, Gerry, *Dublin Nazi No. 1: the life of Adolf Mahr* (Dublin: Liberties Press, 2007).

O'Donoghue, David, *Hitler's Irish Voices: the story of German Radio's wartime Irish service* (Belfast: Beyond the Pale Books, 1998).

Ó Drisceoil, Donal, *Censorship in Ireland 1939–1945: neutrality, politics and society* (Cork: Cork University Press, 1996).

Stuart, Francis, *The Wartime Broadcasts of Francis Stuart 1942–1944* ed. Brendan Barrington (Dublin: Lilliput Press, 2000).

White, Terence de Vere, *A Fretful Midge* (London: Routledge, 1957).

Wills, Clair, *That Neutral Island: A cultural History of Ireland during the Second World War* (London: Faber and Faber, 2007).

The arts in Ireland

Boydell, Brian, 'Remembering Ralph Cusack', *The Recorder* 10/1–2, 1997.

Cusack, Ralph, *Cadenza, an excursion* (London: Hamish Hamilton, 1958).

Cox, Gareth, Klein, Axel and Taylor, Michael (eds.), *The Life and Music of Brian Boydell* (Dublin: Irish Academic Press, 2004).

Freyer, Grattan and Harris, Bernard (eds.) *The Achievement of Seán Ó Riada: integrating tradition* (Ballina: Irish Humanities Centre, 1981).

Kennedy, S.B., *The White Stag Group* (Dublin: Irish Museum of Modern Art, 2005).

—, *Irish Art and Modernism 1880–1950* (Belfast: Institute of Irish Studies, 1991).

Moynahan, Julian, *Anglo-Irish: the literary imagination in a hyphenated culture* (Princeton NJ: Princeton University Press, 1995).

O'Brien, Flann, *Flann O'Brien at War: Myles na gCopaleen 1940–1945* ed. John Wyse Jackson (London: Duckworth, 1999).

Pine, Richard, *Music and Broadcasting in Ireland* (Dublin: Four Courts Press, 2005)

— and Acton, Charles (eds.), *To Talent Alone: the Royal Irish Academy of Music 1848–1998* (Dublin: Gill and Macmillan, 1998).

Richards, Sir J.M., *Provision for the Arts* (Dublin: Arts Council, 1976).

Snoddy, Theo, *Dictionary of Irish Artists: Twentieth Century* (Dublin: Merlin, 1996/2002).

White, Harry, *The Keeper's Recital: music and cultural history in Ireland 1770–1970* (Cork: Cork University Press/Field Day, 1998).

The Irish Times

Brady, Conor, *Up With The Times* (Dublin: Gill and Macmillan, 2005).

Fleming, Lionel, *Head or Harp* (London: Barrie and Rockliff, 1965).

James, Dermot, *From the Margins to the Centre: a history of* The Irish Times (Dublin: Woodfield Press, 2008).

O'Brien, Mark, *The Irish Times: A History* (Dublin: Four Courts Press, 2008).

The Arboretum, arboriculture and silviculture

Allan, Mea, *William Robinson 1838–1935: Father of the English Flower Garden* (London: Faber and Faber, 1982).

Botanic Gardens, Glasnevin, 'Kilmacurra Arboretum: a guide to trees and shrubs', cyclostyled, 17pp., n.d.

Botting Hemsley, W., 'Rhododendron Delavayi', from *Curtis's Botanical Magazine* vol. 3, June 1907.

Forbes, A.C., 'Tree planting in Ireland during Four Centuries', *Proceedings of the Royal Irish Academy* XLI/C/6, 1933.

Hayes, Samuel, *A Practical Treatise on Planting and the Management of Woods and Coppices* (reprint, with a foreword by Thomas Pakenham, Dublin: New Island, 2003).

Hooker, Joseph Dalton, *The Rhododendrons of Sikkim-Himalaya* (London: Reeve and Co., 1849).

Masters, Maxwell T., 'The "Cedar of Goa"', *Journal of the Royal Horticultural Society* vol. 17 part 1.

Moore, David, 'On the successful establishment of *Loranthus Europeus* on Oak Trees in the Botanic Gardens, Glasnevin' – a paper read before the Royal Dublin Society, 20 January 1873.

Nelson, E.C. and McCracken, Eileen M., *The Brightest Jewel: a history of the National Botanic Gardens, Glasnevin, Dublin* (Kilkenny: Boethius Press, 1987).

Pim, Sheila, *The Wood and the Trees: a biography of Augustine Henry* (London: Macdonald, 1966).

Reid, Myles, 'An audit of a current environmental resource: Kilmacurragh Arboretum in Co. Wicklow', unpublished thesis for B.Sc.Hort., National Botanic Gardens, Glasnevin, 2006.

Robinson, William, *The Wild Garden* (London: John Murray, 1870).

Turrill, W.B., *Joseph Dalton Hooker: Botanist, Explorer and Administrator* (London: Scientific Book Club, 1963).

Index